SEXUAL HARASSMENT ON CAMPUS

A Guide for Administrators, Faculty, and Students

Bernice R. Sandler

*National Association for Women
in Education*

Robert J. Shoop

Kansas State University

Editors

Allyn and Bacon

Boston • London • Toronto • Sydney • Tokyo • Singapore

Associate Publisher: Stephen D. Dragin
Editorial Assistant: Susan Hutchinson

Library of Congress Cataloging-in-Publication Data

Sexual harassment on campus : a guide for administrators, faculty, and
    students / Bernice R. Sandler, Robert J. Shoop, editors.
        p.   cm.
    ISBN 0-205-16712-8
    1. Sexual harassment in universities and colleges—United States.
I. Sandler, Bernice Resnick.   II. Shoop, Robert J.
LC212.862.S48   1997
370.19'345--dc20   96-131371
                                                        CIP

Printed in the United States of America
10 9 8 7 6 5 4 3 2 1   00 99 98 97 96

CONTENTS

PREFACE

Although sexual harassment is a relatively old problem, it is a relatively new issue on campuses. The first charges of sexual harassment against a university were filed in 1977; the first national report on campus sexual harassment was not written until 1979.

During the 1980s many institutions developed policies and procedures to deal with sexual harassment. We are now in the second stage of policy development. Across the country institutions are reexamining their policies and procedures, evaluating what has worked and what has not worked, and then revising their policies and procedures. This is not an easy task, and is one that is always accompanied by much campus discussion.

This book is an attempt to help institutions involved in that process. We have included a wide range of chapters covering issues such as the law, the process of developing and changing policies, what policies should look like, and how to deal with complaints, both formally and informally. Because the topic of sexual harassment on campus almost always invites discussion (and dissension), we have also included several chapters to help people as they think about sexual harassment. Finally, we have included the experience of those whose lives have been changed as a result of sexual harassment.

Although, as a whole, the book covers the major aspects of sexual harassment issues, it is not likely that readers will necessarily read it in sequential order; they may browse or select chapters to read at different times. Thus, because some chapters may be read alone and out of the context of the book as a whole, we have allowed some overlapping and repetition between chapters so that key chapters contain essential information and can stand alone.

Because many people have been involved in this effort, agreement on everything was not expected. Some authors see little progress having been made in combatting sexual harassment, others see much improvement since institutions began to deal with this issue. Some authors differ on the how they view the ways in which academic freedom can be reconciled with the concept of an environment free of harassment. Others differ as to whether *all* reports of sexual harassment should have a formal investigation or only those which are presented as formal complaints. Others disagree as to the degree to which sexual harassment is a function of misunderstanding and miscommunication. Some authors also disagree about the use of mediation as a method of dealing with some sexual harassment complaints.

Whatever their disagreements, all authors agree that sexual harassment is a very serious issue, and that institutions need to do much more if they are to provide the kind of productive working and learning environment that is consistent with their mission. We are grateful for the authors who joined us in this endeavor. They have enriched our understanding of sexual harassment, and we hope that they will do the same for our readers.

What the Future Holds

Because sexual harassment is a relatively new issue, the courts will play a major role in clarifying a number of issues, which institutions need to deal with, including the following:

- How shall we resolve the conflict between academic freedom for faculty members and the right of students to learn in an environment that is not hostile or intimidating?
- Are student behaviors outside the classroom (such as wet t-shirt contests) protected by free speech, although the same behaviors in the workplace would clearly constitute a hostile environment?
- What are the criteria for determining a hostile environment? How can we determine if a behavior "interferes" with a person's ability to work or learn, his or her living conditions, or to partake of the opportunities offered by an educational institution?
- What are the determining factors in establishing an institution's liability for the actions of its faculty and other employees?
- What is the institution's liability for peer harassment both on and off campus, including off-campus housing?
- Are colleges and universities responsible for the harassing actions of invited guests and visitors to campus?
- How should the concepts developed by the courts under workplace legislation apply to student-to-student harassment?
- Are punitive damages allowed under Title IX? (Some people interpret the *Gwinnett v. Franklin* decision allowing suits against educational institutions as only allowing compensatory damages. Others believe the decision covers punitive damages as well.)
- What constitutes due process for faculty and employee complaints? For student complaints?
- What rights do victims of harassment have?
- What rights of privacy do alleged and actual harassers have?
- How are the rights of employees to recover damages from sexual harassment affected by workers' compensation programs which also allow workers to collect damages? Does one disallow the other?
- How should other laws such as Section 1983 of the United States Code and various state laws, including those that cover civil suits, be interpreted concerning sexual harassment?

Apart from issues that ultimately will be decided by the courts, institutions can expect an increase in litigation, especially when instances of sexual harassment are not handled well by an institution, including the following:

- A general increase because of increased awareness as people recognize their rights and their ability to recover damages.
- More cases with compensatory and punitive damages awarded to employees and students as courts apply the provisions of Civil Rights Act of 1991, Title IX, and state laws.
- Attorneys may be more likely to take harassment cases on a contingency basis.

- More cases of student-to-student harassment.
- Increased countersuits of defamation, slander, libel, and the like by those accused of sexual harassment, as well as suits based on procedural technicalities.

In addition to increased charges of sexual harassment, in general, both in institutions and in the courts, we can also expect the following at the institutional level:

- Increased use of informal procedures to handle complaints.
- Increased student-to-student harassment and an increase in the number of charges reporting it.
- Increased charges against groups of students such as fraternities and athletic teams.
- Increased training at all levels of the university on a continuing basis, especially more educational programs for students about peer harassment.
- Increased awareness and acceptance by universities and the courts of nonsexual but gender-related behaviors as constituting a hostile environment.
- Increased charges of multiple harassment based on gender and other factors, primarily race and ethnicity, but also including age and disability.
- Increased charges of same sex harassment, especially male-to-male harassment.
- Increased charges by men against women who are administrators, managers, or supervisors.
- Increased charges by male students against female students.
- Increased charges of computer harassment and the development of policies to deal with it such as the one at the Massachusetts Institute of Technology (see Chapter 5).
- Increased incorporation of victims' rights into institutional policies (see Chapter 6).
- Increased policies prohibiting or raising issues about consensual relationships (see Chapters 2 and 6).
- Increased incorporation of multiple kinds of harassment into one policy.
- Increased use of a systematic, comprehensive program dealing with sexual harassment.
- Questions raised about the relationship between policies dealing with sexual harassment and those dealing with sexual assault.

Sexual harassment is a major issue for institutions, not only because of the legal implications and the threat of bad publicity and monetary damages, but because it damages the victims and the learning environment. It makes all of us, women and men, reevaluate the relationships between men and women, what these relationships are, what they might be, and questions the educational institution's role and responsibility for helping its faculty, staff, employees, and students deal with a changing world.

ABOUT THE AUTHORS

Editors

Bernice Resnick Sandler, a Senior Scholar in Residence at the National Association for Women in Education in Washington, DC, consults extensively with institutions and others about sexual harassment and discrimination, and writes the newsletter, *About Women on Campus*. She has given over 2,000 presentations, has written extensively about sex discrimination, and is well known for her expertise in policies and programs. Dr. Sandler also serves as an expert witness in discrimination cases.

She previously directed the Project on the Status and Education of Women at the Association of American Colleges, where she published more than 100 reports, writing the first reports on campus sexual harassment, gang rape, peer harassment, and the ways in which men and women are treated differently in the classroom. She was the first person appointed to a congressional committee to work specifically on women's issues, the first to testify about sex discrimination in education, and played a major role in the development and passage of Title IX and other laws prohibiting sex discrimination in education.

Dr. Sandler was the major contributor to the *Educators' Guide to Controlling Sexual Harassment* (Thompson); her most recent publication is *The Chilly Classroom Climate—A Guide to Improve the Education of Women*.

Her doctorate is from the University of Maryland. She serves on many boards, has received nine honorary doctorates and, in 1994, was awarded A Century of Women Special Achievement Award from the Turner Broadcasting System. She has appeared on national media such as *Larry King Live* and *Good Morning America*.

Robert J. Shoop is a professor of educational law at Kansas State University, Manhattan, Kansas. Prior to earning his Ph.D. from the University of Michigan, he worked as a teacher, community education director, principal, and was the Ohio State Evaluator of Student Rights and Responsibilities. He is the author of over 100 journal articles, eight books, and several monographs and book chapters on various legal issues. His most recent books are: *Sexual Harassment in Our Schools: What Parents and Teachers Need to Know to Spot and Stop It!* and *How to Stop Sexual Harassment in Our Schools: A Handbook and Curriculum Guide for Administrators and Teachers.*

He is also the co-producer of a number of video programs on eliminating sexual harassment. His most recent productions are: *Sexual Harassment: What Is It and Why Should I Care?*; *Preventing Sexual Harassment in High Schools;* and the international award-winning video, *Sexual Harassment: It's Hurting People.*

Dr. Shoop is a recipient of the Kansas State University Outstanding Teacher Award, is a member of the board of directors of the National Organization on Legal Problems of Education, and has consulted with national associations, community colleges, universities, governmental agencies, businesses, and educational organizations throughout the United States. A frequent guest on national radio and television talk shows, he also serves as an expert witness in discrimination cases.

Contributors

Carolyn S. Bratt is the W. L. Matthews Professor of Law, College of Law, University of Kentucky, Lexington. Dr. Bratt earned her J.D. from Syracuse University and a B.A. in history from the State University of New York at Albany. Constitutional law is one of her areas of specialization, and a significant portion of her research and teaching focuses on gender-related law and policy issues. She has published in such forums as the *Family Law Quarterly, Illinois Law Forum, Albany Law Review,* and *Kentucky Law Review.* From 1991 to 1994, Professor Bratt served as a faculty trustee on the University of Kentucky Board of Trustees, and from 1992 to 1993 she was a fellow with the American Council on Education.

Robert L. Carothers is the president of the University of Rhode Island, where he has served since 1991. Prior to his appointment at Rhode Island, he was the chancellor of the Minnesota State University System, and before that, president of Southwest State University. He also served as professor of English, dean of arts and humanities, and vice president for administration and student services at Edinboro University of Pennsylvania. He is the author of the Q7 quality initiative in Minnesota, an effort to define the standards of performance required of both secondary school and college graduates. Carothers received his M.A. and Ph.D. from Kent State University and his J.D. from the University of Akron.

Martha Chamallas is a professor of law at the University of Pittsburgh where she teaches employment discrimination law, torts, and feminist legal theory. She was the chair of the Women's Studies Program at the University of Iowa and served on the Equality in the Courts Task Force for the state of Iowa. Her writings address cultural domination, harassment and stereotyping in employment, and gender and race equity in the civil justice system. Her recent publications include: "Structuralist and Cultural Domination Theories Meet Title VII; Some Contemporary Influences," *Michigan Law Review* (1994): 2370–2409; and "Questioning the Use of Race-Specific and Gender-Specific Economic Data in Tort Litigation: A Constitutional Argument," *Fordham Law Review* (1994): 73–124.

Elsa Kircher Cole has been the General Counsel for the University of Michigan since 1989. She previously served as an Assistant Attorney General for the state of Washington, assigned to represent the University of Washington from 1976 until 1989. She received her A.B. degree with distinction from Stanford University and her J.D. from Boston University. She has served on the Board of Directors of the National Association of College and University Attorneys and edited its second edition of *Sexual Harassment on Campus: A Legal Compendium.* She is a frequent lecturer and writer in the field of higher education law and sexual harassment.

Denise Michelle Dalaimo is currently a Ph.D. candidate in sociology, as well as the director of Sexual Harassment Research and Education at the Jean Nidetch Women's Center at the University of Nevada, Las Vegas. She has published in *Educational Research Quarterly* and her chapter, "The Virtual Construction of Cyber-Selfhood: A Postmodern Ethnography," appears in *Wilderness of Mirrors: Symbolic Interactions and the Postmodern Terrain* (Jon Epstein, editor).

Susan C. Ehrlich is a partner in the law firm of Ehrlich & Oaks with a legal practice devoted to education law. As a school attorney she has worked closely with school districts on personnel and related issues. She has trained school and college administrators throughout the West in documenting employee performance problems and in dealing with sexual harassment issues. She advises school and college districts about sexual harassment policies and assists in investigations, resolution, and discipline of employee and student misconduct. She is developing a standardized computer-assisted approach to investigations of sexual harassment complaints for use by school and college administrators.

Howard Gadlin is university ombudsperson at UCLA, as well as co-director of UCLA's Center for Inter-racial/Inter-ethnic Conflict Resolution. Dr. Gadlin currently designs and conducts training programs in dispute resolution; sexual harassment; and organizational and multicultural disputes for universities, public and government agencies and private organizations. He has published widely in the area of dispute resolution; is past president of the University and College Ombudsman Association; and has been a mediator in a wide range of community, school, business, and family disputes. He is often called in as a consultant/mediator in "intractable" disputes and has trained mediators internationally.

Linda Vaden Gratch is an assistant professor and social psychologist on the faculty at the University of Houston–Downtown. Her areas of research include the study of attributional thinking, self-silencing in intimate relationships, self-silencing in the workplace, and sexual harassment. She is the author of the chapter, "Sexual Harassment Among Police Officers: Crisis and Change in Normative Structure," appearing in *Women, Law, and Social Control* (Merlo and Pollock, 1995); and has written several papers relevant to themes of gender, ethnicity, and intimate relationships.

Susan K. Hippensteele is a research psychologist and the sexual harassment counselor/victim's advocate for students, faculty, and staff at the University of Hawai'i at Manoa (UHM). Active in antidiscrimination research and policy development committees as a graduate student, Hippensteele was hired as the first victim's advocate for this 20,000 student campus shortly after earning her doctorate in psychology from UHM in 1991. Her current research on student and faculty experiences with campus ethnoviolence examines the relationships between victims' experiences of racism, sexism, and homophobia in multiple minority settings. Hippensteele consults with colleges and universities around the country, developing victim advocacy and support programs for students.

Leslie Irvine is a Ph.D. candidate in the department of sociology at the State University of New York at Stony Brook. Her interests include the sociology of emotions, gender, the self, and popular culture. She is writing a dissertation on the popular psychospiritual phenomenon called co-dependency. She is co-author, with James Rule, of "Feminist Theory in Social Science," in Rule's *Theory and Progress in Social Science*, published in 1996.

Joycelyn Landrum-Brown received her Ph.D. and M.A. in clinical psychology from Michigan State University. She is a consultant with her own firm, Landrum-Brown & Associates, which specializes in cultural diversity awareness training. Dr. Landrum-Brown is a manager in student affairs and a lecturer at the Graduate School of Education at the University of California, Santa Barbara.

Robin Oaks is a partner in the law firm of Ehrlich & Oaks, with special expertise in school law issues and sexual harassment complaint resolution. She represents academic institutions throughout the state in education law and personnel matters. Her legal services relating to sexual harassment include representation at hearings, mediation services, investigations, sexual harassment policy/program evaluation, legal advice for complaint resolution, and extensive teaching and training. She was judicial law clerk for the Honorable John Garett Penn who was the trial judge for *Meritor Savings Bank v. Vinson*, the first case where the U.S. Supreme Court recognized a claim for hostile environment sexual harassment under Title VII.

Jayne Richmond is an assistant dean of University College and director of New Student Programs at the University of Rhode Island. She has been a professor of higher education administration since 1982. In 1991, Dr. Richmond became the assistant to the president where her efforts focused on initiatives for change. In 1992, she served as a fellow with the American Council on Education working with the president at the University of Central Florida. She holds a B.A., M.Ed., and Ph.D. from the University of Florida, Gainesville and is also a graduate of the HERS program at Bryn Mawr College.

Mary P. Rowe is one of two ombudspersons for the faculty, staff, and students of the MIT community. In 1982, Rowe was a co-founder of the Corporate Ombudsman Association, now The Ombudsman Association. She has helped to set up ombuds offices in hundreds of corporations, government agencies and academic institutions and consults widely on harassment-related problems. She has written dozens of articles on complaint-handling, design of integrated dispute resolution systems, aspects of workplace diversity, and problems of all kinds of harassment. She is currently working on "second generation" problems in the area of harassment.

Susan Scollay earned her Ph.D. in educational administration from Kansas State University and an M.A. and B.A. from the University of California, Santa Barbara. Currently on the faculty in the College of Education, she previously served the University of Kentucky as the associate vice president for Research and Graduate Studies. Her primary research interest focuses on change processes and governance in educational organizations, especially those dealing with issues of equity and gender. Professor Scollay has published in the *Journal of Higher Education, Review of Higher Education,* and *International Journal of Educational Reform,* among others. She has consulted extensively in the areas of administrative and program development; equity issues; and institutional effectiveness, assessment, and evaluation.

Brenda Seals is a visiting research associate at the Crime Victims Center, Medical University of South Carolina, where she is part of a team investigating relationships between recent trauma and the initiation of HIV risk behaviors. Currently, she is applying symbolic interactionist theory to public health in a study on HIV Partner Notification and Violence. Recent works describe interactions between rapists and victims during an assault and violence in the lives of women infected with HIV.

Anne T. Truax is associate to the director, Office of Equal Opportunity and Affirmative Action, University of Minnesota, Minneapolis. Ms. Truax is active in the National Association for Women in Education and the National Women's Studies Association. She served on the Advisory Committee for the Project on the Status and Education of Women, Association of American Colleges, and is guest editor for a special issue on theory and practice of *Signs: Journal of Women in Culture and Society.* Her responsibilities in the Office of Equal Opportunity include investigating and resolving cases and conducting workshops on sexual harassment.

Nancy A. Wonders is an assistant professor of criminal justice, Northern Arizona University. She received her Ph.D. in sociology from Rutgers University in 1990. Her areas of interest are criminology, gender, and political sociology. Her scholarly work explores the relationship between social inequality and justice. She has authored or co-authored numerous publications including; *Gender and Justice: Feminist Contributions to Criminology, Varieties of Criminology: Readings from a Dynamic Discipline,* and *Understanding the Emergence of Law and Public Policy.* She also serves on the Northern Arizona University Commission on the Status of Women and was a co-author of the university's Safe Working and Learning Environment Policy.

1

WHAT IS SEXUAL HARASSMENT?

BERNICE R. SANDLER   *ROBERT J. SHOOP*

Introduction

It's another typical day on campus. Classes are being taught, research is being conducted and the life of the university goes on. It would be nice to believe that all is well behind the ivy-covered walls. However, in addition to scholars pursuing truth and preparing students to take their place in society, many university campuses are rife with sexual harassment. Although most administrators, faculty members, and students do not harass, sexual harassment is a problem on every campus. The following items represent a sampling of recent incidents of sexual harassment on campuses across the country. Similar events may be taking place on your campus.

> Tenured professors have been sanctioned and fired from colleges and universities because of numerous complaints of sexual harassment.
>
> Graduate students have been coerced into sleeping with their thesis advisors. When they try to break off the relationship, advisors threaten to withhold advice on completing their thesis.
>
> At department parties at a number of different institutions women are given objects in the shape of sexual parts—as a joke.
>
> On many campuses posters about women's organizations, campus committees on women, and activities about or for women are routinely defaced, often with sado-pornographic and antifemale graffiti.
>
> Marching bands, fraternities, and athletic team members have been placed on probation after charges of sexual harassment and hazing have been proven.
>
> Graduate students who file successful complaints against their professors have found themselves isolated in their department. Sometimes these students are forced to transfer to other schools.

Note: Some of the information in this chapter appeared earlier in *No means no: Sexual harassment and date rape* (1993) by Bernice R. Sandler, Association of Governing Boards, Washington DC; *Sexual harassment in our schools* (1994) by Robert J. Shoop and Jack W. Hayhow, Allyn and Bacon, Boston; and *Educator's guide to controlling sexual harassment* (1993), published by the Thompson Publishing Group, Washington DC.

Students use computers and e-mail to distribute sexually explicit materials and to sexually harass other students both in and out of the classroom.

On some campuses professors joke about victims of sexual harassment being overly sensitive.

Some universities spend more time and money attempting to defend themselves from charges of sexual harassment than they do educating their communities about this issue.

Sexual harassing graffiti is routinely placed on university property and often allowed to remain for an extended time, offending generations of students.

Black women students are often openly taunted with the cry of "black meat" or "black bitch."

Women who support women's rights are harassed. Women protesting campus date rape during "Take-Back-the-Night-Marches" or at other campus-sponsored rallies have been mooned, threatened with rape, had beer poured over them, and had obscenities shouted at them.

Women walking past fraternity houses are often whistled or yelled at. Sometimes the men shout obscenities; at other times, they may loudly discuss women's sexual attributes and then rate them on a scale of one to ten.

At one university a large number of women faculty and students do not use the most convenient supermarket because of harassment from fraternity members living in houses next to and across the street from that market.

On many campuses, dormitories are hotbeds of sexual harassment. Obscenities may be scrawled on walls and doors about particular women (i.e., "Mary Smith sucks cock").

Women students have their breasts grabbed at parties and on campus, often by strangers. On one campus a group of men regularly surrounded women and detained them until they bared their breasts.

Most competent university administrators know what sexual harassment is. They also know the potential consequences that may result from charges of sexual harassment. However, even with this knowledge many universities are not doing enough to prevent sexual harassment from occurring. Some are still unaware of the extent that sexual harassment exists on their campus. University administrators have told us that, "if sexual harassment was occurring at my university I would know about it." Some administrators seem to believe that sexual harassment is a fact of life that cannot be changed. Others tell us they are reluctant to sponsor sexual harassment prevention training because they "want to let sleeping dogs lie." These administrators believe that teaching their faculty, staff, and students about sexual harassment will create more problems than it will solve. They are correct in believing there will likely be a rise in awareness and reporting as a result of training. However, we often ask these administrators if they would prefer that people who believe they are being sexually harassed use their university's sexual harassment procedures to solve the problem, or would the university rather learn of incidents of alleged sexual harassment when they receive court papers or a notice of an impending federal investigation.

If a faculty member, administrator, support person, vendor, patron, guest, or student brings a charge of sexual harassment or reports an activity that appears to be a case of sexual harassment, the college or university must respond and have a specific procedure to follow. Simply having a "boilerplate" policy adopted and imbedded in the policy manual will do little to ensure that the university takes sexual harassment seriously.

We are continually surprised by how many university administrators see sexual harassment as a people problem (i.e., sexual harassment occurs when there is an interpretational conflict or an employee or student "behaves inappropriately") rather than an organizational problem (i.e., sexual harassment occurs when there is no clear systemic prevention program). Those who see sexual harassment as a people problem are often content to simply adopt a policy prohibiting sexual harassment and hope that "nothing bad happens." In reality, these administrators don't think about sexual harassment, until a problem arises. They are often shocked by charges of sexual harassment and respond by attempting some form of damage control. The perception that sexual harassment is a people problem leads to a reactionary rather than a proactive posture. This misunderstanding of the issue has resulted in escalating insurance costs, unfavorable changes in coverage limits, critical problems in securing liability coverage for universities, and very unfavorable publicity for the university involved. More important, this perception fosters an educational climate that exposes employees and students to the risk of working and learning in a hostile environment.

Sexual harassment is an organizational and managerial problem, not a people problem. By this we mean that sexual harassment is foreseeable and predictable and therefore should, to a large extent, be significantly reduced through a well-planned, active program of anticipation and prevention. Sexual harassment prevention must be an integral part of an institutions's risk-management program. The risk of having employees or students harmed by sexual harassment will diminish with the expansion of the practice of prevention programs.

In other words, initiating a sexual harassment risk-management program means getting more serious about university safety and security. Such a program provides an accountable means to document a university's commitment to the eradication of sexual harassment. It acts as a testimonial to the fact that the university's standards are reasonable and prudent. Such a program guides the university into a rigorous and continuing examination of its operations to prevent or reduce incidents of sexual harassment and potentially devastating litigation. Such a program can stop most sexual harassment before it begins.

Developing and sustaining a comprehensive sexual harassment prevention program is not an easy task. The individuals selected to manage such activities have a tremendous responsibility. The first step in this process is to become familiar with the educational, sociological, and legal parameters that must guide policy development and staff and student training. A risk-management program must ensure that each student and each employee understands the causes and consequences of sexual harassment. All employees and students should not only know how to file a formal complaint of sexual harassment, but also how complaints are handled, and the variety of informal means that can also be used. It is very important that the investigation procedures used are fair to all parties and do not further the victimization of the person making the claim of sexual harassment. These procedures must also protect the legitimate rights of those accused of sexual harassment.

Typically, university administrators ask experts in sexual harassment prevention to come to their campuses to help them make sure they are in compliance with the law. Many administrators are direct in asking for help to reduce the likelihood that they will be sued. Generally, they ask questions such as: "Will our policy meet the OCR guidelines?" or "How should we handle complaints of sexual harassment?" The question most frequently asked by professors is, "How do I protect myself from false complaints of sexual harassment?" Other professors argue that sexual harassment is too subjective to regulate. Some professors argue that any discussion of sexual harassment prevention is in conflict with the concept of academic freedom. We have had professors tell us that dating students is a private issue between the professor and the student and is none of the university's business.

Sexual harassment occurs much more frequently than is generally assumed. It is devastating to the victim, it can destroy the career of the accused, and it can seriously damage the reputation of the institution.

What Is Sexual Harassment?

Unwelcome sexual advances, requests for sexual favors, and other verbal or physical conduct of a sexual nature constitute sexual harassment when any one of the following is true:

- Submission to such conduct is made either explicitly or implicitly a term or condition of a person's employment or academic advancement.
- Submission to or rejection of such conduct by an individual is used as the basis for employment decisions or academic decisions affecting the person.
- Such conduct has the purpose or effect of unreasonably interfering with a person's work or academic performance or creating an intimidating, hostile, or offensive working, learning, or social environment.

Sexual harassment is a relatively new term and concept under law; however, it is not a new issue on campuses. It has existed, perhaps, as long as there have been educational institutions. But it remained a hidden issue in part because there was no name for the behavior until the early 1970s when a few women at Cornell University came up with the term "sexual harassment." The women had struggled to find a name to describe what had happened to some of them, including an administrative assistant who quit her job with an eminent physicist because of the stress of dealing with his continual sexual advances.[1] Because there was no word to label the behavior, such incidents were seen as aberrations and not as part of a larger pattern.

Although sexual harassment has been illegal for many years, it took the Anita Hill–Clarence Thomas hearing to educate the U.S. public about its prevalence. The hearing acted as a great national teach-in. Official after official, whether they believed Hill or not, decried the fact that any women should have to put up with sexual harassment. Although some may have privately wondered, "What is the big deal about some innocent comments?" most did not say so publicly. Millions watched the hearings, discussed them, and read newspaper and magazine accounts and editorials. Nationally, there was public acknowledgment of a woman's right to a workplace free of sexual harassment.

The dam of silence was broken. Women talked to husbands, lovers, fathers, sons, brothers, friends, and colleagues about their past experiences, often for the first time. Many men commented, "I knew this happened, but I had no idea it happened to people I know." Women gained a new understanding about sexual harassment. This new understanding resulted in their labeling current or past behavior as sexual harassment.

Some men stated they would never be able to talk to women comfortably again; they were worried about charges of sexual harassment. Some professors indicated they were afraid of mentoring women. Others laughed sexual harassment off as a passing joke.

Women, in larger numbers than ever before, began to file charges. In the three months following the hearings, formal complaints against corporate employers filed with the Equal Employment Opportunity Commission (EEOC)[2] jumped from 728 during the same period the previous year to 1,244. Sexual harassment charges filed in the first half of 1992 increased by more than 50 percent over the same reporting period the previous year. Although there are no national figures available for colleges and universities, informal conversations with students, faculty members, and administrators and the emerging research suggest that charges of sexual harassment on campus also increased. Sexual harassment on campus is far more serious and far more prevalent than the number of formal charges would indicate.

Sexual harassment, more than ever before, is a major issue on university campuses. It can be a college president, a dean, a faculty member, a supervisor, or a student sexually harassing colleagues, subordinates, or even superiors. Sexual harassment has become a major problem for educational institutions, with personal, institutional, and societal implications.

Characteristics of Sexual Harassment

The following sections describe these major characteristics of sexual harrassment:

- The behavior is unwanted or unwelcome.
- The behavior is sexual or related to the sex or gender of the person.
- The behavior occurs in context of a relationship where one person has more formal power than the other (i.e., supervisor and an employee or a faculty member and a student) or more informal power (i.e., one peer over another).

Unwanted Behavior

The fact that the behavior is unwanted makes sexual harassment different from other kinds of interaction. Few people would disagree in describing what happened when someone is mugged or robbed. However, in sexual harassment, the behavior, to some degree, is defined by the victim. Thus if the behavior is unwelcome, it can be sexual harassment. If it is welcomed, it is not likely to be sexual harassment.

The laws prohibiting sexual harassment do not prohibit sexual behavior between adults; they prohibit these behaviors only when they are unwanted. How the behavior appears to the victim is the key element. A decision in a California court echoed the dependence on the victim's perception when it ruled that the courts must take into account what a "reasonable woman" would consider a hostile or oppressive environment. Judge Robert Beezer stated: "Men, who are rarely victims of sexual assault, may view sexual conduct in a vacuum without a full appreciation of the social setting or the underlying threat of violence that a woman may perceive."[3] This decision should make it easier to introduce evidence from women about how they feel in certain situations by taking into account the different perceptions men and women may have of the same situation.

The fact that a male may assume that the behavior is welcomed and accepted because the female did not object is no defense to a charge of sexual harassment. A woman may not object to an unwanted embrace or she may smile at an off-color remark for many reasons, such as the fear of offending the harasser, fear of retaliation, difficulty in confronting the offender, and fear of becoming isolated from one's peers.

Women seem less confused about sexual harassment, whether or not they use the term, than men. They know when they are uncomfortable. They know the difference between a witty comment and a sexual joke. They know the difference between flirting and sexual intimidation. They know the difference between professional guidance from a faculty member and being the object of sexual attention. They know the difference between a friendly touch by a fellow student and sexual assault. They know the difference between a voice teacher's appropriate touch to the diaphragm and a touch that lingers too long or wanders to their breast.

Sexual or Gender-Related Behavior

Sexual harassment can be verbal, nonverbal, or physical, the latter sometimes qualifying as sexual assault. Sexual harassment can occur once or several times. It includes, but is not limited to the following:

- Sexual innuendos, comments, or bantering
- Asking or commenting about a person's sexuality
- Humor or jokes about sex or females in general
- Persistent sexual attention, especially when it continues after a clear indication that it is unwanted
- Asking for sexual behavior
- Touching a person, including patting, pinching, stroking, squeezing, hugging, or brushing against his or her body
- Touching or grabbing a person's breasts, crotch, or buttocks
- Giving a neck or shoulder massage
- Leering or ogling, such as "elevator eyes," or staring at a woman's breast or body
- Spreading rumors about a person's sexual activities[4]
- Calling women names such as "hot stuff," "cutie pie," "bitch," "whore," or "slut"[5]
- Making obscene or sexually suggestive gestures or sexual sounds such as sucking or kissing noises
- Sexual graffiti in general or about a particular person[6]
- Using sexual ridicule to denigrate or insult a person[7]
- Sending sexual mail, notes, e-mail, or making sexually explicit phone calls[8]
- Sending, giving, showing, or displaying sexual materials, including pornography, sexual pictures, cartoons and calendars[9]

- Laughing at or not taking seriously someone who experiences sexual harassment
- Blaming the victim of sexual harassment for having caused it
- Making denigrating, sexist remarks about women in general or about a particular woman
- Stalking a person either on or off campus[10]
- Direct or indirect threats or bribes for sexual activity
- Attempted or actual sexual assault or abuse

Peer harassment, especially that of female students by male students, can include all the items in the previous list. We have listed the behaviors that follow separately because they are more common among students. However, if committed by others, these still constitute sexual harassment:

- Shouting obscenities at women as they pass a fraternity house or other place where men gather
- Loudly discussing a woman's sexual attributes and rating her attractiveness, a practice called "scoping"
- Mooning women, whereby men aggressively expose their buttocks
- Pulling down women's shorts or pants
- Creating a sexually demeaning atmosphere, such as displaying posters and pictures that are sexist or otherwise demeaning to women, or having social events focusing on women's sexuality, such as wet T-shirt contests
- Showing petty hostility to women by throwing things, pouring drinks over women's heads or on their breast, heckling women when they enter a room, or making sexual remarks[11]
- Body passing at stadiums
- Biting a woman ("sharking")
- Threatening rape or other sexual abuse[12]

The Context of Power

Sexual harassment has more to do with power and less to do with sex than is generally understood. What makes it different from ordinary flirting is that sexual harassment occurs in the context of a power imbalance. One person has more power than the other and therefore has the power to intimidate. Sometimes the women "chosen" by the harasser are the most vulnerable.

Most people think sexual harassment is simply about sex, when in truth, it has more to do with power than with sex. It is very different from ordinary flirting because it occurs in the context of a power imbalance. The formal power of a supervisor or a faculty member is obvious; both have the power to affect the life chances of employees and students because of their ability to provide or withhold a benefit, evaluation, or service, and their potential to do harm.

It is the power relationship that characterizes the insidious nature of sexual harassment.[13] A person with less power can be easily intimidated by a person with more power. Promotions, raises, perks may be at stake for an employee. For a student, grades, summer opportunities, research positions, fellowships, and access to information and other scholars all may be at stake, making it difficult to say "no" or even to indicate displeasure.

Most discussion of power and sexual harassment have focused on formal power. However, the *informal* power of men over women by virtue of their greater physical size, strength, and status is another factor in sexual harassment, especially when it involves coworkers, or students harassing other students. Indeed, the area of student-to-student harassment is an emerging problem, one which universities have been slow to recognize. All too often, student-to-student behavior is brushed off as "boys will be boys" behavior. In one sense harassing behavior has often been "normalized" and viewed as typical and acceptable behavior for young males. Some institutional policies which prohibit sexual harassment do not even cover student-to-student harassment. When sexual harassment occurs, whether by an administrator, professor, staff member, or student, it creates a chilling affect on the work and learning climate.

Who Is Especially Vulnerable to Sexual Harassment?

Although all women and men can be harassed regardless of their age, appearance, and status, six categories of females may be especially vulnerable to sexual harassment[14]:

1. Women in nontraditional fields, especially when they are few in number and are likely to be seen as "outsiders" who "don't belong" and will now be in competition with men.
2. Women graduate students, who are not only nearer in age to their teachers but also involved in close working relationships with them. Because the students are older, some faculty members may not feel restrained as they might be with younger students.
3. Women of color, who may experience combined racism and sexism (as in being called "black bitch"). They are also vulnerable to stereotypes such as those that depict them as being more sexually available and as having greater sexuality than majority women.
4. Women who appear vulnerable because of their youth, passivity, or social isolation and who therefore are seen as more easily intimidated or manipulated into an exploitive relationship.
5. Lesbian women. Their being "different" may threaten some males who may become hostile and harassing.
6. Women who are physically or emotionally disabled.

Forms of Sexual Harassment

The following three sections describe the basic forms of sexual harassment:

Quid Pro Quo

Quid pro quo means something given in exchange for something else. When the courts first examined sexual harassment, they focused on the kinds of workplace behavior considered quid pro quo—"You sleep with me and I'll give you a promotion." or "If you don't sleep with me, I'll fire you." In terms of students, it might mean "An 'A' for a lay."[15] These kinds of cases are usually the most clear cut but they are the least frequent kind of sexual harassment. Typically the person involved is a supervisor or someone with formal power, such as a faculty member or an administrator who can provide or withhold a benefit, service, or evaluation, and thus has the power to harm the person involved. The threats or bribes may be direct or indirect.

The major elements of quid pro quo harassment are the following:

- The sexual advances were unwanted.
- The harassment was sexually motivated.
- The harassment tangibly affects the target's work or learning.

The institution is generally held liable for quid pro quo harassment even if the institution was unaware of it. The harasser is an agent of the institution (i.e. the harasser is "acting" for the institution) and therefore the institution is responsible.

Hostile Environment

In 1986, in an employment case, *Meritor v. Vinson*, the U. S. Supreme Court unanimously expanded the definition of sexual harassment to include the concept of a *hostile environment*: an environment can be so offensive or hostile so as to interfere with a person's ability to work.[16] Similarly, a hostile environment can interfere with a student's ability to learn or participate in the university environment. This second kind of sexual harassment—offensive environment—is far more prevalent than the quid pro quo type and is harder for people to acknowledge as sexual harassment because it includes many behaviors that are often seen as "normal" or "boys will be boys" behavior.[17]

A hostile environment does not always involve a person with formal power such as an administrator or faculty member; peer-to-peer harassment such as by coworkers, colleagues, and students can be involved in creating a hostile environment. All the behaviors listed earlier, such as sexual innuendos, bantering, unwanted touching, sexual obscenities, computer harassment, exhibiting pornographic materials, and the like, can create a hostile environment. Even behavior that is not sexual but is demeaning, insulting, or intimidating on the basis of sex (e.g., verbal abuse, derogatory comments about women in general, or physical threats) can constitute a hostile environment.

Whether a person objects or does not object to hostile environment behavior is irrelevant if the person later indicates that the behavior was offensive. If the institution knew or should have known the environment was hostile and does not stop it, the institution could be liable. For example, if the harassment is out in the open and many people know about it, the institution may still be liable even if no one mentioned it to people in authority. The Court[18] gave the following guidance for determining liability in hostile environment workplace cases:

- Whether the employer knew or should have known about the harassment
- Whether the employer responded effectively when it learned of the harassment
- Whether the employer had a vigorous policy prohibiting sexual harassment
- If the policy was adequately communicated to employees

Sometimes the line between quid pro quo harassment and that of hostile environment is not all that clear. Threats or bribes for unwanted sexual activity, whether overt or covert, can create a hostile environment for the victim.

Sexual Favoritism

Sometimes favoritism can be considered a form of sexual harassment, although EEOC has concluded that an isolated instance of favoritism toward a lover, spouse, or friend is not sexual discrimination, even though it may be unfair. EEOC's view is that a woman who didn't get a promotion because of that kind of favoritism is no different from a man who did not get the same promotion for the same reason.[19] However, the following are two instances when favoritism can be a form of sexual harassment:

1. Where quid pro quo harassment is involved (a woman is forced to have sexual relations with her supervisor in order to receive a promotion or other benefit) other employees may be able to claim that they would have had to sleep with their supervisor in order to obtain benefits.

2. Where there is widespread favoritism, such as employees who receive benefits because they are providing sexual favors, such as laughing at men's sexual bantering or sleeping with them. This could be a form of hostile environment because other women could claim that the atmosphere was demeaning and degrading because women were being treated as sexual playthings. They might also be able to claim that they were denied benefits or were penalized because they did not partake in the sexual interactions engaged in by the other women.[20]

Questions and Answers About Sexual Harassment

Question: Does the harassed person have to be a female? And if a woman, does she have to be harassed by a male?

Answer: All of the laws prohibiting sexual harassment cover discrimination on the basis of sex. Men and women are protected against sexual harassment. Either a male or female may be the victim or the harasser.

Question: Does the harasser have to be of the other gender from the victim?

Answer: Although most sexual harassment involves males harassing females, same sex harassment can occur and is, in some instances, prohibited. The critical question is whether the harasser is treating a member or members of one gender differently from the other gender. Both can be of the same sex, where the harassment is based on the sex of the victim but not the victim's sexual orientation. Federal sex discrimination laws do not protect against discrimination on the basis of sexual orientation, although some state and local statutes do.

Question: Must the victim indicate to the harasser, a supervisor, or another agent of the institution that the behavior is unwelcome?

Answer: There is no requirement that the victim indicate discomfort with the harassing behavior, or complain to anyone about it for the institution to be held responsible for the conduct when the behavior involves an agent of the institution. When the behavior is committed by a coworker, student, or nonemployee, the institution is not held liable unless it knew or should have known that the behavior was occurring and failed to take appropriate action. The fact that no one complained does not automatically mean the institution did not know or should not have known the discrimination was taking place.

Regardless of how an institution or its agent learns that sexual harassment may be occurring, once it knows or should have known, it must take action. It does not need to wait for a formal or informal complaint.

Question: Does sexual harassment have to be repeated or is one incident enough?

Answer: One incident is usually sufficient for quid pro quo harassment. Generally, a single incident is not enough to prove that a hostile environment exists unless the incident is sufficiently serious. The more severe the incident the less important to show a pattern or series of incidents. For example, if a student or employee is grabbed and fondled in a sexual way and the institution ignores the behavior, the institution is likely to be liable. In the next few years, the Supreme Court will be articulating more precisely the criteria for determining whether an environment is hostile.

Question: What if someone doesn't intend to harass someone else?

Answer: Comments, such as the following, do not excuse sexual harassing behavior: "I didn't mean to harass her." "I was just joking." "I put my arms around everyone." "I would never harass anyone. She just doesn't have a sense of humor." "I always clown around. No one ever complained before." The courts have consistently ruled that the intent of the harasser is irrelevant. It is the effect of the behavior that counts, not the intention of the harassing person.

Question: Can someone complain about sexual harassment even if the harassment was not aimed at them?

Answer: A person can be affected by behavior that is aimed at another person. Harassment can create an intimidating, negative, offensive, or hostile environment for other persons in the workplace or school environment.

Question: Are institutions responsible for the behavior of nonemployees?

Answer: In some instances, institutions can be responsible for the conduct of vendors, contractors, subcontractors, construction workers, and the like when these persons harass employees or students.

Question: What if someone didn't inform the other person that their behavior was offensive? Is it still harassment?

Answer: There is no requirement that a person inform someone else that their behavior is offensive. In *Meritor v. Vinson,* the Supreme Court ruled that a woman who agreed to have sexual intercourse with her supervisor because she was afraid she would lose her job was nevertheless able to press charges of sexual harassment. The Court said the issue was not whether she made a voluntary decision to have intercourse with her supervisor but whether the behavior was wanted or unwanted.

Humor and Sexual Harassment

Sexual harassment often takes the guise of humor. Jokes about women or "funny" comments about individual women or women in general are typical bantering behavior. Although humor can be used to relax a group, humor can also be used to define the "outsiders," the people who are not like us, to express direct or unconscious hostility, and to build solidarity against one or more outsiders. One can readily see the hostility in ethnic jokes that demean various groups as well as in the so-called "locker room" or "dirty" jokes that demean women.

Sometimes such a joke is told in front of women without any awareness that the joke is offensive to them. At other times, jokes are prefaced with "You women probably won't like this joke," and then the speaker goes right on to tell it, clearly indicating that the feelings of the women are irrelevant. Often, if a woman complains about joking remarks, she will be asked, "Don't you have a sense of humor?" as if the fault were hers and not that of the joke teller. Men are more likely to use jokes for the purpose of embarrassing the listener; when humor is used aggressively so that insults masquerade as jokes, the result is sexual harassment.[21] Just as racist humor hurts people of color, sexist humor hurts women and can create a hostile environment.

Some Myths About Sexual Harassment[22]

Myth: Just saying "No" should make it stop.

Fact: Although saying "No" does work occasionally, many men still believe women who say "No" really mean "Yes," and therefore ignore women's protests.[23]

Myth: Harassment will stop if it is ignored.

Fact: Harassers often believe that when a woman ignores harassing behavior, she really likes it. Her lack of response is seen as approval or encouragement. Studies show that in most cases when harassment is ignored it continues and often gets worse.

Myth: If women watched the way they dressed, there would not be a problem with sexual harassment.

Fact: Sexual harassment can happen to anyone, no matter how one dresses. It typically has far more to do with power than with sexual attractiveness or appearance.

Myth: Sexual harassment is no big deal—it's the natural way men and women express affection and friendship.

Fact: Unwanted sexual innuendo, grabbing, and lewd comments are not expressions of affection and friendship, but rather expressions of power, a need to control, and in some instances, hostility toward women. Truly friendly behavior is not hurtful.

Myth: Sexual harassment is less likely to affect women professionals as often as other working women.

Fact: Women professionals report sexual harassment proportionally as often as other working women.

Myth: Sexual harassment is harmless. Women who object have no sense of humor or don't know how to accept a compliment.

Fact: Harassment is humiliating and often frightening. It can undermine careers and economic livelihood. No one should have to endure humiliation with a smile.

Myth: Sexual harassment policies will negatively affect professor's friendly relationships with women students.

Fact: Sexual harassment is not the type of social relationship that professors should be having with students. Friendship and sexual harassment are very different relationships.

Myth: Nice guys could not possibly be harassers.

Fact: Harassers are not perverts, and generally do not fit any particular mold. They come in all forms, including well-liked, talented, respected professionals.

How Pervasive Is Sexual Harassment?

In a study of 235 male faculty members at a research university, 26% reported sexual involvement with students. Only one subject reported that he believed he had sexually harassed a student.[24] In a survey of over 700 undergraduate senior women at the University of California at Berkeley, 34% had experienced some form of sexual harassment from an authority figure while at Berkeley. Forty-nine percent of the authority figures were professors.[25] At the University of Minnesota, 41% to 56% of women (including undergraduate and graduate students, academic employees, and civil service staff) said they had experienced at least one incident of sexual harassment during their time at the university.[26]

Many university administrators do not believe sexual harassment is prevalent because they have had few or no cases reported. In fact, most incidents are not reported; in one study at Harvard, only 5% of students who had an experience they would label as sexual harassment reported it to a college official.[27]

Most of the studies done at individual campuses document that 20% to 30% of undergraduate women have experienced some form of sexual harassment from faculty, administrators, or other staff. Using the lower figure of 20% translates into more than 1.4 million students experiencing sexual harassment.[28] Some studies are showing even higher figures: In the University of Minnesota study mentioned above, 52% of the female graduate students and 42% of the undergraduate students reported they had experienced sexual harassment, compared with 68% of the female academic employees and 59% of the female civil service staff.

About two percent of undergraduate women experience the most severe type of sexual harassment—direct or indirect threats or bribes for unwanted sexual activity from faculty or staff. For graduate women, the incidence for sexual harassment increases; between 30% to 40% report they have experienced some form of sexual harassment from faculty or administrators.

Only a few studies have examined the incidence of female college faculty experiencing sexual harassment, with 20% to 50% of women faculty members reporting some form of sexual harassment from other faculty members, department chairs, or other administrators. About 32% of tenured female professors and 49% of the untenured female professors reported experiencing some form of sexual harassment from someone in authority at least once during their time at Harvard.[29]

There is relatively little data about sexual harassment of nonacademic employees in educational institutions. Because there is greater variation in workplace settings studies of workers generally show greater variability in the incidence of sexual harassment than studies of faculty and students. Workplace estimates of sexual harassment often range from 40% to 75%, with some studies reporting even higher incidences.

In the few studies that have examined student-to-student harassment at the college level, 70% to 90% of undergraduate women report they had experienced at least one negative incident from one or more male students to which they reacted negatively and viewed the incident as serious.[30]

An emerging area of concern is harassment of professors by students. The harassment may be overt such as pornographic graffiti about women faculty. At one campus two male students posted a computerized graphic of a penis on the door of a woman faculty member's office.

Some male students may sexually tease women faculty or use sexual innuendos as a way to avoid issues when the faculty member raises problems such as a late paper.[31] Women faculty may be called "honey" or by their first names or by other inappropriate names by male students. Some male students may make similar inappropriate remarks about a faculty member's appearance, clothing, or sexuality. In one study of women faculty at a large university, nearly half of the respondents experienced behaviors such as the following from male students at least once: sexist comments, undue attention, verbal or written sexual comments, physical advances, explicit sexual propositions, and obscene phone calls believed to be from students. Among those who reported experiencing these behaviors, over 59 percent reported two or more of them.[32]

Although most incidents of harassment involve a male harassing a female, it is important to keep in mind, at least in terms of employees and faculty members, that most men do not harass. Of those who do, almost all are multiple harassers—they harass a number of women either simultaneously or sequentially or both.

Are Men Sexually Harassed?

Most people who are sexually harassed are women, but men can be harassed also. The law covers both men and women. Male students are more likely to be harassed by male teachers than female teachers.[33] Harassment by female faculty members is relatively rare although it can happen. Sometimes male faculty members report that female students come on to them sexually, and they, the male faculty, are the ones who are being harassed. However, because the male faculty member has more power than the student, including having the power to discipline the student, the student's behavior has different implications than the reverse, a male teacher harassing a female student. A male professor who is troubled by a female student's behavior can say something like, "This behavior is inappropriate and must stop or I shall have to report you"—something that a female student could not readily say to a male teacher who harassed her.

Although information about harassment of male employees is scanty, workplace data suggest that as many as 15 percent of male workers may experience some form of sexual harassment. Female students at all levels of education may harass male students, with sexual remarks, unwanted touching, and so forth. Although no data are available, some people suggest that this type of harassment may be increasing. Male students also harass other males. No figures are available although it is clear that harassment may be a serious problem for some males, especially when grabbing and touching are involved.

Student harassment can occur anywhere: in classrooms (even while faculty members are present), hallways, stairwells, cafeterias; at sports events, extracurricular clubs and activities, parties, recreational areas; in dormitories; on university-sponsored trips; in restrooms, and locker rooms (same sex harassment); and in parking lots.

Why Women Delay Complaining or Do Not Report Sexual Harassment

- They may not know that the behavior was sexual harassment.
- They think that because it only happened once it is not serious.
- They may not know there is a policy and that it is against the law.
- They don't trust the policy to be implemented.
- They are fearful of adversarial activity; the formal policy looks very litigious.
- Informal ways of resolving the issue are not apparent or do not exist.
- They are too ashamed or embarrassed to talk about what happened.
- They may blame themselves for "causing" the harassment.
- They are worried that others will blame them for "causing" the harassment.
- They are fearful that no one will believe them, will think they exaggerate, or are overly sensitive.
- They are worried about being humiliated.
- They may be fearful of retaliation from the harasser or his friends.
- They may be fearful of losing popularity for "turning someone in."
- They may be fearful of being labeled a "troublemaker."
- They believe that this is the way males are and that nothing is going to change.
- They don't want to get the harasser in trouble.
- They don't trust their own perception of what happened; they may deny the experience to themselves by believing they "misunderstood" what the harasser was doing.
- They worry about losing their job or getting a bad grade.
- They worry about the long-range impact on their academic life or career.

The Impact and Cost of Sexual Harassment

The impact of sexual harassment on the learning and work environment of universities is widespread. It can affect everyone in the educational institution: students, professors, staff, and administrators. Even potential employees, potential students, and the surrounding community can be affected.

Impact on Females

Like rape, sexual harassment has often been treated as a joke and not been taken seriously. The long history of silence makes many women uncomfortable, ashamed, and embarrassed, so that they are reluctant to talk about it to anyone. Often they may blame themselves for what happened and experience unjustified guilt. They may be fearful of repercussions if they say anything to the harasser or to anyone else. They may be convinced it would reflect badly on their character if they say anything about what happened.

When a boss or faculty member puts pressure on a female for sexual activity, she may fear that refusing these sexual demands will jeopardize her job, her grades, or academic career. She cannot freely choose to say "yes" or "no" in such a situation. Often she fears retaliation and with good reason: rejected males do not always act graciously. Unfair evaluations may be given; perks removed or withheld; promotions and raises may be denied; and the chance of a good recommendation for college or graduate school withheld.

Sexual harassment can be a traumatic ordeal for anyone who is harassed. A woman may be unsure how to handle harassment. Disbelief or denial may occur. Her self-esteem may suffer at several levels; she may feel that she ought to be able to handle it on her own or that there is something wrong with her for responding so strongly to what she and others may view as a common problem. Feelings of helplessness, lack of control, shame, guilt, depression, anxiety, inability to concentrate, and difficulty in handling day-to-day tasks at work or school may occur. Many of these behaviors are typical of posttraumatic stress disorder. Additionally employees may become less productive; students' learning may be seriously affected.

Physical symptoms may also be present, especially those related to stress, such as headaches, backaches, digestive trouble, and the inability to sleep. Females who are not harassed may also be demoralized and feel helpless when they watch or know of others who are harassed, especially when the behavior continues. They too may feel powerless and worry about what they would do if it happened to them. Some students may avoid classes taught by known harassers. Approximately one sixth of the University of Manitoba's female graduate students, for example, changed their study or research plans because of the fear of sexual harassment—they avoided working with faculty members who they "knew or had heard" had engaged in sexual harassment.[34]

Impact on Males

Sexual harassment reinforces stereotypes of women as sexual objects. It makes men less open to working with women and makes it more likely for them to harass and discriminate against women. When faculty members confuse friendly behavior toward students with sexual harassment, they may be fearful of informal interactions, thereby depriving them of the informal mentoring and support that is essential to students' growth and learning.

When male college students harass women in college with impunity, they are learning that harassment is acceptable and that women are fair game. Furthermore, peer harassment may set the stage for sexual assault. When males are accustomed to relating to women as objects of scorn or derision, they may find it difficult to treat females as equal human beings because it is hard to relate to people for whom one has little respect. Thus the relationships between males and females may be damaged when harassment is allowed to persist.

Male students who are allowed to harass women students are not being prepared for a workplace where men and women are colleagues. When they enter the workplace and engage in the same behaviors previously condoned at college, they may be surprised to be criticized by the employer, charged with sexual harassment, or terminated.

Impact on the Institution

In addition to formal charges and costly lawsuits, some schools have had bad publicity or controversy about cases of sexual harassment, especially when the school handled it badly or when the policy was unclear or not enforced consistently.

Some college students have avoided schools which have had bad publicity or when the students learned of incidents by word of mouth. Lower morale often translates into lowered productivity of those who work at the institution. Some may use leave-time to avoid the harasser. Others may quit their job, leading to increased employee turnover.

More important than bad publicity or controversy is the impact of sexual harassment on the learning climate. In an atmosphere where harassment occurs, even if it happens to other people, learning is difficult. Harassment chills the learning climate and subverts the very purpose of the educational institution.

Consensual Relationships

Although almost everyone knows of a professor who married his graduate student and lived happily everafter, most consensual relationships between students and faculty members or between staff are problematic, not only for the parties involved but for others as well. In a relationship between equals, either party is free to end the interaction, but it is difficult to do so in a relationship where one person has power over the other. How can a woman say "no" or indicate her displeasure if she is worried about losing her job or getting a bad grade?

Another problem is that of the student who is "seduced" into a relationship because she is flattered by the attention of an older professor whom she looks up to. Often professors involved in such relationships are "serial" harassers. The potential for exploitation is clear, and explains why many professional organizations have codes of ethics prohibiting relationships between professional and client—a relationship which is analogous to that of faculty member and student.[35]

> A consensual relationship also raises issues of conflict of interest. Can a supervisor or faculty member fairly evaluate someone with whom they are engaged in a consensual relationship?
>
> Moreover, others who know about the relationship are likely to be skeptical of any evaluation, perks, or favors given to the person and attribute them to the relationship, validly or not. Employees or students involved in such relationships may find it difficult to evaluate their own achievements: Did they deserve the positive evaluation, or was it simply the result of the relationship. Finally, colleagues or fellow students may feel uncomfortable and find it difficult to relate to the persons involved in such a relationship.[36]

The potential for abuse and exploitation exists not only during the duration of a consensual relationship between a faculty member and a student, or between a supervisor and an employee, but can worsen after the relationship is ended, especially if the person in power uses that power to try to maintain the relationship (see Chapter 14). It is at that point that the relationship becomes sexual harassment.

But even if there is no harassment, there are other negative consequences, especially for the person with less power. Some women will feel awkward and try to avoid an ex-boyfriend and his colleagues; they may also be fearful of what kind of evaluations they may receive in the future, or how their ex-boyfriend will treat them professionally.[37]

Although neither Title VII nor Title IX prohibit consensual sexual relationships, numerous institutions have developed policies on this issue because of the potential for problems (see Chapters 2 and 6).

Characteristics of Educational Institutions Where Sexual Harassment Is Most Likely to Occur

No institution is exempt from sexual harassment; however, some institutions are more likely to have serious incidents occur, as well as a greater amount of sexual harassment. Some of the characteristics to be aware of follow:

- Does not have the strong support and active commitment of top administrators to end sexual harassment.
- Does not have a well-developed policy in place.
- Does not have an adequate dissemination plan, so that many people do not know about the policy.
- Relies on formal procedures, thus discouraging persons from bringing complaints, or if informal procedures are in place, does not publicize them.
- Does not have a comprehensive prevention and training program targeted at all levels—administrators, faculty members, staff, and students.
- Does not follow its policy, and often does not punish offenders.
- Does not inform the campus population of how complaints are resolved.
- Does not have an ongoing plan and program that responds to change. (Some schools having conducted a program once see no need to do it again.)
- Administrators, such as department heads, division heads, and deans as well as student residence assistants, do not know what their role should be when someone comes to them with problems or how to intervene when they observe sexual harassment.
- Does not have target prevention programs aimed at groups such as new faculty, entering students, athletes, fraternity and sorority members, international faculty, and students.
- Allows and encourages campus activities which are demeaning to women—sexually oriented skits or sexual themes for student activities such as "Hawaiian Night–Come for a Lei."
- Fraternities and athletics play a major role in the social life of the campus.
- Does not respond publicly when sexual harassment occurs as in the case of men mooning women or harassing "Take Back the Night Marchers," thus inadvertently communicating that the behavior is acceptable.
- Does not intervene either formally or informally when harassment of women or others occurs, except perhaps when the behavior is extraordinarily egregious.
- Is an institution that was formerly all male, even though it may have been integrated for many years.
- Has a substantially larger number of male students compared to female students.
- Has no program to inspect and remove or cover up offensive graffiti.
- Has no support program for those who have been sexually harassed.
- Has not integrated prevention programs for sexual harassment with those dealing with sexual assault.

Other Issues

The Typical Harasser

The harasser is typically male. He may be any of the following: young, old, popular, unliked, outspoken, shy and retiring, conservative, radical, married, unmarried, religious or not—in short, there is no "typical harasser." He could be the boy next door or a respected professor. Although there are some instances of women harassing students or employees, they are relatively rare, in part because women are not often in positions of power; and, perhaps, because of gender expectations, women may be less likely to initiate sexual behavior.

Issue of False Charges

Many people believe that women will file false charges against men as a way of getting back at someone with whom they are angry. As mentioned earlier, the vast majority of women are reluctant to file formal charges or tell anyone in a position to help them even when serious harassment has occurred. False charges by students against teachers or staff or employees against supervisors are exceptionally rare, probably accounting for less than one percent of all charges.[38]

Sexuality and Sexual Harassment

For some men, it is difficult to relate to women except in a sexual manner whether the women are students, workers, or professionals. Women's sexuality is often an issue in sexual harassment incidents. When a charge is filed, it is not unusual for people to make comments about the woman's physical appearance, as in "How pretty is she?" That type of comment reveals the belief that sexual harassment is a function of biology rather than of power.

There is a long history of holding women responsible for men's sexual behavior. The comments: "She asked for it" or "Look what she was wearing" indicate that this view is far from gone. Often, when charges have been filed, some people will blame the victim for having caused her own harassment.

Women wear clothing to be in style, for their self-esteem, and to be attractive to other people, including men. Men often assume that a woman's clothing indicates her sexual desire; indeed her behavior may be viewed as sexual even when it is not. In two studies of college students, men were more likely than women to read sexual innuendo into everyday interactions between men and women. In two situations involving a male manager and a female trainee, and a male professor and a female student, men tended to rate the interactions as more sexy, seductive, and flirtatious. Women viewed the same exchanges as merely friendly. Thus, friendly gestures by women are often misinterpreted by men as sexual overtures and suggestive behaviors; men, in turn, may then respond with behavior that can be viewed as sexual harassment.[39]

Clothing and friendly behavior do not give others permission to grab, touch, or engage in other sexually harassing behavior. These behaviors do not signal what a woman wants or what she will do. Focusing on a woman's apparel, attractiveness, or behavior as a "cause" of sexual harassment shifts the blame away from the offender to the victim and ignores the issue of power.

Conclusion

Although protection from lawsuits and fear of false complaints are certainly legitimate concerns, they point to what, to our way of thinking, is a very serious form of myopia. Much of the attention being focused on sexual harassment prevention in our universities is driven by the fear of litigation. Administrators seldom hear questions such as "How can we ensure a safe and nurturing learning environment?" or "What can we do to teach our students and faculty members how to protect themselves from sexual harassment?" or "What can we do to teach our students and faculty members appropriate ways of behaving?" Universities must move away from being motivated by fear of litigation and reclaim the voice of integrity. Administrators must be pulled by the desire to do what is right rather than be driven by the fear of doing something wrong. Solutions to sexual harassment on campuses will not come from law books or court decisions, they will come from a collective effort to ensure that all colleagues and students are treated fairly and that all are guaranteed a safe place to work and learn in an environment free of fear, hostility, and harassment.

Of course, we must all learn how to prevent sexual harassment and how to respond when it occurs. However, it is critical for everyone to understand that *sexual harassment is not wrong because it is illegal, it was made illegal because it is wrong!* Although sexual elements are often involved in sexual harassment, sexual harassment is illegal because it is a form of discrimination that is prohibited. We must put our energy into eradicating sexual harassment because it is the right thing to do.

Endnotes

1. Farley, Lin, *Sexual shakedown: The sexual harassment of women on the job*. McGraw-Hill, New York, 1978, pp. xii, 82–84.
2. The EEOC enforces Title VII of the Civil Rights Act of 1964 which prohibits (among other things) sexual harassment in the workplace.
3. *Ellison v. Brady*, 924 F.2d 872 (9th Cir. 1991).
4. Thompson Publishing Group, *Educator's guide to controlling sexual harassment*. Major contributor, Bernice Resnick Sandler. Washington, DC, 1993. Tab 200, p. 16.
5. Thompson. Tab 200, p. 17.
6. Hughes, Jean O'Gorman and Bernice Resnick Sandler, *Peer harassment: Hassles for women on campus*. Originally published by the Project on the Status and Education of Women, Association of American Colleges, Washington, DC, 1988. Now published by the Center for Women Policy Studies, Washington, DC.
7. Thompson. Tab 200, p. 17
8. Thompson. Tab 200, p. 17.
9. Thompson. Tab 200, p. 17.
10. Thompson. Tab 200, p. 17.
11. The first six bullets are from Sandler, *Sexual harassment and date rape*, p. 5.
12. Thompson. Tab 200, p. 18.
13. Thompson. Tab 200, p. 15.
14. Hughes, Jean O'Gorman and Bernice Resnick Sandler, In *Case of sexual harassment: A guide for women students*. Originally published by the Project on the Status and Education of Women, Association of American Colleges, Washington, DC, 1986. Now published by the Center for Women Policy Studies, Washington, DC.
15. Thompson. Tab 200, p. 25.
16. *Meritor Savings Bank, FSB, v. Vinson*, 477 U.S. 57 (1986).
17. Thompson. Tab 200, p. 26.

18. *Meritor Savings Bank, FSB, v. Vinson,* 477 U.S. 57 (1986).
19. Thompson. Tab 200, p. 28.
20. Thompson. Tab 200, pp. 28–29.
21. Barrecca, Regina, *They used to call me Snow White…but I drifted.* Viking, New York, 1991, p. 65.
22. Sandler, *Sexual harassment and date rape,* p. 8.
23. Indicating one's displeasure at sexually harassing behavior is most likely to work when there is a misunderstanding; in most cases of harassment, however, the harasser *wants* to intimidate and will not stop when asked to.
24. Fitzgerald, Louise F., Lauren M. Weitzman, Yael Gold, and Mimi Omerod, Academic harassment: Sex and denial in scholarly garb, *Psychology of Women Quarterly,* September 1988.
25. *On Campus With Women,* Association of American Colleges, Washington, DC, Fall 1989, p. 7.
26. University of Minnesota Center for Survey Research, as quoted in University of Minnesota documents harassment, *On campus with women.* Project on the Status and Education of Women, Association of American Colleges, Washington, DC, Winter 1990, p. 5.
27. Report of the Date Rape Task Force, Harvard and Radcliffe Colleges, February 10, 1992.
28. Sandler, *Sexual harassment and date rape,* pp. 6–7.
29. Female faculty members and students at Harvard report sexual harassment, *Chronicle of Higher Education,* 27(10), November 2, 1983.
30. *See,* for example, Warren A. Brown and Jane Maestro-Schfeer, *Assessing sexual harassment and public safety: A survey of Cornell women,* New York: Cornell Institute for Social and Economic Research, July 1, 1986, p. 23; Elizabeth Jane Salkind, Can't you take a joke? A study of sexual harassment among peers (Masters's thesis), Massachusetts Institute of Technology, February 1986, p. 63; Assessment of Sexual Harassment Within the URI Community: A Report of an Investigation by the Assessment Task Group of the Sexual Harassment Committee, Kingston, RI: University of Rhode Island, August, 1980; and Barriers to Equality in Academia: Women in Computer Science at MIT, prepared by female graduate students and research staff in the Laboratory for Computer Science and the Artificial Intelligence Laboratory at the Massachusetts Institute of Technology, February 1983.
31. Sandler, Bernice Resnick, Women faculty at work in the classroom, or, Why it hurts to be a woman in labor. Center for Women Policy Studies, Washington DC, 1993, p. 7.
32. Grauerholz, E. Sexual harassment of women professors by students: Exploring the dynamics of power, authority, and gender in a university setting, *Sex Roles,* 21, 789–801, 1989.
33. *See,* for example, Baier, John L. Sexual harassment of university students by faculty members at a southern research university, *College Student Affairs Journal,* 10, 4–11, 1990.
34. Fear of harassment leads students to change plans, *Chronicle of Higher Education,* February 8, 1989, p. A4.
35. Sandler, *Sexual harassment and date rape,* p. 19.
36. Sandler, *Sexual harassment and date rape,* p. 19.
37. *See* What about dating your professor? Hughes and Sandler, p. 8.
38. Stimpson, Catherine R., Overreaching, sexual harassment and education. In Michele A. Paludi & Richard B. Barickman, *Academic and workplace sexual harassment: A resource manual,* State University of New York Press, Albany, 1991, p. 117.
39. Harassment: Just a misunderstanding? In *On Campus With Women,* 17(3), 3–4, 1988.

2

THE LEGAL CONTEXT OF SEXUAL HARASSMENT ON CAMPUS

ROBERT J. SHOOP

Introduction

As the most casual observer has noticed, university communities across the country are embroiled in heated debates about the existence, seriousness, causes, and consequences of sexual harassment on campus.[1] Although sexual harassment is a difficult and complex issue, one thing is clear—sexual harassment is a serious problem and universities must act to prevent it from occurring. As they respond to the challenge of eliminating sexual harassment, university administrators must do so in light of the impact of the laws of sexual harassment on their deliberation. This chapter provides a schema that will permit administrators, faculty members, and students to navigate the partially charted territory of sexual harassment law.

Overview

Sexual harassment is wrong because it hurts people. Sexual harassment is devastating to the victim; it can destroy the career of the harasser, and it can significantly damage the reputation of the university. Through its various legislative efforts, society has made sexual harassment illegal. Universities may be held liable if they do not carry out their legal responsibility to prevent sexual harassment and/or do not respond appropriately when complaints arise.

For more than twenty years legislators at the state and federal levels have been grappling with the issues surrounding sex discrimination. This struggle has resulted in laws being passed that set forth standards and procedures for ensuring

Note: This chapter is designed to provide accurate information regarding the legal issues surrounding sexual harassment. It is provided with the understanding that neither the author, editors, nor the publisher is engaged in rendering legal service. If legal service is required, the services of a competent professional person should be sought.

nondiscrimination. The goal of all these enactments is to ensure nondiscrimination and educational equity for both males and females.

It has only been in the last two decades that courts have addressed the issue of sexual harassment. The first time a court heard a sexual harassment claim was in 1976 when the D.C. Circuit Court held that dismissing an employee for refusal to engage in sexual relations with her supervisor was a violation of Title VII.[2] In 1980 the Second Circuit rejected the first sexual harassment complaint by a group of female students who alleged that Yale University had not taken their complaints seriously, although the court acknowledged that Title IX did prohibit sexual harassment in educational institutions.[3]

Although it is now well established that sexual harassment is a form of sexual discrimination, this understanding is still evolving. As universities have become aware that they are liable for violations of federal law (Title VII and Title IX), they have begun to act affirmatively to avoid liability. However, active debates continue to focus on the validity of women's perceptions of their experiences, the due process protection that is necessary, and the university's liability for any harm that has occurred.

From the first case[4] to recognize a claim for sexual harassment in 1976, to the 1994 case of *Franklin v. Gwinnett County Schools*,[5] challenges in the sexual harassment context have been based on statutory and less frequently, constitutional grounds. Courts continue to be called on to illuminate the legal status of this evolving area of the law. Each new case provides an opportunity for the court to resolve uncertainties and clarify what constitutes sexual harassment. Sexual harassment cases are heard and decided in the context of constitutional challenges under the equal protection clause of the Fourteenth Amendment and the equal protection component of the Fifth Amendment. Recent court decisions have clarified the level of judicial review and the nature of proof required to establish a violation. However, even when courts provide guidance, there is often sharp disagreement in concrete cases. These disagreements generally focus on the questions of truth, sanctions, and university liability.

The Fourteenth Amendment and Fifth Amendment provisions apply only to governmental action. The Fourteenth Amendment prohibits discriminatory actions by the states, while the Fifth Amendment forbids the federal government from denying persons equal protection of the law. The primary statutory bases for sex discrimination questions are Title VII of the 1964 Civil Rights Act, as amended, and Title IX of the Education Amendments of 1972. However, the definition of what constitutes sexual harassment is far from static.

In the hope of achieving harmony, the majority of us voluntarily allow laws to regulate our behavior. Lawmakers and judges are involved in the constant process of attempting to strike a balance that allows individuals as much freedom as possible while at the same time protecting the rights of others. The Constitution protects our individual rights while various state and federal laws protect the general welfare of society and implement the constitutional protection of individuals.

Laws are not made in isolation from what is happening in society. As society changes and new relationships and values evolve, new laws are needed to respond to the emerging view of what is right and what is wrong. As groups of people request or demand legal protection, public opinion interacts with lawmaking to ensure that new laws reflect the values of the majority. Consequently, laws both shape and reflect the values of society.

Because society is made up of people who hold many different values, new rules are not accepted by everyone at the same rate. Some people are way out in front of a value shift. They are the people who are fighting for a new idea before most of us understand what they are talking about. For example, Farley and others coined the term sexual harassment in 1974,[6] but it wasn't until 1986 that the U.S. Supreme Court ruled that sexual harassment was a form of sex discrimination. By the time a new idea is formalized into law, most people have formed an opinion about it, and the majority of the people accept the new law. However, there are always people who continue to fight against a new value, even after it is passed into law. They keep testing the resolve of society to uphold the new law. Some of this testing is taking place on campuses and some is taking place in the courts.

The current understanding about sexual harassment is an example of the complex process of translating a new value into new rules for behavior. While some people are fighting to gain equal treatment for women, others are resisting any change in the role and status of women. Still others argue that the university, although a workplace, is a special kind, one in which the work carried out, by students and faculty alike, is the discovery and assessment of ideas. Some organizations and associations believe that those institutions of higher education that have emulated the Equal Employment Opportunity Commission's (EEOC) Guidelines pay insufficient respect to the unique functions of the academic environment.

When there are conflicting beliefs about appropriate and inappropriate behavior, courts are asked to resolve the controversy. The process is further complicated by the fact that judges, as part of society, have their own sets of values. Therefore, each judge interprets the law through his or her own set of values.

Laws are society's attempt to ensure that consequences will result if certain prohibited acts are committed. Courts were created to interpret the laws and to ensure that all citizens are treated equally and judged by the same standards of behavior when consequences are meted out. The overall purpose of laws and the court system is to produce solidarity, continuity, and conformity within society. The end result of all law is justice.

Because no law can specifically describe all possible actions, we don't always know exactly which specific behaviors are legal and which are illegal until a court makes a ruling on the specific facts of a case. Therefore, the court system has a major influence on all of our behavior. As our attitudes toward men and women have evolved, courts have been called on to provide clarification regarding the laws involving gender.

Sexual Harassment Is Against the Law

The laws that govern sexual harassment of university faculty, staff, and student employees are the same as those that affect all workplaces. For example, whether you are a university administrator, professor, secretary, student worker, graduate assistant, or custodian you are protected from discrimination by Title VII of the

Civil Rights Act. Section 1983 of the United States Code also applies. Title IX of the Education Amendments of 1972 covers students as well as employees.

When I make presentations on the legal rights of victims of sexual harassment and other forms of sex discrimination, I am frequently asked the following questions: Who can sue? How do you file a complaint? How long do I have to file a complaint? Who can make a complaint? How quickly must the investigation be completed? And, what are the punishments allowed? The following sections answer these and other questions.

Legal Interpretation of Sexual Harassment

Sexual harassment is any unwelcome behavior of a sexual nature that interferes with a person's work or education. The term *unwelcome* indicates the action or behavior was unsolicited and nonreciprocal. In other words, the person witnessing or being affected by the behavior didn't desire the behavior. For example, wanted kissing, touching, or flirting is not sexual harassment.

Behavior of a sexual nature includes virtually any conduct that refers to sex. Such conduct can include using profane language or telling off-color jokes. It includes using sexist terms such as "babe," "bitch," or "bimbo" or making comments about body parts. But, it can also include what some may consider to be terms of endearment such as "honey," "baby," "darling," and so on. Behavior of a sexual nature includes leering and ogling, and without question, any kind of unwanted touching such as patting, hugging, and pinching. Finally, any request for sexual favors in return for benefits meets the criteria established for sexual harassment.

Although the concept of sexual harassment is not completely settled in law or fully understood by society as a whole, courts have clearly and consistently affirmed that the workplace and the classroom must be free from sexual harassment. While not legally required to do so, the courts tend to look to the EEOC for guidance on matters relating to sexual harassment. In 1988 the EEOC issued a document to all field offices entitled *Policy Guidance on Current Issues of Sexual Harassment.* The document outlined the behavior that constitutes sexual harassment. The guidelines reminded field personnel that sexual harassment is a form or subset of sexual discrimination and is therefore prohibited by Title VII of the Civil Rights Act of 1964.

The EEOC drew on a substantial body of judicial reasoning in holding that Title VII affords the right to work in an environment free from discriminatory intimidation, ridicule, and insult. The student's workplace is school, and consequently students are afforded this same right under Title IX.

Over the past ten years most sexual harassment cases have been decided on the *EEOC Guidelines on Discrimination Because of Sex.* Under these guidelines, unwelcome sexual advances, requests for sexual favors, and other verbal or physical conduct of a sexual nature is sexual harassment if any of the following is true:

- Submission to such conduct is made either explicitly or implicitly a term or condition of an individual's employment.

- Submission to or rejection of such conduct by an individual is used as the basis for employment decisions affecting such individual.
- Such conduct has the purpose or effect of unreasonably interfering with an individual's work performance or creating an intimidating, hostile, or offensive working environment.

The first two subsections of the EEOC guidelines define quid pro quo harassment. The third subsection describes hostile environment sexual harassment. A subset of the hostile work environment is known as *sexual favoritism.*

Quid pro quo, environmental, and sexual favoritism sexual harassment occur regularly on university campuses. Although all three are forms of discrimination, and it is sometimes difficult to distinguish between the categories, it is important to do so because universities are held to different standards of liability for each. Often these forms overlap or occur simultaneously. However, each is a distinct category and provides for a separate complaint or cause of action. The following sections are overviews of each category of sexual harassment. The Civil Rights Act of 1991 permits an award of limited compensatory and punitive damages against private employers; however, public employers are only liable for compensatory damages.

Quid Pro Quo

Quid pro quo is a Latin term that means, "you do something for me and I'll do something for you." In the context of sexual harassment of university employees or students, quid pro quo may include an offer of special treatment such as awarding a better grade, letter of reference, promotion, or merit raise in return for sexual favors. It can also be a threat of retaliation. For example, quid pro quo occurs if a professor threatens to lower a grade or refuses to write a letter of recommendation or a department chair threatens to withhold a recommendation for promotion or tenure if a sexual request is rejected. Quid pro quo also takes place if a professor threatens a student with some penalty if the student does not consent to have a sexual relationship with the professor. One critical aspect of quid pro quo is that a single event constitutes a violation and courts hold institutions liable for even a single incident. If a professor makes a sexual proposition that involves the student's educational conditions even one time, quid pro quo sexual harassment has occurred. In quid pro quo sexual harassment, the threat or actual deprivation of educational benefits, once it is proven, allows the victim to ask the court to provide relief.

Quid pro quo sexual harassment is the easiest type of harassment to recognize. It occurs when sexual demands are made on a student or subordinate in exchange for educational or professional participation, advancement, or other benefits.

Quid pro quo sexual harassment has received more attention from the media and consequently it is better understood than other forms of sexual harassment. In cases of quid pro quo, the institution is generally held liable even if it had no knowledge of the specific behavior.

Although quid pro quo sexual harassment frequently occurs and the consequences are devastating, hostile educational environment is the most prevalent and misunderstood form of sexual harassment.

Hostile Educational Environment

For practical purposes, any sexually oriented conduct, or any sexually oriented atmosphere that is intimidating or offensive to a reasonable person, can be construed as creating a hostile educational environment. In the workplace this behavior is called hostile work environment sexual harassment; in a university setting, I refer to it as a hostile educational environment. This concept is sometimes confusing because men and women often perceive the same behavior in quite different ways. What a man might consider innocuous, a woman might consider blatantly offensive. It is important to remember that courts examine the behavior in terms of how it would affect a "reasonable person."

One critical dimension of the hostile educational environment category is that sexual harassment can occur even though the victim does not suffer any loss of economic or tangible benefits. Unlike quid pro quo, hostile educational environment generally requires a consistent pattern of behavior. A single event does not necessarily constitute a violation unless it is very serious. For a behavior to be considered to have created a hostile educational environment, it must be "sufficiently pervasive and severe."

Hostile educational environment is a form of harassment that is less tangible, less discrete, and often occurs over a period of time. Unlike quid pro quo which may involve a single incident, sexually hostile or intimidating environments are typically characterized by multiple, varied, and frequent occurrences.

What Constitutes a Hostile Educational Environment

A hostile environment in an educational setting is essentially the same as it is in other workplace settings. In the university setting the hostile educational environment theory is based on the assumption that the relationship between the student and the school and the subordinate and the supervisor is significant and that students and subordinates should be protected from psychological as well as physical abuse. Each student or employee should be able to come to class or work free from fear and free from harm.

It is important to remember that the person who creates a hostile environment does not have to have formal power. Therefore, coworkers and fellow students can crate a hostile educational environment for each other. It is also possible for a subordinate to create a hostile environment for a supervisor and for a student to create a hostile environment for a faculty member.

Sexual Favoritism

A third type of sexual harassment is actually a subset of environmental sexual harassment. Sexual favoritism is also fairly easy to identify. It occurs when a student or employee receives benefits as a result of his or her submission to sexual advances or requests for sexual favors. The victims of the harassment may be the other students or employees who are treated unfairly because they are not objects of the romantic interest of a supervisor. In the workplace, this type of sexual harassment has resulted in successful lawsuits brought on behalf of qualified persons who were denied employment opportunities or benefits. However, courts have required proof of the sexual relationship, not merely rumors or innuendos. Courts have yet to offer consistent views on how to treat sexual harassment cases in which a student is favored by a teacher who has a romantic interest in her or him.

Issue of Intent

Some people are confused about the role that intent plays in determining whether sexual harassment has taken place. Professors who have been accused of sexually harassing students often reply that they did not intend to embarrass, or that they were only teasing. They apparently assume this is somehow a defense against the impact of their actions. Some people who have been accused of sexual harassment preceded their offensive comments with phrases such as, "Now don't be offended by this." or "You will probably think I am a chauvinist pig, but let me tell you a joke." Many people who have been accused of sexual harassment admit they committed the behavior but contend they did not intend the behavior to be offensive. This argument demonstrates a lack of understanding of sexual harassment. The behavior does not have to be sexual in nature. Nor is the *intent* of the harasser relevant. It is the *impact* of the action that determines whether sexual harassment has taken place.

For a behavior to be considered to have created a hostile educational environment, the following four elements must exist:

- **First**, the harassment must be based on a person's sex. (It will be unlikely that a court will find behavior that is equally offensive to men and women to be sexual harassment. This does not mean that a university cannot prohibit such behavior, but a victim will probably not succeed in a sexual harassment suit.)
- **Second,** the behavior must be unwelcome to the victim. The victim must not have solicited or incited the offensive behavior, and the victim must regard the conduct as undesirable or offensive.
- **Third,** the offensive behavior must be sufficiently severe or pervasive to alter conditions of the learning or working climate to interfere with a person's ability to work, learn, or partake in the opportunities offered by the institution by creating a hostile educational environment. One off-color joke or comment will usually not be considered to be sexual harassment.
- **Fourth,** in order for the university to be liable for hostile environment sexual harassment, it must have known or should have known of the harassment and failed to take prompt, effective, remedial action. Because the university is expected to control the campus environment, it is held responsible for sexual harassment.

Some people are confused about the hostile educational environment on a university campus because, in many cases, the harasser is a student who has no formal, recognized authority over the victim. Second, because student victims of sexual harassment often have no obvious loss or physical injury, some people do not recognize that an injury has occurred. And finally, much of the behavior that female students find offensive is behavior that has long been accepted as "normal" heterosexual behavior by many men and boys. It must be remembered that universities are liable for sexual harassment if the behavior creates an intimidating, offensive, or hostile environment regardless of any other impact on the students.

Title VII

Title VII of the Civil Rights Act of 1964 as amended by the Equal Employment Opportunity Act of 1972, the Pregnancy Discrimination Act of 1978 and the Civil Rights Act of 1991 prohibits private employers, state and local governments, and educational institutions employing more than 15 individuals from discriminating on the basis of race, color, religion, sex or national origin in all aspects of employment. It does not cover students, other than those employed by the institution. Title VII covers all aspects of employment including hiring and firing; compensation, assignment, or classification of employees; transfer, promotion, layoff, or recall; job advertisements; recruitment; testing; use of company facilities; training and apprenticeship programs; fringe benefits; pay, retirement plans, and disability leave; or other terms and conditions of employment. The 1972 amendments permit employees and applicants to file suit in federal district court if they are not satisfied with the employer's or EEOC's disposition of their complaints. As amended in 1991, it allows plaintiffs, including those alleging sexual harassment, to sue for monetary damages. This act allows recovery of compensatory damages only in cases of intentional discrimination, and punitive damages only against private employers who act with malice or reckless indifference. The damages are currently capped depending on the number of employees, with a maximum of $300,000. Title VII also prohibits retaliation against a person who files a charge of discrimination, participates in an investigation, or opposes an unlawful employment practice.

In 1986, the U.S. Supreme Court relied on EEOC guidelines when it unanimously held in *Meritor Savings Bank, FSB, v. Vinson*[7] that both quid pro quo and hostile environment sexual harassment are a subset of sex discrimination and are actionable under Title VII. Unwelcome sexual advances, requests for sexual favors, and other verbal or physical conduct of a sexual nature constitutes sexual harassment when submission to or rejection of this conduct explicitly or implicitly affects an individual's employment, unreasonably interferes with an individual's work performance or creates an intimidating, hostile or offensive work environment. According to EEOC, sexual harassment can occur in a variety of circumstances, including but not limited to the following:

- The victim as well as the harasser may be a woman or a man. The victim does not have to be of the other sex.
- The harasser can be the victim's supervisor, an agent of the employer, a supervisor in another area, a coworker, or a nonemployee.
- The victim does not have to be the person harassed but could be anyone affected by the offensive conduct.
- Unlawful sexual harassment may occur without economic injury to or discharge of the victim.
- The harasser's conduct must be unwelcome.

Harris v. Forklift Systems, Inc.

Although, by all accounts, the number of sexual harassment cases is rapidly increasing, *Harris v. Forklift Systems, Inc.,*[8] was only the U.S. Supreme Court's third decision on this issue. Although the Court did not provide the hoped-for tests for hostile work environment claims, it did clearly warn employers that sexual harassment will not be tolerated. This case raised the question of whether employees alleging sexual harassment on the job must prove psychological injury in order to collect damages under Title VII. Although Harris had shown that her boss subjected her to "a continuing pattern of sex-based derogatory conduct," the Sixth Circuit Court of Appeals dismissed the case.[9] The Court said she was unable to prove the abuse affected her "psychological well-being."

In a unanimous decision, the Supreme Court reversed the lower court decision. The Court held that a plaintiff charging sexual harassment does not have to prove psychological harm. The Court reminded employers of the rules it made in 1986 in *Meritor Savings Bank v. Vinson.*[10] According to the Court, "sexual harassment is against the law when it is sufficiently severe or pervasive to alter the conditions of the victim's employment and create an abusive working environment." The environment would be considered abusive if a "reasonable person" would find it objectionable and the victim subjectively found it objectionable. The Court stated that, a mere utterance of an epithet which engenders offensive feelings does not violate Title VII. However, "Title VII comes into play before the harassing conduct leads to a nervous breakdown."

The Court stated that a jury can determine whether or not an environment is "hostile" or "abusive" only by considering all the circumstances that affect an employees psychological well-being. These circumstances would include: (1) the frequency of the discriminatory conduct (2) its severity (3) whether it is physically threatening or humiliating, or a mere offensive utterance and (4) whether it unreasonably interferes with an employee's work performance.

This decision gave all employers a clear warning that they are responsible if they permit abusive or hostile work environments to exist. By focusing attention on the work environment rather than the psychological make up of the victim, this decision will help victims of sexual harassment. Although this case did not provide as much clarity as many had hoped, it provided the ground rules for juries to use in order to determine if the employer crossed the line from rudeness to harassment.

The Court stated that Title VII "bars conduct that would seriously affect a reasonable person's psychological well-being, but the statute is not limited to such conduct. So long as the environment would reasonably be perceived, and is perceived, as hostile or abusive, there is no need for it also to be psychologically injurious."[11]

The effect on the employee's psychological well-being is, of course, relevant to determining whether the plaintiff actually found the environment abusive. But while psychological harm, like any other relevant factor, may be taken into account, no single factor is required. Justice Scalia, in his concurrence, warned that this decision "opens expansive vistas of litigation and will let juries decide whether sex-related conduct engaged in (or permitted by) an employer is egregious enough to warrant an award of damages."[12]

Reasonable Person versus the Reasonable Woman Test

Among the unanswered questions left in the wake of the *Harris* decision is the appropriate perspective from which to evaluate the validity of a hostile work environment claim. Should an employer and courts use the "reasonable woman" standard or the "reasonable person" standard when evaluating an employee's complaint? Although this issue has divided lower federal courts and was discussed in oral arguments, the *Harris* Court clearly avoided deciding the question. Since the court did not deal with the reasonable person issue *per se,* I argue for the validity of replacing the traditional reasonable person standard with a gender-conscious standard.[13]

The Supreme Court made it clear that it will find a person liable for sexual harassment if the actions are unwelcome, and if there is a pattern of severe or pervasive behavior. Until recently, the basis for finding that a behavior is sufficiently severe or pervasive to constitute sexual harassment was the objective standard of "reasonableness." In cases of negligence, the courts have historically asked, "What would a reasonable man (sometimes modified to 'reasonable person') do in a similar situation?"

In early sexual harassment cases many courts examined behaviors offensive to women in light of this test. Because men and women often see the same situation quite differently and many men did not see anything wrong with the allegedly offensive behavior, courts often ruled that the behavior did not violate the "reasonable man" standard, and therefore no harassment took place.

Although, in the *Harris* case, the Supreme Court supported the reasonable person test, earlier lower court decisions indicate an awareness of the gender hierarchy that shapes much of the interaction between women and men in the workplace and at school. That is, women and men often interpret the same behavior differently.

For example, in the case of *Ellison v. Brady,*[14] Circuit Judge Beezer stated that if the reasonable person standards were accepted, victims of sexual harassment would have to endure the harassment until their psychological well-being was seriously affected to the extent that they suffered anxiety and debilitation before they could establish a hostile environment. He said that sexual harassment falls somewhere between forcible rape and the mere utterance of an epithet. "Although an isolated epithet by itself fails to support a cause of action for a hostile environment, Title VII's protection of employees from sex discrimination should come into play long before the point where victims of sexual harassment require psychiatric assistance."

The primary danger of using the reasonable person test is that studies indicate that men and women have different views and perceptions on the issue of sexual harassment. For example, although many studies have documented that women perceive sexual harassment as a serious problem at work, one study reported that approximately two thirds of the male respondents felt the "amount of sexual harassment at work is greatly exaggerated."[15]

The danger of using the reasonable woman, or reasonable victim, test is that by relying on a victim's perspective such a test could be used to censor speech that may be offensive to some but a form of communication deserving legal protection. Schultz warns that such a standard has the potential to allow "the victim the power of a heckler veto, prohibiting another individual from speaking."[16] Another danger of the reasonable woman or victim standard is that it may reinforce stereotypes of women as helpless. Some also argue that "the specter of paternalistic over-regulation of every nuance of interpretation relations fosters a climate of mutual distrust and resentment between male and female coworkers, rather than an environment in which women and men can work constructively toward common understanding and equality."[17]

Although there are differing points of view, the courts are evaluating a hostile environment from the perspective of the victim. There is a broad range of viewpoints among women as a group, of course, but many women share common concerns which men do not. A "reasonable person" standard tends to be male-biased and ignores the experiences of women. Others claim that discriminatory speech is not protected speech.

Beezer states that "by acknowledging and not trivializing the effects of sexual harassment on a 'reasonable woman,' courts can work toward ensuring that neither men nor women will have to 'run a gauntlet of sexual abuse' in return for the privilege of being allowed to work and make a living."[18] Some courts have held that the objective standard asks whether a reasonable person of the same sex as the victim, that is, a reasonable woman, would perceive that an abusive working environment has been created.

In light of the preceding discussion, one point must be clarified. Just because men and women may interpret each others behaviors differently, it does not mean that intimidating, hostile, or offensive educational environments are simply the result of differences of perceptions. In the *Sparks* case,[19] the court stated that "the whole point of sexual harassment claims is that behavior that may be permissible in some settings can be abusive in the workplace." This means that behavior, which may be acceptable in a person's home or in his or her social life, may be considered sexual harassment when it occurs in the workplace. That same behavior in a university classroom or office may be grounds for charges of sexual harassment.

Civil Rights Act of 1991

Shortly after the U.S. Senate confirmation hearings of Supreme Court Justice Clarence Thomas, Congress enacted the Civil Rights Act of 1991 for the express purpose of providing additional remedies under federal law to deter unlawful discrimination. By providing for compensatory and punitive damages relating to punishment and providing for a trial by jury, this act encourages suits charging sexual harassment and should deter employees from discriminating. In addition to the back pay, front pay, reinstatement, and attorneys' fees previously available under Title VII, this act authorizes as much as $300,000 in compensatory and punitive damages. (See Title I, CRA of 91, Sec 102(6)(3) for punitive damages.)

Equal Employment Commission

The U.S. EEOC enforces Title VII[20] and provides oversight and coordination of all federal regulations, practices, and policies affecting equal employment opportunity. EEOC also develops policies, writes regulations, conducts outreach and education efforts, and coordinates all federal issuances affecting equal employment opportunity, and implements approved affirmative employment programs.

If a person believes that he or she has been discriminated against under the protections of Title VII, he or she may file a charge of discrimination with EEOC.

Although the charge can be filed in writing, by phone, or in person, there are strict time frames that must be adhered to. For the Commission to act and to protect the right to file a private lawsuit, charges must be filed with EEOC within 180 days of the alleged discrimination. EEOC's policy is to seek full and effective relief for each and every victim of employment discrimination, whether sought in court or in conciliation agreements before litigation, and to provide remedies designed to correct the discrimination and prevent its recurrence. However, in reality EEOC's caseload is backlogged, and cases can take months or years to be resolved without a lawsuit. If the Commission decides not to litigate a charge, or any time after the expiration of 180 days from the date the original charge was filed, the charging party may request a notice of the right to file a private suit in federal district court. A private suit may be filed within 90 days of receiving a notice of right-to-sue from EEOC.

After a complaint is filed with EEOC, the charging party is interviewed to obtain as much information as possible about the alleged discrimination. If all legal jurisdictional requirements are met, a charge is drafted and the investigative procedure is explained to the charging party. EEOC will then notify the party who is charged with discrimination that a charge has been filed.

EEOC then requests information from the employer that addresses the issues directly affecting the charging party as well as other potentially aggrieved persons. When investigating allegations of sexual harassment, EEOC looks at the whole record: the circumstances, such as the nature of the sexual advances, and the context in which the alleged incidents occurred. A determination on the allegations is made from the facts on a case-by-case basis. Any witnesses who have direct knowledge of the alleged discriminatory act will be interviewed. If the evidence shows there is no reasonable cause to believe discrimination occurred, the charging party and the employer will be notified. At this point or earlier the charging party may elect to bring a private court action.

If the evidence shows there is reasonable cause to believe discrimination occurred, EEOC then attempts to persuade the employer to voluntarily eliminate and remedy the discrimination. Monetary damages may also be available to compensate for future monetary loss, mental anguish, or pain and suffering, and to penalize a respondent who acted with malice or reckless indifference. In addition, the employer may be required to post a notice in the workplace advising employees that it has complied with orders to remedy the discrimination.

Most charges are conciliated or settled, making a court trial unnecessary. EEOC may then file a lawsuit in federal district court on behalf of the charging party.[21] As a result of court action, the Commission's regulations on sexual harassment have been upheld as a lawful regulatory interpretation of Title VII of the Civil Rights Act of 1964. Other court cases have upheld that sexual harassment is a violation of Title IX of the Education Amendments of 1972.

Title IX

In the late 1960s and early 1970s, concerned educators and students intensified the struggle against sex bias and discrimination in our nation's schools and universities. At that time Title VII specifically excluded educational institutions from its coverage. Sex discrimination against students was not prohibited by any statutes.

An awareness of this exclusion and a commitment to equity resulted in the passage of Title IX of the Education Amendments of 1972. The legislative history of Title IX makes it clear that Congress intended to apply Title VII claims standards to Title IX.

Title IX of the Education Amendments of 1972 prohibits discrimination on the basis of sex in educational programs or activities which receive federal financial assistance. Title IX covers both employees and students and virtually all activities of a university or college. The prohibition covers discrimination in employment of professors and other university personnel as well as discrimination in admissions, financial aid, and access to educational programs and activities. Title IX states: "No person in the United States shall on the basis of sex be excluded from participating in, be denied the benefits of or be subjected to discrimination under any education program or activity receiving federal financial assistance." In general, Title IX is enforced by the U.S. Department of Education. Under Title IX students may sue to collect monetary damages from the school or the school may lose federal funds.

Students at all levels of education are protected by Title IX of the Education Amendments of 1972. Title IX is one of the most sweeping sex discrimination laws ever passed. Although it had little early enforcement, it is now the primary tool that defines equal educational opportunity for women in universities. Under Title IX, sexual harassment is defined as "verbal or physical conduct of a sexual nature, imposed on the basis of sex, by an employee or agent of a recipient that denies, limits, or provides different, or conditions the provision of aid, benefits, services, or treatment protected under Title IX" (Office for Civil Rights Policy Memorandum, August 31, 1981).

The courts look to the principles developed under Title VII when they interpret Title IX. Although Title IX law has evolved slowly, it is clear that sexual harassment is sex discrimination under Title IX. In several recent Title IX cases, the courts have continued to clarify how Title VII standards apply to Title IX claims.[22] The first federal case brought under the auspices of Title IX dealt with quid pro quo, hostile environment, and appropriate grievance procedures. In *Alexander v. Yale*, the plaintiff alleged that she received a low grade because she refused to cooperate sexually with her professor.[23] Although leaving this and the other issues undecided, the Second Circuit confirmed the right to sue for quid pro quo sexual harassment. In two 1986 cases, federal courts allowed claims based solely on the allegation of hostile work environments.[24] In the 1992 case of *Franklin v. Gwinnett County Public Schools*,[25] the U.S. Supreme Court unanimously ruled that institutions could be sued for compensatory damages as a remedy for the intentional violation of Title IX.

Office for Civil Rights

Title IX is enforced by the Office for Civil Rights (OCR) at the U.S. Department of Education which has issued a regulation detailing the general requirements of Title IX. Currently in the process of creating guidelines for sexual harassment in education institutions, OCR generally interprets Title IX from the perspective of the EEOC guidelines and what the courts have said concerning sexual harassment.

Some additional guidance can be taken from the 1994 OCR document "Investigative Guidance on Racial Incidents and Harassment Against Students,"[26] created to guide investigators in racial harassment incidents. According to Sorenson, this document identifies five factors to consider when assessing the circumstances of harassment. These factors are: severity, pervasiveness, and/or persistence of the conduct; whether the recipient of federal financial assistance had actual or constructive notice; and whether the recipient acted in a reasonable, timely, and effective manner to eliminate the harassment.[27]

According to the Title IX regulation, each institution must provide a grievance procedure for sex discrimination. Title IX's protection against sexual harassment covers prospective students, students and employees of programs that are operated by the university. Thus employees, including student employees, may file under both Title VII and Title IX. Title IX coverage also extends, with a few exceptions, to all programs and activities whether or not they receive direct federal assistance.

Individuals may file a complaint on behalf of themselves and/or on behalf of another aggrieved party. Generally a Title IX complaint must be filed within 180 days from the date of sexual harassment. A person who files with OCR can go directly into court without having to obtain permission from OCR. Both Title VII and Title IX allow states to be sued in federal court for sex discrimination.

OCR can conduct compliance reviews on its own initiative, and it is required to conduct a prompt investigation whenever a complaint is filed. If, after an investigation is conducted, OCR determines that sexual harassment has taken place, it attempts to secure voluntary compliance from the institution. OCR does have the authority to institute proceedings to suspend or terminate federal assistance or bar future assistance but rarely does so. It may also request the U.S. Department of Justice to initiate court action.

Unlike Title VII, there is no limit placed on Title IX awards. In the case of a student complaint, the court may award monetary damages to cover such things as pain and suffering; emotional distress; attorney's fees; and the cost of past, present and future therapy. The court may also require the university to initiate or change its policy and develop training programs. It may also require the university to waive various time limits for degree completion and/or provide tuition refunds.

In the case of an employee complaint, the court may require the university to reinstate or promote the employee, pay back wages, and so on. It may also award monetary damages to cover lost wages, attorney's fees, and therapy.

State and Local Laws

Because sexual harassment often involves unsolicited, offensive, physical touching and psychological and emotional harm, victims of sexual harassment can bring additional state law civil claims against the harasser as well as the institution. This type of claim for redress of a civil wrong is known as a *tort*. These tort claims include such charges as assault, battery, intentional infliction of emotional distress, defamation, interfering with an employment contract, negligent supervision, invasion of privacy, and wrongful discharge. In addition to tort claims, some forms of sexual harassment may result in criminal prosecution. Various state laws prohibit sexual battery, stalking, terroristic threats, sexual assault, and rape.

Also, every state has some form of gender discrimination law covering employment and in some cases education. Several states have specific laws prohibiting sexual harassment. As mentioned earlier, the amount of attention state legislatures have given to the issue of sexual harassment varies from state to state. To find out the applicable laws in your state, contact the state Civil Rights Commission located in the state capital.

Consensual Relationships

The discussion of quid pro quo in the university setting raises questions regarding consensual sexual relationships and is the focus of much debate. Sexual activity between two consenting adults is not specifically prohibited by either Title VII nor Title IX. Although not illegal in the workplace, a number of institutions are developing policies that attempt to deal with such behavior when it occurs between a faculty member and a student.

As early as 1971 courts began to acknowledge that there were inherent problems associated with teacher–student sexual relationships. In the case of *Board of Trustees v. Stubblefield*,[28] the court recognized that, "Certain professions...impose upon persons attracted to them, responsibilities and limitations on freedom of action which do not exist in regard to other callings. Public officials such as ... school teachers fall into such a category." This court went on to say: "The integrity of the educational system under which teachers wield considerable power in the grading of students and the granting or withholding of certificates and diplomas is clearly threatened when teachers become involved in relationships with students."

In 1984, the Seventh Circuit indicated that when determining if a professor had engaged in sexual harassment the "conduct is not to be viewed in the same context as would conduct of an ordinary 'person on the street.' Rather, it must be judged in the context of the relationship existing between a professor and his students within an academic environment. University professors occupy an important place in our society and have concomitant ethical obligations."[29]

Zalk, Dederich, and Paludi correctly identify the bottom line as one of power: "...the faculty members have it and the student does not."[30] This power imbalance must be kept in mind when discussing amorous relationship policies because, even with the consent of both parties, it may be damaging to the educational process. The stated purpose of consensual relationship policies is to protect students and junior faculty members from being exploited by senior faculty members. These policies attempt to ensure that grading policies are fair and that students are not coerced into sexual relationships. The American Association of University Professors (AAUP) cautions faculty members and staff against entering romantic or sexual relationships with their students. They also warn supervisors against entering such relationships with an employee. "Faculty and staff should be cautious in assuming professional responsibilities for those with whom they have an existing romantic relationship."[31]

The policies that seem to generate the least controversy, and provide the least protection from abuse, are those that are advisory in nature. These policies simply suggest that faculty and students not become romantically involved. A few require that those faculty members or staff engaged in romantic relationships with someone for whom they have professional responsibility must report the relationship to their superior so that an alternate means of performing the professional responsibility can be devised. A more controversial policy is one that prohibits sexual relationships between faculty and those over whom they have grading authority or prohibits all consensual relationships with students.

The policies that include a broad prohibition on sex between faculty and students generate the most controversy. These policies provide a great amount of protection to students and protect the integrity of the grading system. However, some argue that they are too stringent and substantially interfere with the right of people to become romantically involved with the person of their choice. Those who argue against such policies raise issues of individual rights to privacy, freedom of association, and the civil right to engage in intimate relationships without governmental interference. Keller and others argue that "outside the instructional context, the presumption that an intimate faculty–student relationship results from coercion cannot be justified."[32]

The case law on consensual sexual relationships is sparse. *Naragon v. Wharton*[33] is one case that indirectly addresses this issue.[34] This case involved a lesbian relationship between a faculty member and a first-year student. The faculty member had no academic relationship with the student and by all indications the relationship was consensual. After the student's parents learned of the relationship they demanded the university intervene. Although the instructor argued the relationship was a private matter, she was removed from the classroom. In rejecting the instructor's First Amendment right of association claim and her Fourteenth Amendment right of privacy claim, the Fifth Circuit stated that "teachers are role models, good or bad, for students." The court upheld the university's decision to discipline a faculty member for intimacy between a teacher and a student if the university considered it a breach of professional ethics on the part of the teacher.

Because of the special relationship between the universities and colleges and their students, universities have a duty to protect students from sexual abuse by faculty members. Consensual relationships between faculty members and students or between senior faculty and junior faculty or between supervisors and subordinates present potential problems for the university. These relations may be based on mutual attraction; however, these people often do not hold equal positions of power. If and when the relationship ends, coercion, intimidation, or even blackmail can occur.

Consensual relationships also raise the issue of fairness. If a consensual relationship exists between a professor and one of his or her students, it is reasonable for other students to wonder if their grade is dependent on their personal relationship with the professor. It is also likely that the student involved in the relationship may come to question his or her own academic abilities (see Chapter 14). Universities may want to explore the possibility of developing policies covering consensual relationships (see Chapter 6). Absent such policies, it is unlikely that the university will be able to discipline a faculty member for entering into a consensual relationship.

Clearly, the rules have changed. What may have been acceptable behavior even a short time ago is now considered sexual harassment. Many university employees and students are not aware of this change, and they do not understand they are responsible for seeing that sexual harassment does not take place in their universities.

The Concept of Welcomeness

In the *Meritor* decision, the U.S. Supreme Court ruled that sexual harassment violates Title VII if it creates a hostile or offensive environment for the victim, regardless of whether it threatened the individual's job. Although the *Meritor* decision was based on Title VII, Title IX cases will likely follow the same judicial reasoning. In the university setting, this means that in addition to faculty-to-student sexual harassment, student-to-student initiated unwelcome sexual advances, requests for sexual favors, and other verbal or physical conduct of a sexual nature constitute sexual harassment. A key question is whether the sexual advances were unwelcome. In most incidences of sexual harassment involving a student, the student is the victim of the harassment. However, it must be noted that unwelcome sexual attention toward a faculty member by a student is also sexual harassment.

Remarks that simply offend a person's feelings are usually not considered to be sexual harassment. However, if the offending behavior is severe or pervasive enough to actually affect a student's educational environment, then it may be sexual harassment. In this context there is a clear difference between welcome and voluntary. For example, even if an alleged victim agreed to participate in sexual intimacy, the sexual advances are a prohibited form of sexual harassment if it is clear that the victim did not desire to have the sexual relationship, but capitulated under pressure.

Because the 1980 EEOC guidelines do not define "unwelcome," we must look to various court cases to understand the difference between a voluntary activity and a welcome activity. In the *Meritor* case, the victim claimed that she initially refused the sexual advances of her supervisor, but she eventually gave in and engaged in sexual intercourse out of fear of losing her job. The Supreme Court ruled that her participation in a sexual relationship did not establish that the relationship was truly consensual or welcome. The Court ruled that "the fact that the sex-related conduct was voluntary, in the sense that the complainant was not forced to participate against her will, is not a defense to a sexual harassment suit brought under Title VII." Challenged conduct must be unwelcome in the sense that the employee did not solicit or incite it, and in the sense that the employee regarded the conduct as undesirable or offensive.

In 1990 EEOC issued its *Policy Guidance on Current Issues of Sexual Harassment*. These guidelines instructed that when there is conflicting evidence of welcomeness, "the record as a whole and the totality of the circumstances," should be used to evaluate on a case-by-case basis. EEOC suggests that if there is a complaint of unwelcome sexual attention, while not required, the complaint is strengthened if it is made immediately after the event.

Severe or Pervasive

How much sexual harassment must a person endure before he or she has a case that will hold up in court? EEOC has consistently ruled that "sexual flirtation or innuendo, even vulgar language that is trivial or merely annoying, will not usually be considered a violation of law." For example, if a male student calls a female student a "bitch" after a disagreement, it may be rude, it may be inappropriate, but by itself, it is probably not sexual harassment. (Although probably not sexual harassment, this does not mean that a university must approve or permit such offensive behavior.) However, if the above-mentioned male follows the female down the hall shouting obscenities at her, writes vulgar comments about her on the bathroom walls, and spreads sexual rumors about her, then the behavior is probably sufficiently pervasive and severe to qualify as sexual harassment.

Compensatory Damages

Prior to the passage of the Civil Rights Act of 1991, the prevailing plaintiff in a sexual harassment case was only entitled to injunctive relief. Under the Civil Rights Act of 1991, prevailing plaintiffs now have the right to jury trials and the right to recover compensatory damages for emotional distress and mental anguish.[35] If it is found that the employer "engaged in discriminatory practices with malice or with reckless indifference to the plaintiff's rights," the employer may also be required to pay punitive damages.[36] These damages range from $50,000 for an employer with 14 to 101 employees to $300,000 for employers with more than 500 employees.

42 U.S.C. Section 1983 Protection

Causes of action under U.S.C. Section 1983 require the plaintiff to make two allegations. First, that some person has violated the plaintiff's protected rights under the U.S. Constitution or federal law. Second, that the person who allegedly violated such rights acted under color of state law.[37] When the court examines a suit brought under Section 1983, it is the court's duty to examine whether the plaintiff has alleged sufficient facts which, if proved, would comprise an actionable deprivation of a federal right.[38] The plaintiff must include specific allegations of facts showing a violation of rights. Pre-*Franklin* decisions on this issue held that a Section 1983 remedy was not available for alleged Title IX violations. However, the Supreme Court in *Franklin* determined that Congress did not intend to limit the remedies available in suits under Title IX.

In addition to a due process claim under the Fourteenth Amendment, there is also the possibility of an equal protection claim under Section 1983. Such claims would arise if the plaintiff alleged that by depriving her or him of an educational environment free of sexual harassment and other forms of gender discrimination, the university violated a right to equal protection of the law as guaranteed by the Fourteenth Amendment.

The major difference between a Title IX claim and a Section 1983 claim is that Title IX actions must be brought against the agent receiving federal funds. In Section 1983 claims, both individuals and the agent receiving federal funds may be the target of the action, as long as they were acting under color of state law. Many claims of sexual harassment involve claims under Title IX, Section 1983 and various state laws.

Therefore, an employee or student may bring a suit against a public educational institution and individuals if his or her rights, guaranteed under the Constitution or federal law, have been violated. In order to have the allegations supported, the individual must show that the sexual harassment has resulted from a custom, pattern of behavior, or policy of the governing body. Although it is unclear whether a mere failure to act is sufficient to form a custom or policy of sexual harassment, it is clear that a viable sexual harassment policy which is implemented will provide a strong argument against institutional liability.

Rights of Those Accused of Sexual Harassment

Institutions have an affirmative duty to ensure a safe environment to learn and work. There is ample evidence to document that sexual harassment exists on campuses. Sexual harassment seriously interferes with a victim by discriminating against him or her on the basis of gender. However, as with most personnel issues, there are substantive and procedural due process rights that must be protected. As institutions promulgate and enforce policies prohibiting sexual harassment, including regulations pertaining to consensual relations, they must ensure that the rights of both the alleged victim and the alleged harasser are protected. In a number of cases involving charges of sexual harassment, the institution's sanctions against the alleged harasser have been called into question because either the policy, the investigation or hearing process, or the type of sanction violated either a contractual or due process right.[39]

The Intersection of Sexual Harassment and Academic Freedom

Just as the discussion of consensual relationships necessitates considering the legitimate rights of freedom of association, any effort to regulate the speech of students or professors must consider how to distinguish sexual harassment from speech protected by the First Amendment.[40] Most incidents of quid pro quo sexual harassment deal with the conduct of the alleged harasser. However, many incidents of hostile environment sexual harassment deal with speech that in another context may not be seen as not obscene, defamatory, "fighting" words, or otherwise disruptive. Sorenson frames the question as, "Does not sexual harassment law single out particular speech for special treatment based on its content in violation of the First Amendment?"[41] She identifies the problem as distinguishing protected from unprotected speech. She further states that many situations should not present a problem. She notes, for example, sexually derogatory graffiti on university property can be punished as destruction of property independent of the freedom-of-speech issue. And, face-to-face sexual taunting can be prohibited and punished as "fighting words."

However, speech not involving vandalism or "fighting words" presents a more difficult problem for university officials. MacKinnon and Dworkin contend that sexist speech is not protected in the workplace.[42] They claim that those who protect such speech "value speech in the abstract." Content, form, context, and effect are the critical issues to assist the university in determining what constitutes sexual harassment.

In order to try to make some sense of this conflict it is necessary to look at the roots of the concept of academic freedom. In the university setting, academic freedom had its roots in the nineteenth century German university concept of *Lehrfreiheit*, which meant freedom to examine bodies of evidence and freedom to report findings in the classroom.[43] AAUP interprets academic freedom to mean that "[The] teacher is entitled to full freedom in research and in the publication of results."[44]

Over the years courts have interpreted the First Amendment to the U.S. Constitution as protecting academic freedom. In 1957, in his concurring opinion in the case of *Sweezy v. New Hampshire*, Justice Frankfurter quoted the Open Universities in South Africa list of the four academic freedom of a university as the freedom to "determine for itself on academic grounds who may teach, what may be taught, how it shall be taught, and who may be admitted to study."[45] In *Keyishian v. Board of Regents*, the court identified academic freedom as "of transcendent value." This court said that "the First Amendment does not tolerate laws that cast a pall of orthodoxy over the classroom.... [Its purpose is to protect] a robust exchange of ideas."[46]

The U.S. Supreme Court in *Franklin v. Gwinnett County Public Schools*,[47] citing *Meritor Savings Bank v. Vincent*,[48] said that Title IX of the Education Amendments of 1972, which forbids sex discrimination at any college or university receiving federal money, also forbids sexual harassment by a teacher to a student. Because the *Franklin* Court cited *Meritor* in its decision, the definition of sexual harassment in *Meritor* is probably the definition the courts will use with regard to sexual harassment by a faculty member at a college or university. *Meritor's* definition encompasses both quid pro quo and hostile environment sexual harassment, therefore it is arguable that both are forbidden by Title IX on college campuses. Until the U.S. Supreme Court defines hostile or abusive sexual harassment in the classroom, the definition of workplace hostile environment sexual harassment is the best guidance at this time.

To determine if a hostile working environment exists, the Court in *Harris v. Forklift Systems* said the test is whether the conduct in question is severe or pervasive enough that "a reasonable person would find it created an objectively hostile or abusive work environment that altered the conditions of the victim's employment, and the victim perceives that the environment is abusive." According to the *Harris* Court, if the workplace is permeated with discriminatory intimidation, ridicule, and insult that is sufficiently severe or pervasive to alter the conditions of the victim's employment, actionable sexual harassment has occurred. This Court went on to say that conduct that alters working conditions includes that which detracts from employees' job performance, discourages employees from remaining on the job, or keeps them from advancing in their careers.

Although conduct that is merely offensive, such as the mere utterance of an epithet which engenders offensive feelings in an employee, is not actionable sexual harassment, according to *Harris*, no one single factor must be present to find actionable abusive or hostile environment workplace sexual harassment. Such harassment can only be determined by looking at surrounding circumstances such as the following:

1. The frequency of the discriminatory conduct
2. Its severity
3. Whether it is physically threatening or humiliating, or a mere offensive utterance
4. Whether it unreasonably interferes with an employee's work performance
5. The effect on the employee's psychological well-being, which is relevant to whether the victim actually found the environment abusive

In attempting to balance the right of academic freedom with the right to be free from sexual harassment, it must be remembered that both tenured and untenured faculty members enjoy the right to academic freedom in their teaching and research.[49] The *Jeffries* court ruled that, "Academic freedom includes freedom of utterance and action within and without the classroom."[50] However, in *Waters*, the Court said a public employer has the obligation to make a reasonable investigation of the facts before dismissing or disciplining an employee because of a statement he or she made, but the employer may dismiss or discipline based on a "reasonable belief" regarding the accuracy of the facts.[51]

In examining questions of academic freedom in the classroom, it must be remembered that academic freedom does not protect classroom speech that is unrelated to the subject matter at variance with the prescribed curriculum, or in violation of federal or state antidiscrimination laws. Such speech can be the reason for discipline or termination.[52] Further, speech that disrupts the educational environment is not protected by academic freedom. Academic freedom is not a valid defense for noncooperative and aggressive behavior. An institution can discipline a faculty member for such actions.[53] Academic freedom also is not a license for activity at variance with job-related procedures and requirements, nor does it encompass activities that are internally destructive to the proper function of the university or disruptive to its educational program.[54]

In the case of an investigation by the Equal Employment Opportunity Commission, institutions of higher learning do not enjoy a special privilege, grounded in the First Amendment right of academic freedom, to prevent EEOC from having access to confidential peer review materials.[55] EEOC and other governmental agencies may regulate First Amendment rights if they can demonstrate a compelling governmental interest to do so.[56] And, the U.S. Supreme Court has previously determined that the elimination of sex discrimination, of which sexual harassment is a subset, is a compelling governmental interest.[57]

In a widely reported decision discussing academic freedom and sexual harassment allegations, a federal district court judge ruled in favor of a tenured professor on a motion for a preliminary injunction and enjoined a public university from suspending him for his sexually laden lecture comments that had triggered complaints from female students.[58] The *Silva* court cited with approval the test in

Mailloux v. Kiley,[59] for determining the validity of governmental regulation affecting a teacher's classroom speech. *Mailloux* said that free speech does not grant teachers a license to say or write in class whatever they may feel like and that the propriety of regulations or sanctions must depend on circumstances such as the age and sophistication of the students, the relationship between teaching method and valid educational objective, and the context and manner of presentation.

Because the students in the *Silva* case were exclusively adult college students, the court ruled that the classroom statements advanced the valid educational objective of conveying certain principles related to the subject matter of the course, and they were made in a professionally appropriate manner as part of the college class lecture. The court further found that the university's sexual harassment policy was not reasonably related to the legitimate pedagogical purpose of providing a congenial academic environment because it employed an impermissible subjective standard that failed to take into account the nation's interest in academic freedom.

In analyzing this issue Cole concludes that: (1) educational institutions are vulnerable for hostile environment teacher–student sexual harassment cases; (2) to protect the institution and its faculty from such litigation, the faculty must be able to articulate an objective standard of conduct it expects from its peers in this area and make it known; and (3) an additional way to protect against such cases is to have in place an effective complaint procedure that encourages complainants to come forward and results in prompt investigation and action reasonably calculated to end inappropriate conduct.[60] This may also help mitigate any institutional liability.

Negligent Hiring

A student who is sexually harassed by an institution's employee may have a cause of action against the university based on the theory of negligent hiring or retention. Cases of negligent hiring may arise if an employee sexually harasses or abuses a student or other employee, and it can be shown that the university hired or retained the employee with knowledge that the employee had previously committed similar acts. For such a cause of action to exist the following five elements must be present:

1. There must be an employment relationship.
2. The employee must be incompetent or unfit for the position.
3. The employer must have actual or constructive knowledge of this incompetence or unfitness.
4. The plaintiff's injury must have been caused by the act or omission of the employee.
5. The proximate cause of the plaintiff injuries must be the employer's negligent hiring or retention of the employee.

To reduce the likelihood of liability in a negligent hiring suit, the university should be able to demonstrate that it took affirmative steps during the pre-employment investigation of a prospective employee. Lewis, Hastings, and Morgan suggest that educational institutions "establish a written policy which will provide a uniform procedure to be followed and also provide a checklist to make sure all bases are covered."[61] They also suggest that (1) applications and resumes be carefully scrutinized; (2) references and past employers be contacted; (3) responses of those contacted be documented including refusals to divulge information; (4) potential employers require applicants to sign a waiver releasing former employers from liability for disclosing information, personnel records, and appraisals; and (5) potential employers should seek affirmative attestations of the applicant's good character.

A typical scenario is the practice of universities allowing educators to resign amidst allegations or proof of sexual harassment. These resignations often are accompanied by both parties signing a confidentiality agreement. Although it is understandable why the institution and the former employee wish to maintain a low profile in such situations, educational institutions should be cautious about entering into settlement agreements in which the alleged harasser is allowed to leave with no one the wiser. These agreements generally do not require the alleged harasser to admit to any conduct, and the victims agree not to reveal the allegations or the terms of the settlement, if any. There is often a financial incentive for keeping quiet. Generally, such agreements stipulate that if the accuser breaks the pledge of silence, she or he must give back some or all of the settlement money. The arguments in favor of confidentiality agreements include:

1. They allow the victims who wish to remain anonymous to do so.
2. They protect innocent people who were falsely accused of harassing subordinates.
3. They help both parties and the university avoid lengthy and expensive litigation.

The primary arguments against such agreements are the following:

1. They may protect a harasser and allow him or her to continue harassing other people.
2. Other people in the organization may interpret this behavior as condoning harassment.
3. This way of dealing with the harasser makes it impossible to measure how serious the problem of sexual harassment is on your campus.
4. They may mask the seriousness of the problem and result in insufficient attention given to training and prevention.
5. Efforts to change inappropriate behavior will be hindered if the academic community does not see that a problem exists.

Institutions should conduct a proper investigation and inform the university community of the findings when there have been formal changes on public allegations. If the charges of sexual harassment are proven, that fact should be made public. On the other hand, if the charges are not proven, the alleged harasser has the right to expect that the university will publicly confirm this fact. If the alleged harasser chose to resign before the investigation is completed, the university should record the fact that the resignation took place while the person was under investigation for sexual harassment.

Although thus far courts have been slow to recognize suits based on an alleged duty to warn, institutions should carefully consider the potential liability before hiding substantial information or evidence of sexual harassment. In cases where a faculty member resigns as a response to the filing of sexual harassment case, administrators should consider negotiating an agreement that allows the university to include a statement indicating that at the time the faculty member resigned he or she was under investigation for sexual harassment, and that because of the resignation, the investigation was terminated.

Institutional Policies Prohibiting Sexual Harassment

The presence or absence of an effective policy, which specifically addresses sexual harassment, is an important factor in dispelling institutional liability and protecting students and employees from sexual harassment. (For a detailed discussion of policies and the policy development process see Chapters 6 and 7.) Virtually all universities have policies prohibiting sexual harassment. Some universities have adapted EEOC definitions while others have developed their own. AAUP suggests the following guidelines:

> It is the policy of this institution that no member of the academic community may sexually harass another. Sexual advances, requests for sexual favors, and other conduct of a sexual nature constitute sexual harassment when:
>
> - Any such proposals are made under circumstances implying that one's response might affect such academic or personnel decisions as are subject to the influence of the person making such proposals; or
> - Such conduct is repeated or is so offensive that it substantially contributes to an unprofessional academic or work environment or interferes with required tasks, career opportunities, or learning; or
> - Such conduct is abusive of others and creates or implies a discriminatory hostility toward their personal or professional interests because of their sex.[62]

AAUP suggests that universities establish policies and procedures that make it clear the sexual harassment is unprofessional conduct that threatens the academic freedom of others.

Defenses Against Charges of Sexual Harassment

Just as students have a right to be free from incidents of sexual harassment, professors and students have a right to be free from false charges of sexual harassment. The university's policy against sexual harassment should include a prohibition against making a false claim.

Although there are several defenses that may be allowed in sexual harassment cases, many people who have been accused of sexual harassment attempt to defend their behaviors by suggesting that the claimant's failed to verbalize disapproval of the sexually harassing behavior. Others contend that the claimant participated voluntarily in the harassing behavior. Still others report that the claimant exhibited "sexually provocative" behavior, speech, and/or dress.

Defenses against charges of sexual harassment that have been successful for institutions and individual faculty members include: (1) no harassment occurred; (2) any advances that took place were solicited, incited, or encouraged; (3) the harassment was not sufficiently severe or pervasive to alter the conditions of employment and create an abusive environment. Institutions are typically expected to eliminate sexual harassment if they knew or should have known of its existence. Some universities have argued that they had no knowledge of the harassment and there was a grievance avenue for claims. Another defense used by universities is that they took prompt remedial action as soon as they learned of the situation.

As more courts are holding institutions accountable for employees found guilty of sexual harassment, universities and colleges are asking what they can do to protect themselves. The most recent strategy is to sue the offending professor in federal court. Although AAUP believes universities owe professors a defense at least until they are proven guilty, the College of William and Mary has attempted to pass any liability on to the professor, claiming he should pay for any damages awarded in a sexual harassment case. After being sued by a student alleging that the college mishandled her sexual harassment case against a professor, the College of William and Mary claimed that it does not have control over professors on a day-to-day basis.[63]

Adequacy of Corrective Action

Generally courts are hesitant to substitute their judgment for that of the university in matters relating to attempts to disciplinary offending faculty or students. University disciplinary actions have ranged from reprimands, probation, and warnings to suspension and expulsion or termination. The courts do regard the protection of students and employees as a reasonable duty of the university.

Conclusion

Society and the courts are asking university officials to balance the claims of freedom and responsibility on the campus. The breakdown of civility in society is a trend that is evident on campus. Abusive language, sexual misconduct, and sexual assault are occurring more and more frequently. Sex discrimination, although diminishing, still persists.

The existence of sexual harassment on campus undermines the integrity of higher education. The concept of *in loco parentis* clearly has all but disappeared. If the university is not to serve in the place of the parent, what is the new relationship to be? Many are asking, "Is it reasonable to believe that universities can or should impose some code of conduct?"

I do not wish to suggest that colleges and universities have been unresponsive to the new realities of campus life. Many institutions have, in recent years, made serious efforts to respond to these questions. Many are shaping new codes of conduct. However, much needs to be done before universities can reestablish an environment of courtesy and civility that is necessary for learning to take place. The legal boundaries that are developing in the area of sexual harassment are in a state of flux. Each university must establish the goal of equity and opportunity while at the same time protecting the legitimate rights of free and open discourse.

All universities must make preventing sexual harassment a high priority. The first step in this process is to ensure that there is a clear written policy stating that sexual harassment will not be tolerated, and that all students and employees have the right to study and work on campus free of fear, intimidation, and harassment. In addition to defining sexual harassment these policies must define the rights of the victims and the accused. All employees and students must know what their options are if they believe that they have been sexually harassed. There also must be a well-designed grievance procedure that will deal with faculty and student misconduct. Colleges and universities must ensure that adequate training takes place so that all employees and students know and understand the policy. Prompt and through investigating protocals must be in place and investigators must be adequately trained. Although this quest for civility may at first seem quixotic, each institution must establish its ground rules within the framework of the laws of civil liberties and civil rights.

Endnotes

1. According to a report by the United Educators' Insurance Risk Retention Group, the number of sexual harassment claims brought against colleges they insure has approximately tripled over the past three years. Neary, C. B. (1994). Unique issues in sexual harassment litigation. Annual conference of National Association of College and University Attorneys; Stokes, J. D. & Vinik, D. F., in Consensual sexual relations between faculty and student in higher education, 96 Ed. Law Rep. [889] (March 23, 1995), report that "survey's conducted in the 1980s found that anywhere from 10% to 33% of female students at a number of campuses believed they had been subjected to sexual harassment at some time during their college careers."

2. *Williams v. Saxbe*, 413 F.Supp. 654 (D.D.C. 1976).

3. *Alexander v. Yale University*, 631 F.2d 178, 183 (2d Cir. 1980).

4. *Williams v. Saxbe*, 413 F.Supp. 645 (D.D.C. 1976).

5. 120 S.Ct. 1028 (1992).

6. Farley, L. (1980). *Sexual shakedown*, Warner Books, New York; *see also* Sandler, Bernice, Important events in the history of sexual harassment in education, in *About Women on Campus* 3(2), 5, 1994.

7. 477 U.S. 57 (1986).

8. 114 S.Ct. 367 (November 9, 1993).

9. Teresa Harris was a rental manager at Forklift Systems. Harris proved in the trial court that Charles Hardy, the company's president, targeted her with unwanted sexual- and gender-related comments throughout her employment. Harris quit and sued Forklift for sexual harassment under Title VII of the Civil Rights Act of 1964. Forklift Systems argued that she left work for other reasons. The Tennessee trial court ruled in favor of Forklift Systems because Harris did not show serious injury to her psychological well-being. The Sixth Court of Appeals agreed. The U.S. Supreme Court reversed the lower court decision.

10. 477 U.S. 57 (1986).

11. *Harris*, 114 S.Ct. at 371.

12. *Id.* at 372 (Scalia, J., concurring).

13. *See* Meads, M. A. (1993). Applying the reasonable woman standard in evaluating sexual harassment claims: Is it justified?, *Law and Psychology Review*, 17:209–223; Shoop, R. J. (1992), The reasonable woman in a hostile environment, 72 Ed. Law Rep. (703) (April 23, 1992); and Lester, T. (1993), The reasonable woman test in sexual harassment law—Will it really make a difference? 26 Ind.L. Rev. 227.

14. 924 F.2d 872 (9th Cir. 1991).

15. Collins, E. G. & Blodgett, T. B. Some See It… Some Won't. *Harv. Bus. Rev.*, Mar–Apr, 1981.

16. Schultz, D. (1993). From reasonable man to unreasonable victim?: Assessing *Harris v. Forklift Systems* and shifting standards of proof and perspective in Title VII sexual harassment law, *Suffolk University Law Review*, Vol. XXVII: 717.S.

17. Brief of Amicus Curiae for Feminists for Free Expression at 5, *Harris v. Forklift Sys. Inc.*, 114 S. Ct. 367 (1993).

18. 924 F.2d 872 (9th Cir. 1991).

19. *Sparks v. Pilot Freight Carriers, Inc.*, 830 F.2d 1554 (11th Cir. 1987).

20. The popular interpretation of the addition of "sex" to Title VII is that it was the result of a deliberate ploy of foes of the bill to scuttle it. An alternative explanation is that this inclusion is a typical example of "incubated" legislation. For an extensive analysis of the over forty-year process of seeking equal rights for women *see*: Freman, J., "How sex got into Title VII: Persistent opportunism as a maker of public policy." *Law and Inequality: A Journal of Theory and Practice*, Vol. 9, No. 2, March 1991, pp. 163–184.

21. Material regarding EEOC was drawn from EEOC documents that are in the public domain. Information on all EEOC-enforced laws may be obtained by calling toll free on 800-669-EEOC.

22. *See Lipsett v. University of Puerto Rico*, 864 F.2d 881, 897 (1st Cir. 1988); *O'Connor v. Peru State College*, 781 F.2d 632, 642 n. 8 (8th Cir. 1986); *Doe v. Petaluma City Sch. Dist.*, 830 F.Supp. 1560, 1571–72 (N.D. Cal. 1993); and *Nagel v. Avon Bd. of Educ.*, 575 F.Supp. 105, 106 (D. Conn. 1983).

23. 631 F.2d 178 (2d Cir. 1980).

24. See *Moire v. Temple University of Medicine*, 613 F.Supp. 1360 (E.D. Pa. 1985). aff'd 800 F.2d 1136 (3d Cir. 1986) and *Lipsett v. University of Puerto Rico*, 864 Fd 881 (1st Cir. 1988).

25. 112 S.Ct. 1028 (1992).

26. 59 Fed.Reg. 11448 (1984).

27. Sorenson, Gail, Peer sexual harassment: Remedies and guidelines under federal law, 92 E. Law Rep. [1] (Sept. 8, 1994).

28. 16 Cal. App. 3d 820, 824–27 (1971).

29. *Korf v. Ball State University*, 726 F.2d 1222 (7th Cir. 1984).

30. Zalk, R., Dederich, J., & Paludi, M., Women students' assessment of consensual relationships with their professors: Ivory Power reconsidered. In *Academic and workplace sexual harassment: A resource manual*, edited by M. A. Paludi & R. B. Barickman, pp. 99–111. State University of New York Press, Albany, 1991.

31. American Association of University Professors, Sexual harassment: Suggested policy and procedures for handling complaints. *AAUP Policy Documents & Reports* 113, 133 (1990).

32. Keller, E. A. (1988). Consensual amorous relationships between faculty and students: The constitutional right to privacy. *Journal of College and University Law* 15:21–42.

33. 737 F.2d 1403 [18 Ed.Law Rep. (574)] (1984).

34. For a detailed discussion of the issue of consensual relationships, *see* Stodes, J.W.D & Vinik, D. F., *Consensual Sexual Relations Between Faculty and Students in Higher Education*, 96 E.Law Rep. [899] (March 23, 1995).

35. 42 U.S.C. § 1981a (Supp.III 1992).

36. 42 U.S.C. § 1981a (Supp.III 1992).

37. *Gomex v. Toledo*, 446 U.S. 635.

38. *Robinson v. City of Mount Vernon*, 645 F.Supp. 170.

39. *See* Jury ignores judge to set award in suit, *New York Times*, July 24, 1994.

40. The legal research and concept development in this section is derived from Elsa Kircher Cole's speech entitled "The Intersection of Sexual Harassment and Academic Freedom." The speech was presented to the Association of Governing Boards of Universities and Colleges, March 25, 1995, Seattle. (Used with permission.)

41. Sorenson, p. 1.

42. MacKinnon, C. A. (1987). *Feminism unmodified: Discourses on life and law*, Harvard University Press, Cambridge MA; and Dworkin, A. (1981). *Pornography: Men possessing women*, Putnam Books, New York.

43. *See*, Hostadter, R. & Metzger, W. (1995). *The development of academic freedom in the United States*, pp. 367–412, Columbia University Press, New York.

44. *AAUP Bulletin*, Vol. 60, No. 2, Summer 1974, 269–72.

45. 354 U.S. 234, 263 (1957).

46. *Keyishian v. Board of Regents*, 385 U.S. 589, 603 (1967).

47. 112 S.Ct. 1028 (1992).

48. 477 U.S. 57 (1986).

49. *Perry v. Sindermann*, 408 U.S. 593 (1972).

50. *Jeffries v. Harleston*, 820 F.Supp 741 (SONY 1993); aff'd 21 F. 3d 1238 (1994); cert. granted and case remanded, 115 S.Ct. 502 (1994) for reconsideration in light of the Supreme Court's ruling in *Waters v. Churchill*, 114 S.Ct. 1878 (1994).

51. *Waters v. Churchill*, 114 S.Ct. 1878 (1994).

52. *Clark v. Holmes*, 474 U.S. 292 (7th Cir. 1972); *Hetrick v. Martin*, 480 F.2d 705 (6th Cir. 1973).

53. *Harden v. Adams*, 760 F.2d 1158 (11th Cir. 1985); *Kelleher v. Flawn*, 761 F.2d 1079 (1985); *Adamian v. Jacobsen*, 523 F.2d 929 (9th Cir. 1975); *Chitwood v. Feaster*, 468 F.2d 359 (4th Cir. 1972); *Jawa v. Fayetteville State Univ*, 426 F.Supp 118 (EDNC 1976).

54. *Statsny v. Bd of Trustees of Central Washington University*, 647 F.2d 496, 32 Wash.App. 239 (1982).

55. *University of Pennsylvania v. Equal Employment Opportunity Commission*, 110 S.Ct. 557 (1990).

56. *United States v. Lee*, 455 U.S. 252 (1982).

57. *Board of Directors of Rotary Int'l v. Rotary Club*, 481 U.S. 537, 549 (1987).

58. *Silva v. University of New Hampshire*, 1994 WL 504417 (DNH 1994); the case was settled by reinstating professor, no appeal.

59. 448 F.2d 1242 (1st Cir. 1972).

60. Cole, 1995.

61. Lewis, John F., Hastings, Susan C., & Morgan, Anne C., *Sexual harassment in education*. National Organization on Legal Problems of Education, Topeka, KS, 1992.

62. American Association of University Professors, Sexual harassment: Suggested policy and procedures for handling complaints. *AAUP Policy Documents & Reports* 113, 133 (1990).

63. Wilson, R. William and Mary seeks to shift liability for damages to professor in federal sexual-harassment case. *The Chronicle of Higher Education*, June 9, 1995, A 20.

3

STUDENT-TO-STUDENT SEXUAL HARASSMENT

BERNICE RESNICK SANDLER

Georgie Porgie, pudding and pie,
Kissed the girls and made them cry.

Do you remember when it was OK for the boys to tease the girls? People laughed, or at least the boys did. The girls may have been uncomfortable, but nobody took this kind of teasing very seriously. In fact, many people thought of it—and some still do—as "boys will be boys" and as "natural" and acceptable behavior.

The old nursery rhyme about Georgie Porgie takes on new meaning in light of sexual harassment law and policies. Such behavior is no longer acceptable. What was previously allowed, or at least ignored, is no longer behavior that universities can allow to be tolerated. Peer-to-peer harassment, often unnoticed, is potentially one of the most explosive areas of sexual harassment. The dangers are as follows:

1. Some institutional policies do not specifically prohibit student-to-student harassment.
2. Training programs and materials often omit student-to-student harassment so that many students, faculty, and administrators are not aware of either the legal or policy implications for the university. Faculty, administrators, and student personnel, such as residence assistants, often inadvertently ignore such behavior, do not take complaints about it seriously, or know how to deal with it.
3. Since 1992 when the Supreme Court unanimously ruled that plaintiffs may sue their institution for damages under Title IX,[1] universities can be liable for unlimited damages if they fail to stop discriminatory behavior including sexual harassment.[2] Institutions that do not respond to complaints of peer harassment do so at their own peril.
4. As a result of the recent publicity about sexual harassment cases, female students are increasingly likely to recognize sexual harassment when their peers engage in it.
5. Peer harassment, if unchecked, sets the stage for campus sexual assault.

Ideally, college experiences as a whole should help students not only acquire knowledge but also build skills and confidence, how to make good choices in life, and particularly how to handle differences, including those of race, class, gender, and sexual orientation. Yet all too often institutions are failing to meet the challenge of helping male and female students learn to get along with each other; many women students experience hostility, anger, and sometimes even violence from male students.

College is a lot more than just going to classes. The social learning that happens outside the classroom is often as important as what happens inside it. The wide range of experiences students have with friends and acquaintances are not only complementary but critical to how students see themselves, and to the development of their ability to get along with others.

There is a darker, typically unnoticed, side to college life or if acknowledged, it is often brushed off as "normal behavior." That darker side of college includes all forms of peer harassment, whether it is men harassing women, or women harassing men; students harassing racial and ethnic minorities, and gay and lesbian students. This chapter is limited to peer harassment based on gender; however, many of the concepts will be applicable to other forms of peer harassment.

For many students the relationships between men and women are not always positive, with some men treating women in ways that can only be described as emotional and psychological harassment. The behaviors are often invasive and disrespectful, and they can poison the college experience for women.

When these behaviors occur again and again, and when they are unnoticed or condoned by peers and even some college officials, men and women alike receive the message that women can be treated with disdain, a lack of respect, and that this does not matter to anyone. It makes coeducation less than equal.

What Is Peer Harassment?

Peer harassment is generally a form of hostile environment harassment. In other words, an environment can be so hostile or offensive that it interferes with a student's ability to learn, his or her living conditions, and the ability to partake in any and all of the opportunities offered by the institution. Very little has been written about peer harassment. The first national report was written by myself and Jean O'Gorman Hughes in 1988.[3]

Peer harassment covers a wide range of behaviors. At one end of the scale, peer harassment consists of so-called teasing, sexual innuendos, obscenities, and the like—a sort of sexual bullying, both physical and verbal, often made in the guise of humor. At the other end is explicit sexual aggression, with rape as the most extreme form of peer harassment. Stalking can also be a form of sexual harassment.

Here are some examples of peer harassment (the names of schools have been omitted when the incidents were not made public[4]):

• Women members of the Texas A&M University Corps of Cadets complained that they were subjected to constant verbal abuse, social ostracism, and threats of physical assault and rape.[5]

• Four first-year male students at a prestigious school of liberal arts worked in pairs, one blocking a female student from the front while the other grabbed her genitals from behind. (When brought individually to the Dean of Students, each of the men was astonished, stating "but everybody does this in high school."

• A Southern school has a tunnel under the campus where students typically paint pictures and graffiti on the wall. For several months, there was an almost life-size painting of a Raggedy Ann doll, legs spread apart with blood flowing out, with the words, "I raped Raggedy Ann."

• Men of the coeducational marching band at the University of California at Davis yelled sexually explicit cheers during games and told female band members that "virgins aren't appreciated."[6]

• Sexist graffiti at the University of Houston's College of Architecture included a headless and armless woman sitting bare-breasted with her legs spread apart.[7]

• Fraternity men on many campuses rate women as they pass by, sometimes loudly describing the women's sexual characteristics (such as size of breasts) and appearance. Some men hold up signs ranging from one to ten.

• Sometimes campus computers contain offensive graffiti which students have added to the sign-in process, so that women must view them in order to use the computers.

• Male students leered at and made derogatory comments about women who were participating in an aerobics class at a large state institution in California.

• A fraternity at Occidental College mooned a sorority house. Between 40 and 50 members dropped their pants and flaunted their naked backsides in front of the house.[8]

• In many classrooms when a female student raises an point about women's issues in class, some of the men hiss or boo, or otherwise ridicule her. She is effectively silenced, especially if the faculty member says nothing, even though theoretically, in a classroom, students are supposed to feel free to bring up related topics.

• At a large state university, a group of men regularly sit at a table facing the cafeteria line. As the women go through the line, the men loudly discuss the women's sexual attributes and rate them on a scale of one to ten. Some women only get on line if they have a friend with them so together they can ignore the men's comments; other women skip their meal if the men are there.

• At a technical institution in New England, men in the cafeteria often make comments about women being "too fat" when they go up to the dessert table. Some women are too intimidated to get dessert when the men engage in such comments.

• Women who support women's rights have been harassed on many campuses. It is not unusual for women who rally against date rape to be mooned, have beer poured on them, or hear shouts aimed at them such as "Let's rape her," or "I'll take that one."

Other common examples of peer harassment include the following:

• Sexual innuendos, such as comments about a person's body, appearance, activities
• Whistling or making suggestive sexual sounds such as sucking noises or catcalls
• Pestering a person for dates long after she has indicated no interest
• Spreading rumors about a person's sexual activities or feelings
• Direct sexual propositions
• Leering, ogling, staring about a person's sexual parts
• Inappropriate touching, grabbing or groping (some of this is considered sexual assault or abuse under most state laws)
• Brushing against someone's body

- Blocking a person's path
- Giving an unwanted neck or shoulder massage
- Graffiti about a person's sexuality
- Name calling such as "bitch," "whore," and "slut"
- Insulting and belittling a person through sexual ridicule
- Sending letters, notes, telephone calls, or sending materials of a sexual nature
- Laughing at or not taking seriously a person who experiences sexual harassment
- Pejorative (sexist or stereotyped) comments about females
- Blaming the victim of sexual harassment for having caused it
- Displaying pictures, calendars, cartoons or other materials with sexual content within the institution
- Coerced sexual intercourse

Peer harassment can be a single serious incident or a series of incidents. Legally the behavior must be serious enough to interfere with a student's ability to learn, her or his living conditions, or any of the opportunities provided by the institution. However, institutions need to deal with all levels of peer harassment whether they rise to the legal definition or not.

It is the issue of power that makes sexual harassment so insidious. Most often, when people think about sexual harassment, they think of the official, formal power of a boss over an employee or that of a faculty member over a student. Equally important, however, is the informal power that males often hold over females. Although it is beyond the scope of this chapter to explore the dynamics of male and female power, one can merely note that males are generally physically larger, and that numerous studies have documented how men dominate socially in mixed groups; they speak more than women and generally control the topic of conversation. Indeed, often the aim of peer harassment is to intimidate and to show power and dominance.

Although the behaviors usually seem to be individual, unrelated acts, they are part of a larger pattern of unwanted behavior, often sexually tinged, on the part of male students toward females. The behaviors are not universal, nor do they occur all the time. Certainly not all college men bother or harass women students, and many women do not experience these incidents. Even though both sexes can be harassed, females make up the majority of peer harassment victims. While not all harassment is *sexually* related, harassment on the basis of gender alone is equally illegal. Additionally, even though women are harassed by men because they are women, not all women recognize the behavior as harassment.

Peer harassment occurs at virtually all schools: large and small, Ivy League, public and private, religiously affiliated, and community colleges. Although some institutions may have fewer instances than others, none are immune.

Humor

Although humor is often used to lighten up a situation and to relax people, it is also a way to mask hostility: cruelty by caricature. Almost all jokes about women are jokes which at best portray women in an unfavorable manner, or at worst, degrade them. Some women may enjoy this form of humor, but many do not and can feel uncomfortable, embarrassed, or angry; yet if they protest this kind of humor, they are likely to be told, "What's wrong with you? Don't you have a sense of humor?" Thus a woman is made to feel she is at fault rather than the person who offended her.

Women are left with little recourse; no one wants to be accused of lacking a sense of humor. Yet the "humor" they experience is often intimidating and discomforting. Jokes about rape, about women of color, and that demean women are very common on campus; occasionally faculty also partake in such jokes, unaware of the chilling effect of such remarks.

Who Is Likely to Harass?

It is unlikely that many men have grown up in our society without having sexually harassed some female(s) at some point in their lives. Nevertheless, some people are more likely to continue to harass than others.

Men in Groups

Men in temporary or permanent groups may be more likely to harass than others, because for some men, harassing women is a way to prove to other men how "masculine" they are. It is, for some, a way to bond with each other.

• **Fraternities**. Fraternities are increasingly being charged with sexist behavior and harassment. Much of what is seen as "friendly fun" by the brothers may be viewed very differently by women. The brothers are having a good time with each other at the expense of women.

Fraternities often sponsor events that result in the harassment and degradation of women or in which women are viewed primarily as sexual objects—"Come for a lei on Hawaiian night." At one party, the face of a female mannikin was smashed, with red paint smeared on the face and breasts to resemble blood. The mannikin was then hung from a balcony as a decoration.

• **Athletes**. Harassment by athletes is sometimes exacerbated when coaches support harassing behaviors, as in the case of a coach who allowed his players to wear T-shirts that showed a woman being dragged away by her hair by a male. He thought the T-shirt was funny.

• **Temporary groups.** Groups can be as temporary as a group of men standing in front of the student union or men at a party, a cafeteria, or dormitory. Men in a class may also constitute a group. When women are few in number, harassment may increase, as in the case of women in classes when men predominate.

Individual Men

Although the men who harass their fellow students are as varied as the students themselves, some are more likely to do so:

• **Men who hold traditional views of women**, especially those who believe that the relationships between men and women are adversarial. Some men are angry at women, either individually (such as at a woman who rejected them) or at women in general. Some are angry at the women's movement.

- **Males from cultures where women are treated poorly** and where it is common for men to harass women. They may continue similar behavior on the campus.
- **Men who are primarily comfortable relating to women in a sexual manner**. Many of these men believe that women like any form of sexual attention. The situation is compounded especially because many women do not articulate their displeasure at unwanted sexual attention, preferring to ignore it instead. (Women may ignore unpleasant behavior because they think it will then cease and that if they respond in any way, the behavior will get worse. In contrast, the lack of response on the part of women is often viewed by men as confirmation that the women **like** the behavior.)
- **Men who shore up their "masculinity" by bullying those they perceive as weaker such as women.** These men may use "sexual bullying" as a way to demonstrate their "masculinity" to other men as well.

In What Situations Is Peer Harassment Likely to Occur?

Peer harassment can occur anywhere on campus, especially where college personnel are either absent or where they ignore the behavior, do not intervene, or encourage it. For example, a professor who jokes about "women's libbers," when a female student raises an issue concerning women, is giving license to other students to ridicule her as well.

Alcohol and drug use whether by individuals or by groups, whether by men or by women exacerbates peer harassment. It impairs judgment of both genders, and makes women appear as more vulnerable targets. Others under the influence of drugs or alcohol are also less likely to intervene when they observe offensive behavior.

Some of these situations or places likely to be hotbeds of harassment are: fraternity and athletic events, in front of fraternity houses, dormitories, parties, and cafeterias. Additionally, universities that have not recognized or publicized the issue, do not have a policy or fail to enforce it, have failed to train personnel and students (including targeted groups such as fraternity members, athletes, and new international students), do not intervene when it occurs or punish those engaged in such behavior, or have not removed offensive graffiti about women are more likely to have a higher incidence of student-to-student harassment than those who do otherwise.

Peer harassment sets the stage for campus rape. One fourth of college women report that they have been forced to have sexual intercourse at least once.[9] For men disposed to rape, tolerance of sexual harassment is a powerful predictor.[10]

How Prevalent Is Peer Harassment?

Most women on campus who have been sexually harassed by anyone—perhaps 90 percent of them—will not talk to anyone in a position of authority. And, of those few that do, perhaps 90 percent or more do not want to file a formal complaint. So the absence of complaints does not mean the absence of a problem. In order to put peer harassment into a proper perspective, listed below are some figures about campus sexual harassment in general. The range of information provided is based on an informal examination of studies of sexual harassment.

- Some 20 to 30 percent of women undergraduates are harassed by a male faculty member, administrator, or staff person.
- About two percent will face direct or indirect threats or bribes for unwanted sexual activity.
- Of graduate students, 30 to 40 percent will experience some form of sexual harassment, primarily from faculty members.
- In the workplace, the figures vary because the workplace itself is varied—some 40 to 90 percent of women workers will experience some form of harassment.
- Some 20 to 50 percent of women faculty will experience some form of sexual harassment from colleagues and supervisors.
- Between 70 and 90 percent of women students will experience harassment from fellow students, behaviors from males which they saw as serious and to which they reacted negatively.
- Although a number of campuses have surveyed students to determine the extent of harassment by faculty and administrators, only a few have examined student-to-student harassment, although by far it is the most common form of sexual harassment experienced by women students.

Who Gets Harassed?

Although any woman student can be the object of harassment, some women may be more likely to be harassed than others. Women who appear weak and more vulnerable are one such group; women who are assertive and perhaps viewed as threatening male superiority are another. Others include the following:

- Naive, inexperienced, unassertive, or socially isolated females because they may be less likely to defend themselves.
- First-year students.
- Women from foreign countries who may be viewed as more passive than U.S. women.
- Women of color who may be more prone to peer harassment than white women. They may be seen primarily in terms of sexuality, especially African American and Hispanic women who may be viewed as "erotic exotics." Among some fraternity men, a man is not considered a "man" until he has slept with an African American or Hispanic woman. Asian American women may be teased more often because they are perceived as passive and thus more vulnerable. Anger about their receiving better grades may also make them a target. Sometimes racism and sexism are so intertwined that it is hard to tell which is which, as in the case of the taunt "black meat" or "black bitch."
- Women active in women's issues.
- Women who participate a lot in class.
- Women who are a minority in any class and especially in classes where men predominate.
- Lesbians, whose harassment stems, in part, from homophobia.

- Women who are physically impaired in some way.
- Female graduate assistants.
- Women who work in dormitories as resident assistants.
- Women who have been sexually abused or assaulted previously, including victims of incest.

What Is the Impact of Peer Harassment?

Just as racial slurs, epithets, and other forms of harassment hurt minorities, sexual slurs, epithets, and other forms of harassment hurt women. Peer harassment sends a message that a woman is not equal to a man in terms of being a person. She is an object of scorn or derision. She is not taken seriously as a person with dignity; she is not valued.

Even if a woman does not experience it herself but sees it happening to others, she receives the same message—a message that can weaken her self-esteem or self-confidence, and can undermine her academic, vocational, or personal goals.

Women may feel uncomfortable or annoyed; they may feel embarrassed, humiliated, or degraded; they may feel alienated, helpless, and unsure about how to respond. At times they may feel angry, insulted, and fearful of violence. They may also feel guilty or blame themselves for "causing" the men to harass them.

The cumulative effect of repeated peer harassment can reinforce self-doubt and affect a woman's entire college experience. The more pervasive forms may make it difficult for a woman to trust or have friendships with men. She may begin to believe that this is how men act in general, a belief with profound consequences for future relationships. And when harassment comes primarily from classmates in a particular class or department, particularly in fields in which men predominate, some women may drop classes, change majors or schools, or drop out of college altogether.

The impact of student-to-student sexual harassment is not limited to women. When men harass women with impunity, they are learning that women are fair game and that such harassment is acceptable behavior. It becomes a socially approved way of bonding with other males at the expense of women.

Pervasive harassment may make it difficult for a man to form a healthy committed relationship with a woman because it is hard to be committed to someone for whom he and others have so little respect. When men view women as objects to be demeaned, they may find it difficult not only to relate to women as equal human beings, much less as friends, potential romantic partners, or colleagues at work.

Lastly, men who are allowed to harass in college are likely to continue the behavior in the workplace where is it less likely to be tolerated and can be a cause for dismissal and/or a lawsuit.

Why Peer Harassment Is Typically Unreported

Some women are unaware that others have had similar experiences with harassment, and thus believe their experiences are individual and unique. Some, as mentioned earlier, believe that somehow they are responsible for the harassment they experience.

Sometimes, women believe nothing can be done. They either do not know that their institution has a policy and legal obligation to deal with the situation or they may believe the only way their institution can deal with a complaint is with a formal legalistic and adversarial process, a process in which they do not want to be involved. They may be unaware that good informal procedures are far more likely to be used and to be more successful. Worse, they may not trust the institution to take their complaint seriously, deal with it fairly, and protect them from retaliation.

Some women, while not condoning the behavior, "accept" it as "the way things are" and therefore do not view it as something worthy of a complaint. Some are fearful, often realistically, of retaliation from the male who harasses her, his friends, and even from other women who may chastise her for "getting poor Jim into trouble."

What Can Campuses Do About Peer Harassment?

A climate that tolerates peer harassment can inhibit academic learning, social growth, and psychological well-being. The following recommendations, although by no means comprehensive, are designed to help institutions deal with peer harassment and to create an atmosphere in which such behaviors are neither tolerated nor condoned. The following list contains a wide range of strategies that can be adapted for individual institutions.

Educating the Campus Community

- Require that student leaders, including fraternity and sorority leaders, attend peer harassment workshops or programs.
- Inform faculty members about what constitutes peer harassment, especially in the classroom, and suggest ways to deal with it directly or how to refer the complaint to someone designated to deal with peer harassment.
- During orientation discuss peer harassment and stress values such as respect for others, tolerance, and freedom from harassment or intimidation for all members of the academic community.
- Develop specific materials about peer harassment: brochures, posters, and flyers; distribute them widely and often.
- Inform students about the legal definitions of, and punishment for, indecent exposure; lewd, obscene, and harassing behaviors; and sexual assault.
- Incorporate student-to-student harassment issues into other existing educational programs such as sexual harassment, sexual assault, and diversity programs.
- Include peer harassment information in alcohol education programs and develop rules for the use of alcohol on campus. Require that nonalcoholic beverages be available whenever alcohol is served.
- Develop educational programs for all-male groups such as male athletic teams and fraternities which often perpetuate predatory attitudes toward women.
- Develop educational programs or incorporate into existing programs information about peer harassment for international students, both male and female.
- Encourage interfraternity councils and individual fraternities and sororities to develop and present programs on peer harassment.

- Encourage men to develop support groups to talk about interactions and relationships with women.
- Encourage student government organizations to sponsor, publicize, and conduct programs on peer harassment.
- Encourage campus racial, ethnic, and religious organizations such as African American student unions, campus ministries, and Hillel Foundations to publicize, sponsor, and conduct programs, and to pass resolutions concerning harassment of women in general and of women from their particular group.
- Gather information about peer harassment by survey, interviews, focus groups, and other methods. Train a few students (female and male) about peer harassment and ask them to write down all incidents they observe during the following week. The list could be printed in the student newspaper or as part of a report on peer harassment.
- Report annually on peer harassment. The report might be presented separately or incorporated into an existing report on sexual harassment or student life. One university issued an annual chart showing all reported incidents of sexual harassment, deleting identifying information. The chart described each incident, how it was handled and what happened subsequently. The information helps people understand what kind of behavior is prohibited and demonstrates how the institution is taking an active role in ending these behaviors.

Developing and Implementing Policies and Procedures

- Make sure that the code of student conduct expressly prohibits sexual harassment of one student by another; sexual assault and other forms of sexual exploitation; and intimidating or threatening behaviors. The University of Florida bars "actions or statements that amount to harassment or intimidation or hazing," and actions "including those of a sexual nature that are intimidating, harassing, or abusive."[11]
- Ensure that policies prohibiting sexual harassment specifically prohibit student-to-student sexual harassment.
- Expand policies prohibiting racial harassment to include sexual harassment. Specifically mention women of color as a group that experiences harassment.
- Appoint a task force, which includes students, to examine peer harassment by gathering information, evaluating current policies and procedures, and to make recommendations for improvement.
- Be sure that informal procedures are available as an option so that complaints can be handled without formal charges where appropriate, and if desired by the person harassed. Informal procedures can protect the privacy of the individuals involved and give the harassers an opportunity to change their behavior. Sometimes the accused and accuser can agree on a penalty such as community service. Sometimes all that is needed is an apology to the victim and a promise not to repeat the behavior. Informal methods are also useful when incidents are disputed or unable to be proved.
- Respond when students anonymously report incidents of peer harassment that happened to them or to others. Depending on the seriousness of the incident, institutional response could range from talking to the alleged harasser to conducting a full-scale investigation.
- Ensure that whatever committee or other body, which administers the student conduct code, includes a substantial number of women and that all members have received training about peer harassment issues.
- Inform persons reporting incidents about the institution's policy on retaliation. (In some instances men have tried to intimidate women to drop charges.)
- Warn the accused to refrain from any contact with the accuser during the time charges are being investigated or otherwise dealt with.

- Specifically inform the alleged harasser that any retaliation by him or his friends against the person who reported the incident will be a serious offense.
- Although mediation can sometimes be helpful, it should not be required. A student, seeking redress of a wrong, who is forced into mediation may feel doubly victimized; to force her to negotiate with the person who is harassing her implies that she is part of the problem that needs to be resolved. Peer harassment is not a failure of interpersonal communication (see Chapter 11).
- Write policies that enable a school to pursue charges in a case of a serious alleged violation of the student conduct code, even if the victim does not do so. (Some students who would not bring a charge on their own are willing to be a witness at institution-initiated proceedings.) If a victim is reluctant to file a formal charge, and the institution feels it is to her best interest for the institution not to pursue a formal charge, it should at least have someone speak to the alleged harasser to inform him that his behavior violates the school's policy and that he will be in serious trouble if he repeats the same behavior. In some situations in which a school has taken action against an individual, several women who were reluctant to bring charges earlier came forward with additional complaints against the student.
- Develop a clear and consistent policy on appropriate sanctions for those individuals who commit serious peer harassment offenses, such as the following:
  - Require the perpetrator to attend peer harassment workshops;
  - In cases involving excessive drinking, require those involved to attend programs on alcohol abuse;
  - Require relevant community service such as helping to alleviate the problem of peer harassment by preparing posters or disseminating information about harassment;
  - Require those involved to inform their parents;
  - Require the perpetrators to write a letter of apology to the victim;
  - Deny use of campus housing;
  - Place a letter in the person's permanent file;[12]
  - Place on probation for a specified time;
  - Suspend for a specified time; and/or
  - Expell the student.

  Counseling may also be required but it is not a substitute for disciplinary action.
- Develop a clear and consistent policy of appropriate sanctions for fraternities who commit serious peer harassment offenses, such as the following:
  - Loss of campus housing;
  - Suspending rushing for a specified time;
  - Prohibiting all social activities including parties, participation in sorority socials, Greek Week, Homecoming, etc., for a specified time;
  - Suspending intramural activities, including both fraternity and independent league play;
  - Prohibiting pledges and members from holding office in student government or any other campus leadership and status position;
  - Requiring community service such as participation in peer harassment education programs;
  - Restricting female guests to the downstairs area during social functions;
  - Probation; and
  - Disbanding of chapter.
- Develop written guidelines for dealing with peer harassment if it occurs on campus when school is not in session such as after classes end.

- Develop written guidelines for dealing with peer harassment for persons likely to handle such incidents, such as resident advisors and fraternity and sorority faculty sponsors.
- Should serious harassment occur and both parties reside in the same living unit, consider moving the harasser to another unit. Should the victim prefer to move, provide alternative arrangements with no penalty for moving.
- Ensure that the student code clearly states that the use of alcohol will not be accepted as an excuse for abusive behavior or for lessening sanctions for unacceptable acts.
- Ensure that the policy covers harassment via computers (see Chapter 5).
- Develop a procedure whereby buildings and equipment, such as tables and library carrels, are periodically inspected for graffiti that is sexist, racist, anti-Semitic, homophobic, or otherwise offensive. Develop ways to remove or cover such graffiti.
- Distribute the policy or statement about student-to-student harassment to all new and transfer students.
- Encourage or require inter-fraternity councils as well as individual fraternities to develop codes of behavior regarding interpersonal behavior concerning women.
- Require individual fraternities and sororities to establish their own policies on peer harassment. The policies should be reviewed periodically by members and should be posted in the houses. Pledges should be asked to sign a statement that they have read the policy and will abide by it.
- Encourage dormitory residents to establish codes of behavior regarding interpersonal conduct.
- Periodically review the extent of peer harassment on campus via open hearings, interviews with student groups and individual students, and other methods such as surveys to ensure continued awareness of the issue and to monitor the effectiveness of policies and procedures.
- Develop a coordinating mechanism to ensure that topics related to sexism and peer harassment are the responsibility of a particular office, several offices working together, or a single individual.
- Train counselors, residential assistants, and other student personnel administrators to deal with peer harassment, including helping students handle it themselves where desired and appropriate.
- Take harassment seriously. When two male students posted a computer-generated obscene picture on a woman faculty member's office door, Bates College faculty members canceled all classes and activities so that students could attend a series of workshops and seminars on harassment. (There had also been a series of incidents involving female students being harassed by male students.)

Response to Students Who Are Harassed

Although many administrators are increasingly sensitive to complaints about peer harassment, some campus personnel are still unaware that peer harassment is a problem. Others, while acknowledging that "inappropriate" behavior occurred, do not recognize the behavior as harassment, as discrimination and needing institutional response. They may view the problem as a "personal" or "individual" one—a "miscommunication" among two individuals rather than a violation of law and institutional policy, and thus provide no resources or special help for those students who are harassed and may need assistance. Although most students who are harassed may not need any special help, some may. The following recommendations may be of help in developing or using existing resources:

- Be sure that personnel in existing resources are aware of and trained to deal with peer harassment. Such resources might include the counseling center, women's center, student affairs office, and resident assistants. Providing an array of resources encourages women to come forward and talk about their experiences.
- Be sure that counseling as well as medical care and protection, if needed, are available either on or off campus.
- When students bring forth formal or informal complaints of peer harassment, be sure that the information given them includes information about available services.
- In cases of severe harassment, support systems should be extended to help the person harassed handle any academic problems that may arise after the harassment. Such support might take the form of offering to provide the student with a letter to faculty members explaining her situation, or a support person who can accompany her while she talks to her instructors.
- Inform peer harassment victims of the possibility of countercharges being filed by the person she is filing against. At one school a woman was involved in an altercation with a male student at an off-campus bar. Both were drinking, started to argue and ended up shoving each other. After she complained about the incident, the male student filed a charge against her. At another school, a male student accused of rape filed a suit charging defamation of character against his accuser. To the extent an institution can file charges on its own, it may encourage others to bring forward additional information that would lessen the likelihood of countercharges.

The Use of Public Shaming to Deal with Peer Harassment

When community values are thwarted or ignored, public shaming may be a useful tool for administrators. Although "public shaming" may conjure up images such as colonial stocks, shaming can be a way to reassure the academic community that its basic common values of human respect and dignity will be upheld and that those who do not observe those values are people to be scorned.

For example, when students conduct "Take Back the Night Marches" to call attention to the issue of sexual assault, it is not uncommon for them to be harassed as they march. Male students may heckle and ridicule or call out, like in the following chant, "We can rape you anytime, anytime we want." Typically these behaviors are ignored by the campus community; at best they may be reported (with one or two lines) in the campus newspaper.

At Princeton University after men and women who marched in a "Take Back the Night" observance were threatened, harassed, and mooned, campus officials met with the march leaders that evening and the next morning issued a strong statement, making it clear that such behavior would not be tolerated and that it was not the kind of behavior expected from Princeton students. A second march was immediately scheduled that evening and took place without incident.

The campus statement became a way to educate the community about the issues as it became the focus of discussion among many students. Most impressive was that some men who had ridiculed the women during the first march, apologized and marched with them during the second one.

Public shaming is especially useful when free speech issues may be involved. For example, when a fraternity at a public institution asked for permission to show *Deep Throat* (a pornographic movie) as a fund-raiser, the administrator who gave them permission told them he did so because of their First Amendment rights. But he also added that he planned to write an open letter to the campus newspaper condemning them for showing it. He did so, and his letter sparked discussion throughout the campus.

Such public shaming reassures those who oppose such behaviors that the community at large is supportive. It also tells those who engage in such behaviors, even in instances where they may have a right to do so, that there are consequences to their acts.

Peer harassment is a serious problem but with institutional commitment, a comprehensive educational program, and clear effective policies, administrators can make their institutions a more hospitable place for all of its students.

Empowering Students to Deal with Peer Harassment

When students report peer harassment, they need to know that the behavior they have encountered violates institutional policy and that there are a number of options they can consider. They might want to handle it themselves informally or they might want to file a formal charge. The institution might act in an informal manner to stop the behavior (such as talking to the perpetrator) or file charges on its own.

Most students who report peer harassment do not want to file a formal charge; they just want the offending behavior to stop. In such instances, helping a woman to handle the situation herself may be the most effective way to deal with peer harassment. Empowering her by providing a series of options for responding to an uncomfortable situation makes her less of a victim and also teaches her skills that may be useful throughout her life.

Here is a brief list of some options for individuals[13] that might be considered:

- Informing the offender in a strong voice that his behavior is offensive and not welcome. ("I don't like what you are doing. Please don't do that anymore!") This can be combined with labeling or describing the offending behavior. ("This is the third time you put your arm around me. I want you to stop it now!")

- Indicating shock and surprise, as recommended by Miss Manners ("I beg your pardon!" or "Why in the world would you want to say [or do] something like that!")

- Sending a copy of the institution's peer harassment policy to the offender after highlighting or underlining the relevant parts. (This could be done anonymously.)

- Sending a special type of letter to the harasser.[14] The letter is low-key, polite, and detailed, and consists of three parts:
    1. A factual account of what happened, without any evaluation, as seen by the writer. Most people agree with the facts, but not the interpretation. (This letter separates the facts from the feelings.) It should include date, time, place, and any other relevant

facts: "Last week you called me a slut and a whore when I entered the lounge on our dormitory floor. Yesterday, you did the same thing when you passed me in the hall."

2. A description of how the writer feels about what happened, expressing her anger, dismay, disgust, fear, or whatever: "I am very angry at what you said and feel disgusted with your behavior. I look at you and want to throw up."

3. What the writer wants to happen next. "I want you to stop calling me names. I want you to treat me in a respectful manner."

The writer keeps a copy of the letter. Sometimes the letter is sent by certified mail, return-receipt requested, as a way to call attention to the seriousness of the letter. The letter is a private communication; it does not show that copies were sent to anyone, although the writer may, if she wants, give a copy of it to the person who advised her to write the letter. Sometimes that person may also help her write the letters.

What usually happens is that the harasser says nothing but stops his offensive behavior. Occasionally, he wants to discuss, explain or apologize, and it is best to advise women to say something like "I'm not going to discuss it; I just want your behavior to stop, and then walk away."

Because the letter can be read and reread without having to respond (as in a conversation), it gives the harasser a new perception of how his behavior is experienced by others. It also provides the writer with a sense of doing something constructive about the situation and helps her feel in charge of her life.

The letter is most effective with individual harassers. It will not work if the harasser is extremely aggressive, nor is it appropriate if group harassment is involved.

• Using a "sexual harassment notebook": This is sometimes effective with individuals and with groups, particularly when the harassment is repeated in the same place. The woman purchases a large notebook and writes on it in large visible letters "Sexual Harassment." When the harassment begins, she takes out her notebook and a pen, and begins to write what was said, asking questions such as "Could you repeat that, I want to write it down," "What is today's date?" If asked what she is doing, she should say something like: "just keeping records" and to be noncommittal; alternatively she can say she is doing "research" but cannot discuss what it consists of. The aim here is to break the cycle of harassment by doing something unexpected and that also shows the harassment is not intimidating the woman as intended; she comes across as calm, cool, and collected. In rare instances should the notebook be grabbed, the woman should give it up and walk away.

• Using the "confrontation survey." The woman who is harassed looks the harasser in the eye and in a very businesslike manner says, "I'm so glad you said that. Women are conducting a survey on sexual harassment and I want to include you in the survey. I'd like a few minutes of your time since this is important research."

The survey includes questions such as "Why do you do this?" "Do you do this to all kinds of women or just certain kinds?" "Do you remember how old you were when you first said something like this?" A copy of the survey appears in Martha J. Langelan's book, *Back Off* (see previous footnote), or can be obtained from Confrontation Survey, D.C. Rape Crisis Center, P.O. Box 21005, Washington, DC 20009. A group of students or the staff at a Women's Center could also devise their own survey. As in the previous option, the aim is to show that the intimidation is not working.

Not all women want to handle peer harassment on their own; they should not be required to do so. As in any kind of attempted resolution, someone should follow-up with the individual within a week or two to see if the harassment has stopped, if there has been any retaliation, or if any other intervention is needed.

Peer harassment is emerging as a controversial and troublesome area on campuses—one which is expected to engage more and more attention and institutional resources. Helping young men and women learn to get along better is a legitimate and important goal of college life—one which must be dealt with if we are to make possible the basic mandate of educational institutions: providing a positive learning climate for all of its students.

Endnotes

1. Title IX of the Education Amendments of 1972 prohibits discrimination on the basis of sex in educational institutions receiving federal funds.
2. *Franklin v. Gwinnett Public Schools,* 112 S.Ct. 1028 (1992).
3. Hughes, Jean O'Gorman and Bernice Resnick Sandler, Peer harassment: Hassles for women on campus. Originally published by the Project on the Status and Education of Women, Association of American Colleges, Washington, DC, 1988. Now published by the Center for Women Policy Studies, Washington, DC.
4. These incidents were reported to the author either in conversations or during her campus visits.
5. *About Women on Campus,* Spring 1992, Vol. 1, No. 2. National Association for Women in Education, Washington, DC.
6. *AWOC,* Summer 1992, Vol. 1, No. 3.
7. *AWOC,* Spring 1993, Vol. 2, No. 2. The dean of the college arranged for its immediate removal, called a school meeting, and condemned the graffiti.
8. *AWOC,* Spring 1995, Vol. 4, No. 2.
9. Survey by the American Social Health Association, reported in the *Washington Post,* Health Section, April 4, 1995, p. 7.
10. *See,* for example, Bernice Lott, Sexual harassment: Consequences and remedies, *Thought*

and Action, National Education Association, Washington, DC, Winter 1993, Vol. VIII, No. 2, pp. 89–103.
11. Fields, Cheryl M., Colleges weigh liability in alcohol and sexual harassment cases, *Chronicle of Higher Education,* 3 February 1988, Vol. 34, No. 21, p. A–14.
12. At one school where a gang rape occurred, the sanction for the perpetrators was written as follows:

   …Have a letter written by [dean] about these matters to be placed in their permanent record, to be transmitted to any college, graduate school, professional school, or employer, with any transcript requested. Upon a sufficient showing of growth and development in coming to terms with the issues involved, [dean] would expect to destroy these letters. The College has an obligation to help its students with educational and vocational placement, but it also has obligations to those who ask for recommendations or educational records. (Should a student select separation [from the college] we will not send the letter but would respond honestly to inquiries.)

13. For an excellent compendium of strategies women have used to stop sexual harassment, *see* Langelan, Martha J., *Back Off,* Simon & Schuster, New York, 1993.
14. Rowe, Mary P., Dealing with sexual harassment, *Harvard Business Review,* May–June 1981.

4

FACULTY-TO-FACULTY
SEXUAL HARASSMENT

BRENDA SEALS

Introduction

Research on sexual harassment at universities and colleges has focused on documenting the prevalence of such behaviors among students, faculty, and staff; examining perceptions of what constitutes sexual harassment; describing why some people report sexual harassment and others do not; explicating the consequences of sexual harassment for individuals and organizations; and identifying factors correlated with sexual harassment. However, beyond these numbers and correlations are real people with real problems. Research focusing on how it occurs and the process of complaining about sexual harassment is needed to understand the personal meaning for faculty members who experience sexual harassment and to direct policy aimed at preventing and adjudicating such harassment.

This chapter briefly reviews sexual harassment literature as it applies to higher education faculty, describing gaps in the understanding of sexual harassment and examines five cases of junior faculty members who filed charges against senior faculty members. The chapter concludes with a summary and recommendations.

Although estimates vary, approximately 40% of female and 18% of male faculty at colleges or universities report experiencing some behavior from other faculty members or staff that could be labeled sexual harassment (Carroll & Ellis, 1993; Fitzgerald et al., 1988a; Gruber, 1990; Goodwin et al., 1989; McKinney, 1990; Rubin & Borgers, 1990).[1] Further, in a study by Grauerholz (1989), about 48% of women faculty members described experiencing harassment behaviors from students (contrapower harassment), some of which could be defined as sexual harassment. Approximately 3% of faculty members reported incidents of sexual bribery from students (Grauerholz, 1989; McKinney, 1990).

Note: An earlier version of this paper was presented at the Sociologists Against Sexual Harassment meetings, Pittsburgh, August 20, 1992. I would like to acknowledge Bob Shoop, Phoebe Stambaugh, Greg Seals, and other anonymous reviewers for their help and support with this paper.

Using the Equal Employment Opportunity Commission's (EEOC) definition of sexual harassment, Carroll and Ellis (1993) estimate that 31% of the women and 5% of the men have experiences that could legally be labeled sexual harassment, with 18% (not broken down by sex) experiencing physical advances. Of those who describe such incidents, only 12% of the women and 5% of the men label their experiences as sexual harassment (Goodwin et al., 1989).

The reported percentage of faculty members who have ever experienced sexual harassment from other faculty members or administrators in their current positions underestimates the total extent that sexual harassment has affected faculty members. Fitzgerald and Shullman (1993) estimate that as many as half of all women serving as higher education faculty have experienced some form of sexual harassment in their academic preparation or career. Further, it is unknown how many women over their careers as undergraduate students, graduate students, university employees, and, ultimately, as faculty members have been repeatedly harassed sexually or by how many different persons.

Higher education faculty members are more likely to label specific behaviors as sexual harassment than are graduate or undergraduate students (Fitzgerald & Ormerod, 1991), but few officially report incidents (McKinney, 1990). Of those faculty members who self-identified as experiencing sexual harassment, only 22% reported the incident to a university authority (Goodwin et al., 1989). Common reactions to sexual harassment among working women in general include ignoring the behavior, confronting the harasser, going along with the harassment, and joking (Cammaert, 1985; Goodwin et al., 1989; Grauerholz, 1989; Gutek & Koss, 1993; Lach & Gwartney-Gibbs, 1993). Reasons given for not formally reporting sexual harassment consist of fear of retaliation, fear of being accused of provoking the incident, fear of being blamed, lack of knowledge about how to register a complaint or a belief that no result would come of the complaint, and not wanting to hurt the accused harasser (Gutek & Koss, 1993; Rubin & Borgers, 1990).

Women who did formally report sexual harassment said they did so as a last-ditch effort to stop the harassment, because the severity of insult was increasing, and because they perceived their environment as supportive (Lach & Gwartney-Gibbs, 1993). However, the results from formal complaints may not be positive and the threat of retaliation may be real (Coles, 1986; Lach & Gwartney-Gibbs, 1993; Russell, 1984). In Terpstra and Baker's (1988) study of formal complaints, only 31% received a favorable outcome and the average remuneration was only a little over $3,000.

Sexual harassment in the workplace takes a high toll. Psychologically, sexual harassment may result in anger, frustration, anxiety, and posttraumatic stress disorder (Cammaert, 1985; Gutek & Koss, 1993). Productivity may decrease and the harassed person may forfeit work, research, and a career (Dziech & Weiner, 1984; Russell, 1984). Based on a sample of federal employees, Russell (1984) estimates that sexual harassment may cost well over $189 million in lost productivity over two years.

In higher education, lost productivity because of sexual harassment may decrease the number of women who seek academic careers, and for those who pursue academic careers, decrease the number of women gaining promotion or choosing to stay in academia. Sexual harassment in academe may undermine the ability of female faculty to effectively teach, conduct research, mentor, and act as role models. Ultimately, sexual harassment may contribute to sex segregation in the university, indirectly contributing to sex discrimination (Dziech & Weiner, 1984).

The relatively high percentages of faculty affected by sexual harassment is not surprising given the organizational context of colleges and universities. Faculty careers are based on long-term relationships, where subjective recommendations and job evaluations are crucial for hiring and promotion (Lach & Gwartney-Gibbs, 1993). A certain amount of collegiality necessitating complex, cross-gender inter-actions with administrators, faculty, and students is expected (Grauerholz, 1989; Lach & Gwartney, 1993; Lobel, 1993; McKinney, 1990; Stanko, 1993; Stockdale, 1993). Women are often minorities in academic departments and are concentrated in the junior professor and lecturer positions where the power differentials may make them particularly vulnerable to sexual harassment (Bond, 1991; Cleveland & Kerst, 1993; Dziech & Weiner, 1984). Also, female faculty may be more likely to be unmarried and young (Russell, 1984). These factors make female junior faculty especially vulnerable to sexual harassment from administrators, faculty, and students (Grauerholz, 1989; Tangri, Burt, & Johnson, 1982).

This research along with increasing charges of sexual harassment has advanced an understanding of sexual harassment to the point where it is recognized as a valid problem to which universities and other organizations must respond (Elza, 1993). The variety of research to date suggests the importance of strong policy and prevention programs in order to decrease sexual harassment in the university and college environment and to bring redress to those victimized by it (Paludi & Barickman, 1991; Remick et al., 1990). However, to better inform theory and policy on sexual harassment, research must address two gaps in our current understanding of this phenomenon. One gap is the lack of discussion of sexual harassment complaints; this gap must be filled to clarify definitions of sexual harassment and to specify professional ethics. The second gap is the lack of research on policy in action—the detailed explication of resolution processes based on actual complaints and hearings. Institutions could improve issues of jurisdiction and policy if such research were available.

Studies of the phenomenology of sexual harassment can address these gaps in understanding because such studies focus on the sexual harassment experiences of people in university and college settings. Beyond bridging research and policy as suggested before, phenomenological studies may help to integrate theories about vulnerability and oppression with those of sexual harassment. Although this chapter presents a brief iteration of sexual harassment complaints, the primary focus of this research is to explicate the resolution process.

Five Cases

The following cases portray five different universities in public and private, urban and rural settings. All the participants self-identified as having been sexually harassed and all were junior faculty insofar as they were in untenured, assistant professor or lecturer positions at the time the harassment occurred. All of the alleged sexual harassers were tenured at or above the associate professor level. For purposes of convenience, I refer to those who self-identified as having experienced sexual harassment as junior professors and the people they alleged to have sexually harassed them as senior professors.[2]

The cases presented here are not representative of the full range of sexual harassment cases. The cases and the information from them should be interpreted descriptively. All twenty-one of the sexual harassment cases reviewed were unique in regard to the events. However, participants' descriptions of how institutions handled the cases were similar with only a few differences. These cases are titled by where the harassment occurred.

Case #1: Professional Meetings

During an wine/cocktail reception at the society's national meetings, a senior professor "followed" a junior professor around and repeatedly fondled her. The junior professor tried to use avoidance techniques such as going to talk to other people and staying in the bathroom. She finally left the cocktail hour. Back at the university, the junior professor felt embarrassed and could not comfortably work with the senior professor although his demeanor toward her was professional. Because they were working on a number of projects together, she thought that this incident and fear of future incidents impaired her ability to make progress. She complained to the department chair almost a year later—the year before she would come up for review.

Case #2: General Office Areas

A number of senior professors in the department repeatedly sat on the secretary's desk and would look down her shirt regardless of who was in the room. The secretary seemed uncomfortable at work and often complained to a junior professor. Although the junior professor was not treated in this manner, one of the senior professors frequently stared at her "breasts" during conversations, which made her uncomfortable. The junior professor attempted avoidance techniques such as always carrying a notebook to hold over her chest area. One day, these senior professors made suggestive comments about the secretary's clothing and joked about taking her to lunch to a place where they would have to sit on the floor and have an opportunity to look up her dress. The junior professor publicly complained, telling the senior professors to stop saying things like that and to treat women with more respect.

Almost two years later the junior professor was denied tenure with one of the factors being noncollegiality. The junior professor could not understand this accusation and, on investigation, found that the men in the department cited her public complaint as an example of her lack of collegiality because she unnecessarily embarrassed them in public. The junior professor made a formal complaint about the sexual harassment she received (staring at her breasts). The secretary had moved to another position and refused to make any accusations against her former employer, although on the phone to the Dean, she confirmed the story regarding the incident at her desk where the junior professor "embarrassed" the senior professors.

Case #3: Private Office

The spring before a junior professor came up for promotion, she was called into the office of a senior professor. He said that he wanted to discuss funding for new graduate students. He asked her to shut the door. After a little while someone knocked on the door. The junior professor was sitting closest to the door and she got up and opened the door. The secretary handed her two files, got "wide eyes," and fled down the hall. The junior professor was surprised and turned to the senior professor to ask what he thought was the matter. She found that he had unzipped his pants and was tucking in his underwear. She fled the office herself. She was embarrassed about the incident and avoided the office. About a week later she attempted to discuss the incident with another professor. The professor would not talk to her. She realized that no one in the department would talk to her—especially the secretary who had handed her the files. Claiming sexual harassment, the junior professor complained to the dean.

Case #4: Graduate School and Faculty Meetings

The junior professor was sexually harassed as a graduate student where she got her degree. After the junior professor was on the faculty at a different university for about a year, she heard that another student was being harassed by the professor who harassed her and decided she couldn't "live" without doing something. The junior professor filed a formal complaint at the university she had graduated from. To attend the hearings on the case, she traveled extensively, which decreased her ability to publish, and under the stress of this case, her teaching suffered as well. On her yearly review, these two problems were cited as reasons *not* to renew her contract, even though the hearings on the case where she was a graduate student was, by then, finished.

In the departmental debate on this topic, the junior professor asked whether the faculty would have treated her differently had she had a death in the family. Some faculty members claimed that would be an acceptable reason for leniency because a death in the family was understandable and the junior professor would not have chosen that to happen to her. In the heated argument that ensued, some professors claimed she had earned her degree by "sleeping around" and should she be "thankful" she had been hired in the first place. The junior professor formally complained that these comments and assumptions about the quality of her work constituted another form of sexual harassment.

Case #5: Dates and Private Office

In the semester that the junior professor came up for promotion, a famous professor in her department repeatedly asked her to go out. Although a bit uncomfortable with the relationship because she had a steady partner whom she was commuting with, she agreed. However, one night when she was working late the senior professor came into her office at work and said he wanted to have sex; she told him she did not want to. He began taking off his clothes. She finally threatened to call the campus security and he angrily left. Two weeks later, she was denied the promotion. She filed a formal complaint of sexual harassment within three months of the denial.

Results

Information from the five cases was organized chronologically by the steps junior professors took in the complaint, investigation, and hearing processes. The results from the analysis of the data are presented, following the steps from complaint to hearing, noting variations in cases. Where possible, the terms and phrases from participants' narratives are presented.

Because participants emphasized negative aspects of their experiences, presenting combined results represents a worst case scenario for processing sexual harassment charges. Although this worst case scenario is certainly extreme and does not describe the experiences of any one participant, these cases are instructive from a policy and practice standpoint.

Complaining

All of the junior professors tried avoidance techniques to stop the sexual harassment and two tried "confronting their aggressor." In the two latter cases, both junior professors verbally asked the senior professor to stop and one went on to write a letter to the senior professor explaining the negative consequences of the harassment for her.

In general, the complaint process started at the department level. That is, the junior professors verbally complained to the chair of their department prior to considering more formal procedures. Two junior professors initially complained directly to the dean of their school or college. Reporting initially to the dean was deemed "appropriate" in one case because the senior professor was the department chair and "inappropriate" in the other because the dean instructed the junior professor that complaints were to originate at the department level following a "chain of command."

Four junior professors requested private meetings with their department chairs. The meetings began with the junior professors recounting "the problem" to their department chairs in what was described as awkward, halting terms. Department chairs asked questions about the recounted event(s). Junior professors characterized most of the questions as being "matter of fact"; however, all of these junior professors said the department chairs asked what the junior professors had done to encourage the behavior of the senior professors. One junior professor said that, at this time, she felt she was being blamed for the sexual harassment.

The actions of the department chairs were multifaceted including counseling, lecturing, advising, recording, and referral.[3] Department chairs counseled junior professors by exploring ways to stop the current or anticipated future behavior. Tactics were recommended for junior professors to follow like discussing the situation verbally with the senior professors involved, writing to the senior professors, and avoiding future situations. The department chairs frequently tried to make the junior professor understand and forgive the untoward behavior, assuming the problems were a result of miscommunication.[4]

With lecture overtones, department chairs would caution junior professors that complaining about sexual harassment was a serious matter. The chairs explained how difficult allegations about sexual harassment are to handle and how stressful pursuing a formal complaint would be. Department chairs advised that pursuing the complaint process might jeopardize (or further jeopardize) the junior professors' positions. Most department chairs noted that the time and energy spent in the complaint process would threaten the junior professors' ability to publish; thereby jeopardizing promotion or the ability to get another job in academia.

Two department chairs went further in their advice to point out that it might be difficult for the junior professors to get good letters of recommendation if their involvement in such a case became generally known,[5] which one of them perceived as a veiled threat. It is important to note that three of the junior professors already had been denied promotion in one form or another. In one case, the department chair insinuated that the junior professor was trying to penalize the department for not promoting her. Two of the junior professors said their department chairs' emotional reactions were surprise and dismay. All the junior professors said their department chair was not very supportive.

Once the department chair or the dean was convinced that the junior professor was committed to proceeding with the complaint, a formal record of the complaint was established. Most commonly, this included a summary of the meeting, a written description of the sexual harassment incidents, and the completion of several forms by either or both department chairs and junior professors. To maintain confidentiality and avoid jeopardizing their case, junior professors were cautioned against discussing their case with anyone.

Last, department chairs referred junior professors to affirmative action officers to fill out formal complaints involving a form and an incident description. In one case, the dean's office had someone officially designated to hear sexual harassment incidents. All of the junior professors were asked to document the complaint again by producing a detailed written statement with exact dates, times, places, and possible witnesses. Most interviews with the affirmative action officer or appropriate personnel took 2 to 4 hours to complete and were described as "very draining."[6]

Complaints were then referred from the affirmative action office to the dean's office to determine how the cases would be processed. This referral necessitated meetings between junior professors and deans to go over their cases. In four cases, junior professors showed up for meetings with deans to find out that their departmental chairs and/or other departmental personnel were also invited. In one case, the dean met with the junior professor in the company of his secretary.

All the junior professors described themselves as being nervous going into the meetings with their deans. However, for the four cases where someone else from their department was also in attendance, this meeting was described as extremely stressful.[7] All of them wondered about the confidentiality of their cases; three of the junior professors noted that they didn't mind the departmental person being there but thought they should have been notified of this before the meeting. Another professor thought her case was compromised because the departmental person was known to be a good friend of the senior professor accused of sexual harassment. Two of the junior faculty quipped that they thought the dean considered them unsafe to be with given their complaint.

Junior professors described themselves as feeling particularly uneasy in front of their department chairs when they were discussing the case with the dean. This uneasiness was especially true for those who had received a negative review by their department. Three of the junior professors said they were unable to present their cases as well as they would have liked because of the unexpected presence of a person from their department. One junior professor said she wished she had been able to bring someone with her for this meeting to give support and to be a witness to the proceedings.

In these meetings with deans the cases were reviewed, options for handling the cases were discussed, and advice was given to junior professors. Because this meeting about the case was the second or third so far, junior professors said that no new knowledge was gained. Junior professors were advised to pursue all possible informal and formal avenues within the university to resolve their charges before seeking help outside the university. The rationale for this was that if the cases ultimately were heard by courts outside the university, such courts would be more sympathetic to plaintiffs who tried to resolve sexual harassment charges within their organizations.

Sometime after these meetings with deans, senior professors were interviewed by deans and asked to submit written reports of their side of the story. Deans later informed junior professors in person or over the phone that meetings with senior professors had occurred. In these conversations with deans, junior professors were given opportunities to respond to further questions and to make some decisions about their cases. On the one hand, the junior professors said that deans tried to negotiate proper reprimands with senior professors. If these negotiated reprimands were not satisfactory to both junior and senior professors involved, then junior professors had to decide whether to go on to a hearing or to drop their cases. Although none of the deans were described as trying to discourage junior professors from going forward with cases, their advice was not perceived as encouraging. Junior professors in this study all requested a hearing.

Preparation for the Hearing

The deans of the schools or colleges also had discretion over the kinds of evidence or data allowed in hearings. Prior to hearings, junior professors had to prepare case portfolios including copies of the charges, descriptions of the event(s), listings of relevant university or other organization policies (such as the American Association of University Professors or discipline-specific codes of ethics), explanations of harm to the junior professors and lists of other evidence to be used during the hearing including what witnesses would appear and what the witnesses were prepared to say. Case portfolios were due approximately two weeks to one month before hearing dates. During this time period, case portfolios were shared with senior professors. *Note that none of the junior professors knew anything about information or testimonies that senior professors would present.* Junior professors were advised by the deans' offices about the relevance of certain policies to their cases and were advised to exclude some kinds of evidence from their cases with the justification that focusing on the least ambiguous evidence would strengthen their charges; however, notifications regarding evidence were sent the day of the hearing, often only hours before.

Junior professors were told what witnesses could come before the hearing boards. In general, witnesses testifying to the women's good character and witnesses serving as experts in sexual harassment were not allowed for junior professors. Junior professors were allowed to bring three types of witnesses: (1) people to whom they had disclosed the event prior to initiating charges (2) people who saw an harassing or unprofessional event; and (3) people who admitted to being harassed similarly by senior professors.

Identifying and bringing others who had been harassed by the senior professors was particularly troublesome for junior professors. First, only two of the junior professors personally knew anyone who had complained about sexual harassment by the senior professors involved in their cases. And, these complaints by other people were not specific or detailed. Two junior professors had heard some rumors about sexual harassment in the department but did not know who was involved or exactly what happened. Second, because junior professors were cautioned against discussing their cases with anyone outside the complaint process, they did not know how to ethically gather information regarding the possibility of other sexual harassment behaviors by senior professors.

Two of the junior professors called a few graduate students or other women faculty to generally solicit information. However, both junior professors thought this method was unsuccessful because they were not good friends of the people they were calling, which made asking personal questions difficult. Plus, they were unable to mention why they needed the information which made them feel uncomfortable. One professor described this experience as, "...calling you out of the blue to see if you had sex with anyone in the department. No, no one in particular." Interestingly enough, both of the junior professors said that a number of the women they talked to freely admitted to having sexual relations with the senior professors involved in their cases; albeit, they described it as consensual.

All of the junior professors asked deans if it was possible or advisable for them to have lawyers or other legal representatives at the hearings. However, in all but one case, outside legal representatives were not allowed in hearings but junior professors were advised that they were welcome to seek professional advice to prepare their cases at their own expense. The rationale given for this policy was that hearings were an "informal" matter inside the university and closed to outsiders. For the junior professor who got to bring a lawyer to her hearing, the lawyer's participation was limited to observing the hearings.

Three of the junior professors contacted one or two outside lawyers requesting advice about how to prepare their cases. All three junior professors were very dissatisfied with this legal advice primarily because the outside lawyers knew little about sex discrimination, less about sexual harassment, and virtually nothing about university procedures. In short, monies were spent but junior professors thought no expertise was gained.

The Hearing

Hearing boards were usually composed of five to nine faculty and/or staff, drawn from either a standing university board (grievance committee or some other committee) or an impromptu committee usually appointed by a dean or provost. A representative from the affirmative action office or the office of general counsel was often present as a nonvoting member. Note that beyond these general comments, the hearing boards were unique in composition and procedures. In all the cases, the organization of the hearing was similar to a criminal case; that is, prosecutors (junior professors) presented their cases and defendants (senior professors) presented their cases. In general, anyone on the board could ask questions at any time.

The hearings began with a statement from the chair of the committee or an appropriate university representative, which included an introduction of the committee members, a reading of the charges, and instructions to the committees regarding their role. Committees were generally responsible for weighing the merits of the charges and deciding whether the charges held in the case before them. Committees did not have to give their decisions immediately and some kind of committee report or summary was to be prepared shortly after the conclusion of the hearing. In only one case was the committee instructed that, in the event they decided sexual harassment had occurred, they would be required to write recommendations for appropriate actions to be taken. Otherwise, responsibility for actions, presumably, would lie with the dean, provost, and general counsel of the college or university.

After these preliminary statements, junior professors were directed to describe the relevant events, to present any witnesses or supporting evidence, and to summarize by discussing the relevance of their case to the appropriate sexual harassment policy. This presentation done, senior professors were asked to similarly present their side of the events, with witnesses, supporting evidence, and a summary.

All the junior professors said that few questions came up in the presentation of their charges and that the questions that did arise were generally for clarification of the sexual harassment events. In all the cases presented here, the events were reported fairly consistently by both junior and senior professors. Because there were few discrepancies in the descriptions of the events (i.e., few instances of "he said" versus "she said") and because senior professors had been previously informed of the kinds of information junior professors would present, but not vice versa, junior professors thought the hearings focused exclusively on the cases as written by them. That is, discussions in the hearings ignored the statements of senior professors but consistently called into question case facts as presented by junior professors.[8]

For senior professors, the questions brought up by hearing boards focused on the intentions of their behavior such as "Did [senior professor] really mean to do this or that?," the foreseen consequences of the behavior such as "Could [senior professor] have anticipated any harm?" and the present consequences such as "Was the event linked to the lack of a promotion of [junior professor]?" and "Was the consequence of the event sufficient to really harm [junior professor]?" In a couple of the cases there was also some discussion about whether doing anything about the event would be worthwhile.[9]

Hearing Surprises

The preceding details the general process of the hearings as described by junior professors; however, junior professors described five surprises they thought largely determined the outcomes of their charges. The first and most subtle surprise was the tendency for senior professors, at some time during the proceeding, to refer to some hearing committee members by their first names. Beyond breaking away from the formality associated with hearings, referring to committee members by their first names indicated that senior professors were familiar with board members beyond what the junior professors were, perhaps reminding board members of past relationships or affirming an equality of status.

The second surprise was that three of the senior professors brought an attorney or legal advisor with them to the hearings. During introductions, explanations were given to junior professors that this attorney was working for the university (usually from the law school or the political science department) and as such was available as an informal consultant to professors. Although none of the attorneys present for senior professors asked questions directly, they did take notes and sometimes whispered to senior professors during the hearing.

None of the junior professors were informed by deans prior to the hearing that, if available, they could have had similar representation. One of the junior professors said that a friend suggested she consult with a lawyer inside the university system. However, this junior professor said she did not know such a lawyer well enough to request assistance and she did not know that the senior professor involved in her case would have such assistance. In the case where an outside lawyer was admitted for the junior professor, she felt this lawyer's advice was less helpful than that available to the senior professor because her lawyer was not very familiar with university policy and the advice she received was not helpful. Although junior professors could not ascertain how helpful having a lawyer in the hearing was to senior professors, they characterized their cases as underprepared compared to those of senior professors.

The third surprise to junior professors was that character and expert witnesses were allowed to talk in support of senior professors. Junior professors assumed that, because they could not have such witnesses, senior professors were comparably limited. All the junior professors were surprised by the presence of other faculty from their department at the hearings. In what may be an extreme case, all the tenured professors from the department involved and two upper administrators of the university served as character witnesses for one senior professor.

Because junior professors had been cautioned not to discuss their cases with people who were not directly involved, they assumed senior professors were given a parallel constraint. However, in gathering character witnesses, senior professors had obviously informed many people in the college or university about the hearing. Three of the junior professors said that, prior to the hearing, they were aware of other people "eyeing" them strangely or that some people stopped interacting with them, but the three junior professors initially attributed these changes in behavior to their own negative feelings or paranoia.

The fourth surprise to three junior professors was the presence of character witnesses intending to testify to their traits. Although junior professors were not allowed to choose character witnesses, senior professors were. In three cases, senior professors brought in witnesses who claimed to be friends of the junior professors. These witnesses testified to at least one of the following:

1. Junior professors had not disclosed the event to them.
2. Junior professors showed no changes in personality or behavior before or after the purported event.
3. They saw no signs of sexual harassment themselves even though a few had worked with the senior professors in question.
4. There were inconsistencies in the events charged by junior professors.
5. Junior professors had some personality problem such as hating men, not knowing how to appropriately interpret cues from men, or being generally unstable or untrustworthy.

The fifth surprise was that senior professors used other kinds of evidence, which junior professors thought was professionally confidential and irrelevant to the current charges. For example, in two cases senior professors referred to junior professors' teaching evaluations. In one case, a few students had written in that the junior professor was a feminist or had man-hating tendencies. In the other case, students wrote that the junior professor seemed nervous and preoccupied during class.

Two senior professors presented as evidence letters from graduate students whom they had contacted and asked to write down their opinions of the junior professors. In one case, none of the graduate students who submitted letters had taken classes with or worked with the junior professor. In another case, the boyfriend of one of the graduate students said he had met the junior professor twice in public places and had noticed her unstable personality and bad attitude toward men.

Comments, jokes, and words taken out of context, such as excerpts from departmental meeting minutes, were used by senior professors as other evidence to indicate the abnormal attitudes or behaviors of junior professors. In short, junior professors thought that anything ambiguous or bad on the record about them was brought up. Four of the junior professors said that the vast majority of comments they were quoted as saying were things they did not remember saying or had been taken out of context. The junior professor who had a legal advisor present at the hearing said her advisor was shocked by what was allowed as evidence for that senior professor.

All of the junior professors described themselves as stunned by the representations of their personalities created by the senior professor and his witnesses. Four of them said this was the worst part of their hearings. Junior professors anticipated that most of the hearing would center on the sexual harassing behavior. However, because the behavior was admitted and agreed on by both parties, the hearings centered on the personalities of the women who defined such behavior as unprofessional. Junior professors were painted as being, to quote one respondent, "Vixens who misconstrued every gesture, every word that was uttered [by senior professors]." Four of the junior professors mentioned that they thought much more was said about their personalities than was needed for senior professors to win their cases. Three of the junior professors said that the length of time and effort put in to misconstrue their personalities was another form of degradation and punishment.

All the junior professors claimed to be so affected by the representation of their personalities and the kinds of evidence allowed that they could not think of questions to ask and could not analyze inconsistencies in senior professors' cases. That the hearing could be so different from their preparations and expectations created a silencing process that deeply disturbed these women who described themselves as aggressive, quick on their feet, and accustomed to tough arguing.

Junior professors claimed that, by the end of the hearing, they could barely present a good summary of their cases. They were exhausted by the length of the meetings, which generally went two to four hours beyond what they were told to expect. They were shocked at the hearing itself and what was said about themselves. They felt let down by the university for not seeing sexual harassment and professional ethics as "that important." They felt double-crossed by hearing systems that violated their perceived civil liberties and their rights to due process and confidentiality. They felt betrayed by the other people who served as witnesses for senior professors. And, they felt embarrassed and were unsure how they were going to go to work the next day with their office frequently just down the hall from the those who participated in the hearing.

Aftermath

Waiting for results of hearings took from a few days to a couple of weeks. In three cases, "nothing" was done; that is, the hearing committee decided there was insufficient evidence to substantiate sexual harassment charges. In one case, a letter was put into the senior professor's file; it discussed his inappropriate behavior in a public setting but had no mention of sexual harassment. In the last case, the senior professor was obligated to write an apology to the junior professor. In none of their cases was their behavior labeled sexual harassment by hearing committees.

Via letters or meetings with deans or other university officials, junior professors were advised that they could appeal the outcomes of their cases. Appeals variously would go to other hearing boards, to university or college senate committees or, in two cases, to meetings of the faculty of the whole university or college. No junior professors were advised that they could go to EEOC or to another agency "outside" the university for further case processing or help.

Two of the junior professors went to EEOC on the advice of legal advisors outside the university. These junior professors reported waiting a long time, meeting with an EEOC officer, and filling out a lengthy report. Toward the end of the meeting, they had to decide whether they wanted EEOC to investigate their cases. Both junior professors said that EEOC, as an organization, did not know how to handle sexual harassment charges within the unique organization of a university for two primary reasons.[10]

First, EEOC required that claimants [junior professors] document how they have been harmed.[11] The primary way of indicating harm was through showing loss of wages, demotion, or firing. Neither junior professor could show that their wages had been reduced or that they had been specifically demoted. Both junior professors who went to EEOC had a letter saying their contract would not be renewed, but it did not take effect until approximately a year and a half after the letter's date. From EEOC officers' perspectives, this was a long time to find a new job, a job that could possibly be better than their current job.

Second, both junior professors said EEOC expected a written document detailing criteria that would be used in job evaluations, but no such documents applied to junior professor positions in the university or college where they worked. Neither junior professor had a document specifically delineating job responsibilities and performance criteria applicable to each job. Further, EEOC officers expected to see written periodic evaluations. Both junior professors described annual meetings with departmental chairs and vague advice they were given in those meetings as their only periodic evaluations. Part of the problem was, as quoted from one junior professor, "I know I have to do service, research and teaching, but I don't know how to prove I've done a good job. A couple of publications each year really doesn't reflect what I do in an average work week. The EEOC officer didn't know what to do."

Beyond these difficulties, both junior professors said EEOC seemed very understaffed. They reported having to repeatedly call the EEOC officer to make them work on their case and often found a new person had been assigned their case. EEOC did investigate both cases but their decision seemed irrelevant to the junior professors; officers had just sent them letters saying that the EEOC had concluded their investigation. In both cases, the EEOC officer said the university demonstrated that the junior professors had not published enough in the last year and that was the sole criterion for promotion at the university. There was a sentence in both letters stating that EEOC did not find any sex discrimination.

Two of the junior professors called their professional organizations for help. One was discouraged because "everyone thought someone else was responsible for handling such cases," and she could find no one who would. One was discouraged because the organization said it would "investigate" the case but she never heard what happened or whether an investigation took place. To date, none of the junior professors in this study have pursued their cases any further than what has been described here.

Conclusions

Current movements in case law holding colleges and universities liable for eliminating sexual harassment have placed an emphasis on developing good policy and effective infrastructures to encourage harassment reporting. However, emphasis on policy and infrastructure will not solve problems in hearing and resolving cases (Ehrenreich, 1990). What is needed, and what this study is a first effort toward, is an evaluation of policy in action (Brandenburg, 1982; Fitzgerald & Shullman, 1993; Lach & Gwartney-Gibbs, 1993).

Policy in action, or the study of how complaints are processed by a university, is a crucial step in understanding the organizational and personal dynamics of sexual harassment (Schilling & Fuehrer, 1991; Vaux, 1993). Universities and colleges are organizations that stand on a long history of inequalities in power, variously discriminating along race, gender, class, and ability lines (Benson & Thomson, 1982; Fitzgerald et al., 1988b; Hoffman, 1986; Paludi, 1990). The hierarchial power inherited by male professors endows an ascribed status with incumbent discretion. On a personal level, this ascribed status allows senior professors to differentially prepare and present their cases with an ultimate advantage in case outcome (Olson & McKinney, 1991).

If universities are going to take on the responsibility of formally and informally resolving sexual harassment cases, their policies must address inequalities in status and provide fairness in the complaint, investigation, hearing, and resolution processes for students, staff, and faculty (Brandenberg, 1982; Elza, 1993; Markunas & Joyce-Brady, 1987; Remick et al., 1987; Somers, 1982; Stimpson, 1991). Specifically, junior professors need access to complaint processes that will enhance their ability to consider their cases and make decisions about case processing. An investigation process should be clearly specified and must include ethical and confidential measures to collect evidence relevant to the case, particularly if information about other cases involving the senior professor is required (Eason, 1988; Olson & McKinney, 1993; Paludi & Barickman, 1991).

Institutional regulations should address issues of admissible evidence. The kinds and types of evidence presentable by accuser and accused should match. Further, hearing boards should be impartial, but because of the familiarity with faculty and staff that senior professors may have compared to junior professors, hearing boards composed of university personnel may not be able to provide impartiality. Hearing boards need training in issues of sexual harassment and hearing processes so that more emphasis can be placed on the behaviors identified as sexual harassment as opposed to the personalities of those involved in the case process (Eason, 1988).

Harder to resolve is the issue of making the university more understandable to agencies like EEOC, especially with regard to documenting success on the job as a professor and harm to junior professors (Pollack, 1990). Admittedly, changes to accomplish this end would require revolutionary innovations in university policy beyond sexual harassment issues. However, until institutions can fall under the scrutiny of outside, regulatory agencies for policy and case investigation, process, and outcome, sexual harassment will remain alive and well in the university and college setting.[12]

Much can be done within institutions to increase the equity and fairness of the hearing process such as providing administrative support for hearings, offering more avenues for complaints appropriate to faculty and staff, offering knowledgeable counsel for junior professors, and making information on hearings available. Regarding the latter, institutions could publish information on the number of complaints made and the number of cases that go to hearing boards. Information on the hearing process should be standardized and published. Finally, professional ethics ought to address relations among university and college employees, even with regard to participation in hearings as witnesses (Tuana, 1985). Without addressing sexual harassment issues, institutions will not be able to provide a safe environment for learning, researching, and teaching, whether by student, faculty or staff.

Lessons to Learn for Equity in Hearings

Organizational Issues

- Provide confidential support for both accuser and accused in the complaint, investigation, hearing, and after-hearing processes. Both accusers and those accused should have equal access to friends, advocates, and, where appropriate, university and non-university legal representatives. For example, where one party to the complaint has legal representation, the institution ought to take steps to help the other party secure equal representation.

- Recognize that sexual harassment is not a form of miscommunication. The burden is on the institution to stop sexual harassment behaviors, not make victims "understand."
- Realize that sexual harassment complaints and hearing processes are stressful. Referrals to appropriate mental health services should be provided to both parties. Also, organizations should understand the realities of lower productivity and should develop guidelines for appropriate allowances.
- Institute training programs for all administrators, faculty, and staff who handle sexual harassment complaints so they can sympathetically listen to complaints, fully inform both parties of their legal rights, and initiate referral and investigation processes within the institution. Such personnel should be warned that discouraging complaints may be illegal.
- Provide training for panel or committee members who hear sexual harassment cases, including a background in the issues of sexual harassment, questions to ask and to avoid, and what kinds of evidence is allowable.
- Derive investigation procedures that provide for training of personnel on how to promptly respond to complaints, to confidentially collect relevant information, and to objectively present information for review. Both accused and accuser should have equal access to this information.
- Ensure that conflicts of interest do not influence investigation and hearing processes so that due process and civil liberties are protected. Universities and colleges should consider developing liaisons with independent organizations to investigate and hear cases. However small colleges may find it impossible to eliminate all conflicts of interest.
- Develop professional ethics to improve fairness.
- Understand that informal processes exist not only to minimize formal complaints, but to provide complainants options to stop sexual harassment. Done well, informal processes can confidentially provide education that allows both parties to "win." If Barbara Gutek (1993) is correct in claiming disputes are an integral part of organizations, then informal processes' goals can moderate levels of conflict to the benefit of organizations.

Hearing Procedure Issues

- Allow one or more advocates or friends to provide support and be present at hearings and meetings concerning the case.
- Avoid arguments that focus on the personalities of claimants instead of the behavior or events of the claim. Credibility issues ought to focus on behaviors or events, not personalities of accuser and accused. Insofar as character witnesses' roles focus on personalities, these witnesses should be prohibited from participating in hearings on behalf of both parties.
- Extend policy to include the kinds of evidence allowed in hearing and ensure that the policy is equitable to both accused and accuser. Specifically, if the accused is allowed to review charges and other points of evidence in advance of the hearing, the accuser should be allowed to review the accused's response.
- Inform both parties well in advance about the general organization of the hearing and its procedures, including who will be present.
- Invite expert witnesses to provide background and to answer questions, especially if panel members have had limited training in sexual harassment issues.

References

Benson, Donna J. & Thomson, Gregg E. Sexual harassment on a university campus: The confluence of authority relations, sexual interest and gender stratification, *Social Problems* 29(3), 236–51, 1982.

Bond, M. E. Division 27 sexual harassment survey: Definitions, impact, and environmental context, in M. Am. Paludi & R. B. Barickman (Eds.), *Academic and workplace sexual harassment: A resource manual* (pp. 189–198). SUNY Press, Albany, 1991.

Brandenburg, J. Sexual harassment in the university: Guidelines for establishing a grievance procedure. *Signs* 8, 320–36, 1982.

Cammaert, L. How widespread is sexual harassment on campus? Special Issue: Women in groups and aggression against women. *International Journal of Women's Studies* 8, 388–97, 1985.

Carroll, L. & Ellis, K. L. Faculty attitudes toward sexual harassment: Survey results, survey process. *Initiatives* 46, 35–41, 1993.

Cleveland, J. N. & M. E. Kerst. Sexual harassment and perceptions of power: An under-articulated relationship. *Journal of Vocational Behavior* 42, 49–67, 1993.

Coles, F. S. Forced to quit: Sexual harassment complaints and agency response. *Sex Roles* 14, 81–95, 1986.

Dziech, B. & Weiner, L. *The lecherous professor: Sexual harassment on campus.* Beacon Press, Boston, 1984.

Eason, Yla. When the boss wants sex. In Paula S. Rothenberg (Ed.), *Racism and sexism: An integrated study* (pp. 139–147). St. Martin's Press, New York, 1989.

Ehrenreich, N. S. Pluralist myths and powerless men: The ideology of reasonableness in sexual harassment law. *The Yale Law Journal.* 99(6), 1177–1234, 1990.

Elza, J. Liability and penalties for sexual harassment in higher education, *Education Law Reporter*, 631–42, 1993.

Fitzgerald, L. F. & Hesson-McInnis, M. The dimensions of sexual harassment: A structural analysis. *Journal of Vocational Behavior* 35, 309–26, 1989.

Fitzgerald, L. F. & Ormerod, A. J. Perceptions of sexual harassment: The influence of gender and academic context. *The Psychology of Women Quarterly* 15, 281–94, 1991.

Fitzgerald, L. F. & Shullman, S. L. Sexual harassment: A research analysis and agenda for the 1990s. *Journal of Vocational Behavior*, 42, 5–27, 1993.

Fitzgerald, L. F., Shullman, S. L., Bailey, N., Richards, M., Swecker, J., Gold, Y., Ormerod, M. & Weitzman, L. The incidence and dimensions of sexual harassment in academia and the workplace. *Journal of Vocational Behavior*, 32, 152–75, 1988a.

Fitzgerald, L. F., Weitzman, L. M., Gold, Y., & Ormerod, M. Academic harassment: Sex and denial in scholarly garb. *Psychology of Women Quarterly* 12(3), 329–40, 1988b.

Garvey, M. S., The high cost of sexual harassment suits. *Personnel Journal* 65, 75–8, 80, 1986.

Goodwin, M. P., Roscoe, B., Rose, M., & Repp, S. E., Sexual harassment: Experiences of university employees. *Initiatives* 52, 25–33, 1989.

Grauerholz, Elizabeth. Harassment of women professors by students: Exploring the dynamics of power of authority, and gender in a university setting. *Sex Roles* 21(11–12), 789–801, 1989.

Gruber, James. Methodological problems and policy implications in sexual harassment research. *Population Research and Policy Review*, 9(3), 235–54, 1990.

Gutek, B. A. *Sex and the workplace.* Jossey-Bass, San Francisco, 1985.

Gutek, B. A. & Koss, M. P. Changed women and changed organizations: Consequences of and coping with sexual harassment. *Journal of Vocational Behavior* 42, 28–48, 1993.

Hoffman, Frances L. Sexual harassment in academia: Feminist theory and institutional practice. *Harvard Educational Review* 56(2), 105–21, 1986.

Lach, D. H. & Gwartney-Gibbs, P. A. Sociological perspectives on sexual harassment and workplace dispute resolution. *Journal of Vocational Behavior* 42, 102–15, 1993.

Lobel, S. A. Sexuality at work: Where do we go from here?" *Journal of Vocational Behavior* 42, 136–52, 1993.

Markunas, P. V. & Joyce-Brady, J. M. Underutilization of sexual harassment grievance procedures. *Journal of NAWDAC* 50, 27–32, 1987.

McKinney, K. Sexual harassment of university faculty by colleagues and students. *Sex Roles* 23(7/8), 421–38, 1990.

Olson, C. & McKinney, K. Processes inhibiting the reduction of sexual harassment in academe: An alternative explanation. *Initiatives* 46, 7–14, 1993.

Paludi, M. A. *Ivory power: Sexual harassment on campus.* State University of New York Press, Albany, 1990.

Paludi, M. A. & Barickman, R. B. *Academic and workplace sexual harassment: A resource manual.* State University of New York Press, Albany, 1991.

Paludi, M. A. & DeFour, D. C. Research on sexual harassment in the academy: Definitions, findings, constraints, responses. *Initiatives* 46, 43–49, 1993.

Pollack, W. Sexual harassment: Women's experience vs. legal definitions. *Harvard Women's Law Journal* 13, 35–85, 1990.

Remick, H., Salisbury, J., Stringer, D., Ginorio, A. B. Investigation of sexual harassment complaints. *Women's Studies Quarterly* 1/2, 207–21, 1990.

Rhodes, Deborah. Gender, race and the politics of supreme court appointments: The import of the Anita Hill-Clarence Thomas hearings. *Southern California Law Review* 64, 1459–65, 1992.

Rubin, L. & Borgers, B. Sexual harassment in universities during the 1980s. *Sex Roles* 23, 397–411, 1990.

Russell, D.E.H. *Sexual exploitation: Rape, child sexual abuse, and workplace harassment.* Sage Publications, Newbury Park, 1984.

Schilling, K. M. & Fuehrer, A. The organizational context of sexual harassment. In M. Am. Paludi & R. B. Barickman (Eds.), *Academic and workplace sexual harassment: A resource manual* (pp. 123–132). SUNY Press, Albany, 1991.

Somers, A. Sexual harassment in academia: Legal issues and definitions. *The Journal of Social Issues* 38(4), 23–32, 1982.

Stanko, E. A. Reading danger: Sexual harassment, anticipation and self-protection. Paper presented to the American Criminological Society, Phoenix, November, 1994.

Stimpson, C. R. Overreaching: Sexual harassment and education. In M. A. Paludi and R. B. Barickman (eds.). *Academic and workplace sexual harassment: A resource manual* (pp. 115–122). SUNY Press, Albany 1991.

Stockdale, M. S. The role of sexual misperceptions of women's friendliness in an emerging theory of sexual harassment. *Journal of Vocational Behavior* 42, 84–101, 1993.

Tangri, S. S., Burt, M. R., & Johnson, L. B. Sexual harassment at work: Three explanatory models. *The Journal of Social Issues*, 38(4), 33–54, 1982.

Terpstra, D. E. Organizational costs of sexual harassment. *Journal of Employment Counseling* 23, 112–19, 1986.

Terpstra, D. E. & Baker, D. D. Outcomes of sexual harassment charges. *Academy of Management Journal* 31, 185–94, 1988.

Tuana, N. Sexual harassment in academe: Issues of power and coercion. *College Teaching* 33(2), 53–63, 1985.

Vaux, A. Paradigmatic assumptions in sexual harassment research: Being guided without being misled. *Journal of Vocational Behavior* 42, 116–35, 1993.

Endnotes

1. The following estimates suffer from different definitions of sexual harassment, survey methodologies, and time frames (Fitzgerald & Hesson-McInnis, 1989; Paludi & DeFour, 1993).

2. This nomenclature reflects the author's belief that power dimensions are the most important factor in sexual harassment cases, not necessarily the gender of those harassed or harassing.

3. Although departmental chairs may have been trying to give, what they might define as, good advice to the junior professors, taking such a stand at this stage in the process and giving advice, which may discourage reporting, may be illegal.

4. I call this phenomenon, "Making sure all the dirt is under the rug without sweeping." *See* Gutek (1985) about assumptions of misunderstanding.

5. I have labeled this process "Shaking the rug without sweeping the floor."

6. This process could be labeled "Beating the rug without sweeping the floor."

7. Perhaps, "Gang beating the rug without sweeping the floor."

8. In many respects this represents a subtle linguistic process. Committees referred to "her statement" although "both statements" would have been more accurate because there was not disagreement on the particular issue at hand. The implication was that the credibil-

ity of the junior professor was being called into question even when there was no difference in the events described. *See* Deborah Rhodes (1992) regarding contests of credibility in the Anita Hill/Clarence Thomas hearings.

9. This argument went something like, "This event was unfortunate, but it is all water under the bridge and nothing will help the current situation."

10. *See* Paludi (1990) for further discussion of the uniqueness of the university.

11. Both junior professors said they experienced emotional harm, but they thought that was difficult to argue as the sole criterion for harm.

12. Please note that, as Terpstra and Baker (1988) have documented, the ability to have the EEOC hear cases in no way provides guarantees of hearing success or remuneration of economic inequalities. *See* Garvey (1986) for estimates of social costs associated with hearings.

5

ELECTRONIC SEXUAL HARASSMENT

DENISE M. DALAIMO

Electronic mail (e-mail) is fast becoming an educational necessity whether you are the president of a university communicating with faculty and staff, or a first-year student "surfing" the Internet. At most universities any student, staff, or faculty member may obtain an e-mail account by filling out a short application at the computer services center on campus. E-mail allows users to access facts, figures, databases, public archives, libraries, and information from around the world, and also enhances both professional and personal relationships by providing a fast and efficient way to communicate with colleagues and friends, whether they live next door or half way around the globe. In fact, an increasing number of social and professional relationships are initiated and sustained through electronic mail (Elza, 1994; Fox, 1994; Johnson, 1994; Tannen, 1994).

The prevalence of this increased interaction through computer-mediated communication has given rise to issues regarding inappropriate behavior and harassment (Costello, 1993; Fox, 1994; Jackson, 1993, 1994; Johnson, 1994; Monson & Dalaimo, 1994; NBC, 1994). On June 16, 1994, NBC ran a segment on its *Dateline* series entitled "Predators On-Line," which discussed seduction, preying on naive victims (often young boys), intimidation, harassment, stalking, and even rape as issues relevant to electronic communication. However, the young and naive are not the only victims of electronic harassment. Recently the Microsoft Corporation won an e-mail harassment suit against a former female employee who was sending Bill Gates frequent, hostile, and unwelcome messages after her termination (Elza, 1994). A student from The University of Michigan was freed from jail on March 10, 1995, after first being denied bail for posting a sexually violent story to an electronic bulletin board. Because the author used the name of an actual person and stated privately to another list user "...just thinking about it doesn't do the trick, I need to do it...," he was charged with the federal crime of transporting

Note: I would like to dedicate this chapter to Mel and Mer, whose enduring support and commitment to feminist and multiculturalist ideals has been nothing short of inspiring, as well as gratefully acknowledge the contribution of Melissa J. Monson in the preparation of this manuscript.

threatening materials across states lines (Lewis, 1995). The fact is, all of the major computer-mediated communication providers (NBC, 1994) and many scholars in the field (Costello, 1993; Ehrlich, 1992; Elza, 1994; Jackson, 1993; Monson & Dalaimo, 1994; Peterson, 1994) report that inappropriate behavior and harassment on-line *is* a problem.

The Electronic Privacy Information Center in Washington, D.C., advises colleges and universities to examine their harassment policies and state antistalking laws to determine how they deal with students and staff who electronically harass or threaten other system users (Sandler, 1995). The Massachusetts Institute of Technology (MIT) has pioneered a program to address issues of electronic harassment, appropriately named *Stopit*. In the first year of the program's existence, Stopit handled 89 incidents, including pornographic images used as screen backgrounds (27%), harassing e-mail messages (23%), improper use of the system (19%), and obscene or harassing interactive messages such as "I'm stalking you" (10%) (Costello, 1993, p. 286). The *Stopit* program is discussed in greater detail in the Policy Implications section of this chapter.

What follows is a personal account of an incident of sexual harassment that occurred through electronic mail; a discussion of some practical and theoretical explanations that have been offered for the increase in uninhibited behaviors and harassment through computer-mediated communication; and an examination of MIT's *Stopit* program, including its implications for policy.

Part One: The Incident

Prologue

There were six graduate teaching assistants, three women and three men. I was the only single woman; but following a failed four-year relationship, I swore in a public statement to all who would listen that I would never date again, and for a year had kept my promise. "Sonia" was married to a wonderful older man, "Geena" lived with her long-term significant other, "Charlie" was also married, "Jack" could always be spotted talking with a different woman at the Student Union, and "Dan" rarely dated. We all spent a lot of time together, both professionally and socially.

It was great at first. We shared the same "grad-school reality"—and all of the pain, the pleasure, and the trauma that went with it. We all communicated through our e-mail accounts, whether it was to ask a technical question, to tell a joke, to offer words of support and encouragement, or to announce "I've had enough! I'll be at the pool hall!"

Dan and I were best friends. When I first met him, his physical presence (more than six-feet tall and 300 pounds) intimidated me, but his helpful and eager-to-please attitude was disarming. Dan became a sort of big brother and protector to me. He said he understood my desire not to date, and I could always count on his presence to scare off any potential suitors. Dan was the fatherly type; he always planned the social events, he always insisted on paying for drinks when we were out (amidst protests from all), and he always drove. During times when we were all swamped with deadlines, it was Dan who would check in with each of us. His phone calls and e-mail messages helped us to maintain a feeling of "connected-ness" to the rest of the group. He acted as the communicative hub of the cohort. Dan was the first to tell you he was "there" if you needed him.

We all worked together, and we played together…which means we often went out for a drink together. There would always be some heated conversation about politics, philosophy, the economy, or who stuffs the little pimentos in the olives. And, as is common with close friends, the conversation sometimes turned to sex. It was rarely about anything specific or personal; rather, it was usually either a comment said in jest or a question to ponder in a critical or analytical way. Later I learned that it was conversations such as these that led my harasser to think I wanted to have sex with him.

Betrayal

In the Spring of the following year, Dan became depressed. He drank excessively, he slept for days at a time, and he began to talk about suicide. As his friends, we were quite worried about him. We made repeated attempts to cheer him up and tried to get him out of his house. One weekend afternoon I logged onto my e-mail account as I do every day and found a six-page letter from my "best friend" that changed my life forever.

The first page was full of kind words about what a great friend I'd been to him and how he felt he could tell me anything. He wrote that he was unsure as to whether he should be sending me this letter, and that if I didn't want to "listen," I should stop reading. Well, I didn't stop reading. I had no idea what he was going to say, and I wanted to be a good friend and "be there" for him like he had been for me. The next three pages told the history of his sexual life, which he said began as a child when he was molested by a friend of the family. I felt devastated for this poor man. What he must have gone through! I read on. He described in detail three separate sexual experiences he had, each of which had a humiliating or tragic end-ing. I felt many things while reading this confession. I felt sympathy and humilia-tion for Dan, but also nausea and disgust because of the graphic nature of the details and the imagery it conjured up. I felt so bad for my friend, relieved that he finally had told someone, but uncomfortable that it was me. I felt responsible for him now that he had shared his secrets.

The next two pages described Dan's sexual dysfunction, and his desire to "get past it." He again praised me and my enduring friendship. It was because of my caring and loyalty that he thought I was the one to help him get through it. The let-ter then took a disturbing twist that at the time made me feel very guilty, but now I realize it was nothing short of emotional blackmail. He said I was the only one who could help him. That he couldn't "perform" for anyone in his past, but he knew I would be the "inspiration" he needed. He wanted me to teach him how to have sex and to show him how to "please a woman." Dan suggested a weekend at his place, that we would stay in bed for days, and I could teach him the ropes. He said he knew I was still getting over a long-term relationship and that I didn't want to get involved with anyone. He let me know I didn't have to be his girlfriend, just his sexual mentor. There was one more request. He referred to a conversation a few of us had earlier in the week about body piercing. There was a specific part of the female anatomy that he did not know the location of, and wanted me to show him mine. He said he'd understand if I didn't want to.

My first reaction was total pity and complete disgust. I silently reprimanded myself for being disgusted. After all, he had come to me for help and it was my duty as a friend to help him. I also realized how hard it must have been for him to tell his story and I felt horrible, thinking my rejection of him might exacerbate his depression. Nevertheless, there was no way I was going to be his sexual slave and mentor. I paced my apartment for hours, looking at my computer terminal with disgust, as if it had been responsible for the violations it transmitted—a postmodern version of killing the messenger. Finally, I deleted Dan's letter from my account because the thought of it being there was too much. I felt as if he were actually *in my apartment* as long as that letter was *in* my computer. I just wanted it to disappear. The letter was gone with a keystroke, but the violation, the betrayal, and the imagery remained.

Dan had presented himself as a caring, generous, and thoughtful person. He had never made any inappropriate advances or suggestions in my presence. I remembered a time I had defended him to a woman who had alleged he had "come on" to her over e-mail. I told her Dan was "a wonderful man" and that she must have misinterpreted his intentions. Everything I knew about Dan at the time led me to believe he was well liked and respected. I was devastated by the realization that Dan, one of my best friends and a confidant, had misrepresented himself and taken advantage of our friendship.

Reactions

I felt an intense pressure to respond. Unlike the U.S. Mail, where it is a matter of days to exchange a letter, e-mail is virtually instantaneous. I knew Dan could tell when I had picked up my mail by "fingering" my account through our e-mail system. By typing the command "finger" and then my user name, he could see exactly when and for how long I was last on the system, which meant he could tell when I was home. If I was on the system at the time he did this, he could initiate a real-time conversation by using the "talk" command. If he did this, I would have to either respond to his request by interacting with him electronically, or I could ignore him, the rejection which I feared might send him "over the edge." I was also afraid that if he knew I was home, he might call, or worse, come over. This thought disturbed me intensely. Every time the phone rang, or someone knocked at the door, I became very anxious, hoping it wasn't Dan. I knew it was common practice for him to "finger" all of us in the group, because he would make comments like, "You sure were up late last night. I noticed you were on the system at 3:00 A.M." In my haste to alleviate any anxiety Dan might have waiting for a response, I sent him the following short e-mail message several hours after I received the letter:

> I'm sorry for the horrible things you've been through. I'm flattered that you think I could help you with your problems, but I think of you as a big brother or a father. The thought of being with you in that way is incestuous. Maybe you should seek professional help.

I don't know why I told him I was flattered—I could kick myself for it now. I was many things at the time: confused, disgusted, hurt, frightened, violated; but, I *was definitely not flattered*. I guess it was my way of being polite and "letting him down easy." His answer to me came almost immediately after I sent the message, proof that he had been "watching" me electronically. He thanked me for "listening" to him and said he hoped we could still be friends. I wasn't sure that was possible. Over the next few days I didn't log on to my e-mail account. I felt like he was stalking me. I not only avoided him, but I avoided all of my friends from school. I was extremely disturbed about the letter. I felt violated and betrayed, but I didn't tell anyone about what had happened. I felt to do so would be a betrayal of my friendship with Dan.

Three days after Dan sent this letter, I received a phone call from an under-graduate in our department, a woman I'll call "Kate." Kate had met Dan the previous semester when he had been the graduate assistant in a class she was enrolled in. Since then, Kate had occasionally joined us when we went out socially.

Kate was very upset on the phone. She said she wouldn't have called, but that Dan had told her he had "propositioned" me too, and she needed someone to talk to. She began to tell me about an e-mail message Dan had sent her and we realized he had sent Kate *the same letter* he had sent me. Dan later defended himself by saying the letters were not *exactly the same*. He had written a different introduction and conclusion—a different sales pitch—for each of us. Kate also told me that Dan had sent this letter to an out-of-state woman before he sent it to me. I finally let myself become angry. Here I was feeling sorry for Dan and guilty that I had betrayed him. While I was feeling responsible for the fact that he might never have a normal sex life, he was sending this same e-mail message around to different women, apparently hoping to find a taker. I later found out he had called and/or e-mailed many of our mutual friends, telling them all that I hated him but never telling them why. Eventually, all these people came to me with questions and I told them my version of what had happened.

The reactions among our cohort varied. Jack and Charlie could both understand how Dan might have gotten the wrong idea, after all I *"was* a little *friendly"* with him. True, I often gave Dan a hug to make him feel better, or a compliment to boost his morale, as I did with many of my friends. Neither Jack nor Charlie believed the letter could have been *that bad*; after all, it was only e-mail, "just delete the message." Jack was very upset because if anyone "got" me *he* should, and he had confided as much to Dan. Jack perceived Dan's letter to me as an insult to *him*, an invasion of *his* territory and a betrayal of *their* friendship. The reactions from my feminist friends ranged from inspiring to disappointing. This incident proved to be one of those rare moments in life when theory meets practice and our values and beliefs are put to a test. Those of us personally involved found out who was preaching feminism and empowerment and who was actually practicing it.

It was an extremely uncomfortable and stressful time for all of us, wondering what would happen, when we would see Dan next, and about the fate of "the gang." Many of Dan's friends were disgusted and confused by what he had done; he had called himself a feminist! They too felt betrayed by this violation of our friendship. Dan's e-mail message had permanently changed the dynamics of our group of friends, but that was only a small part of it. The fact that he had sent this same letter to other women, including a former student of his, lent a sense of jeopardy to the situation. I was a strong, independent, and educated woman, yet I was experiencing anxiety and shortness of breath caused by the stress of the incident. What if his next victim wasn't as strong as I was? What would happen to her? Would she go along with him for fear of reprisal? Would she feel forced to drop a class, or worse, to drop out of school? Would it disrupt her life as it had mine?

In the meantime, Dan repeatedly e-mailed our friends, asking if they hated him, saying that if they did he didn't know if he could go on living. Sonia and Geena didn't answer his messages, hoping he would stop trying and leave them alone. He didn't. Finally, Geena sent him a response to his pleas. She knew he was stalking her electronically, and she had been avoiding her e-mail account so he wouldn't know when she was home. When she could no longer handle the stress, she e-mailed him and said she didn't feel comfortable with what he'd done and she needed time to rethink their friendship. She asked him to stop trying to contact her. He forwarded this message, without Geena's consent, to others, claiming this was proof of my campaign to make everyone hate him.

Dan continued to brood dramatically around the department. It took less than a week for other students and staff to learn Dan was suicidal, and that it had something to do with me. People began to ask questions: "What did you do to Dan?" "Have you seen Dan? Why are you avoiding him?" "You know, Dan really needs his friends right now." "I heard you hate Dan." I was trying to deal with my own problems at the time: the anxiety, the nightmares, the daily vomiting, the crying spells, and the feeling of being stalked. There were many different issues involved. As a graduate assistant, I felt a responsibility to Dan's future students. As a feminist, I felt a responsibility to every other woman Dan came into contact with. I also felt responsible for the division within our cohort and the end of what I believed at the time were some great friendships. Another concern of mine was my reputation in the department. I was quite familiar with the stigma attached to people who report sexual harassment, and I didn't want my professors and future employers to think I was a troublemaker.

Institutional Handling

A few weeks after I received the letter, members of the faculty began questioning me about my involvement in Dan's troubles. One evening during a graduate seminar, somehow the lecture turned into a discussion of "this sexual harassment case," and the professor questioned me about particulars *in front of 6 other graduate students.* I was mortified! I was angry and humiliated, and I felt forced to defend myself. I felt I had to do something, but I didn't know what.

I went with Geena to a faculty member whom we both trusted. "Dr. B" was quite disturbed when she heard the details of the incident. Dan had been to see her, told her he was depressed and suicidal, that I and others in the group were alienating him, but had failed to mention the harassing letters he had sent. Although she was visibly upset by what we told her that day, and by Dan's ongoing public brooding and suicide threats, she did not know what to do. No one wanted Dan to harm himself. She asked if it was OK to share this information with a colleague, who was also a feminist…and a friend of Dan's. I felt safe in saying it was all right if it would get Dan some help and keep him from doing this again.

The colleague's greatest concern was to "normalize relations" in the department. She called in a mediator and together with Dr. B, they had a meeting with Dan. He admitted to them that he had "propositioned" me in the letter, but didn't see what "the big deal was." He felt everyone was ganging up on him. The outcome of the meeting was an agreement that he would seek professional help, discontinue his barrage of pleas for friendship to members of our cohort, as well as the forwarding of letters without consent, and stop his electronic surveillance practices. He was also asked to read and sign a copy of the student conduct code. I learned of these terms the next day when I, too, was asked to meet with this committee to "normalize relations."

They told me about their agreement with Dan, and asked if he held up his end of the agreement, would I be *satisfied* and attempt to normalize relations with Dan. Suddenly I felt defensive. It was not my responsibility to make Dan feel better about his violation of several women. I could tell they felt bad for Dan, and just wanted it all to go away. It was then I was handed a document. It was the university's student conduct code. I thought they were giving it to me so I could see what Dan was asked to sign. I was wrong. One of my mentors asked *me* to read and sign it.

I don't think I heard another thing that was said in that meeting. I was in a state of shock, of disbelief. Did she just ask *me* to *sign a copy* of the Student Conduct Code? What had *I* done? Why am *I* being made to sign documents? These women had taught *me* about retaliation and secondary victimization, and now they were perpetuating it. It took about twenty-four hours to get over the shock of this slap in the face by my "feminist supporters." I felt betrayed by my own department, especially by those who preached feminism and empowerment. Another "feminist" professor, on hearing of the sexual content of the e-mail, had proclaimed, "Well, I'm sure he didn't mean it *that* way."

The next day I went to the director of the Women's Center on campus with Kate, one of the other women who received Dan's pornographic e-mail. "Ms. C" was a strong woman who had a reputation for saying what she meant. Kate logged onto to her e-mail account, and retrieved Dan's letter for Ms. C to read. Thankfully she had kept a copy; she had not made the mistake of deleting the evidence like I had. Ms. C was visibly disturbed by the contents of the letter, as well as the manipulative way in which sexual favors were requested, and advised us to make a formal complaint with the administrative officer on campus; she offered to be involved in the process if it would help. Kate still felt sorry for Dan, and didn't think she could go through the process of a sexual harassment case, and so never took action against him.

I struggled with myself long and hard about filing a complaint of sexual harassment against Dan. I asked myself if I was doing it for the "right" reasons. Was I just being vindictive? Was I overreacting? In the end, I felt I had no choice but to file. If I did nothing, he would be free to continue harassing women. I didn't really want to punish him, I just wanted to try and prevent him from harassing me or others again. If I filed a complaint and there was something on record, maybe next time he wouldn't get off so easy.

The first thing I did was go to the campus computer services center. I wanted to see if I could prevent him from sending anyone else this disturbing letter. I also wanted to see if I could block my e-mail account from being "fingered" by Dan. I spoke with "Ellen," the woman in charge that day, who was both helpful and supportive. The first thing she said to me was that they took these types of complaints very seriously, and that I had done the right thing in coming to them. Apparently harassment over e-mail was relatively common. She immediately went into my harasser's account to see if the letter was still there, and if there was a record in his "sent-mail" folder of who else he'd sent it to. He had deleted the evidence from his account.

I explained to Ellen how Dan would "watch" us by fingering our accounts, and that several of us felt like we were under surveillance and consequently had been avoiding using e-mail altogether. Ellen was quite disturbed by Dan's abuse of his e-mail privileges, not only by his request for sexual favors, but also by his continued electronic stalking and practice of forwarding others' messages without consent. Within twenty-four hours, Dan's university e-mail account was canceled. He eventually got an e-mail account elsewhere, but because he was not on the same system as us, he could no longer "stalk" our accounts.

I was trembling when I knocked, with a sweaty palm, on the door of the administrative officer to file my complaint. A white man in his early forties opened the door and waved me in as he finished a telephone conversation. His manner was businesslike and almost gruff. I found myself wishing that this had been a woman, or at least a minority male. I was sure he would be on "Dan's side." I told him Ms. C had advised me to come to him. As I began to explain the situation to "Dr. S," I found myself on the defensive. I was shaking, my voice was quivering, and I kept saying things such as "I don't want to cause any trouble" and "I don't want to be vindictive." He was silent while I told my story. Occasionally he would ask a question for clarification, or scribble something on the note pad in front of him. I became embarrassed and flustered when I came to the more graphic details of the letter, but Dr. S's expression never changed. When I stopped speaking, there was a dreadfully long silence and then, "What do you want me to do?" For a moment I thought I was going to break down in tears. Then I thought I would run screaming from his office. What I did was sit staring at him in disbelief. Was this man mocking me?

Despite first impressions, Dr. S took his job seriously. He gave me a list of formal and informal options, ranging from not filing a complaint, to Dr. S having "a talk" with Dan, to having him fired, to bringing formal charges against him. Basically, the more serious the sanction, the more lengthy and stressful the process would be. He asked *me* what I wanted the punishment to be. He told me that *if* what I said was true, and *if* I could prove it, I should be able to win my case, whatever *I chose* to do. I thought about it overnight, and discussed it with several friends and family members the next day. It didn't seem fair that the victim should have to name the punishment for her harasser. The responsibility of Dan's future, whether he was allowed to remain in the program and to keep his job, was largely in my hands. In the end, I felt the most important thing was to try to keep him from harassing other women. I knew Dan was scheduled to instruct a class the following term, and the thought of him having the power of evaluation over a classroom full of students—half female—frightened me. I knew I would feel responsible if another woman had to endure what I had to because I did *nothing*. Maybe if he had realized the severity of his offense it would have been different, but he was still insisting what he'd done was "no big deal."

The next day I went to see Dr. S. I told him how I felt about Dan teaching, but that I didn't want to be the reason he lost his job, or got kicked out of the Ph.D. program. Even though this meant I would have to continue to see my harasser on a regular basis, I couldn't handle the responsibility of ruining his future, whether he deserved it or not. I also wanted to give Dan the option of voluntarily stepping down from teaching, rather than both of us having to endure a stressful and embarrassing hearing. Ultimately that's what happened. Dan was informed by Dr. S and our department chair that he could either voluntarily step down from teaching the following term or have the case put through the proper channels. He was advised that there was compelling evidence—although I had deleted it from my account, Kate still had a copy of the letter. Dan stepped down from teaching and continued on as a research assistant for the same salary. This lasted for one term, after which "poor Dan" was put back in the classroom and is once again a very visible part of the department, his "little indiscretions" apparently forgotten. Mutual acquaintances have told me Dan felt he was "ganged up on" and he "didn't see what the big deal was." The department had a sexual harassment training seminar almost a year later; Dan was not in attendance.

Even though Dan only received a "slap on the hand" for his offenses, I still believe I did the right thing in filing a complaint of sexual harassment against him. Regardless of how difficult both the decision to file and the process itself had been, I *did* something—I stood up for my principles. More important, my complaint will be in his file; so if he harasses again, the consequences will be much more serious.

Discussion

Part of the reason sexual harassment is so difficult to prove is the subjectivity that surrounds its circumstances. In the most commonly accepted definitions of sexual harassment, the harasser has power over the victim. Colleagues and coworkers can cause an equally illegal hostile environment. My experience has shown that the victim does not have to be subordinate to his or her harasser for the incident to cause not only a hostile work or school environment, but a *hostile emotional environment* from which there is no escape. My harasser was a coworker and a fellow graduate student. He had no formal power over me or my colleagues, yet we were all dragged into, and affected to varying degrees, by the situation.

It is my hope that by examining this experience we can learn from and improve on the ways in which we deal with harassment on campus. The faculty at the department level were not familiar with the best way to handle a complaint of this nature, so they did what they thought was best. However, their well-intentioned mediation of the problem with Dan only served to exacerbate it. By asking me to sign a copy of the student conduct code, they implied that this was a case of miscommunication between us rather than sexual harassment. There should have been no attempt to normalize relations. The faculty member who told me Dan "didn't mean it that way" did not understand what sexual harassment was and completely denied its impact on me. They all should have been better informed about the university sexual harassment policies. The faculty at the department level tried to keep the incident out of my harasser's file, and at the same time tried to appease me by "having a talk" with him. However, by trying to be *fair* to my harasser, they made me feel to blame for all the trouble, thereby revictimizing the victim.

This situation should have been kept confidential, should *never* have been the topic of classroom discussion, and should have immediately been directed to the campus official who handles complaints of sexual harassment. The director of the Women's Center, though supportive and empathetic, did not notify anyone else to intervene. Her advice to file a formal complaint implied that the institution would do nothing unless a formal complaint was filed, yet institutions have a responsibility to **stop** sexual harassment when they know about it, whether or not a complaint has been filed. The staff at the university computer center, on the other hand, by acting swiftly in revoking my harasser's computer account *as well as calling him in for "a talk,"* sent a clear message that electronic harassment would not be tolerated.

I was never informed in writing about what the institution had done to stop the harassment and how it was dealt with. There was no follow-up from any administrator or faculty member to see if the harassment had stopped or if I needed any help or support in the way of counseling or support groups. As far as I know, Dan was not even required to become better informed about sexual harassment as evidenced by his absence from the departmental training seminar.

Part Two: Theoretical and Practical Explanations

Many believe electronic mail elicits a more personal and informal type of communication, often resulting in the loosening of inhibitions because of a lack of visual and physical reminders of status (Elmer-Dewitt, 1994; Johnson, 1994; Monson & Dalaimo, 1994; Tannen, 1990, 1994). Several explanations have been offered for the increase in uninhibited behaviors and harassment that occur over e-mail and other types of computer-mediated communication. This section summarizes the more commonly discussed explanations and discusses several elements unique to electronic communication: message coordination and feedback; absence of visual and contextual cues; impression manipulation; and deindividuation, as well as cultural norms and gender differences in communication—all of which may aid in the perpetuation of uninhibited behavior and harassment via e-mail.

Ambiguities Unique to Computer-Mediated Communication

One way in which e-mail communication differs from face-to-face interaction is that it is asynchronous in nature. An individual may send off a message and almost immediately receive a response, or he or she may wait days or weeks to hear from a correspondent. There is often no way to tell whether someone has checked an electronic mailbox, and this may lead to problems of message coordination and feedback.

Message Coordination and Feedback

As Goffman (1959) notes:

> When individuals are unfamiliar with each other's opinions and statuses, a "feeling-out" process occurs whereby an individual displays his [*sic*] views or statuses to another a little at a time. After dropping his guard just a little he waits for the other to show a reason why it is safe to continue to do this, and after this reassurance the person can safely drop his guard a little bit more. (p. 192)

Because electronic mail lacks the contextual and reflexive nature of face-to-face interaction, the feeling-out process Goffman describes occurs differently. Over e-mail, information is communicated in monologues, with one person giving some information and then asking questions. Then the other reciprocates, answering the former's questions and asking a few of his or her own. There can be no midstream interjections or requests for clarifications. The sender and the receiver do not share the same temporal or spatial milieu. Because e-mail lacks the constant feedback about one's self and the visual communication that occurs in face-to-face interaction, images of message senders develop in a different, often more spontaneous manner. Cues necessitating image revision and adjustments are not as readily available electronically as they are in person.

Absence of Visual and Contextual Cues

In addition to problems with message coordination and feedback, communication over e-mail lacks several important visual and contextual cues that can reveal information about a person. These cues include, but are not limited to, voice tone and speech patterns, facial expressions, and body language, which can imply things such as mood, emotion, attitude, and intent. Also lacking in computer communication are cues from a person's conduct and appearance that allow us to employ our previous experience with similar individuals by applying stereotypes (see Goffman, 1959). Some contextual cues, which are absent from e-mail communication, include insignia of office or rank, clothing, gender, age, racial characteristics, size, posture. All these contextual cues allow us to ascribe meaning to interactions in face-to-face situations, help us make sense out of a situation, and predict how the other will act based on past experiences. As social beings, we are always developing relationships with others by employing generalizations or stereotypes that aid us in predicting behavior, share meanings and experiences, and develop a common basis from which to interact (Schutz, 1962). These cues help to define the situation and clarify mutual expectations.

In a face-to-face situation, a victim of harassment has the potential advantage of visual and contextual cues with which to assess the perpetrator's actions and the situation. Over e-mail, the perpetrator has the advantage of being able to control what information the victim receives, thereby allowing no secondary or inferential information for the victim to work with. In this way, the harasser has the ability to manipulate the victim's opinion of him or her. Left with no social or contextual cues, the victim is forced to rely more heavily on subjective experience to make up for the lack of observable behavior to assess the harasser on the other side of the computer screen.

Impression Manipulation

A first impression may be more easily manipulated over e-mail because there are no contextual cues to indicate the creation of false impressions. We often speak of "getting off on the right foot." Once made, the first impression is much harder to change with subsequent interaction (Goffman, 1959). Therefore, after making a good initial impression, a harasser may be permitted to get further than she or he would have in a face-to-face situation. Goffman stresses the fact that "the initial definition of the situation projected by an individual tends to provide a plan for the cooperative activity that follows" (1959, p. 12); in other words, once a harasser gains the trust of a victim, that person can be easily manipulated.

Because of the visual anonymity of communicating over e-mail, it is very easy for an individual to shift personas and to present himself or herself as someone or something other than what is actually true. One man "dated" a "woman" through electronic mail and even had "virtual sex" (a lot like phone sex, but through computers) with "her." After this virtual relationship went on for several months, "she" experienced some financial troubles so "her" "virtual boyfriend" sent "her" $1,000. A few weeks later, the man learned his "girlfriend" was really another man.

In this situation a man formed a friendship over e-mail with a man who had presented himself as a woman. After making this initial impression, a few "gender slips" probably would not make the man suspicious of his new "girlfriend." In real life, a gender-switch would be much harder to pull off, but the visual and vocal anonymity of electronic communication makes it relatively easy. Stories like this one are common among the Internet community, but unfortunately "pranks" such as these are rarely harmless.

The visually anonymous nature of e-mail seems to be a large part of why inappropriate behavior and harassment are so prevalent. A harasser can guide and control the impression the potential victim forms. The e-mail harasser can play the role of the "nice person" in electronic messages, and can easily avoid anything that is inappropriate. Because there are no contradictory contextual cues, it is relatively easy for the harasser to manipulate the victim. In the words of on e-mail user, "you can make the character behind the alias exactly like you, nothing like you, a combination of both, or even make it vary depending on the situation" (quoted in Myers, 1987, p. 256). When the harasser is not on-line, he or she may practice and perfect the techniques of managing the impression he or she wants to create. The victim, armed with only false information obtained from the harasser, may likely perceive someone totally unlike a person they believe might harass. The victim, therefore, is unprepared to deal with harassing behaviors once they begin, and may then cope with the situation by ignoring the perceived "out-of-character" behavior of the harasser. However, because the strategies of the harasser are influenced by the victim's response, a lack of response, which means "leave me alone" to the victim, can be perceived as approval or at least that he or she "didn't say 'no'" to the harasser. Much like other forms of harassment, miscommunications over e-mail increase the possibility of some behavior being perceived as inappropriate or as harassment.

Deindividuation

The social psychological concept of deindividuation is useful to explain the increase in uninhibited behavior demonstrated in electronic communication (Kiesler, Siegel, & McGuire, 1984; Kiesler, Zubrow, Moses, & Geller, 1985; Orcutt & Anderson, 1977). Defined classically, *deindividuation* is "the process whereby submergence in a group produces anonymity and a loss of identity, and a consequent weakening of social norms and constraints" (Lea & Spears, 1991, p. 284). The size of the cyber-community of e-mail users, in addition to the visual and vocal anonymity, add to this loss of identity. However, deindividuation may also occur when an individual's attention is *removed from the self and social context* as it becomes consumed by the communication task itself. Many e-mail users report feelings of "becoming one" with their computer and being in "another time and space—completely anonymous." An individual using e-mail might lose her or his sense of public and private self-awareness which may lead her or him to act "more impulsive and assertive and less bound by precedents set by societal norms" (Kiesler et al., 1984, p. 1130). Not only can a user who is absorbed in computer-mediated communication become deindividuated, but "submergence in a technology, and technologically induced anonymity and weak social feedback might also lead to…a loss of identity and uninhibited behavior" (Siegel et al., 1986, p. 183).

However, while electronic communication may lower *public* self-awareness, *private* self-awareness may actually be enhanced (Franzoi, Davis, & Young, 1985; Matheson & Zanna, 1990; Spears, Lee, & Lee, 1990; Turkle, 1984). The computer can become an extension of the self, rather than a substitute for it, serving as individual expression, not as an oppressor of self-awareness. In the words of one e-mail user (quoted in Turkle, 1984):

> When you type mail into the computer you feel you can say anything…sometimes it gets pretty personal…I don't feel I am even typing…I am thinking it, and there it is on the screen…I feel totally telepathic with the computer. (p. 211)

Research addressing differential self-awareness has shown that individuals who demonstrate greater levels of self-focus tend to be less easily influenced by perceptions of others (Scheier, 1980). In other words, e-mail users who demonstrate an increased sense of self-awareness and/or egocentrism may write things they would not ordinarily say in face-to-face conversation without worrying about reprisals or repercussions. As Matheson and Zanna (1990) state:

> An increased sense of self-focus may lead e-mail users to reveal their own positions, without a great need to support or explore them, as this would require an understanding that other people's perspectives are important and that they may be quite different from their own….This could lead to an escalating cycle of conflict and disagreement, and it could increase the display of affect and uninhibited behavior characteristic of computer users. (p. 9)

Rather than the lowering of both public and private self-awareness, then, the combination of the *lowering of public self-awareness* and the *heightening of private awareness* leads to uninhibited behavior. In the words of one frequent e-mail user, as long as "you use an alias, you can say pretty much what you want without others pinning what you say to your real name. In 'real life,' you have to wear a mask, trying not to say the wrong thing....Under an alias, it doesn't matter" (quoted in Myers, 1987, p. 256). According to Sproull and Kiesler (1986):

> When people feel less empathy, less guilt, less concern over how they compare with others, and are less influenced by norms [and when] social definitions are weak or nonexistent, communication becomes unregulated. People are less bound by convention, less influenced by status, and unconcerned with making a good appearance. Their behavior becomes more extreme, impulsive, and self-centered. (p. 48)

Sanctioned by Subculture

The two previous explanations—deindividuation and heightened private awareness—rest on the assumption of a lack regulation of public norms and values. A third explanation that has gained recent recognition refutes this claim that the "community" itself (i.e., "cyberspace") displays conditions of normlessness and anomie. Scholars have proposed that rather than lacking customs and beliefs, Cyberspace constitutes a subculture with its own set of unique normative prescriptions and values (Lea & Spears, 1991; Myers, 1987). The argument is that "antinormative behavior, where it has a clear and directional form precisely describes a norm (albeit an extreme of negative one)," or more simply, the very absence of norms is a norm in itself. In group discussions, "if behavior was really socially deregulated...then a haphazard and random distribution of decision responses...should be expected" (Lea & Spears, 1991, p. 286). Cyberspace, from this perspective, comprises a subculture "...which rejects conventionality and social restrictions" (Kiesler et al., 1984, p. 183). Uninhibited behavior becomes the rule rather than the exception. *Flaming* (the sending of insulting and degrading messages), self-righteous monologues, and argumentative speech are all inherent elements of the virtual environment. The rules may be unwritten but they do exist.

Electronic mail is not isolated from, but rather deeply embedded in, the broader social and cultural practices of society. The norms that govern the "net" were set by computer hackers who typically, "subscribe to a sort of anarchistic ethic" and tend to practice antinormative behavior (Elmer-Dewitt, 1994). Furthermore, there is more than just computer culture to contend with; cultures from all over the world utilize e-mail. In fact, a survey randomly sent to Internet users found that 34% of all respondents ($N = 300$) were from countries other than the Unite States (Monson & Dalaimo, 1994). The effects and implications of this meshing of cultures in cyberspace on computer-mediated harassment is relatively unresearched and too expansive a topic to discuss here, but certainly warrants closer examination as to the impact on computer harassment.

Gender Differences in Communication Styles

Differences in communication styles because of gender are present in e-mail, just as they are in face-to-face interaction. Researchers have identified typically feminine methods of communication as more relational and cooperative, and less direct and confrontational than the traditionally masculine style of communicating (Richardson, 1988; Tannen, 1994). Linguists studying e-mail communication found that women tend to be less adversarial, less assertive, and more likely to use personal experiences for support. Men were less likely to take personal offense from comments and to be more self-promotive (Herring Report, cited in We, 1994). This same report also found the following:

- Men wrote longer messages than women.
- Men wrote more messages than women.
- Messages from men received more responses than those written by women.
- Men threatened to leave the [discussion list/newsgroup] if there was prolonged discussion where women contributed 50 percent or more of the comments.

Tannen believes that, similar to co-ed classrooms and meetings, discussions on e-mail networks tend to be dominated by male voices. But unlike classes or meetings, "on-line, women don't have to worry about getting the floor (you just send a message when you feel like it)" (1994, p. 53). Linguists Susan Herring and Laurel Sutton, however, report that even though a woman may have the opportunity to send off a message, she still has the same problem of having her messages ignored or attacked (cited in Tannen, 1994). The idea here is that the same inequalities and differences that are present in the social environment of face-to-face interaction carry over to computer-mediated communication (Frissen, 1992; Troung, 1993). E-mail is not the cause of harassment, rather, it serves as a tool that may be *used for harassment*. However, the complexities, ambiguities, and virtual anonymity of electronic communication may provide an environment that is more conducive to inappropriate and harassing behavior.

Part Three: Policy Implications

Electronic harassment should not be considered any less harmful than harassment in a face-to-face situation. Although many victims of electronic harassment may never actually see their harasser, they experience many of the same feelings as those who are harassed in person, including fear, anxiety, embarrassment, powerlessness, and anger. Victims of both forms of harassment share common reasons for not filing complaints: fear of retaliation; the desire not to be labeled as emotional, oversensitive, or vindictive; the general lack of support for victims, and the fear that harassing behaviors will be viewed as acceptable (Paludi & Barickman, 1991, pp. 124–25).

MIT's *Stopit* program addresses problems such as these in an intelligent and aggressive manner. *Stopit* was initiated after several incidents of "harassment via electronic messages, displays on public workstations offending other users, and improper use of scarce public workstations for other than intended academic work" (Jackson, 1993, p. 1). The purpose of the program is to both educate system users as to what is appropriate electronic behavior and also to offer avenues of recourse to users who have been offended and/or harassed. As Gregory A. Jackson, Director of Academic Computing at MIT explains, the *Stopit* "mechanisms" are based on the proposition that *"most offenders, given the opportunity to stop uncivil behavior without having to admit guilt, will do so"* (1993, p. 1). These mechanisms were designed to (1) discover harassment, improper use, and other uncivil behavior rapidly; and (2) to communicate effectively with its perpetrators (i.e., to "Stopit").

The first mechanism of the program is the *Stopit* poster (see Figure 5.1), which is displayed prominently in all of the campus computing facilities as well as reproduced in printed and on-line documents. This poster both encourages victims to call for help and/or file a complaint and provides clear instructions on how they go about it. The second *Stopit* mechanism is the *stopit@mit.edu* address. Messages and complaints sent to this address go to the senior directors at academic computing, who respond swiftly and professionally, taking appropriate measures as necessary. The third mechanism of the program involves the standard notes, which are sent by *Stopit* officials to alleged perpetrators of harassment, inappropriate behavior, and/or improper use. The standard note states, "Someone using your account did [whatever the offense is]," and then goes on to explain why the behavior is offensive or violates university policies, rules, or other guidelines. It continues, "Account holders are responsible for the use of their accounts. If you were unaware that your account was being used in this way, it may have been compromised." The letter requests that the account holder notify officials if he or she knows who has compromised the account, and states clear instructions on how the user's password may be changed. There are standard responses for complaints regarding, for example, harassment, chain-letters, the posting of offensive graphics or letters, and forged mail. In extreme cases of harassment, the fourth and fifth Stopit mechanisms may come into play—namely, the harasser may be invited to have a "discussion" with the Info Systems administrator, or face disciplinary procedures.

Although the incidence of unreported harassment is unknown, the Stopit program has proven to be a highly effective way to deter, track, and control electronic harassment *when a problem is brought to the attention of officials*. Program officials report having only a few repeat offenders, which they believe supports their "basic tenet that most offenders intend no offense, and are responsive once they are aware of how their behavior has affected others [and this has] reinforced [their] belief that education is the critical factor in promoting proper behavior" (Costello, 1993, p. 287).

Jackson reports two interesting outcomes of MIT's *Stopit* program. First, many recipients of the standard letter report that their accounts have been compromised and change their password, *even when there is clear evidence that they have engaged in harassment*. Even more significant, however, is that recipients of this letter virtually never repeat the offending behavior (1993, p. 4). Joanne Costello, Manager of Network Support Services at MIT, offers some sage advice. She asserts that all university computing center personnel "must realize that in addition to teaching our students how to use new technologies, it is imperative for us to teach them the proper ethical and social uses of those technologies" (1993, p. 287).

Conclusion

At first glance, electronic mail might seem to provide an ideal environment to gain access to people and information, and a place where one might have an equal chance to argue and question, without those who are more dominant, confident, or prestigious having unequal power. The capability to control settings (like using

---

DON'T IGNORE HARASSMENT

> SOME DO IT　Harassment of any kind is
> SOME DON'T　unacceptable at MIT and in
> SOME SEE IT　conflict with the interests and
> SOME WON'T　policies of the Institute.

> This is MIT Policy. See *MIT Policies & Procedures*, Section 3.16.

STOP IT!

Is it harassment? Ask yourself these three questions:
- Did the incident cause stress that affected your ability, or the ability of others, to work or study?
- Was it unwelcome behavior?
- Would a reasonable person of your gender/race/religion subjected to this behavior find it unacceptable?

If you answer yes to these questions, please don't ignore the situation.

HERE'S WHAT TO DO

- If you are in danger or want to register a complaint,
  call Campus Police at xxx-xxxx (24 hours)
- To talk to someone off the record during the academic year,
  call Nightline at xxx-xxxx (for students only) (7 PM-7 AM)
- To talk to someone off the record Monday thru Friday, all year,
  call a Counseling Dean at xxx-xxxx (for students only) (9 AM-5 PM)
- To file a complaint with Office of the Dean for Student Affairs
  (ODSA), Monday–Friday, call at xxx-xxxx (9 AM-5 PM)
- If you want help from IS/Athena, send e-mail to <stopit@mit.edu>

(Responses will be sent Monday–Friday, 9 AM to 5 PM)

FIGURE 5.1　**The *Stopit* poster** (cited in Jackson, 1993, p. 2)

e-mail) is one of the major prerogatives of power (Giddens, 1983, pp. 206–9), and this power is available to anyone with an e-mail account. However, a closer look reveals that the same types of inequalities and discrimination that plague the physical world are also present in the virtual world. Power is inherently unequal, and electronic communication is no exception. "Cyberspace, it turns out, isn't much of an Eden after all. It's marred by just as many sexist ruts and gender conflicts as the Real World" (Kantrowitz, 1994, p. 48).

The work done by those involved in MIT's *Stopit* program has been revolutionary. Many colleges and universities have guidelines and policies for issues of traditional forms of harassment, but few address the forms of harassment introduced by new technology, especially electronic networks. The *Stopit* program at MIT addresses this crucial problem of electronic harassment, and shows that strict guidelines, quick response, and education can and do help. College and university computer centers would do well to institute programs similar to the Stopit program.

It is through the act of communicating that society actually operates and evolves, and our evolution will bear the signature of the increased use of computer-mediated communication around the world. If the social order is the "result of past human activity [and] exists only insofar as human activity continues to produce it" (Berger & Luckman, 1966, p. 52), then it should be possible to "recreate" a more effective, less conflictual, and less alienating computer-mediated environment.

References

Berger, P. & Luckmann, T. 1966. *The social construction of reality*. Doubleday Anchor, New York.

Blumer, H. 1969. *Symbolic interactionism: Perspective and method*. Prentice-Hall, Englewood Cliffs, NJ.

Costello, J. 1993. "StopIt!" *Toward New Horizons* ACM SIGUCCS XXI:285–87.

Ehrlich, R. 1992. "Sexual harassment an issue on the high-tech frontier." *Macweek*, December 14.

Elmer-Dewitt, P. 1994. Battle for the soul of the Internet. *Time Magazine*, July 25.

Elza, J. 1994. A question of harassment: E-mail and the academy. Unpublished paper. Department of Political Science, Valdosta State University, Valdosta, GA.

Fox Television Network. Playgrounds of the 90s. *A Current Affair*, June 9, 1994.

Franzoi, S. L., Davis, M. H., & Young, R. D. 1985. The effects of private self-consciousness and perspective-taking on satisfaction in close relationships. *Journal of Personality and Social Psychology* 48:1584–94.

Frissen, V. 1992. Trapped in electronic cages? Gender and new information technologies in the public and private domain: an overview of research. *Media, Culture and Society* 14:31–49.

Giddens, A. 1983. *Central problems in social theory*. University of California Press, Berkeley.

Goffman, E. 1959. *Presentation of self in everyday life*. Doubleday Anchor, New York.

Habermas, J. 1979. *Communication and the evolution of society* (trans. by Thomas McCarthy). Heinemann Educational Books, London.

Jackson, G. A. 1993. *STOPIT@MIT.EDU: Mechanisms for reducing computer-based harassment, improper use and incivility at MIT*. Massachusetts Institute of Technology, Cambridge.

Johnson, K. 1994. On-line romance: Office workers feel cupid's byte. *New York Times Metro*, March 26.

Kantrowitz. 1994. Society, men, women, computers. *Newsweek*, May 16.

Kiesler, S., Siegel, J., & McGuire, T. W. 1984. Social psychological aspects of computer-mediated communication. *American Psychologist* 39:1123 –34.

Kiesler, S., Zubrow, D., Moses, A., & Geller, V. 1985. Affect in computer-mediated communication; An experiment in synchronous terminal-to-terminal discussion. *Human-Computer Interaction* 1:77–104.

Lea, M. & Spears, R. 1991. Computer-mediated communication, de-individuation, and group decision making. *International Journal of Man–Machine Studies* 34:283–301.

Lewis, P. H. 1995. An Internet author of sexually violent fiction faces charges. *New York Times*, February 11, p. 7.

Matheson, K. & Zanna, M. 1990. Computer-mediated communications: The focus is on me. *Social Science Computer Review* 8:1–13.

Monson, M. & Dalaimo, D. 1994. *E-mail harassment: A workplace hazard for the 90s*. Paper presented at the Annual Meeting of the American Sociological Association, Los Angeles, August.

Myers, D. 1987. Anonymity is part of the magic: Individual manipulation of computer-mediated communication contexts. *Qualitative Sociology* 10:251–66.

National Broadcasting Company. Predators On-line. *Dateline*, June 16, 1994.

Orcutt, J. D. & Anderson, R. E. 1977. Social interactions, dehumanization and the "computerized other." *Sociology and Social Research* 61:380–97.

Paludi, M., & Barickman, R. 1991. *Academic and workplace sexual harassment*. State University of New York Press, Albany.

Peterson, R. 1994. Harassment by electronic mail. *Synthesis: Law and Policy in Higher Education*, 402(3):416.

Richardson, L. 1988. *The dynamics of sex and gender: A sociological perspective*, 3rd ed. Harper & Row, New York.

Sandler, B. (Ed.) 1995. "*The MIT solution: stopit@mit.edu,*" in *About Women on Campus* 4(1). National Association for Women in Education, Washington, DC.

Schutz, A. 1962. *Collected papers I: The problem of social reality*. (trans. Maurice Natanson). Martinus Nijhoff, The Hague, Netherlands.

Siegel, J., Dubrovsky, V., Kiesler, S., & McGuire, T. W. 1986. Group processes in computer-mediated communication. *Organizational Behavior and Human Decision Processes* 37:157–87.

Spears, R., Lea, M., & Lee, S. 1990. De-individuation and group polarization in computer-mediated communication. *British Journal of Social Psychology* 29:121–34.

Sproull, L. & Kiesler, S. 1986. Reducing social context cues: Electronic mail in organizational communication. *British Journal of Social Psychology* 29:121–34.

Tannen, D. 1990. *You just don't understand: Women and men in conversation.* Ballantine Books, New York.

———. 1994. High-tech gender gap. *Newsweek*, May 16.

Troung, H-A. 1993. Gender Issues in Online Communications. Paper presented at the 3rd Annual Conference on Computers, Freedom, and Privacy, San Francisco, March.

Turkle, S. 1984. *The second self.* Simon & Schuster, New York.

We, G. 1994. Cross-gender communication in Cyberspace. *Electronic Journal of Virtual Culture* 2:3.

6

ELEMENTS OF A GOOD POLICY

BERNICE RESNICK SANDLER

Having a policy and program about sexual harassment, in some instances, may shield an institution from liability by indicating its concern about the issue, but more important, a policy will help address and prevent the problem more effectively. Institutions have been most successful responding to sexual harassment when they have a broad plan that includes the following:

- A comprehensive policy prohibiting sexual harassment.
- The development of informal procedures to supplement the formal complaint process.
- The development and implementation of an ongoing education and prevention program.
- A process to continually monitor all aspects of the program.

Additionally, institutions need to determine how they will respond to victims as complainants and as people who may need services, ensure that the rights of all parties are protected, and how public response will be managed.

There may be assorted policies already in existence, such as antidiscrimination policies, which cover sexual harassment, as may affirmative action and human relations policies. Nevertheless, it is important to have a specific policy to cover sexual harassment. Title IX requires that educational institutions have grievance procedures to deal with sexual discrimination, and technically, any policy dealing with discrimination would also cover sexual harassment. However, because of the nature of sexual harassment and some of the special problems it involves, universities have found it essential to develop a separate policy dealing with sexual harassment, although the policy may also cover other forms of harassment.

Most institutions of higher education have sexual harassment policies and often are in the "second stage" of policy development: they are refining or "fine tuning" their policy in light of their experiences with it.

Note: This chapter appears with minor modifications, as Tab 400 of the *Educator's guide to controlling sexual harassment*, © 1993, 1994, 1995, and is reprinted here with the permission of the publisher, Thompson Publishing Group, Washington, DC. The *Guide* is a looseleaf volume which is updated monthly and includes a monthly newsletter. This chapter's author was a major contributor to the *Guide*.

Developing or Reevaluating a Sexual Harassment Policy

Whether your institution already has a policy, is reevaluating a policy, or is just beginning to develop one, it is useful to examine policies that other institutions have developed. You can obtain copies by writing or calling other institutions. Often it helps to contact institutions similar to your own, although examining policies from different kinds of institutions can also be helpful.

Policy Development

The process of how a policy is adopted or changed is directly related to how well the policy is accepted by the educational community it will serve. Policies that are revised or developed elsewhere and simply adopted by the top administrators without input from the educational community are not likely to have widespread support. In contrast, policies that are adopted or revised with the input and involvement of many people are better understood and are more likely to be supported and implemented by wide segments of the community. The policy development process can itself serve as a tool for educating members of the educational community (see Chapter 7).

Elements of a Good Policy

The purpose of the policy is to:

- Demonstrate the school's commitment to prevent and deal with sexual harassment,
- Educate employees and students about the issue,
- Set forth the procedures and sanctions for dealing with instances of sexual harassment, and,
- Encourage persons to come forward with problems.

Thus, it is important that the policy be written simply and with as little "legalese" as possible. (This is not the place to describe the harasser or victim as "the party of the first part.") The University of Rochester in New York redesigned its sexual assault policy with the express purpose of making it "user friendly" without abridging anyone's rights. When reviewing or developing a policy, try to read it from the point of view of someone who is feeling helpless and victimized, and needs some help. Should the policy omit any aspects covered by law, the law still applies. Thus, even if a policy does not mention that retaliation against a complainant is prohibited, the complainant is still protected by the law. Similarly, the fact that a policy does not mention student-to-student harassment does not mean that student-to-student harassment is not prohibited by law. It is important for institutions to include issues such as these because having a comprehensive policy in place can educate individuals to their responsibilities (and liabilities) and help prevent sexual harassment.

Policies vary among institutions because of different histories and ways to resolve conflicts. Some schools have short policies with appendices at the end. Others develop long policies, and then develop a shortened version for widespread dissemination. Because policies are complex, it is useful to summarize them in a brochure or another format. The elements described in the following sections need not appear in the order listed, other than the first one.

1. A Statement of Commitment

This part is usually short, stating the commitment to have a positive learning and working environment, and that the institution will not tolerate any sexual harassment of its members.

Example:

> This university is committed to having a positive learning and working environment for its students and employees and will not tolerate sexual harassment or sexual violence.[1]

2. A Statement Describing Sexual Harassment as Illegal

Sexual harassment should be described as violating federal and state laws. Title VII and Title IX should be mentioned as well as sexual abuse and assault laws, civil laws, and any other state prohibitions.

Some policies include the relevant clauses of all the various laws in the body of the text; others include text from Title VII and Title IX in the policy and include other statutes in an appendix; still others simply cite the names of the federal and state statutes and include the text of all the statutes in an appendix. It may be helpful to note that in some instances individuals who harass may be personally liable under civil suits. It is unwise to make the institution's policy weaker than the law because the law still prevails. However, educational institutions are not precluded from developing policies that provide greater protection than that required by law.

3. A Definition of Sexual Harassment, with Examples

There are almost as many definitions of sexual harassment as there are institutions.[2] Some institutions include the legal definition from the Equal Employment Opportunity Commission (EEOC), which enforces Title VII. That statement, however, only covers sexual harassment of workers. It can be adapted, however, to cover student harassment. It may be difficult to translate the legal definition into behaviors prohibited; therefore, many universities craft their own definition of sexual harassment in addition to or instead of the legal ones. Note that the first example here could proceed a legal definition.

Example:

Sexual harassment consists of:
- Unwelcome sexual advances, requests for sexual favors, and other verbal or physical conduct of a sexual nature when submission to such conduct is made either explicitly or implicitly a term or condition of an individual's employment or academic advancement or submission to or rejection of such conduct by an individual is used as the basis for employment or academic decisions affecting such individual.[3]
- Verbal or physical conduct which interferes with an individual's work, professional or academic performance, productivity, physical security, participation in living arrangements, extracurricular activities, academic or career opportunities, or services or benefits.

Example:

Sexual harassment consists of unwanted sexual behavior including overt or implicit threats or bribes, which interfere with an individual's ability to work, learn, or otherwise participate in the services and benefits of institutional activities and programs.

Whatever definition is used it should cover quid pro quo and hostile environment and be broad enough to cover harassment of students by faculty and by other students. Some policies also mention that the institution prohibits harassment based on other factors such as color, ethnicity, religion, disability, sexual orientation, or age. Sexual harassment is sometimes associated with one or more of these other forms of harassment, and persons who belong to one or more of these groups may be more likely to be sexually harassed than others. Including other forms of harassment in the sexual harassment policy allows institutions to deal with sexually harassing behaviors that may be based on more than a single factor and eliminates the need for someone to file, for example, two complaints, one for sexual harassment, the other for racial harassment.

Example:

MIT defines sexual harassment as any conduct verbal or physical, on or off campus, which has the intent or effect of unreasonably interfering with an individual's or group's educational or work performance at MIT or which creates an intimidating, hostile or offensive educational, work, or living environment.

Harassment on the basis of race, color, gender, disability, religion, national origin, sexual orientation, or age includes harassment of an individual in terms of a stereotyped group characteristic, or because of that person's identification with a particular group.

Sexual harassment may take many forms. Sexual assault and requests for sexual favors, which affect educational or employment decisions, constitute sexual harassment. However, sexual harassment may also consist of unwanted physical contact and requests for sexual favors, visual displays of degrading sexual images, sexually suggestive conduct, or offensive remarks of a sexual nature.

The policy of Florida State University College of Law notes that,

Sexual harassment is not easy to define…[We] do not attempt to establish a definition but rather to inform the University community of expected standards of…conduct.

The policy might also include a statement about nonsexual behaviors constituting sexual harassment:

Example:

Nonsexual conduct, such as intimidation. hostility, rudeness. name-calling, can be abusive and therefore harassment.[4]

A lengthy list of offending behaviors is critical, because many people can read official definitions and not make the connection to specific behaviors. The list should be preceded with something like: *Sexual harassment is illustrated below but is not limited to the following examples.*

The list should include some examples of harassment of men, as well as harassment based on color, ethnicity, religion, disability, sexual orientation, and age.

4. A Clear Prohibition of These Behaviors
Where appropriate, the policy might refer to faculty and student codes of conduct, or to existing statements of students' and staffs' responsibilities.

5. A Statement About Confidentiality

Because of the sensitive nature of sexual harassment charges and the need to protect the privacy of the parties, guard against retaliation, and avoid adverse publicity and possible defamation lawsuits, institutions should do all they can to maintain information in as confidential a manner as possible. The policy statement should indicate this:

> *Example:*
>
> The confidentiality of the reporting party will be observed provided it does not interfere with the institution's ability to investigate or take corrective action.

Committing the institution to *absolute* confidentiality could act to preclude an investigation that is fair to all parties. Also if formal charges are filed, the complainant may be asked to testify, precluding any possibility of strict confidentiality. In addition, state open records and freedom-of-information laws can require public institutions to provide copies of complaints and reports of investigations, redacted to exclude personally identifiable information, or to open them for inspection to members of the public (see additional comments after No. 21).

6. A Statement About Intent

It is important for individuals to know that intent generally is not relevant to determining if sexual harassment has occurred.

> *Example:*
>
> The fact that someone did not intend to sexually harass an individual is no defense to a complaint of sexual harassment. Regardless of intent, it is the effect and characteristics of the behavior that determine whether the behavior constitutes sexual harassment.

7. A Strong Statement Prohibiting Retaliation or Reprisals Against Anyone Reporting Sexual Harassment Behaviors

> Retaliation against anyone reporting or thought to have reported sexual harassment behaviors or who is a witness or otherwise is involved in a sexual harassment proceeding is prohibited. Such retaliation shall be considered a serious violation of the policy and shall be independent of whether a charge or informal complaint is substantiated. Encouraging others to retaliate also violates this policy.

The statement should include examples of retaliation such as the following:

- Unfair grading
- Unfair evaluation
- Unfair assignments
- Having information withheld or made difficult to obtain in a timely manner such as class information, recommendations, or grades
- Not being informed about important events such as meetings or changes in policies
- Ridicule (public or private)
- Oral or written threats or bribes
- Refusal to meet with person even though that person has a right to do so
- Name calling
- Further harassment of any nature

8. Scope of Coverage

The policy should state that *all* persons—administrators, faculty, teaching assistants, staff, and students—are covered. Because many people think of sexual harassment as occurring in the workplace, the policy should clearly state that harassment of students by faculty or staff as well as by other students is also covered, as is harassment of faculty and staff by students. Prospective and former students as well as visitors to the campus should be included.

The policy should also state that harassment of students and employees by vendors, including contractors, is prohibited. An educational institution is required to provide a nondiscriminatory environment, so it is responsible for the way vendors and contractors treat students and employees. The policy should state that men as well as women are covered by the policy, as well as same-sex harassment.

9. Coverage of Other Forms of Harassment

Discrimination on the basis on sexual orientation is not prohibited by federal anti-discrimination laws. Where state or local laws prohibit this form of discrimination, the policy should mention the appropriate legislation and be clear that discrimination on the basis of sexual orientation is prohibited. Where state or local legislation does not exist, the institution may want to consider prohibiting such discrimination in its policy anyway, because harassment of any kind should not be tolerated.

10. Coverage of Off-Campus Violations

Off-campus violation at campus-sponsored events or programs, such as athletic events or internships,[5] should be covered by the policy. The policy should also make it clear that the institution will not tolerate harassment of its students or employees by noninstitutional personnel in programs sponsored or supported by the institution.

The issue of institutional jurisdiction often arises in connection with student-to-student harassment at off-campus fraternity houses. Although some institutions claim they have no jurisdiction over off-campus activities, it is difficult to justify such a stance when the institution gives recognition and provides services, such as advisers to off-campus organizations, thus leaving the institution open to liability claims.

More complicated is the issue of harassment when it occurs in off-campus situations where there is no nexus or relationship with the institution such as in someone's private living quarters or at a private party. However, harassment off-campus, or outside a university's grounds, can have a chilling effect on the individual's behavior inside the university. A professor who sexually harasses a student at her or his home makes it impossible for that student to relate freely within the university environment. Students harassing students outside of the university can create a similar chilling effect.

Some institutions have a code of behavior for students to follow, whether they are on or off campus; other campuses cover some off-campus violations relating to health and safety such as fraternity hazing. To the extent that off-campus rules exist, sexual harassment should be incorporated into them.

11. Impact of Sexual Harassment

Include a brief description of how sexual harassment affects individuals.

Example:

Sexual harassment is demeaning and degrading. It affects an individual's self-esteem and can have a negative impact on performance at work or in class. It can make an individual feel angry, powerless, and fearful.

12. Statement About False Charges

A short statement should note that false charges will be treated as a serious offense. However, it is important that this section *not* be among the first few issues covered, or it may give the misleading impression that the institution is more concerned about false charges than about real charges.

13. List of Sanctions

Sanctions for a person found guilty of harassing behavior should be listed. The sanctions may differ for staff, faculty, and students and should be reasonably calculated to end the sexual harassment, punish the harasser, and prevent recurrence of incidents. Some examples of sanctions follow, although others might be added. All have been used. Consult with legal counsel for confirmation that the sanctions fall within the institution's legal bounds, union constraints, and student's rights.

- Written warning letter of reprimand
- Loss of choice assignments
- Suspension, probation, termination, or expulsion
- Change of job or class assignment (remove the person from being in a position to retaliate or further affect the victim)[6]
- Loss of travel dollars
- Advice and counseling (Although advice and counseling are occasionally appropriate, they should never be the only sanction.)
- Require attendance at a sexual harassment training program
- Police involvement—when sexual assault or sexual abuse is involved
- An apology to the victim

Any of the following may also be listed in the policy statement in connection with individual students or student groups (such as fraternities) guilty of harassing:

Additional Sanctions for Students

- Prohibit the student(s) from holding office or participating in student activities, including sports, for a specified time
- Transfer the student to another class
- Disband or suspend a fraternity or other student group involved in sexual harassment
- Transfer the student(s) to different housing or banish from institutional housing facilities
- If alcohol was involved, require attendance at a program on alcohol abuse
- Require relevant community service such as preparing posters or disseminating information about peer harassment
- Require perpetrators to attend workshops on peer harassment (Like counseling, community service and attending workshops should never be the sole sanctions.)

14. A Statement About Consensual Relationships

A growing number of institutions are developing policies concerning consensual relationships between students and faculty or staff. The policy needs to be clear regarding who is covered: Will all faculty–student relationships be covered, or only those in the instructional context? Will all relationships be covered, including employment relationships, where there is a benefit, service or evaluation? Will teaching assistants be covered? In all cases, will such relationships be prohibited or simply viewed as problematic? Many people believe that a truly consensual relationship may not be possible between two people when there is a large power differential because the relationship is potentially exploitive. Institutions that have developed policies to deal with the issue in either of two ways:

> **A. Consensual relationships are neither banned nor accepted but are described as problematic.** The University of Michigan's policy does not prohibit "romantic or sexual relationships" but points out that such relationships can raise "serious concerns." Consensual relationships between faculty or staff and students require disclosure to the appropriate administrative supervisor so that arrangements can be made for objective evaluation and decision making with regard to the student. In addition, the policy notes that romantic or sexual relationships outside the instructional or supervisory context can also lead to difficulties.
>
> The University of Wisconsin System condemns romantic and/or sexual relationships between faculty or other instructional staff and students or between supervisors or subordinates. The policy focuses on conflict of interest and abuse of power.
>
> The Massachusetts Institute of Technology requires that anyone who has a supervisory or educational responsibility for an employee, other faculty member, or student should divest himself or herself of that responsibility if a personal involvement develops between the two people.
>
> At the University of Minnesota, the fact that a relationship was consensual at one time cannot be a defense to a subsequent charge of sexual harassment. The policy acknowledges that consensual relationships can turn into sexual harassment when the person with more power refuses to let the person with less power end the relationship.
>
> **B. Consensual relationships are prohibited.** The Vermont State College System, The University of Virginia, and the University of Iowa prohibit amorous relationships between a student and an individual with professional responsibility for that student.

15. A Statement and Description of the Formal Complaint Procedures

Because more than 90 percent of individuals who experience sexual harassment do not want to file a formal charge, it is critical that institutions include in their policy a statement indicating that: (1) most complaints are handled informally; (2) informal procedures are optional, and individuals can choose to bypass them, discontinue them or initiate a formal complaint while using them; (3) the purpose of dealing with a complaint informally is to stop the offending behavior and to resolve the matter as expeditiously as possible; and (4) institutions cannot take disciplinary action using informal procedures—disciplinary action requires a formal charge. It is important to avoid using the word "charge" or "formal charges" when describing how informal procedures are initiated.

16. A Description of the Formal Complaint Procedures

Because of the heavily formal nature of these procedures they are often off-putting to individuals who are experiencing sexual harassment. Therefore some sexual harassment policies do not include them in the policy itself but simply refer to the procedures and where they can be obtained.

Institutions generally use the same policy prohibiting sexual harassment for all individuals whether they are employees or students but the general procedures for formal complaint resolution often differ for different categories of individuals such as administrators, faculty members, unionized personnel, and students. Some schools have one procedure for employees, another for faculty members, and use the regular student disciplinary procedures for sexual harassment by students. Although it is possible to use the same formal complaint resolution processes that are used for other infractions, institutions have found it helpful to develop a single and separate procedure for handling sexual harassment complaints; this helps ensure that the people who implement the procedures gain experience with sexual harassment and provide a consistent response. Formal procedures for dealing with sexual harassment need to be coordinated with tenure policies, existing grievance procedures, and procedures mandated by union contracts.

Although it is beyond the scope of this chapter to discuss all the elements of a good grievance procedure in detail, the formal policy, at the very least, should list the following procedural elements:

- *Who decides to pursue the complaint*: the institution and/or the individual?
- *Complaints by third parties are allowed.* Some institutions allow a person who is not harassed but is affected by harassment of others to file a complaint of harassment. Rice University (Texas) states that a "third party may also file a complaint…if the sexual conduct of others in the education or work environment has the purpose or effect of substantially interfering with the third party's welfare, academic or work performance."
- *Time frames for filing and responding* to formal complaints, including when an investigation begins, when it must be completed, and when the results of the investigation must be transmitted to the proper person(s);
- *Time frames for scheduling and completion* of hearing; making recommendations and decisions about sanctions if any; when the decision is transmitted to involved parties; appeal and response to appeal.
- *Time frames for filing* should not be less than the federal standard, 180 days. Provision should be made so that timelines for reporting can be extended in unusual circumstances such as illness, and so on. Optimally, formal complaint procedures should be completed within one to two months, including appeals.
- *Who handles complaints?* It is helpful to have a person designated to be responsible for seeing that the policy is followed, that time frames are observed, and that questions from all parties are answered.
- *Who does the investigation?* At some schools there is a person appointed whose job responsibilities includes investigation. At other schools, a hearing panel, whether specific for sexual harassment cases or not, does the investigation.

- *Who makes the ruling* that the accused violated or did not violate the policy? In many instances a panel makes the decision.
  - *Who is allowed at the hearing procedure* following the investigation?
  - *Whether parties are allowed representation* at the hearing and, if yes, whether attorneys are allowed. Some schools bar attorneys from all formal proceedings, including hearings, reasoning that their presence makes the process more adversarial. Other schools allow attorneys to participate in hearings when employees are involved but not when the hearing involves students. Still others allow lawyers to participate in the process at any time. Another possibility, utilized at some schools, is to allow lawyers to be present but not to be part of the proceedings. Client and attorney may speak to each other at any time, but the lawyer is not allowed to participate in the hearing process in any manner. The school's policy should be clear about the role of lawyers.
  - *The standard of proof required.* People conducting investigations or making decisions about sexual harassment charges should be aware that the standard of evidence in investigations of sexual harassment is not the one often seen on television: beyond a reasonable doubt. Although that is the standard for cases involving criminal penalties, the standard for administrative procedures, such as those occurring in educational institutions, is different because the penalty is less severe than in a criminal case. The standard is that of "a preponderance of evidence"— that is, a reasonable person would assume that the events did or did not occur given the preponderance of evidence.
  - *Who can testify?* Allowing information or testimony from "fresh complaint" witnesses—persons to whom the victim spoke shortly after the incident occurred—should be allowed. Statements about a person's character should not be part of the investigation or subsequent procedures.
  - *The relationship of informal procedures to formal procedures*, that is, that the use of informal procedures is not required to use the formal procedures, and that not using formal procedures will not influence the outcome of a formal proceeding.
  - *Who decides the penalty?*
  - *The appeals process.* Who can overturn the findings?
  - *Reporting procedures* for the hearing.

17. A Description of the Person(s) to Contact If an Individual Is Experiencing Sexual Harassment

Many institutions have multiple points of access such as a dean, members of a sexual harassment committee, student volunteers, and others. Having more than one point of access makes it easier for victims to choose a point of entry into the system for handling sexual harassment. Include a description of the kinds of help these persons will provide. In addition, provide information about other forms of help such as counseling from the mental health center, advice and information from the affirmative action office and women's center, advice on formal procedures from the affirmative action office and the student life office. Be sure there is one person or office, however, that can provide all the information a person needs. Although employees may be encouraged to report incidents of harassment to their supervisor, provisions should be made for people to report incidents to other persons, because sometimes the supervisor is the harasser.[7]

18. Reporting Requirements

Some institutions require that administrators and faculty members, as agents of the institution, report all instances of sexual harassment that are reported informally, just as they are obligated to report other instances of improper or illegal behavior. Because this can create problems of confidentiality and have a chilling affect on whether people will report sexual harassment, some institutions do not require reporting the name of the person who was harassed; only the incident and the name of the alleged harasser needs to be reported. The policy might read as follows:

> Because this institution takes sexual harassment seriously, it requires that its faculty and administrators report, confidentially, all incidents of sexual harassment to (name of office). Administrators and faculty will not include the names of victims without the victim's permission unless there is a threat of physical harm.
>
> Such reporting enables us to identify problem areas that we can, in some instances, eliminate by initiating educational efforts for a particular unit without identifying the information that makes the educational efforts necessary. Such reporting also helps us identify persons who may have a history of harassing, which requires stronger institutional intervention.

Additionally, some institutions designate a particular person or office where people can anonymously report incidents such as an ombudsperson; this location should be included in this policy section as well as in the section on reporting sexual harassment.

19. The Name, Title, and Phone Number of the Person or Administrative Group Responsible

This person, or office, should be capable of dealing with all aspects of the institution's sexual harrassment policy and educational efforts.

20. A Statement About Other Legal Remedies Available to Complainants

Many institutions are reluctant to list other rights that students and employees have in dealing with sexual harassment; they are fearful that by mentioning various laws individuals will be more likely to file formal charges against the institution. In fact, people who are upset by a school's lack of responsiveness are likely to look to alternative solutions. These people will find out their legal rights with or without the institution's help. Listing other legal remedies in the policy suggests a strong commitment to ending sexual harassment. Some policies mention the rights of the accused such as the right to: (1) due process if a hearing is conducted—state law may require due process, as may a union contract; (2) reasonable time frames; (3) be informed about specific charges; and (4) present information and rebut evidence.

There is a recent trend to include a statement about the following rights of the complainant to:

- Remain present during the entire hearing
- Have a person of their choice accompany them throughout the disciplinary hearing
- Not have past sexual history discussed during the hearing—this right is established in many state criminal codes involving charges of sexual assault

- Make a "victim impact statement" during the hearing
- Suggest an appropriate penalty if the accused is found in violation of the institution's policy or code of behavior
- Complete alternative work assignments outside of a class or be assigned to another class with a different professor if the accused is the accuser's professor
- Transfer to a different class or employment situation
- Be granted an alternative living arrangement if the alleged harasser is in the same dormitory or employed at the same facility
- Be informed immediately of the outcome of the hearing
- Appeal a decision made by a panel hearing a formal complaint

21. List of Resources

A short list of articles, books, and videos that are readily available from the library or other campus offices should be included.

Additional Thoughts About Policies and Procedures

Confidentiality

Most complainants desire confidentiality and some will not tell anyone about sexual harassment if they believe their name will be divulged. Often they just want to tell someone about their experience and are ambivalent about what they want to happen next. They may also want to know what can be done about the problem. They may need reassurance about the institution's commitment to protect them against retaliation and just how the institution will protect them.

Often, if individuals can be reassured about being protected against retaliation, they may be more likely to deal with the harassment even if it means allowing their name to be used in resolving the problem. If a student is worried about retaliation by a faculty member, she or he needs to know that a transfer to another class is possible and that grades can be evaluated by another teacher. An employee may need reassurance that her job will be protected and that she can have her evaluation redone by another supervisor. If it is a case of student-to-student harassment, students need to know that they will be protected against further harassment, that the other student can be transferred. Most important, they need to be reassured that the institution views retaliation as serious an offense as harassment itself.

Sometimes, the issue can be resolved in a number of ways without divulging the victim's name. Some institutions, conscious of their need to respond when they have knowledge of sexual harassment whether or not there is a formal complaint, require that records of informal complaints be kept but the name of the complainant can be omitted if she desires.

There are times, however, especially in instances of severe harassment, when the institution must intervene (as in the case of a sexual assault) to address a serious situation and to protect itself from future liability. The victim's name, as well as that of the perpetrator, should not be divulged except on a "need-to-know" basis. Although the institution can require its agents—faculty and staff—to not divulge information about individual cases, it cannot necessarily prohibit victims, their friends and parents, or the alleged harasser from divulging information to others. An exception to this might be a "gag" rule imposed during the course of a hearing until the matter is resolved.

Maintaining Records

Issues of confidentiality are also involved in the maintenance of records and efforts to identify instances of multiple harassment by the same person. In many educational institutions it is difficult to recognize repeat offenders because no record of informal complaints is kept, records may be scattered throughout the institution, or those in a position to know—a dean, an affirmative action officer, or director of personnel—are no longer in that position.

Institutions need to develop some sort of system to keep track of complaints, especially informal reports of harassment. Some schools have developed a central locked file with information about informal complaints. Only one person, such as a dean, has access to information in the locked file. The information may be used in subsequent complaints against the same person to assess whether a pattern of harassment exists. This is often a controversial issue. Faculty and staff may resent the existence of a file about them without their knowing what is in it. Certainly, if such a file exists, no formal action (such as refusing promotion or a suspension) based on the information in the file could be taken without telling the person about the information and providing them with an opportunity to respond.

The faculty at the College of Arts and Sciences at Cornell University has devised a procedure to deal with this issue. Students who are harassed can speak with one of two sexual harassment senior counselors, a man or a woman (both tenured) who are appointed by the dean and have undergone special training for the position. If a student does not want to file a formal complaint immediately, she or he can file a written complaint that can be pursued at a later date—at the end of a semester, after graduation, or if other people complain about the same person. Complainants are more likely to file a formal charge when others are willing to do so against the same person.

The complaint is kept in a locked box or file to which only the senior counselors have access. Before putting the complaint in the locked box, the senior counselor determines if the complaint has merit and marks it as such. The locked box preserves institutional memory of informal complaints. However, if an institution adopts such a procedure, it will still need to respond in some way to such complaints, even if they are not formal charges because of the institution's legal obligation to stop harassment.

Confidentiality Regarding Outcomes of Complaints

Some institutions have tried to keep the settlement of formal charges confidential, simply saying that the matter was addressed and is now closed. Many people object to this, claiming that it is analogous to a court's failing to reveal the sentence for an offender. When outcomes are withheld, morale is affected negatively, rumors typically abound, and often, the inaccurate assumption is made that the institution did nothing and is not responsive to sexual harassment issues. Moreover, it is difficult to keep such matters totally confidential, and it is not uncommon for part or all the details to leak out in ways that are damaging to the institution, particularly if the information is inaccurate. Generally, it is better for the institution to control the flow of information rather than to assume it will remain confidential. Additionally, the U.S. Department of Education's Office for Civil Rights, which enforces Title IX, requires prompt notice of the findings and the disposition of issues.

Liability Issues

Institutions have a responsibility under the law to provide a nondiscriminatory environment. Although the extent of liability in hostile environment cases is not yet settled, having a strong policy which encourages people to come forward, and enforcing the policy is good protection against charges of sexual harassment.

Responding to information about sexually harassing behavior is critical. Once an institution knows or should have known that harassment has occurred, it should address the situation if it is to avoid liability. Whether a formal complaint has been lodged or information merely reported, the institution needs to respond. Although standards of institutional liability are still evolving in the areas of harassment, it is clear that when acts of harassment are serious and repeated and an institution takes no preventive measures, the likelihood of institutional liability increases substantially.

Institutions may also incur liability when information about sexual harassment allegations or formal charges is withheld from a prospective employer of the alleged harasser in the event that a third party is later damaged by the employee. For example, a teacher leaves an institution in part or solely because of allegations or charges of sexual harassment. Because the first institution gives excellent references, the second institution hires him. The professor again harasses students, one of whom attempts suicide as a result of his harassment. Is the first institution liable? Possibly, especially when the first institution knew or should have known about the danger posed by the employee and could reasonably expect the former employee to continue the same kind of behavior.

Mentioning charges or allegations of sexual harassment in a reference—even if no formal charge is filed—is not an invitation to a defamation suit when the information is true, when there is no intent to harm the employee, and the prospective employer has a "need to know" the information.[8]

Freedom of Speech Issues

The freedom of speech issue has been raised in various contexts concerning sexual harassment. Some faculty, prompted by concerns about sexual harassment, have claimed that any restraints on their behavior toward students are an infringement on their freedom of speech and academic freedom. Academic freedom, however, involves the free discussion of ideas and does not include asking students for sexual favors or intimidating them because of their gender.

The free speech issue has also been raised as schools and colleges grapple with issues of student-to-student harassment, particularly racial harassment. Some schools have promulgated speech codes to deal with student-to-student harassment. Some of these codes in public institutions have been found to be in violation of the First Amendment, although no such case has reached the U.S. Supreme Court. Private institutions, however, are generally not required to follow constitutional standards and may be able to enact such codes.

About 100 colleges and universities have such codes. Although detailed discussion of this issue is beyond the scope of this chapter, it is important to keep in mind that freedom of speech is not absolute and that the courts have upheld some restraints on free speech.

The issue of a sexually harassing hostile environment in an educational setting as a constitutional issue has not yet reached the U.S. Supreme Court. One could speculate whether the court, which ruled unanimously in 1986 that a hostile environment *in a workplace* violated sex discrimination laws[10] would rule that a similar hostile environment *in an educational setting* would not violate sex discrimination laws because of constitutional constraints. The argument can be made that educational institutions should be held to an even higher standard than employers.[11] It is unlikely that the court would consider direct or indirect threats or bribes for unwanted sexual activity as a free-speech issue. Whether speech that creates a hostile environment *interfering with a person's ability to learn* is constitutionally protected may ultimately be decided by the Supreme Court.

Whether or not speech codes can be crafted in such a way as to be valid under the Constitution, schools, however, are not prohibited from dealing with offensive speech and behaviors in other ways, such as the following:

- Other rules, such as prohibitions against vandalism, uncivil behavior, trespassing, littering, threatening behavior, intimidation, harassment, and the like, can still be invoked as well as state laws prohibiting discrimination.
- In some instances where free speech issues have arisen and institutions have been hesitant about invoking formal sanctions (as in some cases of peer harassment), institutions have remained silent. Unfortunately, such silence is often construed as condoning the behavior. Schools and colleges, however, can do much to help educate their community institutions by taking a public stand against the behavior (see discussion on public shaming in Chapter 3).
- Create a positive atmosphere with policies and programs that promote civility, respect, and tolerance.
- Develop programs to increase awareness and responsibility about these issues.

How to Deal with Sexual Harassment When There Is No Formal Charge

An institution is in a common bind when they know about sexual harassment and no one wants to file a formal charge. It may be liable if it does nothing, yet it cannot invoke its formal procedures without a formal charge. What are the institution's options?

1. The Institution Can Provide Students and Employees with Techniques to Handle It on Their Own If They are Willing to Do So.
See suggestions later in this chapter.

2. The Institutions Can Initiate Activities to Increase Awareness of Sexual Harassment.
In some schools, especially when the victim has not wanted her name known, the dean or president has sent a letter to every member of the particular department or unit stating that there is a concern about sexual harassment within the department or unit and that, because of legal liabilities, staff are invited (or required if possible) to attend a workshop on sexual harassment.

3. A Supervisor or Administrator Can Speak to the Alleged Offender.
If possible, obtain the permission of the victim before doing this, unless the harassment is so severe, as in the case of sexual assault, as to merit this kind of intervention without permission.(Even then, the victim should be informed in advance of the intervention and the reason for it.) In many instances, a department chair, a dean, or other supervisor speaks to the alleged harasser (sometimes without naming the woman), noting that his behavior is being perceived as sexually harassing, and reminding him that sexual harassment is prohibited by law and by institutional policy.

The person is also told that because there is no formal charge, there will be no investigation. Whether the alleged offender admits or denies the charges is not important. If he denies the harassment, the administrator can state that without an investigation, it is not possible to know if the allegations are true or not and that what is important at this stage is for the alleged offender to recognize how his behavior is being perceived.

The administrator should also note that no action is being taken other than to inform him of how his behavior is perceived, that no record is being put in his personnel file, but that the information will be available should there ever be a formal charge of sexual harassment. In addition, the person is reminded that the institution's policy prohibits any retaliation. The administrator who talks to the alleged harasser should write a confidential memo about the conversation for his or her own files to be used in the event there are subsequent allegations of sexual harassment.

4. The Institution Could Bring Its Own Charges Against the Alleged Harasser.
Most institutions establish a neutral forum that hears formal charges of sexual harassment. Another alternative is for the institution to bring charges against the harasser, particularly in egregious cases and where victims would be willing to testify as witnesses, even though they might not be willing to bring charges on their own. Institutions can usually bring such third-party charges against employees and students when they violate certain institutional policies.

What to Do When Someone Comes with a Complaint

Individuals come to see someone about sexual harassment (although they may not label it as such) when the harassment has made them feel helpless, vulnerable, and/or angry. Persons who are likely contacts should be trained in responding. Some of the people who are likely to be contacted about harassment are:

- Women faculty
- Department chairs
- Deans and other administrators
- Women's center staff
- Affirmative action officer
- Ombudsperson
- Health center personnel
- Counseling center staff
- Committees or commissions on the status of women
- Sexual harassment committee
- Persons officially designated to handle sexual harassment
- Resident assistants in dormitories
- Women student leaders

Not everyone will be comfortable dealing with someone who comes to them with a sexual harassment complaint. But, all faculty, administrators, and staff should at least know how to respond minimally by (1) showing sympathy ("That's such a shame"); (2) informing the persons that kind of behavior is not allowed ("We have a policy against that kind of behavior and it is against the law"); (3) not blaming the person or allowing him or her to accept the blame; (4) knowing whom to refer the person to and encouraging a meeting with the designated person ("I'm not the person to talk to about this. Mary Smith had been helpful to a lot of people who have faced the same kind of problem. Let me give her a call right now and see when she can see you"); and (5) providing for follow-up ("If that doesn't work out, get back to me and we'll figure out what to do next").

For others who can or must respond more extensively, the purpose is primarily not to advise but to help empower the person to figure out what they want to do next. When people are anxious or upset, it helps them regain their sense of autonomy if they can make decisions and have some things to do. Although not necessarily in this order, the following actions may be helpful:

- Show sympathy
- Ask questions in a nonjudgmental way ("What happened then?" not "What were you wearing when it happened?")
- Inform the person that that kind of behavior is not allowed ("We have a policy against that kind of behavior and it is against the law")
- Don't blame the person or allow her to blame herself
- Ask what they want to happen next
- Tell them there are a number of ways the problem can be handled: they might be able to do some things to stop the behavior; there are some informal actions the institution can take; and there are formal charges that can be brought

against the offender under institutional policy and/or under law. (If the problem is not resolved readily, at some point a victim may seek information about her legal rights. It is better to inform victims so that they and others do not feel the institution was trying to discourage them from pursuing their legal rights. Keep in mind that most people don't want to file a lawsuit unless they feel nothing else is possible.)

- Offer to tell them about some of the actions people have found helpful in dealing with similar incidents.
- Ask if they have indicated that they did not like the behavior to the other person and wanted it to stop, adding that sometimes this stops the behavior. ("Could you say something like 'This makes me uncomfortable. I want it to stop.'") If the person relates that they have already done that and it didn't work, go on to another option; some harassers continue even when given strong messages that their behavior is not welcome. If they indicate that they do not want to do this, accept their decision without criticism and go on to another option. If the person indicates interest in this option, you might coach or work with them on what they want to say. Rather than end the interview at this point, however, suggest you have another way (see next item) to handle the incident(s) that they also might want to consider.
- Describe the technique of using a "special" letter (see below)
- Describe informal actions the institution can take such as:
  - Send a letter to everyone in the unit indicating concern about sexual harassment and enclosing a copy of the policy
  - Conduct a workshop on sexual harassment for the unit
  - Have someone speak to the offender
  - Have her meet with the offender with a third party present
- Mention that the person can file a formal charge either within the institution or under various laws. Often the victim does not want to hear about all of the details of formal procedures, especially if she is considering informal options. However, if she is interested, how they operate should be described.
- Ask what the person thinks she wants to do, or does she need some time to think about this. Whatever her decision is, offer your assistance and support.
- If you sense hesitation, you might ask if she is worried about retaliation and/or confidentiality. If so, reassure her about the institution's policies on these issues.
- Make another appointment to talk with her to provide additional help. Tell her if she needs to talk to you earlier you will be available. If she decides to talk to the offender on her own or to use the letter, be sure to make an appointment to follow-up and to see if any other help is necessary.
- Urge her to write everything down—a description of what happened, how she responded, where and when the incident(s) occurred, and the names of witnesses, if any. (This may help clarify her feelings and act as evidence should she bring charges against the harasser in the future.)
- Urge her to talk to other people. She needs support and she may also find other victims of the offender.
- Provide her with written materials about sexual harassment such as the institution's brochure, materials on the letter, and a copy of the policy.

Using a Letter to Deal with Sexual Harassment

The letter technique is a powerful technique developed by Mary P. Rowe at the Massachusetts Institute of Technology. It has been extraordinarily successful in many institutions of higher education; in approximately 90 percent of the cases it stops the harassment of that particular person and seems to prevent the future harassment of others by the offender.[12] It has also been used successfully in cases of one-to-one peer harassment with college students and those in other settings. The letter is polite, low-key, and consists of the following[13]:

* *Part I* is a factual account of what happened, without any evaluation, as viewed by the writer. It should include details, including time, place, and a description of the behavior(s). For example, "Last month when I came to your office you asked me to come to your apartment that night to discuss how to improve my grade." Often the harasser agrees with the facts but not with the interpretation.
* *Part II* describes how the writer feels about what happened such as misery, fear, revulsion. For example, "I'm frightened whenever you come near me" or "When you walk into the room, I want to throw up." As in Part I, there are no evaluative words or accusations, only a description of how the writer feels.
* *Part III* describes what the writer wants to happen next. This part is usually short because most people just want the harassment to stop. For example, "I want your behavior to stop" or "I want to treated the way a student has a right to be treated" or "I don't want you to make sexual remarks to or about me anymore."

The letter is best delivered in person or by certified mail with a return receipt requested. This ensures that the harasser receives the letter. A copy should be kept by the writer; should there be any subsequent retaliation or continued harassment, the letter can be used as evidence.

Copies are not sent to anyone else. A letter copied to someone in authority such as a dean or department head is likely to lead to the recipient's contacting that person, denying the incident and denigrating the writer's credibility. If the letter is to work, it should be a private communication between the two people involved.

If the student is interested in writing a letter, you might ask the student to give you a copy, but tell the student that it is not required. You can also offer to look at the letter before it is sent but that is the student's decision.

Because the letter gives the recipient an opportunity to read the letter several times without having to respond immediately (as in a conversation), and because it is low key and nonaccusatory, it provides the recipient, perhaps for the first time, with a view of how the behavior is perceived by the writer. In most cases, the recipient is astonished that the behavior is viewed in the way the writer sees it. He may also fear a formal charge and worry about who else has seen the letter, and thus be less likely to engage in retaliation such as bad evaluations or further harassment.

The letter is apparently more powerful than a verbal request to stop. Usually the recipient says nothing and simply stops the harassing. Should he want to apologize or discuss the situation, the writer does not need to discuss it; she can say: "I'm not going to discuss it; I just want your behavior to stop," and then walk away.

The letter has many advantages: it avoids formal charges and a public confrontation; keeps the incident confidential; and bypasses issues of legality, evidence, due process, and his-word-against-her-word. Except in the rare instance where the recipient is extremely aggressive or sadistic, it usually works. Generally, it should not be used in the case of peer group harassment as in the case of a fraternity because, as a group, they are likely to ridicule the letter rather than take it seriously.

The letter is effective even if the writer misinterpreted a friendly action as being sexual. Equally important, the letter helps the writer to regain a sense of control. It must be voluntary, however, and follow-up with the writer is essential to determine if other action is needed. A number of schools have publicized the letter in materials they have developed concerning sexual harassment.

Sometimes victims find it helpful in terms of sorting out their feelings about the experience to write the letter even if they do not send it.

Using the Sexual Harassment Notebook as a Technique for Handling Recurring One-on-One or Group Harassment

Often harassment by an individual or a group is not limited to a single incident but occurs again and again. One informal way that individuals can handle such harassment is the use of the Sexual Harassment Notebook.

The harassed person labels a notebook in big letters "Sexual Harassment." When the harassment occurs, she responds by pulling out her notebook with a pen, looks at the harasser(s), and asks him/them to repeat what was said as she proceeds to write it down. She might also ask what the date is, verbally describe where she is ("Let's see, this is on the campus in front of the administration building"). She can also ask how the harasser(s) spells his (their) name. Her attitude should be very matter of fact. When asked what she is doing or why she is writing everything down, she simply responds with something like "I'm just writing things down" or "I'm just keeping records" (best accompanied by a smile). She does not give any other information. Another alternative is to say that she is doing research on sexual harassment.

This kind of action has the potential of breaking the cycle of harassment in part because her response is not one of vulnerability but of strength; it is unexpected; it labels the behavior as socially unacceptable; and it implies that she might take additional formal action.

As in the case of the letter, the technique may not work with extremely aggressive or hostile individuals. Should the notebook be grabbed, she should not indicate any distress but simply walk away. She can also calmly say, "I knew you would do that, I predicted it to myself a few moments ago." The notebook technique should be voluntary, and follow-up is needed to see if additional intervention is needed.

Responding to Victims

People who have been harassed often need to know what has happened to them is not their fault; that sexual harassment violates the law and institutional policy; that they have a right to feel angry; and that they have a number of options to use in dealing with the behavior. They need to be informed about their legal rights, the institution's formal procedures, and informal ways of dealing with the problem. They also need to be reassured that the institution takes their complaint seriously and will do everything possible to protect them from retaliation.

Additionally, victims of sexual harassment, whether they file a formal charge or not, often feel helpless, ashamed, or worried, and may suffer stress-related symptoms. Letting victims know they can obtain help is important, but it is equally important that the person giving help is familiar with sexual harassment and its impact and has specific training on how to deal with sexual harassment victims.[14]

Victims should be allowed to bring a person of their own choice with them during all interviews, meetings, and formal proceedings. Keeping the victim informed at all stages of the process, including any formal or informal action taken by the school is essential, whether she is a student or college employee. Victims should be encouraged to report any further incidents or retaliation.

Especially when formal charges have been filed and/or when harassment has been particularly egregious or repeated, someone should periodically check with the victim during the following year to see if any other help is needed or if any other incidents have occurred.

Provisions should be available, if needed, for redoing job evaluations in the case of employees, or having a grade reevaluated, in the case of students. This should be done by someone other than the alleged harasser. When either the harasser or victim transfers to another situation, it is important that steps be taken to ensure that the harasser understands why the transfer is occurring so that he does not continue to harass.

Help should be available to facilitate an employee who has been harassed to transfer from a job to one of equal or better status without penalty, or a student's transfer or dropping of courses, when the victim requests it. Students should be able to obtain a refund when a course is dropped because of harassment. Should an employee or student wish to take a leave of absence, this should be facilitated without penalty. Some colleges have provided funds for psychotherapy to mitigate the aftermath of sexual harassment.

Educational and Preventive Measures

No matter how comprehensive or well written a policy is, educational programs and activities are essential in helping to prevent sexual harassment. The first step in any educational program is dissemination of the policy. Here are some ways that institutions have used to ensure that all members of their educational community know about the policy:

• Reporting annually to the community about sexual harassment, although incidents may be sanitized to protect privacy. One university does this annually in the form of a chart published in the school newspaper. The behavior is described as well as how the incident was resolved. This short description might relate how a professor put his arm around a student; she complained to the sexual harassment committee; a member of the committee spoke to the department chair who then spoke to the faculty member who subsequently apologized to the student. This kind of reporting educates the community as to what behaviors are prohibited, and how many incidents can be resolved without resort to formal procedures.

- Sending a letter from the president to all faculty and staff members at the beginning of each school year, reminding them about the policy.
- Creating a brochure aimed at all members of the educational community. The brochure explains in simple terms what sexual harassment is, prohibitions, and what to do if one experiences harassment.
- Including information about sexual harassment in orientation for students, staff, and faculty.
- Printing the policy in the student newspaper at the start of each school year.
- Including the policy in student, faculty, and employee handbooks.
- Ensuring that peer harassment is given sufficient emphasis in student handbooks.
- Including information about sexual harassment in materials given to new employees and transfer students.
- Passing out bookmarks that define sexual harassment and list a resource to call for information.
- Creating and displaying posters on sexual harassment. Some schools have held poster contests. The Hawaii Department of Education developed a poster which said, in part, "When you were a kid you and your friends may have teased the girls, made them cry, maybe even hurt some of them. 'Boys will be boys' was the excuse. Let's call it what it is: Sexual harassment. Domineering, tough, abusive behavior is not 'masculine.' It's unhealthy. It's uncool."
- Posting the policy or an abbreviated version of it in prominent places.
- Incorporating sexual harassment issues into other policies—faculty professional ethics code, human rights and antidiscrimination policies, student code of honor, or behavior students rights.

Many institutions have developed educational programs to sensitize members of the academic community. A number of films and videos have been developed for help in training. The following activities have been undertaken at many schools:

- Establishing a permanent committee to monitor the issue, whether the policy is working, and make recommendations about sexual harassment. The committee should include representatives from different segments of the school or school system such as students, staff, and faculty. People of color, women, and men should be represented. In some schools, the same committee is the panel for hearing sexual harassment cases.
- Establishing a special committee on peer harassment. Student groups may consist of dormitory residents, members of Greek organizations, and so on.
- Appointing a specific person to be in charge of sexual harassment activities and programs.
- Providing training programs about sexual harassment for the entire educational community.
- Providing training separately for specific segments of the educational community, such as faculty, graduate assistants, staff and specific departments or units, and students.
- Providing training for administrators, with emphasis on their responsibilities and how they should and should not handle complaints.
- Providing training for those most likely to be contacted by people with complaints about sexual harassment such as counselors, advisors, health personnel, resident assistants, mental health personnel, women's center staff, and student life personnel.

- Providing training for those with specific responsibility for addressing sexual harassment issues such as a sexual harassment committee or persons involved in hearing complaints.
- Developing training and special materials for faculty members from other countries. Some of these faculty, including graduate assistants, may have very different ideas about what constitutes acceptable behavior toward females, especially females who are alone. Others may be unaware of U.S. law. Special materials may need to be developed for students from other cultures as well.[15]
- Providing training for faculty members on how to deal with peer harassment, including intervention techniques.
- Including material on sexual harassment in other related programs such as faculty development training, training for graduate assistants. If a school includes programs on conflict resolution, peer harassment should be included.
- Including training about peer harassment in all sexual assault education programs.
- Training students to be peer educators.
- Involving men in training activities. If there are no qualified men, have men introduce the trainers.
- Documenting the seriousness and extent of the problem through surveys of students, staff, and faculty members; campuswide presentations; and conferences.
- Evaluating fraternity life for evidence of peer harassment.
- Including items about sexual harassment and sexist remarks in teaching-evaluation questionnaires.

Endnotes

1. Adapted from Susan Strauss with Pamela Espeland, *Sexual harassment and teens.* Free Spirit Press, Minneapolis, 1992, p. 24.
2. Fitzgerald, Louise F., *Sexual harassment in higher education.* National Education Association, Washington DC, p.13.
3. Based on EEOC Policy Guidelines on Sexual Harassment, 29 CFR Sec. 1604.11 (1986).
4. Unpublished "Final Memorandum" by Evan Stolove, member of the Section of Women in Legal Education Committee re. "Preliminary Ideas for Policy," 7/1/92 on Model Anti-Harassment Policies and Procedures. American Bar Association, Chicago IL.
5. Institutions are prohibited by Title IX from allowing sex discrimination in off-campus educational programs such as internships or other similar activities.
6. The institution needs to be certain it is not just moving the problem to another setting. However, if moving is necessary, the focus should be on moving the harasser rather than the victim, although occasionally this may be necessary, especially if that is what the victim desires.
7. The U.S. Supreme Court in *Meritor Savings Bank v. Vinson* criticized the bank's policy, saying that it offered the bank no protection from liability because it required all employees to first complain of sexual harassment to their supervisor and would therefore discourage complaints if the supervisor was the harasser, as he was in *Meritor*.
8. *See* Kenneth L. Sovereign, Labor relations, pitfalls of withholding reference information, *Personnel Journal,* March 1990, 119–121; and Terri L. Regotti, Commentary, negligent hiring and retaining of sexually abusive teachers, *Education Law Reporter,* May 21, 1992, 333–340; and *Negligent hiring,* Office of Public Instruction, State Capitol, Helena, MT 59620, nd.
9. *See* "Report of the Date Rape Task Force, Harvard and Radcliffe Colleges," February 10, 1992, p.5.
10. *Meritor v. Vinson,* 1986.

11. *See*, for example, Ronna Greff Schneider, Sexual harassment and higher education, in Elsa Kircher Cole (ed.) *Sexual harassment on campus: A legal compendium*. National Association of College and University Attorneys, Washington, DC, pp. 46–49.

12. Conversations with Mary Rowe, numerous campus affirmative action officers, presidents, and other administrators across the country.

13. See Mary P. Rowe, Dealing with sexual harassment, *Harvard Business Review*, May–June 1981; Bernice R. Sandler, *Writing a letter to the sexual harasser: Another way of dealing with the problem*, 1983; and Jean O'Gorman Hughes & Bernice R. Sandler, *In case of sexual harassment: A guide for women students*, both available from the Center for Women Policy Studies, Washington, DC, 1986.

14. Training in dealing with victims of sexual assault is excellent preparation for dealing with victims of sexual harassment.

15. SUNY-Binghamton has developed materials concerning sexual harassment for international students.

7

POLITICS OF
THE POLICY PROCESS

NANCY A. WONDERS

In 1994, Northern Arizona University (NAU) officially approved a new, comprehensive policy entitled the "Safe Working and Learning Environment Policy." The policy covers sexual harassment, various forms of discrimination, sexual assault, and consensual relations, and provides a description of formal and informal procedures available to address violations of the policy. This policy is the result of four years of hard work and negotiation within the NAU community. The new policy originated with a task force of the university's Commission on the Status of Women, a group charged with the task of assessing the status of women on NAU's campus. I was a member of the Campus Climate and Safety Task Force during the four years the policy was developed and, along with other members of the Task Force, I learned an enormous amount about sexual harassment on our campus, sexual harassment policies, and the political context within which policy-making occurs.[1] As a faculty member in the Department of Criminal Justice, I frequently teach about sexual harassment issues. But as a principal writer and negotiator for the new policy, I learned more about the politics surrounding the development and revision of sexual harassment policies than I could have ever learned in a Ph.D. program or from the existing literature on sexual harassment.

In this chapter, I share what it took me (and many others on my campus) four years to learn. Creating a sexual harassment policy is no easy task, but it is made harder by the absence of information about successful strategies for negotiating the policy process within an academic setting. Although what makes a strategy "successful" is highly dependent on the local context within which policy is created and implemented, it is my hope that this chapter will save others precious time as they seek to create and improve harassment policies on their own campuses, to create a safe working and learning environment for their colleagues, for their students—for themselves.

Understanding Policy and Politics

Developing a sexual harassment policy within an academic environment is an inherently political process. Like other forms of policy, sexual harassment policies reflect, and sometimes alter, existing power arrangements within the university or college. The provisions contained within sexual harassment policies will almost inevitably be viewed as privileging some members of the university community while disadvantaging others. A stronger document is often viewed as a "victory" for women at the "expense" of men. A weaker policy is often seen as the reverse. And every policy choice is charged with political ramifications. Even the absence of an effective policy is a significant political statement, because it reflects a choice on the part of administrators to ignore a problem that has serious consequences for many employees and students.

For those interested in successfully negotiating the politics surrounding the policy process, there are two types of information that are important to have. First, it is important to be familiar with the policy process, especially how policy is created within universities and colleges, and points of access for those wishing to create or change policy. Second, it is useful to know the kinds of barriers that may prevent policies from being created, and successful strategies for overcoming these obstacles. Participants in the policy process who understand the stages and hurdles policies must maneuver around are likely to be at a distinct advantage compared to those who do not have this information. This chapter addresses both the nature of the policy process and myths that create barriers for those wishing to create an effective sexual harassment policy.

The Policy-Making Process

At all stages of the policy process, political negotiation and strategizing occurs. A quick glance at the literature on policy creation is instructive for those unfamiliar with the policy process. Although policy creation in an academic environment differs in some ways from other contexts, the stages policies must move through are strikingly similar. Anderson (1984) identifies five stages of the policy process: (1) problem identification and agenda setting, (2) policy formulation, (3) policy adoption, (4) policy implementation, and (5) policy evaluation.[2] What follows is a brief description of the stages and their relevance for sexual harassment policy.

Within the policy process, the first thing that must happen before a policy change can occur is for people to organize together to define an issue as a public, rather than a private, problem worthy of placement on the agenda of policymakers. To achieve this, those concerned about the issue must organize and mobilize sympathetic groups and individuals so that the issue is perceived to have wide impact. How this is done and who constitutes the "public" that the problem affects has consequences for policy success. If the issue of sexual harassment is defined narrowly as a "women's" problem, it may be more difficult to obtain support from within the campus community. If sexual harassment is defined more broadly or is linked to other issues, it may have a better chance of gaining a wide range of supporters for policy change.

Once the issue is defined as a public problem and a coalition is assembled to support a policy change, proposed solutions to the issue must be brought to the formal agenda of policymakers. Because policymakers must make choices among issues competing for their attention, it is critical that proponents of a new sexual harassment policy be prepared to explain why their issue is a priority. It is also important for proponents to offer some realistic strategies for resolving the problem to aid policymakers in their effort to formulate a policy solution. In a college or university setting, most policymakers are administrators, although it is common for faculty (and sometimes staff and students) to have access to policy-making bodies. This access creates the possibility that initiatives for policy change can come from below, from employees, rather than only from above, from the administration. Policies created by those the policy will affect may be more likely to be effective because they may be viewed as more legitimate than policies imposed on employees from above by administrators. Initiatives for policy change around sexual harassment might begin within groups or committees on campus that already have some access to the policy-making process. Because administrators must decide how to allocate their time among competing demands, the more work proponents of a new or revised sexual harassment policy have done to draft a policy, the more likely administrators are to place the issue on their agenda for consideration. It is much harder to ignore a concrete proposal than it is a mere idea or suggestion.

Once an issue is on the formal agenda of policymakers, various strategies for responding to the issue may be considered. At this stage, the goal is policy adoption. However, several possibilities exist: a policy solution that proponents of the issue favor may be adopted, a different policy solution may be agreed on, or policymakers may be unable to arrive at an acceptable solution. Access to the policy process is again important to ensure that proponents of a new or revised policy are pleased with the outcome. Policies that have been drafted by those interested in seeing the policy created are more likely to contain elements that proponents support.

The final two stages, policy implementation and policy evaluation are in some ways conclusions to the policy process. However, as will be pointed out later, a good policy is useless without a commitment to and strategy for implementation. Regular policy evaluation is similarly important since static policies quickly lose their relevance given the rapid pace of change in contemporary society. Indeed, at our university it was at the point of policy evaluation—evaluation of our *old* policy—that new "problems" were identified, creating a circle back to stage one, the identification of issues that we believed should appear on the policy agenda.

At each stage outlined here, "politics" enters into the policy-making process. At each stage there is the possibility of a struggle between different actors desiring to have their interests heard and represented within the policy process. Those who understand the stages the policy process must move through have a better chance of mobilizing appropriately for each stage of the process to ensure success; they also have a better chance of anticipating potential problems.

Myths that Cause Trouble, and Strategies for Ensuring Success

Because policies emerge out of political struggle and negotiation, it is particularly important to be aware of the barriers that might loom before those wishing to create or alter sexual harassment policies on their campuses. Many of these barriers consist of myths that prevent people from acting to change the status quo. In the United States, it is easy to see that the mythology that "voting doesn't matter" has helped to create a situation where only a small percentage of the population decides presidential elections (and an even smaller percentage of the population decides local elections).[3] Similarly, the mythology surrounding sexual harassment policies often creates barriers that seem insurmountable to those seeking to create more effective policies. What follows is an outline of some of the myths that serve as obstacles to the development of sexual harassment policies, and a discussion of strategies that help to ensure success for those committed to the creation of effective policy on their campuses.

"There She Goes Again!"

One myth that makes the development of an effective sexual harassment policy difficult is the idea that initiatives for change or action by women really are just another form of complaining, typically complaining by one woman or a few women who are perceived to be chronic troublemakers. People who believe this myth can then argue that it does not matter what action is taken because nothing will please these women; such women will always find something to complain about.

To debunk this myth before it creates a barrier that dooms a sexual harassment policy requires wise organizing and strategic thinking from the beginning. The claim that it is just a few women who are complaining, can only be made when those pushing for a sexual harassment policy are few in number, homogenous, and/or exclusively female. If at all possible, those wishing to develop an effective policy should have the weight of an organized group or committee behind them so that their effort is viewed as representing broad interests. Within the policy literature, "interest aggregation," or the development of broad-based support for a policy change, is recognized as a critical component of the policy process.[4]

Diversity within the organizing group can also be critical for debunking this myth. In addition, it is useful to have people representing different constituencies who are willing to serve as spokespeople on behalf of the policy. At my university, the push for policy change emerged from the Commission on the Status of Women. This group includes faculty, staff, students, administrators—women and men—people from different racial and ethnic backgrounds—people with different political viewpoints. Although this group does not represent the entire university community, it does represent diverse interests that are shared by a large cross-section of the university community. Key spokespeople for our policy included individuals representing very different constituencies within the university. This diversity ensured that a large number of groups and individuals could "hear" or connect with what we were advocating.

"You're Just a Bunch of 'Faculty' or 'Staff' or 'Students,'
What Do You Know About Sexual Harassment?"

One myth that inhibits people from entering into the policy-making process is the perception that they lack expertise in the particular policy area. It is often the case that those on campus who are most concerned with the problem of sexual harassment have little expertise or formal training on the topic. However, this should not discourage people from writing policy; several strategies to remedy this weakness can be used to prevent criticism later on.

The first strategy for developing expertise is to know your community. Become informed about sexual harassment on your campus. There are many ways to obtain information about the incidence of harassment, the kinds of harassment, and the strengths and weaknesses of your university or college's procedure for responding to complaints. Many institutions of higher education have surveyed their campuses to assess the prevalence of sexual harassment as well as perceptions about remedies.[5] Rather than devoting a great deal of time to creating a survey from scratch, it might be wise to borrow a survey used on another campus and then spend time tailoring it to fit your local needs. Although it may be difficult to obtain funding for a survey, the data obtained can be useful for creating expert knowledge about sexual harassment in your local context. One way to lower the cost of this type of evaluation research is to use research services that may already exist on the campus.

At NAU, our organizing efforts were aided by a survey that was conducted by the statewide Commission on the Status of Women that found that:

> Approximately 28 percent of the female respondents indicated that they had experienced unwanted teasing, jokes, remarks or comments of a sexual nature at one of the three [Arizona] universities within the past three years. Among full-time faculty women, who comprised half of the respondents to this question, 40 percent answered the question Yes, as did 35 percent of the women administrators responding.[6]

This information clearly evidenced that sexual harassment was not just an academic issue, but affected large numbers of people on our campus.

In addition to surveys, information can also be obtained from the Affirmative Action Office (or its corollary) about the number of people who have filed harassment charges and the nature of their claims. This information can only be released in aggregate numbers to protect the confidentiality of complainants, but it may provide useful information about the nature of formal complaints. Information about informal complaints or about victims of harassment who fail to come forward at all is more difficult to obtain, but is clearly just as critical for understanding sexual harassment.

On NAU's campus, some of the most useful information provided to those of us working to revise our sexual harassment policy resulted from conversations with individuals who had been harassed and/or had taken their complaint to the Affirmative Action Office. We did not solicit these conversations, but once people on our campus heard we were reviewing the policy, victims of harassment sought us out to see what we might do about harassment in their unit or department. The value of these conversations was that they provided first-hand information about specific kinds of problems on our campus and about specific fears and experiences people had regarding reporting and retaliation. The conversations also provided us with detailed information about the weaknesses of the existing harassment policy and current procedures for responding to complaints. This information was invaluable and aided us in becoming local experts on the topic. Others might know more about sexual harassment at an abstract level, but members of our Task Force came to know more than almost anyone about sexual harassment on OUR campus. Although we did not systematically record the stories told by individual women, it might be useful to do so and distribute these stories to others to help the campus community understand the lived experience associated with sexual harassment.[7]

Expertise can be gained in other ways as well. If possible, any group organizing to create or alter a sexual harassment policy should contain some individuals with expertise in the area. We had several people who regularly deal with sexual harassment, discrimination, or sexual assault (all included in our policy) on our committee, including an Assistant Dean of Students who frequently hears student complaints, a faculty member with expertise in sexual harassment, and the director of the student health center. These individuals were helpful in directing other committee members to outside sources of information about sexual harassment that they might not have been aware of otherwise, and their own expertise helped to make the claims of the Task Force more credible.

Another strategy for developing expertise is to become familiar with laws about sexual harassment. This can be accomplished by reading the literature or attending conferences on sexual harassment.[8] A relatively new way to learn about sexual harassment is by participating in computer discussion lists such as the Sociologists Against Sexual Harassment (SASH).[9] The SASH list contains excellent information about current policies, laws, and training programs and welcomes questions about any of these topics.

Laws that are critical to review include: Title VII, the Civil Rights Act of 1964; Title IX, the Education Amendments of 1972; and the Civil Rights Act of 1991. It is important to become familiar with these pieces of federal legislation because they outline the minimum requirements for an effective sexual harassment policy under the law.[10] Relevant state antidiscrimination and sexual assault/abuse laws should also be reviewed.

Although it is unreasonable for those who want to create or alter a sexual harassment policy to become legal experts, basic knowledge of the law is extremely useful. For example, on the NAU campus there were those who objected to inclusion of the phrase "hostile environment" within our sexual harassment policy. The debate about its inclusion was shortened when we had those raising this concern read the section of the Equal Employment Opportunity Commission (EEOC) policy outlining hostile environment as it is defined under Title VII. Regardless of personal opinion, the law is the law, and knowing the law is power in a negotiating situation.

"It's a Good Idea But It'll Never Work" or "It's a Good Idea But It'll Never Work HERE."

Another kind of myth that can prevent policy change from occurring is the belief that proposed changes are a good idea—in the abstract—but that the effort to make the change is not worth it, given the local reality of sexual harassment. People might say that the change is a good idea but it just is not workable or it is not practical. A corollary concern is that the proposed changes sound good, but they are not likely to work *here*, given the idiosyncratic nature of this particular institutional context.

To combat this attitude, it is valuable to propose policy changes that are drawn from policies already in existence elsewhere. If they are working at another institution, it is difficult for others to argue that the policy change is utopian. It is especially helpful if you can evidence that the policy is in place at an institution similar to yours. We obtained sexual harassment policies from all our peer institutions, other universities within our state, and from many other universities and colleges we had heard have model policies. By looking at these policies, we became familiar with the range of policy options available to us. Many of these options are outlined in Chapter 6 of this book, but reviewing actual policies may make it easier to identify policies that exist in institutional contexts like your own. Our review of policies gave us national "expertise" about sexual harassment policy within academic institutions and enormously increased our legitimacy on campus.

"We Don't Need MORE Policies!"

Anyone who works in higher education can sympathize with those who object to more rules, more documents, more committees—more policies. Even those wishing to create a more effective sexual harassment policy may feel frustrated at the way policy creation and revision seems to perpetuate, rather than simplify, bureaucratic excess. However, on many campuses where people wish to strengthen their sexual harassment policy, it is possible to reduce policy proliferation by revising an existing policy and, in some cases, merging several policies together into a new, more comprehensive policy.

At NAU, when we first reviewed our sexual harassment policy, we realized there were separate (though somewhat redundant) policies for students, faculty, and staff. Additionally, we realized that discrimination and sexual assault were discussed in other documents, though the procedures for addressing these harms were in some cases very similar to the university's response to sexual harassment. Because our new policy combines elements of several policies into a single policy, no one could argue that we were merely contributing to bureaucratic growth.

"You've Got a Great Policy But It'll Never Be Implemented Like You Intended!" or "How in the World Will You Get the Administration on Board?"

Mistrust between faculty, staff, students, and administrators is all too common within colleges and universities. People may be unwilling to work on policy changes they believe will never be implemented or will be sabotaged during the process of implementation. This fear is not without cause, but it can be addressed in ways that prevent it from becoming a barrier to change.

One way to ensure that this myth will not prevent people from working to create a strong policy is to consider implementation an integral part of the policy process. Concerns about implementation can be remedied, in part, by including procedures for implementation in the policy itself. For example, language might be included in the policy that outlines responsibility for prevention programs, specific educational strategies, or mechanisms to inform new employees about the policy.

In addition, it is also important to include those who will be implementing the policy in the process of creating it. The form that their involvement takes may vary from institution to institution. At NAU, the Affirmative Action Office and the president have the greatest responsibility for implementing the new policy. When we began to work on policy revision, we felt it was important for our initial discussions NOT to include representatives from the affirmative action office. We wanted our first draft to reflect a wish list of employee and student interests. Once we had a working document, however, we spent many hours in negotiation with affirmative action officers and the campus attorney. We recognized that no policy would be successful without the full support of the affirmative action office and the university president.

Much of the negotiation involved explaining WHY we thought a particular change was important—informing the affirmative action officers and attorney about what we had learned through research on our own campus and other campuses. We also learned a great deal from them about the constraints placed on the university by EEOC, the Title IX regulation, and limited budgets. Although the process was tedious at times, in the end every major change we wanted was included in the document. Language was sometimes reworded, but very few significant substantive changes were made throughout this process. Although this process of negotiation slowed down passage of the document, our work with the administration and it representatives gives us more confidence that they will help to ensure effective implementation of the policy.

The process of negotiation can be aided by several factors. As mentioned earlier, having diverse representation within the policy-making group (or negotiating team) helps to ensure that the group's claims will be heard and that they will be viewed as representing broad interests. Having the support of administrators across campus also helps. For example, one of our negotiators was an associate dean who was also the chair of the Commission on the Status of Women, and one dean and several other administrators on campus were strong advocates of the policy. The clout that administrators carry on campus was important because they could be heard, at times, in a way that some of the rest of us might not have been. And, as has already been mentioned, our ability to document and provide evidence for our policy suggestions, either by relying on the law, other universities' and colleges' policies, or the academic literature, was invaluable in the negotiating process.

Finally, ensuring that you get what you want requires patience. Our policy took several years to develop. For many, this may seem too long to wait for a policy change. At our university, those working on the policy agreed that the revision was meaningless without certain substantive changes, and we were unwilling to support a policy that did not contain these items.[11] Different groups might make different decisions, depending on their context; in our case, we believe patience paid off.

"You've Got a Great Policy, But People Will Never Read It—
It Will Just Go into the Circular File Anyway!"

Many people are reluctant to create or revise a sexual harassment policy because they do not believe policies really matter anyway. This can be a particularly difficult obstacle to overcome if there is already a policy on the books that has never really been put into action on campus. It is true that policies alone rarely create significant change, but a well-written sexual harassment policy can provide an important foundation for change in several ways. Being able to explain how a *new* policy can create change may help to persuade people, who would otherwise be unwilling to put forth the effort, to work on the endeavor.

First, a new or revised sexual harassment policy provides a vehicle for implementing a campuswide education program. Some have argued that sexual harassment policies cannot be effective without campuswide education.[12] An educational program can be implemented without a policy change, but a change in policy provides a compelling reason to extend educational programs to all sectors of the campus community, including groups that might otherwise be reluctant to participate.

At our university, the president has supported the initiation of a campuswide training program that will ultimately reach all faculty and staff members. Because our policy change is significant, the president intends to ensure that the campus community is informed about recent changes in the policy, as well as the consequences for violations of the policy. This push to educate the campus community is critical for the success of any sexual harassment policy. Once people have been educated about what constitutes sexual harassment, claims of ignorance about the law, a common excuse for justifying harassing behavior,[13] will cease to be acceptable. Additionally, there will be greater clarity about what constitutes sexual harassment, increasing the likelihood that harassing behavior will not occur in the first place, and that, when it does occur, it will be identified and addressed.

It is important to understand that campuswide education must be an ongoing effort. Although rates of employee turnover from institution to institution vary, universities and colleges employ large numbers of people, guaranteeing that there will always be new employees. Ideally, sexual harassment policies should provide guidelines that guarantee that all new employees and students are educated about the policy and about sexual harassment.

"I'm Not Going to Support This Policy—There's
Nothing in It for Me!"

Another myth about sexual harassment policy is that such policies benefit only women. This myth can become a significant problem for those seeking to create an effective sexual harassment policy because some people may attack the policy as a special interest policy; this may heighten campus tensions between women and men rather than reducing them. There are several methods that can be used to directly respond to this myth so that it does not have currency on your campus.

It is important to remind people that a good sexual harassment policy benefits men too. First, men can be victims of harassment within an academic setting. Although sexual harassment directed toward men is clearly less common than harassment of women,[14] sexual harassment policies protect the safety of men on campus as well as women. Second, a good sexual harassment policy ensures fair procedures that protect the rights of those accused of harassment, most frequently males.[15] Although false claims of harassment are uncommon, there is great fear that sexual harassment policies will protect the rare individual who files a claim to be vindictive or mean.

Protection of the rights of the accused is a critical component of an effective sexual harassment policy because it guarantees that the policy will be viewed as "fair" and "just" by the entire campus community. A policy that is perceived as fair, and a process for resolving complaints that is perceived as just, are more likely to be used and, therefore, are more likely to be effective. A good sexual harassment policy benefits the entire campus community by clearly outlining prohibited behavior, as well as formal and informal procedures for complaints to be handled. This clarity reduces the likelihood of misunderstanding and grievances along the way. As Ehrlich Martin (1989, p. 72) points out:

> Clear prohibition of sexual harassment is an important first step toward recognition of the problem the latter poses for women. It provides victims with legal redress, establishes employer responsibility, and encourages employees to resist harassment.[16]

Another way to gain support from the campus community is to make the policy as inclusive as possible. Policies that combine other forms of discrimination with sexual harassment may have a better chance of obtaining a broader base of support. At NAU, we developed a common grievance and complaint procedure for all forms of harassment and discrimination to avoid ghettoizing women by defining them as a special group requiring special treatment.[17] Any member of the university community can use the procedures outlined in the policy to resolve discrimination or harassment complaints they may have against others.

Additionally, it is important that all groups on campus have an opportunity to critique the policy before it is approved. Send drafts of the policy to governing groups, administrators, and those likely to implement the policy early on to get advance warning about their concerns.[18] As the policy nears completion, seek approval of governing groups within the campus community to ensure that the document is supported by as many members of the campus community as possible.

At NAU, we made the document available to the entire campus community early on in the process. This made it difficult for opposition to arise later. The document was also sent before the Faculty Senate and the student governing body for approval. Although the process of making changes to accommodate these groups' interests late in the process was sometimes frustrating, the unanimous passage of the policy by both groups increased the legitimacy of the policy and the likelihood that it would be implemented in a way that ensures its effectiveness.

"Sexual Harassment Is Such a Huge and Complex Problem; a New Policy Can't Possibly Make a Difference!"
It would be difficult to dispute the claim that sexual harassment is a huge and complex problem. Indeed, this book makes much the same point. However, it is a myth that a new policy cannot affect the problem of sexual harassment in a significant

way. Many of the advantages of policy change have already been outlined, but a quick summary is in order.

A new policy that is widely distributed as required reading can achieve several ends. It can initiate a campuswide dialogue about an issue that too often is not discussed and, indeed, frequently silences people. The research and expertise accumulated by those working on the policy can form the basis for an educational campaign that can raise awareness about the problem and about potential solutions. In addition, the distribution of a new policy puts people on notice that sexual harassment will not be tolerated, paving the way for an initiative to more strongly enforce laws against sexual harassment.

A new sexual harassment policy, which is up-to-date and reflects current knowledge about the issue, sends a message to some individuals on campus, especially women, that they are valued members of the university community who deserve to be free from hostile working and learning conditions. The importance of this climate for retaining good female faculty and staff members cannot be overstated.[19]

A policy change can also send a message to the campus community that policy is not static. Policies that are not working or are out of date need to be revised, and all policies should be reviewed regularly to ensure that they are relevant for the current context. Because change is a process, it is important to know in advance that you may not get everything you want in the first policy revision. But, because change IS a process, the changes you are able to make may lay a foundation for other changes in the future that can have tremendous impact on the problem of sexual harassment.

Conclusion

In the end, it is true that policies alone rarely make change. But, fortunately, policies rarely occur in isolation. Because policymaking is highly politicized, the success of a policy is typically a reflection of the success of a particular group or coalition of people who sought to have their interests represented in the policy process. Ultimately, policy success depends more on the commitment of those desiring change than the words on a piece of paper. Commitment to change means working to ensure that policies achieve the ends they were meant to achieve. It means monitoring implementation, ensuring campuswide education, remaining vigilant to problems, and retaining a willingness to pursue other avenues if needed. Ultimately, the success of a policy depends on courageous individuals willing to push for change. As Zinn (1994, p. 10) puts it:

> People are practical; they want change but feel powerless, alone, do not want to be the blade of grass that sticks up above the others and is cut down. They wait for a sign from someone else who will make the first move, or the second. And there are intrepid people who, at certain times in history, take the risk, that if they make that first move others will follow quickly enough to prevent their being cut down. And if we understand this, we might make that first move.[20]

I encourage you to make the first move to create a strong sexual harassment policy on your campus; to start a wave of change that others can ride along with you. We owe it to each other, and we owe it to ourselves to work to ensure a safe working and learning environment for all.

Endnotes

1. Membership on the Task Force changed each year. In the end almost all members of the Commission had a hand in "creating" the policy because many editorial and substantive changes were made by both Task Force and Commission members (and, as I will mention later, changes were also made by other groups and individuals within the university community). The work of several individuals, however, was critical to the creation and eventual passage of the policy. These include several Commission chairs—Pat Baron, Mary Ann Steger, and Julie Schimmel; individuals who helped to draft the document, Donna Nelson, Susan Deeds, and Ilana Landes; university president Clara Lovett who approved the policy within a year of her arrival; and Cindy Anderson who, like me, was there from the beginning and there at the end, and without whom, I genuinely believe, the policy would never have been created.

2. James Anderson, *Public policymaking: An introduction*. Boston: Houghton Mifflin, 1990.

3. Michael Parenti, *Democracy for the few* (6th ed.). New York: St. Martin's Press, 1995.

4. Anderson, op. cit.

5. Some of these surveys are reviewed in Michele A. Paludi & Richard B. Barickman (Eds.), *Academic and workplace sexual harassment: A resource manual*. Albany: State University of New York Press, 1991; and in Billie Wright Dziech & Linda Weiner, *The lecherous professor: Sexual harassment on campus*. Chicago: University of Illinois Press, 1990.

6. Arizona Board of Regents' Commission on the Status of Women, "Reaching the Vision: Women in Arizona's Universities in the Year 2000," Phoenix, 1991.

7. Of course, anonymity can be difficult to ensure since stories are often recognized by others. This strategy is only suggested when victims give their permission for their stories to be told and when great care is taken to protect their anonymity.

8. The annual Sociologists Against Sexual Harassment (SASH) conference is excellent for learning about current laws and policies regarding sexual harassment.

9. Thanks to Phoebe Stambaugh for creating this valuable resource. Persons wishing to join the list should contact Sociologists Against Sexual Harassment (SASH-L) at SASH-L%ASUA-CAD.BITNET@cmsa.Berkeley.EDU.

10. Our policy sets a standard that is higher than this minimum. It is important to know that local standards for conduct can exceed the federal standards. For more information about legal issues related to sexual harassment, see Chapter 2 of this book.

11. These included the creation of a deadline within which the affirmative action office must respond to complainants (previously there was no such deadline) and inclusion of sexual orientation as a protected category, along with several other items we believed essential to an effective "Safe Working and Learning Environment" policy.

12. *See* Wright Dziech & Weiner, op. cit.; and Paludi & Barickman, op. cit.

13. Wright Dziech & Weiner, op. cit.

14. Paludi & Barickman, op. cit.

15. Paludi & Barickman, op. cit.

16. Susan Ehrlich Martin, Sexual harassment: The link joining gender stratification, sexuality, and women's economic status. In Jo Freeman (Ed.), *Women: A feminist perspective*. Mountain View, CA: Mayfield Publishing, 1989.

17. Wright Dziech & Weiner, op. cit., argue that this ghettoizing effect is common with sexual harassment policies. Although some would argue that sexual harassment IS a unique phenomena requiring a separate policy, it is my view that the BEST policy for each university or college will depend on the local context; for some contexts a policy focusing only on sexual harassment may be best, for others a more comprehensive policy may be best.

18. Ideally, the draft should be relatively polished before distribution to the campus community to minimize speculative objections, as well as time-consuming editorial work by others. Drafts should be accompanied by

materials supporting controversial points with documentation, where possible.

19. Martin, op. cit.

20. Howard Zinn, *You can't be neutral on a moving train: A personal history of our times.* Boston: Beacon Press, 1994.

8

FORMAL COMPLAINTS

ELSA KIRCHER COLE

An institution may decide to use its formal complaint process to resolve an allegation of sexual harassment for several reasons. The alleged victim or the institution's complaint administrator may be dissatisfied with the progress a complaint is making in the institution's informal complaint process or the outcome of that process. The type of disciplinary punishment available under the informal complaint procedure may be too limited to satisfy the alleged victim. The institution itself may feel strong sanctions are necessary, wish to pursue a formal complaint to demonstrate the importance it attaches to complaints of sexual harassment, or want to warn potential harassers of the severe consequences of such behavior.

Creating a Formal Complaint Procedure

In creating a system to handle formal complaints, the institution should consider if a single procedure is best to handle complaints against all segments of the campus community, or if different elements of that community are best served by having separate complaint procedures. In part, this may be determined by existing institution procedures for handling complaints of misconduct, such as procedures for removal of tenured faculty, that have to be followed or included in a formal complaint process. If faculty or staff are unionized, their union agreements may dictate what procedures must be used.

It is not necessary to have a single, institutionwide procedure for handling formal complaints of sexual harassment, but having several different procedures can create confusion and uncertainty for what may already be a reluctant complainant. To the extent that formal complaint procedures against faculty, staff, and students can be harmonized with each other, it is more likely they will be perceived as encouraging the reporting of sexual harassment activity.

In drafting complaint procedures, care must be given to respecting the rights of all parties—the alleged victim, the alleged harasser, and witnesses who may be brought in willingly or unwillingly—involved in such proceedings. At public institutions, the procedures must also provide for basic due process. *Basic due pro-*

cess means that before disciplinary action is taken, the alleged harasser is given adequate and timely notice of what the allegations are and an opportunity to respond to them before some neutral and unbiased individual or panel. Private institutions may, through their internal policies, have guaranteed equivalent due process protections to their students, faculty, and staff that need to be considered in drafting procedures. Beyond these basics, the complexity of the procedures should be governed by balancing the need for a thorough, fair investigation and hearing, and the duty to act promptly to resolve complaints.

The Intake Process

A complainant should be able to easily find out from the institution's procedures which office or offices at the institution can receive formal complaints. Often, it takes a long time for a person to become ready to come to such an office with a complaint, and therefore it is important not to hurry the complainant when he or she finally comes in to talk to someone. Complaint administrators should be trained to allow ample time for the intake process.

The complainant should be assured at the outset of the intake process that the institution has a strong policy of disciplining those who retaliate or threaten to retaliate against someone who has filed a complaint, and that it will do so in this case. The intake administrator should explain the way a complaint is processed and the time needed to complete each step.

No promises of absolute confidentiality should be given. Instead, it should be explained that, to the extent permitted by law, only those with a need to know will be shown the complaint, but that includes the accused. The complainant should be advised that if the accused contests any disciplinary action that is the result of the complaint, it is likely that the complainant will have to testify about the allegations in a hearing at the college or university and be cross examined about them. Moreover, the alleged harasser does not have to keep the accusation confidential. This information should be given in as supportive a way as possible. Although what has to be conveyed can be intimidating, it must be said. It is a misuse of everyone's time and institutional resources to conduct a formal investigation if the institution knows it will be unable to take disciplinary action at its conclusion because its chief witness will be unwilling to stand behind his or her accusations when necessary. If that is the situation, alternative methods short of a formal complaint to resolve the harassment must be used.

The complainant should be required to put his or her formal complaint in writing and to sign it, affirming the truth of the statements made. Writing down allegations helps to clarify them so that the investigator of the complaint knows what to examine and the alleged harasser has fair notice of what the accusations are in order to be able to prepare a defense. The written statement should be prepared by the complainant, but the complaint administrator can assist if there are literacy or communication problems. If the administrator helps to draft the complaint, care should obviously be taken that the administrator's own perception of the allegations does not color the statements. When completed, the complainant should always read a complaint carefully, and, as stated before, sign it and affirm that the statements within it are true.

Most institutional procedures require that complaints be filed within a certain amount of time after the incident in question occurred, generally, within six months to a year. This is to prevent the passage of too much time between the incident and its investigation, which can result in memory losses, departure of key witnesses, and destruction of evidence, any of which can prevent a complete investigation and a fair opportunity for the alleged harasser to defend against the allegations.

If a complaint appears on its face to be untimely, it is first necessary to be certain when the last incident occurred. If the complaint still appears to be untimely, it may be possible, under some policies, to expand the normal time limit to file complaints because of unusual circumstances such as a student being in an overseas program or a faculty member being on sabbatical. If this is not possible and the complaint appears to be valid, then the institution needs to determine what mechanism it has available, other than the formal complaint process, to address the incident.

The untimeliness of a complaint does not mean an institution can do nothing about apparent inappropriate behavior. The alleged harasser can still be confronted with his or her actions and warned not to continue them and the harasser's unit can receive educational training about the institution's policies against sexual harassment. A sealed envelope can also be placed in the alleged harasser's file in the complaint administrator's office, not to be opened unless there are new allegations of sexual harassment against him or her.

The Investigation

If a complaint appears timely, the investigation of it should begin as soon as possible. It is critical that the investigation of a formal complaint be fair and thorough. Objective and comprehensive investigations prevent unfair results for all parties involved. Additionally, they demonstrate the institution's commitment to eliminate sexual harassment. They also limit the chance that the institution will be held to have been negligent in its investigation or to have failed to take prompt corrective action for behavior that it knew or should have known was taking place.

Note that sometimes, in addition to filing a formal complaint with an institution, a complainant will file a separate complaint about the sexual harassment with an agency external to the institution, such as the Equal Employment Opportunity Commission (EEOC), the Office for Civil Rights (OCR) of the U.S. Department of Education, or a state human rights agency; some even file a lawsuit in a state or federal court. The fact that an outside civil rights agency is investigating a matter or that litigation is proceeding must not be the reason to stop the campus' independent investigation or to not hold a hearing if disciplinary action is proposed. To do so is considered retaliation for filing the complaint or action and is a violation of law.

The investigation of a formal complaint on campus can be done by an individual, several individuals, or a committee. Although there may be political reasons why an institution decides to use investigatory committees, such as lack of trust in the sexual harassment procedure or those administering it, generally it is preferable to use a few trained individuals rather than committees for several reasons. First, investigators must be very knowledgeable about sexual harassment, how to conduct an investigation, and how to determine the credibility of parties and witnesses. It is difficult and time-consuming to train a large number of people to do this well, especially if a new committee is formed for each investigation. Second, it is hard to give a large group sufficient, frequent experience in conducting investigations for them to gain the expertise necessary to do an effective investigation. Third, investigations need to be conducted promptly, and it is not easy to assemble a large group of people quickly or often given their other time commitments and obligations. Lastly, because consistency in methods and approaches is important in validating a sexual harassment investigatory procedure, using the same team of investigators over and over again is preferable to large committees whose members only occasionally are called on to serve in an investigatory capacity.

Although a single investigator may conduct an excellent investigation, an investigatory team with both sexes represented may be advantageous because men and women can have different viewpoints about the nature of sexual harassment and some people will react differently to males and females in interviews. Investigators should be individuals with sufficient autonomy and stature within the institution so that they have credibility with the campus community. They have to be people who can make tough decisions, including the truthfulness of the parties and the witnesses. They should be skilled at asking the type of questions that extract needed information from reluctant individuals. Good investigators know that they are neutral and represent the institution, not the alleged victim or the alleged harasser. They do not come to any conclusion until the investigation is complete. They refer alleged victims to counseling, if needed, and do not attempt to perform that role themselves.

To begin an investigation, investigators need to set up a confidential file. They should prepare their strategy, including identifying the issues to be decided, the witnesses to be interviewed and in what order, and what documents to collect. Although relevant documents may include records from the personnel or student files of the alleged harasser and alleged victim, care must be taken not to prejudge the validity of the complaint based on information contained therein. The investigators should proceed with open minds and should be prepared to modify their investigation plan as the investigation moves along.

From the beginning, investigators should create their investigatory file with the assumption that everything in it might be subject to disclosure some day, perhaps as part of discovery in a lawsuit against the institution or, at another public institution, because of a public records or freedom-of-information request. Therefore, the file should be an accurate reflection of the investigation, but should not contain extraneous information such as personal conjectures or speculations about the facts or witnesses. The investigators' notes should be factual and not venture opinions. Additionally, investigators must be conscious and consistent from the onset of the file's creation about keeping its contents private and confidential. Allowing those who do not have a need to know the file's contents or to read it may lead to charges of defamation by the alleged harasser against those who shared the file.

Investigators need to notify the alleged harasser of the complaint, but generally this will follow notification of the appropriate campus administrators in order to alert them to be watchful so as to prevent any retaliation by the harasser once he or she learns of the complaint. The formal complaint procedures may describe which administrators have to be notified. If not, generally the institution's affirmative action officer, the alleged harasser's supervisor, and the unit head or dean should be told. If the matter involves faculty or staff, the appropriate human resources officer should be notified, if students, the student affairs administrator. The institution's central repository of statistics on such complaints ought to be informed of the complaint as well. Those notified should be told that it is inappropriate for them to interfere in the ongoing investigation or to discuss the investigation with others, and that they should keep an open mind about the allegations until the conclusion of the investigation. They also must prevent any retaliation from occurring. Should they observe any retaliation, they should be advised to report it to the investigators or someone else in authority.

When informing the alleged harasser's supervisor of the complaint, it is important that he or she understand that no disciplining of the alleged harasser is appropriate until the investigation is complete and the alleged harasser has had an opportunity to be heard on the issues. Depending on the nature of the complaint and the alleged harasser's day-to-day interaction with the complainant, or those in a similarly vulnerable situation, the supervisor may have to relocate the alleged harasser or assign him or her different duties within the same job classification until the completion of the investigation and hearing. The supervisor should be told to inform the investigators and complaint administrator should it become apparent that retaliation against the complainant is occurring.

Immediately after informing the appropriate administrators and the alleged harasser's supervisor, the alleged harasser should be notified that a complaint, which alleges sexual harassment, has been filed against him or her and that a formal investigation of the allegations will occur. The alleged harasser should be given a copy of the complaint, as well as a copy of the institution's policy against sexual harassment. He or she should be warned about retaliating against the complainant in any way, be given examples of retaliation, and told to have no unnecessary contact with the person. An early interview date should be arranged as well; then, the investigation should begin. Chapter 10 contains a complete discussion of how to conduct the investigation.

During the investigation of the formal complaint, the complainant should be asked what resolution of the matter he or she would like to have occur and the file should reflect the complainant's response, but no promises that a particular resolution will occur should be made. Because complainants often suffer from stress, the complainant should be asked if he or she would like to use the institution's employee or student counseling center. If he or she declines, that should be documented in the file to protect the institution later against possible claims of emotional distress by the complainant.

After conducting interviews with the alleged harasser, the complainant, and any witnesses and the gathering of relevant documents, the evidence must be reviewed. At some schools, the investigators do this; at others, the investigators give the information gathered to an administrator or panel for the review. The institution's procedures may say that reviewers are to use the preponderance of the evidence standard to review what the investigators have gathered, that is, whether it is more likely than not that sexual harassment occurred; or an institution may use the higher clear and convincing evidence standard to conduct the review. The reviewers must decide whether they can make a good faith determination, based on the relevant evidence standard, that sufficient cause exists to discipline the alleged harasser for sexual harassment.

If there are questions of party or witness credibility, the reviewers must look for corroborating evidence such as whether any witness saw the alleged event or any changes in behavior of either party that occurred thereafter, and whether the complainant told anyone about it and when. Internal inconsistencies must be examined. The reviewers should consider when the complaint was made in relation to the alleged harassment and, if there was a delay, what events might explain it. They should obviously pay particular attention to the existence of other complaints against the accused.

The institution's legal counsel should be consulted at this point if the alleged incident is serious or if there are legal issues needing resolution. The institution's human resources department should be consulted about the appropriate level of discipline, which is consistent with the past disciplinary practices for similar incidents of harassment, to recommend.

Post-Investigation Actions

Whether an institution's procedures provide that the investigators are empowered to make a conclusion as to whether sexual harassment occurred, or if they are only to pass the information along to others, the investigators should prepare a written report. If the reviewers of the investigation's evidence find it inconclusive, the final report of the investigation should so state, but it should also say that serious allegations were made and, if similar allegations occur in the future, appropriate action will be taken. If sexual harassment is believed to have occurred, under some institution's policies, the reviewers of the evidence are authorized to recommend action to correct the situation, disciplinary or otherwise, to the appropriate administrator. Under other institutions' procedures, that recommendation comes from a different administrator or panel.

A copy of the report should be sent to the same people who were alerted to the original complaint with instructions not to duplicate the report or share it with anyone other than someone with a legitimate need to know its contents. A copy of it should be kept in a central repository of such complaints. Separate meetings with the alleged harasser and complainant should then occur. In the meeting with the complainant, he or she should be told whether the allegations have been substantiated and what corrective action is recommended. The complainant should again be told that any retaliatory acts against him or her should be reported, as well as any further acts of sexual harassment.

Some institutions' procedures allow for the investigators' report itself to be given to the complainant, others allow it only to be read but not copied for the complainant, and others just allow a written summary of the report to be given to the complainant. In all of these cases, it should be stressed to the complainant that in order to respect the privacy rights of all concerned, the results of the investigation should not be shared beyond those who need to know, or the small number of friends and family who have been the complainant's support group. The institution should then document in writing how it informed the complainant of the outcome of the report and a copy of what it shared with the complainant should be placed in the investigatory file.

When the investigators meet with the alleged harasser, they should share the results of the investigation with him or her and document that they have done so. If the investigators could not determine whether sexual harassment occurred, they should warn the alleged harasser that if such charges are serious and if similar ones are received again, the appearance of a pattern of harassment will be weighed heavily against him or her. As with the complainant, it should be stressed to the alleged harasser that in order to respect the privacy rights of all concerned, the results of the investigation should not be shared beyond those who need to know, or the small number of friends and family who have been his or her support group. Because an inconclusive result may seem to be a lack of commitment to eradicating sexual harassment, the administration may wish to schedule a workshop for the alleged harasser's unit to demonstrate the administration's continuing concern about sexual harassment. To ensure good attendance, the administration could announce that those not present will be held to know everything about sexual harassment covered at the workshop.

If there is not sufficient cause to believe sexual harassment occurred, the administration should take appropriate steps to restore the reputation of the alleged harasser. Such steps should include informing all of those involved in or notified of the investigation that sufficient cause was not found. In such a situation as well, a workshop might be held to educate the alleged harasser's unit about the subject and to demonstrate commitment to ending sexual harassment on campus.

If it is determined there is reasonable cause to believe sexual harassment has occurred, the institution must take prompt remedial action reasonably calculated to end the harassment and to inform the complainant what steps it is taking. For example, if the complainant resigned his or her job because of the harassment, the institution should consider making an unconditional offer of reinstatement. Such an offer should expressly state that acceptance does not waive the complainant's right to pursue legal claims, or else it will not prevent the complainant's claims for back wages and future compensation from continuing.

If the alleged harasser is the complainant's supervisor and he or she is not going to be terminated, the complainant's reporting relationship needs to be changed. Alternatively, a substantially equivalent job should be offered the complainant or the alleged harasser may need to be moved elsewhere in the organization. To remedy harassment of a student by a faculty member, the alleged harasser needs to be removed from any position of authority over the student. This may mean, for example, taking the harasser off of the complainant's dissertation committee and adding a different faculty member instead, even if it has to be someone from another institution. It may mean accepting a substitute class for degree requirements rather than the one taught by the alleged harasser or having a different faculty member grade the complainant's work in a course. Counseling for the student can also be offered. Such corrective actions may be seen as the institution admitting sexual harassment occurred. However, that risk must be weighed against the likelihood that the institution will be exposed to greater liability if it does nothing to remedy a bad situation.

In all the above situations, it is the harasser's unit head or dean rather than the investigator or complaint administrator who should decide what the appropriate sanction is for the alleged harassment. Although termination may be the correct sanction for the severest sexual harassment, a unit head or dean has other disciplinary actions available to deal with less egregious forms of sexual harassment. These include written reprimands, salary reductions, denial of sabbatical or other leave, demotions to nonsupervisory positions, placement on probation, reassignments, transfers, and suspensions.

In situations where the matter investigated was harassing speech or ambiguous physical actions, an oral or written warning to the alleged harasser may be sufficient to remedy the situation. A written warning has the advantage of clearly recording what the harasser has been told to do and what to change. Such a written warning should say that a complaint has been made concerning behavior by the alleged harasser that was inappropriate, abusive, unwelcome, and possibly illegal. This warning should contain, if possible, references to the institution's own standard of conduct and the ethical standards of behavior of the alleged harasser's profession. The alleged harasser should be warned that if the behavior is repeated, disciplinary action, up to termination, will occur. The letter should describe the federal and state laws that such conduct violates and alert him or her that he or she could be sued for such behavior. The alleged harasser should be encouraged to examine his or her conduct and to take actions to ensure that no ethical, legal, or professional standards are being violated.

A letter stating that the alleged harasser will be severely disciplined if he or she engages in a future incident of sexual harassment may be appropriate. Such a "last chance" letter usually is preceded by a face-to-face meeting with the alleged harasser to discuss the behavior and to tell him or her that any further incident will result in a specifically named disciplinary action. Such a letter may say the institution expects the alleged harasser to seek professional, medical assistance and to follow any treatment plan prescribed. It could say that failure to do so will be a factor heavily weighed against the alleged harasser should another incident occur. Including a recommendation that medical treatment be sought forestalls the alleged harasser from using a medical condition, such as alcoholism, as an excuse if a subsequent incident occurs.

Similarly, while required counseling is generally not a disciplinary sanction that can be ordered, nor should it alone ever be a sanction, in a last chance letter the institution can say that a lesser disciplinary sanction will be imposed if the alleged harasser seeks counseling and follows through on recommended treatment. The alleged harasser's failure to do so should preclude the institution from having to offer counseling as a remedy should another incident of sexual harassment occur with the same individual.

If termination is the appropriate sanction, it is preferable for the supervising administrator, unit head, dean, or legal counsel to announce this in a face-to-face meeting with the alleged harasser. In such a meeting, the alleged harasser needs to be informed about the results of the investigation and how his or her behavior violated the institution's policy and/or state or federal law. If requested, the alleged harasser's attorney can attend such a meeting. Often, the attorney will be much more realistic than the harasser about the appropriateness of the sanction and can convince his or her client about the wisdom of accepting it.

Resignations

At the end of the investigation or soon afterward, the alleged harasser may offer to resign rather than be terminated. Generally, an institution is willing to accept a resignation because it guarantees the individual will no longer be employed and in a position to harass someone else. Failure to accept a resignation runs the risk that a court will disagree that adequate cause existed for it, resulting in monetary damages and the chance of additional claims, such as defamation, being brought against the institution and its administrators.

It is preferable to have the complainant acknowledge in writing that resignation is an acceptable resolution of the matter. The alleged harasser should be told that a condition of the institution's accepting the resignation will be a letter in his or her personnel file stating that he or she resigned while an allegation of sexual harassment was pending, and that the letter will be sent to anyone requesting a letter of recommendation about the alleged harasser. The alleged harasser's personnel file should also contain a copy of the investigation report.

As a condition of accepting the resignation, an institution should obtain a waiver from the alleged harasser of all claims he or she has against the institution as of the date of the resignation agreement. In addition, it is often wise to have a provision regarding what will be said publicly by either side about the resignation. Sometimes such provisions say that nothing will be said publicly and that any questions will be referred to the human resources department, which will divulge only the dates of employment, titles held, and the fact that the person resigned. If this is preferred by the institution, careful consideration should be given as to how the institution will handle inquiries if the matter is leaked to the media, as it might be by a complainant. The complainant should be informed about the alleged harasser's resignation but cannot be required to maintain confidentiality.

If the alleged harasser does not or is not allowed to resign and a disciplinary sanction is recommended, at a public institution the alleged harasser must be informed of his or her procedural rights, and the institution should document that this has been done. At a public college or university, alleged harassers, whether students or employees, have a right to a hearing before disciplinary action is imposed, unless the individual is in a probationary period or at the end of his or her contract of employment with the institution. Private colleges and universities, through their personnel or disciplinary procedures, union contracts, or sexual harassment policies, may have also committed to having a hearing prior to implementation of discipline.

Mediation

Before going to a hearing, a determination should be made by the parties and the institution as to whether mediation is appropriate to resolve the matter. Mediation may be preferable to a hearing because it generally is a shorter process and is not as adversarial. The complainant may be able to get the harassing behavior stopped and the alleged harasser avoids the publicity a hearing can bring. The institution benefits from a prompt resolution of a sexual harassment complaint. Mediation can only be successful if there is some agreement between the parties as to what occurred between them. If there is a dispute about material facts, the formal hearing route is probably the one that should be pursued (see Chapter 11).

If mediation is successful, the institution needs to document the agreement between the parties and do follow-ups after certain periods of time—one week, one month, and six months—to be certain that the agreed remedy has ended the harassment and there have been no retaliatory acts. If the mediation fails, the next step in the formal process is the drafting of the notice to the alleged harasser that outlines the allegations and the proposed disciplinary sanction, and also informs both parties that a formal disciplinary hearing will be conducted.

Notice and Hearing

The notice of the allegations and proposed sanctions can be drafted by the investigator, the complaint administrator, the institution's attorney, a personnel officer, or the unit head or dean. It should be signed by the unit head or dean, however. The notice should describe the allegations with sufficient specificity that the alleged harasser knows what the accusations are in order to prepare a response, if he or she chooses to make one. A good way to do this is to state the work rule or conduct policy section that the alleged harasser is believed to have violated and the evidence that exists to support the allegation. The person who drafts the notice should also specifically reserve the right to amend it later if additional allegations are discovered or received prior to the hearing.

After the notice is served on the alleged harasser, either in person or by certified mail, return receipt requested, the next step is to proceed to the hearing. The institution should choose a hearing date that allows the alleged harasser a reasonable amount of time to prepare a defense. Generally, the length of time varies, depending on the seriousness of the offense and the penalty proposed. The Policies and Procedures Manual of a college or university may describe in great detail when the hearing is to be held and how it is to be conducted. It may, however, merely outline the "bare bones" of a hearing procedure.

One of the first decisions for a college or university to make is who the parties to the hearing will be. Generally, it is preferable for the institution, or the unit head or dean, to be the party bringing the charges rather than the complaining witness. It can be too intimidating for the complainant to have to present the case and to feel responsible for the effect of the disciplinary action.

The institution's procedures manual usually will determine whether a hearing officer or a hearing panel will conduct the disciplinary hearing. Whichever is used, the officer or panel needs to be knowledgeable about sexual harassment laws. If more education on this subject is necessary, it should be done before the hearing by someone who is independent of any preparing of the evidence against the alleged harasser. Additionally, the hearing officer or panel should be educated about the procedures to be followed, what is admissible evidence, and the standard of proof that must be met by the college or university administrator—generally, a preponderance of the evidence standard, but some institutions may chose the higher clear and convincing standard. The hearing officer or panel must also decide whether hearsay will be allowed, if witnesses will be excluded except when testifying, and who can be present from both sides during the hearing.

Before the hearing begins, the hearing officer or committee should resolve any procedural issues such as the timeliness or sufficiency of the complaint, challenges to the hearing officer's or panel members' ability to hear the matter, witness logistics, and evidence disputes. The officer or panel also should determine if the hearing is to be opened to the public and to what extent anyone is allowed to discuss the hearing. Generally, to avoid the possibility of comments resulting in defamation claims, a "gag" order is preferable. The gag order should be invoked against the parties for the duration of the hearing, and it can be invoked against the institution's employees forever.

The institution's policy should be clear about the degree to which attorneys may participate in the hearing—to be present just to advise, but not speak on behalf of the client, which is all due process requires, or to have a more active role. If the institution's procedures are silent about this, the hearing officer or panel should rule on this before the hearing begins. Generally, if significant disciplinary sanctions may occur, participation in the hearing by attorneys in some fashion is allowed. Such participation is more likely to result in the perception that the hearing was fair if challenged later in court and may prevent a challenge altogether.

The hearing officer or panel also must decide the mechanics of the hearing—who sits where, and whether the hearing will be taped or if a court reporter will be hired. The officer or panel should also be responsible for ensuring the presence of witnesses deemed necessary to the proceeding.

The most important evidence at the hearing will be the testimony of the complainant and the alleged harasser's denial or explanation of events. The credibility of these two individuals is an essential determination for the officer or panel to make. Corroborating evidence from coworkers, fellow students, or others might assist in determining credibility. In making that determination, the officer or panel should also consider such things as the timing and nature of the complaint, whether the complainant's behavior changed after the event, the alleged harasser's prior conduct with regard to issues of sexual harassment, and the general sexual atmosphere in the complainant's workplace or academic setting. Character evidence usually is not helpful in determining credibility. Of more use is expert testimony as to whether the complainant's behavior was consistent with that of a sexual harassment victim. The officer or panel should also determine if a reasonable person would be offended by the alleged behavior.

During the hearing, the administrator representing the institution, or the attorney assisting him or her, should keep the complainant and the institution's witnesses informed as to the progress of the hearing if they are not allowed to be present. This often means frequent meetings or calls so that frustration does not occur over the length of time that the hearing may take. It also means exercising discretion as to how much sensitive information to divulge—enough that the relevant individuals feel informed, but not so much that they can intentionally or unintentionally disclose to others information damaging to the institution or anyone else.

At the conclusion of the hearing, it is helpful to the hearing officer or panel to receive a written summary prepared by each party outlining how the evidence and witness testimony supports that party's position. The officer or panel may also find it useful to have each side prepare draft findings of fact and conclusions. The desirability of such written materials, however, should be weighed against the fairness of requiring them if the parties have unequal experience or skills in preparing written materials. For example, it is highly unlikely that a student complainant who presents his or her own case will have the same skills as an attorney representing an alleged harasser, and a hearing officer or panel may wish to forego written summaries, findings, and conclusions in such a situation.

The hearing officer or panel will then determine if harassment occurred, and, if so, depending on the institution's policy, if the sanction proposed by the unit head or dean should be imposed or if a different one should occur. A college's or university's procedures may make the decision of the hearing officer or panel the final one or procedures may allow for an appeal to a senior administrator or the institution's board.

Role of a University or College Legal Counsel

Throughout this entire process, from investigation through hearing, consultation with the institution's legal counsel is essential. In particular, legal counsel should be consulted if there is the potential of threats, stalking, or intimidation of the alleged victim or witnesses. If any of the parties retains an attorney, legal counsel should be apprised of that because it may affect the way reports are written or procedures are explained. Additionally, counsel needs to be involved early in any case where the nature of the sexual harassment is particularly serious or where litigation may result. The institution should consult with its legal counsel whenever First Amendment rights of free speech, freedom of association, or academic freedom issues could be affected by the institution's actions. It is also extremely important to keep legal counsel alerted to the investigative and hearing procedures contemplated to avoid any due process problems.

Long before any incident occurs, the institution's sexual harassment policies and procedures should be reviewed by counsel for their legal soundness. In particular, counsel should make sure that the policy or procedures are realistic in what they commit the institution to do such as the degree to which confidentiality is promised, or how soon they say the institution will hold a hearing and render a decision in a matter. Such statements form the basis of a contract between the institution and the complainant, as well as one between the institution and the alleged harasser. Failure of an institution to comply with its own policies or procedures can provide the basis for a successful breach-of-contract action or other action against the institution by the complainant or the alleged harasser.

Once a sexual harassment complaint is made, legal counsel should be available as the facts develop to discuss what their legal consequences are. It may be advisable to consult with the institution's attorney about the sufficiency of the evidence uncovered in the investigation and to receive suggestions about what additional information is needed to decide if cause exists to recommend a disciplinary sanction. The particular sanction to be chosen is also an area where legal input can be helpful.

It is not recommended that legal counsel conduct the actual investigation. Although there may be some initial appeal to cloaking the investigation with the attorney–client privilege or protecting it from discovery under the attorney work-product rule, it is likely that a court would order that the results of the investigation be turned over to the alleged harasser anyway. Even more important, if the attorney acts as investigator, he or she might have to become a witness in any subsequent hearing and therefore statements made to him or her during the course of the investigation would lose the attorney–client privilege. Additionally, an attorney investigator would not be available to act as the institution's counsel in the hearing.

After the investigation concludes, if the incident's resolution includes a negotiated agreement between the institution and the alleged harasser, the attorney should review that agreement and any letters of resignation or recommendation that are part of the resolution of the matter. If, instead, a disciplinary action is contemplated, legal counsel should review the notice of disciplinary action to the alleged harasser from the unit head or dean for completeness.

The institution must avoid giving an attorney conflicting roles during the hearing process. Although the same legal counsel can provide advice to the investigator and the unit head or dean, that attorney cannot also be counsel to the hearing officer or panel, or counsel to reviewing administrators or boards. Each of those decision makers needs separate legal counsel to preserve the appearance of fairness and to avoid a conflict-of-interest situation. Even though, in some situations, this may mean additional expense for the institution, to not do so risks having a court invalidate the whole procedure and order the institution to start all over again at great cost in time as well as money.

It is preferable to have attorneys who will play the different roles in the investigation and/or hearing from different law offices or firms to avoid any appearance of impropriety. However, if it is not possible to do this, courts have allowed attorneys from the institution's legal office or the same law firm to have different roles in a disciplinary proceeding as long as "chinese walls" are maintained within the office or law firm; that is, the attorneys who have these different roles do not speak or communicate in any way with each other about the matter throughout its pendency.

Dealing with the Media

Another important role played throughout the investigative and hearing process is that of media spokesperson. Dealing effectively with the media during an investigation, hearing, and resolution of a sexual harassment complaint can be extremely demanding. Because both the alleged harasser and complainant have privacy rights, the institution will be limited in what it can reveal about the way it has handled a matter.

In these situations, it is best for the institution to appoint a single spokesperson to handle all media inquiries regarding a particular event. This ensures that the information the institution can reveal will be uniform and consistent. The institution may also wish to have different spokespersons designated to deal with different types of harassment situations (e.g., student-to-student, faculty-to-student, staff-to-staff), or different types of harassment (e.g., sexual assault versus sexually offensive remarks in the classroom). People involved with the complaint process should be told to refer all questions to the media spokesperson.

The spokesperson should know what the institution's public relations objectives are as it deals with a sexual harassment matter. He or she should know which media best reach the audience for each objective and how to tailor his or her actions and remarks to best impact that audience. The spokesperson should establish a reputation for openness and candor with the media. However, the spokesperson must not unknowingly volunteer information and should not speculate or guess about facts. The spokesperson should understand that nothing is ever truly "off the record" and that he or she should be quoted only if it is clear for whom he or she is speaking.

The spokesperson should avoid saying "no comment"; this is overused and seldom advances any institution's objective. At the least, the institution can say it takes sexual harassment very seriously and can describe the process for reviewing a complaint if it cannot discuss the facts. There are times when the spokesperson can say that commenting would just be speculating or inappropriate. The spokesperson should know that every question does not have to be answered and sometimes none should be. There may be times when, because the amount of adverse publicity is so great, the institution will choose to take some risk and reveal more of the facts in a matter. This needs to be done only after consultation with legal counsel and a careful assessment of the risk of incurring a defamation lawsuit.

Negotiated Resolutions

At some point during the formal complaint process, and sometimes before, the administration may determine that it best serves the needs of the institution to enter into an agreement with the alleged harasser to resolve the matter before completing the investigative or hearing process.[1] Alternatively, the alleged harasser may approach the institution with such a proposal. In negotiating an effective agreement, several things must be kept in mind.

First, the institution must have a clear idea about which terms it believes are essential, which are preferable or desirable, and which are not as important and therefore may be negotiated or traded for more important provisions. The institution should know the complainant's views on settlement and, to the extent possible or practicable, include them in its settlement proposal. To facilitate effective negotiation, a good first proposal will contain some of each type of the terms described here.

Generally, an institution should take the position that it is willing to listen to reasonable settlement offers. A reasonable offer is one that reflects the seriousness of the alleged incident. Its attractiveness will also be measured by whether or not the institution is anxious to settle. Sometimes, even though an offer is reasonable, it will be refused because the institution wishes to make a particular point or example of the discipline of the alleged harasser by following the formal complaint process through to completion.

Sometimes a settlement will involve the payment of money by the institution to a complainant or alleged harasser, such as when one or both have filed a lawsuit against the institution and the institution believes it has liability or when an institution wishes to buy out an alleged harasser to get rid of him or her without litigation.[2] In negotiating an agreement that includes a monetary settlement, it is rarely a good idea to begin negotiations by offering the most money the institution is willing to pay. It usually is assumed there will be a counteroffer and perhaps several further offers before agreement on the size of the settlement. Sometimes negotiations begin with the institution making a very low offer and receiving a very high counteroffer. The parties, then, demand that each other be serious about the negotiations, and some real numbers begin to appear.

To be a credible negotiator for the institution, it is good to have from the outset of negotiations an explanation as to how the institution arrived at the dollar offer made to the alleged harasser. For example, if the institution wants to have the alleged harasser leave its employment but it knows it has some weaknesses in its case, its offer might include the institution's assessment of the alleged harasser's out-of-pocket losses, such as income that will not be earned, benefits lost, or medical bills incurred, over a reasonable period of time. A credible explanation of how the amount offered was computed may make the offer more palatable to the alleged harasser. The institution should likewise demand an explanation of how the alleged harasser arrived at the figure he or she is seeking. This explanation will then provide points of attack for the institution to use to whittle the number down.

The parties may be so far apart that it is not possible to reach closure on an agreement. Sometimes, if a little time passes, the negotiations can begin again. Often, it is best for the institution to wait until the alleged harasser is feeling more vulnerable, which may occur as the date of the hearing approaches, publicity increases, or attorney fees mount up. These same factors may also be pushing the institution to settle so that the negotiator may receive more flexibility from the institution in the terms it requires. The institution should avoid making empty threats. To some extent, bravado is important in negotiations, but bluffing is generally inadvisable because it is very risky.

A good agreement should resolve all issues arising out of the alleged harasser's relationship with the institution up to the date of the agreement. Because particular state laws may govern the degree to which the institution can be released from liability, the institution's attorney should review the agreement before it is signed. Generally, however, the agreement should state that the alleged harasser releases the institution and all its employees, officers, and agents from any liability for any cause of action or complaint arising out of the incidents that occasioned the agreement. If money is to be paid, it should be clearly stated in the agreement that the amount negotiated satisfies all monetary amounts owed by the institution to the alleged harasser, including his or her attorney's fees.

The agreement should state that if either party breaches it, that party will be responsible for all court costs and fees incurred in the enforcement of the agreement. The agreement usually should also specify what information will be released to the media; prospective employers; or institutions about the alleged harasser, the agreement, and the incidents that occasioned it. The institution should carefully consider what information it is agreeing not to disclose because any release of it without the other party's permission will be a breach of the agreement. Thus, for example, if the institution wants to publicize how it resolved an incident of sexual harassment, it should be sure it has left itself the opportunity to do so under the language of the agreement.[3]

Conclusion

Whether a formal complaint of sexual harassment is resolved through negotiation, mediation, or completion of a formal hearing and appeal, the time and energy required to deal appropriately and thoughtfully with such an allegation is immense. Those dealing with a complaint need to be realistic about the time commitment required to do a thorough and complete job and arrange their schedules accordingly. The time-and-energy commitment is made more difficult by the fact that there is seldom a resolution to a formal complaint of sexual harassment that satisfies all the individuals involved. Those dealing with such a complaint, therefore, must be content with meeting their own expectations as to whether a good investigation was conducted and a fair and complete hearing occurred.

Endnotes

1. The term "alleged harasser" is used for convenience in this section although at the point a negotiated agreement is contemplated there may have been a finding that harassment did occur.
2. The institution should weigh the possibility of negative publicity should the monetary payment be made known, something that can be beyond the institutions' control, despite an agreement to keep it secret. At one institution when word of a $40,000 payment to an alleged harasser became public, the campus "joke" became "$40,000 for sexual harassment; how much for a rape?"
3. It is important that the agreement allow the complainant to know the key elements of the agreement. Otherwise the complainant is likely to feel that "nothing happened" or that the institutional response was inadequate. Sometimes negotiating a separate agreement with the complainant is helpful.

9

INFORMAL COMPLAINTS

ANNE TRUAX

Introduction

An informal complaint is any method of resolving a sexual harassment complaint which does not utilize the institution's formal grievance procedure. The complaint may be settled in a single meeting or may have to involve the assistance and cooperation of several people. It includes instances in which complainants decide to handle the problem themselves. Sometimes a complainant is content in the knowledge that he or she has called the bad behavior to the attention of authorities, believing that if there is another complaint against this person the previous record may stand as corroboration. The institution still has the obligation to stop the behavior even if the complainant is content to let things ride. Complainants may decide to handle matters themselves, by writing a letter or by confronting the harasser, with or without an advocate by their side. Some campuses have dispute-resolution services, which provide assistance in mediation for students or even between employees (see Chapter 11).

The advent of a sexual harassment complaint brings into play complicated human interactions which involve more than the complainant and the respondent. Accusations of sexual harassment can arouse strong feelings in others as they empathize with either principal or worry about their roles in the resolution of the complaint. To help restore the department or classroom to a more favorable atmosphere, the person working to find a solution must take the broadest possible view of the situation.

It is almost always preferable to handle a complaint informally, if possible. Informality allows for greater flexibility in how the matter is approached and resolved. Because it is not dependent on the measured steps of the formal process described in Chapter 8, and usually includes fewer people, the process moves more quickly and easily. Because the informal process depends on the consent of the people involved, there are fewer surprises, and the results show less resentment and fewer repercussions. If the attempt at an informal solution fails, the complaint can always be upgraded to formal if necessary.

This chapter is written from the standpoint of the sexual harassment officer—the person charged by the institution with receiving and investigating complaints of sexual harassment. In most cases this person will make recommendations for the outcome of the problem, but if any discipline is agreed to, it will be carried out by supervisors or managers.

Assumptions

Certain assumptions are made when a complaint is received, including the following:

- It is legally and ethically necessary to respond to all complaints.
- Even minor complaints are important to the individual complainant for the sake of her or his comfort; to the individual respondent to correct his or her behavior so there may be no repetition; and to others to improve the climate, set decent standards, and encourage all to join in the mutual enterprise of eliminating discrimination.
- Due process is important to preserve everyone's rights, but also because the complaint may be continued, appealed, or grieved. During each stage of the process, it is important that all parties receive all of the due process protection they deserve. Some of the items that must be attended to include: (a) prompt attention to the complaint, (b) stopping the harassment, (c) giving the alleged harasser information about the nature of the complaint and an opportunity to present his or her side, (d) keeping both parties informed of their options under the institutions' policy, (e) keeping both parties informed about what is happening, and (f) promptly reporting the results of the investigation.
- Everyone involved deserves respect. In many cases no one is likely to be completely right or absolutely wrong.
- Most people—respondents, witnesses or administrators—will be cooperative.
- Prevention is possible and should be emphasized.
- Some of the stories will be the most surprising tales imaginable, human behavior being infinitely variable. But these stories do not necessarily reflect any unwillingness on the part of the complainant or respondent to deal with them. Sometimes problems will be allowed to fester while feeble or useless attempts are made to correct the situation. These problems often demonstrate a lack of communication between employees and supervisors. Difficult situations can be allowed to trouble a unit for many months before anyone tries to cut through the problems and look for closure.
- Flexibility is necessary so plans can be changed to take advantage of new possibilities for assistance or resolution.

Analysis

The kinds of people, problems, and politics presented by a complaint must be analyzed to decide on the best strategy to follow. Details, which have the power to alter how one looks at a situation, may include a respondent who has tenure or some kind of "permanent" status, membership in a union whose processes are in potential conflict with the institutional ones, a respondent who is known to have violated the policy before, or a situation in which physical danger seems likely. Issues like these can be contraindications for an informal settlement. If the problem appears to be intractable, the complainant may be better served by a formal approach that forces certain specific actions to take place, actions that are designed to be protective of the rights of both parties and can bring clarity to more difficult complaints.

What other complicating factors might exist? Keep in mind the shadows that may haunt any situation—the previous experiences individuals bring into it, or the norms operating in that unit. A complaint can be simultaneously about a current sexual harassment problem and a reference to other problems connected to the people who are part of the situation. Is anyone in the unit taking advantage of a complaint situation as a way to disguise a different intent, such as getting rid of a unit employee who is difficult to get along with, but when the administrator can find no other cause to terminate? Most educational institutions must go through convoluted processes to get rid of employees once they have passed the required probationary period. Complainants and administrators, anxious to be free of an obstreperous person, often confuse sexual harassment with ordinary, nonsexual harassment, which may be difficult to bear and irritating, but not illegal and not subject to the sexual harassment policy.

Another part of the evaluation of the complaint must look at the likelihood that an informal resolution will succeed. Any of the following factors may make an informal resolution more difficult:

- Have complainants complained because there is a nonsexual problem in their unit they are tired of putting up with? If an individual files a complaint, is the problem really sexual harassment? Can it be pursued successfully?
- From the standpoint of the complainant, is the complaint autonomous or is it on behalf of others? Is the complainant responding to subtle pressures to take action and acting out problems the others don't want to take responsibility for? If there are multiple instances of harassment occurring to several people, the most suggestible one may complain, but the actual strength of the complaint may be found with another's complaint.
- Is the complaint a means of postponing a threatened adverse personnel decision? Would she have filed if she didn't think she was losing her job? A complainant may accept or even participate in an office atmosphere that is offensive, but file a complaint if her probationary reviews are marginal.
- Is it a clear-cut complaint? It is possible for it to be "real" and influenced by outside circumstances at the same time. It may take careful sorting out to discern the facts. Is the complaint complicated by other things such as:
  - Multiple complaints against the same respondent—unless the complainants are willing to act as a group and likely to agree as to what they want to happen, informal resolution may be inappropriate in many instances
  - Previous incest or sexual assault experiences
  - Issues of sexual orientation (of complainant or respondent, especially in units dominated by one sex)
  - Complaints of one kind of discrimination are countered by claims of another kind such as a situation in which a religious fundamentalist complains that the actions of a person's different sexual orientation are a violation of her religious rights
  - Overwhelming anger, in which an individual files against another individual but is really angry at the cultural milieu of sexism and racism and tries to demonstrate that

- Unclarified personal needs that lead a person to take actions to alleviate them such as a lonely person who writes personal notes to someone who has expressed a sympathetic response
- A complaint which is too late or too weak so that an agreement would not be possible
- Problems with emotional illness (fantasy, attribution of own actions to the harasser, inability to distinguish reality)

None of these factors mean a complaint is more or less viable or important, but they are factors that may need to be taken into consideration in deciding whether to handle the complaint informally.

From the standpoint of the respondent, what needs to be thought about? Is it a serious form of harassment—stalking or forced kissing and grabbing—and best handled formally? In what context did it arise? If it was a minor infraction, such as a casual remark, an informal settlement may be best. If the activity was unexpected and sudden, such as coming up behind someone and kissing her while she is on the telephone, the formal process provides a stronger platform for discipline.

Have there been other reports or rumors about this person? A formal investigation is more likely to turn up other instances of misbehavior. An employer needs to know if it is dealing with a one-time problem or one of long-standing. What is the atmosphere of the unit? Is it casual, with an "anything goes" atmosphere? Areas in which students work performing mostly routine duties are likely to have a lot of laughter and joke telling. Or are behavioral expectations more formal? What is the respondent's attitude toward the complaint? What kind of reaction did he or she have to notification of the complaint? Respondents who are especially cavalier might respond better to the more structured system of a formal complaint.

From the standpoint of the unit, does the situation exceed or fail expectations that are used as guidelines in similar units? Is it a service unit, with workers of relatively little sophistication, or a large research-oriented academic department with highly educated personnel? Is it a unit women have only recently entered, and if so, was anything done to prepare personnel for the change in atmosphere?

Is the complainant or investigator looking for a behavior change, or an attitude change? Complainants often have unrealistic ideas about what the process can accomplish for them. Has there been any kind of training or education presented to the unit? Is anything known about the administration of the unit? Are its leaders supportive of enforcing the policy or not? Have they had any previous experience with complaints? Are they willing to commit time and resources to demonstrate support? If the analysis indicates that an informal settlement is possible, decide on a strategy, notify everyone involved of what you plan to do, and then proceed.

Management of the Complaint

Based on the analysis, what can be done? Ask the complainant what it is he or she wants to have happen next. Determine if it is realistic; if the complainant wants the person fired, a formal procedure may be necessary. Determine whether this is an appropriate resolution. Determine who should be involved in negotiating a resolution. In some instances, the resolution of the complaint is between the complainant and the respondent, although they may not meet together to work it out; in other instances, particularly where voluntary but severe disciplinary action will be taken, such as suspension or termination, university counsel may be involved in the negotiation. If the complainant is not involved, it is important that she or he be kept informed of what is happening and that the settlement allows her or him to know what the resolution was.

Level 1: Speak to complainant and respondent separately to see if an agreement can be reached. This involves helping either party understand the limitations and advantages of an informal method of settlement, and that in this situation both parties may have to compromise. The parties do not have to meet together; the person crafting the agreement may travel back and forth between the parties, bringing information from one to the other, until an agreement is worked out. If both parties are willing, they might meet together (see Chapter 11).

Level 2: If agreement between the two is not possible, will the assistance of a supervisor (often acting as consultant) enable an agreement? A manager at the department head level or above may be able to put pressure on a serious offender to sign an agreement or even take early retirement.

Level 3: Get assistance from auxiliary people when attempting to settle. These may include a counselor, instructor, department head, the employee assistance program. It may be necessary to go back and forth between people several times to accomplish anything. The strategy may have to change as new facts or information are discovered.

At any level, let auxiliary people act as go-betweens or solvers if it appears they have more influence or better rapport.

Throughout the Process

- Keep in mind the preferred outcome expressed by the complainant.
- Get approval from the people involved of any actions before carrying them out.
- Be open about intent. Always keep complainant and respondent informed of what you plan to do. Let them know whether your plan works out.
- If new information turns up that seems to implicate respondent, he or she must be informed. The information may also make informal attempts to settle impossible.
- Keep records! If proposals do not work, you may have to move to a formal complaint.

What Outcomes Are Possible?

The complaint may be dismissed. If you cannot find a preponderance of evidence, you have no choice but to dismiss it. You do not have to give any reason, other than lack of evidence, for the dismissal. Even if you feel strongly that harassment occurred, you probably should not try to explain your decision. These matters are emotionally charged, and any explanation will not make the complainant feel better and may give undeserved justification to the person accused. If you believe you must give an explanation to the complainant, it is better to do it verbally than to put it in writing.

If the case is strong enough, an agreement can include discipline. Respondents may sometimes agree to disciplinary action, such as a written reprimand, or even resignation, especially when the case is very strong in order to avoid a formal complaint with its resultant hearing. The outcome should be determined in part by what the complainant wants and what the institution's representative thinks is appropriate, given the full context of the harassment. Typical agreements may include several of the following—some are more appropriate for faculty and employees, others for students or for both students and employees, and other possibilities can also be worked out:

- An apology, written or oral, or a promise not to do anything like that again
- The respondent undergoes sexual harassment training
- The respondent undergoes counseling (counseling by itself should not be sufficient)
- Suspension, termination, or resignation—if a faculty member is allowed to resign, the agreement should include a promise not to teach again
- A letter of warning in the respondent's file
- Loss of committee assignments
- The respondent's undergoes related community service
- An agreement that contains clauses giving administrators the right to discipline or termination immediately if another violation is proven
- In the case of students, transfer of housing or denial of campus housing
- Denial of campus privileges, such as computers (in the case of computer harassment), participation in leadership opportunities, participation in athletics
- Loss of scholarship monies or denial of renewal
- A promise of no retaliation by the respondent
- A reevaluation of a grade or other evaluation to be done by someone other than the respondent
- A statement about future behavior of both parties

The agreement should be written, and signed by both parties. If it is not written formally, the facilitator should write up their verbal agreement, and send it to both parties, saying this is what they agreed to, and if this is not accurate, to respond within a certain time limit. The complainant should be encouraged to return if there is any breach of the agreement, including retaliation by the respondent or his or her friends. Termination or expulsion from an institution without a formal complaint is possible, but only under egregious, and probably assaultive, circumstances.

Even when an agreement is reached to everyone's satisfaction, the investigator, depending on his or her responsibilities in the institution, may have to deal with the aftermath of some complaints. When a complainant and a respondent have to continue to work together, they may not be cooperative. Supervisors may have a great deal of trouble restoring the workplace to its normal productivity because people often refuse to speak to one another or try to get coworkers to side with them. This agitation may not rise to the level of demonstrable retaliation, but it can be irritating to everyone involved. It is a good idea to keep these potential problems in mind when writing agreements and in conversations with both parties. Any sign that one or the other may bear a grudge should be brought out in the open and discussed, and if possible, prevented.

10

THE INVESTIGATION PROCESS

SUSAN C. EHRLICH

The investigation of a formal claim of sexual harassment in the academic setting, when properly done, permits the college or university to resolve the claim according to standards of fairness and due process; minimizes the risk of exposure for failure to take prompt action reasonably calculated to end any harassment; and avoids creating liability for violating the privacy rights of the complainant, the accused, and witnesses. For the inexperienced supervisor or administrator who must investigate a claim, tightrope walking may seem far easier and less risky than balancing the competing rights and interests evoked when a claim of sexual harassment is made. The investigator must obtain necessary information without interfering with privacy rights, produce closure while recognizing rights of speech and academic freedom, be timely without sacrificing thoroughness, and suggest disciplinary measures that are consistent with conclusions drawn.

Issues that arise in the formal investigation of sexual harassment claims at the college and university level typically include problems involving excess delay in beginning the investigation, incomplete investigations, unnecessary or unauthorized disclosure of confidential or privileged information, and lack of skill in interpreting and weighing evidence. Speech and academic freedom issues may capture media attention and require sophisticated legal analysis, but the most common error is flawed investigation procedures. The following discussion highlights critical steps in an investigation of a complaint of sexual harassment.

Timeliness and Advance Preparation

Administrators charged with investigating are often more aware of the potential for mistakes and the negative consequences their errors may create for their college or university than they are of the specific steps they can take to avoid making these errors. The natural reaction, to delay initiating the investigation because of uncertainty, can be the first misstep, because timeliness of the institution's response to the complaint is evidence of the institution's serious commitment to the elimination of sexual harassment in the academic environment and has significant consequences on the liability of the institution.

The most thorough of investigations may be of little assistance to the complainant and may leave the employer unnecessarily exposed to liability if the investigation is not timely. The guidelines for determining how soon an investigation must be initiated, how soon it must be concluded, and how soon any discipline or remedial measures must be initiated involve a standard of reasonableness. One court found that a delay of more than twenty-four hours in beginning an investigation was unreasonable based on the particular facts the situation presented. Another court determined that a four-week delay in investigating was an indication that the employer "did not take reasonable measures to enforce antiharassment policies." In general, the promptness and adequacy of an employer's action to correct instances of alleged sexual harassment must be evaluated on a case-by-case basis. Although there is no precise, absolute standard of timeliness, clearly, it is not sufficient that the institution relegate a complaint alleging sexual harassment to the bottom of a "To Do List." The timeliness standard is based on the facts of the complaint, not the other work demands of the institution's administration.

General guidelines and policies about the complaint procedure are rarely sufficient to guarantee that administrators will be prepared to begin an investigation within a reasonable time. They do not deal with or describe the steps of investigations of sexual harassment at the level of detail necessary to implement a successful investigation. An analysis of these necessary details reveals much that can be done ahead of time to ensure against unnecessary delay.

A institution should implement certain procedures whether or not any complaints are pending. Those procedural steps are described here in general terms, but they must be reconciled with existing state laws before a institution can be sure that its investigation procedures are legally sound. The investigation of discrimination claims is complicated because there are both federal statutes and rules and state statutes and rules that define and regulate employer, employee, and student behavior with respect to discrimination. A institution must comply with *all* applicable laws; federal law does not apply to the exclusion of state law—both must be followed. In addition, negotiated labor agreements and administration–faculty understandings unique to each college or university must be taken into consideration. If applicable state laws or labor agreements or institution policies offer fewer procedural safeguards than those provided in federal laws and regulations, then the federal standards should be met. Frequently, there is considerable similarity in the laws and with only slight differences. These differences may still have significance, however, and may create additional and alternative criteria for evaluating a sexual harassment claim. The variation in wording may create different definitions of harassment, different standards of proof, different criteria for evaluating liability, and different remedies. An awareness of these differences in wording will help investigators identify critical areas of inquiry in investigations where the details obtained from witnesses must be precise enough to permit the investigator to accurately apply each standard.

The safest way to develop an investigation procedures that meets all applicable legal standards is to ask legal counsel to review them before they are finalized.

It is vital to develop procedures that are specific to investigation of sexual harassment or at least of discrimination complaints. Do not rely on the general faculty, employee, and student discipline procedures for dealing with sexual harassment complaints. Multiple procedures create confusion and inconsistency and may emphasize the rights of the accused to the exclusion of the rights created to protect victims under federal and state legislation dealing with discrimination and specifically with sexual harassment. Use of the following steps is recommended:

• Develop a detailed, written investigative approach that is consistent with the institution's policies on sexual harassment.

• Train investigators in legal issues related to sexual harassment, and have them review the procedural steps for investigation by checking them against all applicable institution policies, procedures, labor agreements, and other relevant documents. Many institutional policies seem less clear, inconsistencies or flaws becoming evident, when the policies are reviewed by someone who has the actual responsibility for investigating a complaint.

• Assign multiple investigation teams. The number of teams needed will depend on the size of the institution and should take into consideration the history of complaints filed. It is not uncommon for more than one complaint to be pending. A team member may be disqualified from a particular investigation because of other pressing work commitments. An investigator's relationship to the complainant or accused, or some other bias that may exist with respect to a particular complaint, could also be a basis for disqualification.

• Teamed investigators will provide a check on each other. They can corroborate each other if the matter goes to court. Investigation findings and decisions will be more reliable. Assign a minimum of two investigators to a team. More may be desirable for certain types of complaints.

• Choose investigators who are well respected, credible, and would make good witnesses. Expect that alleged victims and witnesses and those who are accused will be emotional and distrustful; select investigators who have "people skills." They need to be empathic but objective, and skilled in reading nonverbal behavioral cues.

• The administrator responsible for sexual harassment investigations should interview and evaluate prospective investigators for bias before assigning them to an investigation team. Biased investigators, even those who will not make ultimate disciplinary decisions, may overlook or misinterpret evidence, or they may be unable or unwilling to recommend certain disciplinary actions. An inquiry into bias should consist of at least one face-to-face interview and should involve a detailed discussion of attitudes toward sexual harassment. A faculty member may have no problems investigating harassment claims against non-teaching staff but may believe that there should not be any limits on what may permissibly be said by an instructor or professor. Such bias must be discovered before such an individual is included in the investigation team.

• The responsible administrator should clearly delineate individual responsibilities for the investigation such as developing the initial investigation timeline estimate; taking notes; interviewing; maintaining files, securing interview rooms, scheduling interviews; communicating with the administrator who will make the ultimate decision; assuring that the investigation progresses according to the time-line; controlling rumors, gossip, and unauthorized leaks; and making a written list of those who have a need to know about the progress and results of the investigation.

• At what point do the investigation team's responsibilities end? Who will review the facts determined through investigation and make the final decision about whether harassment took place and what discipline and remedies are appropriate?

Failure to recognize and address all these advance preparation steps can be detrimental. When these details have been attended to ahead of time, it is much less time-consuming for an administrator, after a complaint is made, to screen potential team members for bias unique to the facts of a particular complaint, analyze other critical work commitments, and assign a team to begin investigating immediately.

Determine Whether a Specific Complaint Can Be Investigated

Investigators are confronted with two problems in making the initial evaluation of a complaint of sexual harassment: (1) They may be inclined, out of fear that they will be accused of being nonresponsive, to initiate a full investigative process when it is unwarranted and would be very unlikely to produce substantive information; (2) They may also fail to recognize a complaint that, although vague or seemingly unspecific, provides enough information that *some* level of investigation should be conducted.

Complaints, which usually cannot be investigated, are those that are totally anonymous; neither the victim nor the alleged harasser is identified by name or title or position. "My professor harassed me in class and humiliated me and made me lose sleep and now my grades have dropped," is an example of an anonymous complaint alleging some sort of misconduct by some academic person against some particular student. The problem with investigating such a complaint is that all the necessary detail is missing. "I am tired of this institution's practice of discriminating against female students in its instructional programs," submitted anonymously, is a example of a complaint against some general institutional practice. Like the first example, it does not notify the institution of the offending conduct or activity in a manner that requires or permits the conduct to be investigated.

If a complaint appears to be too vague to require or permit an investigation, test this assumption by asking, "What else would I need to know before I would have an obligation to investigate this complaint?" Then ask whether the missing information is available and how readily it is available. An unsigned complaint that alleges, "I am the only student who dropped Physics 210 this semester because of the instructor's conduct toward women" may provide an avenue for further inquiry. A check of institution records may show that only one or two students dropped Physics 210 and warrant a general inquiry of those students to determine whether they have a complaint. Victims of sexual misconduct within the institutional setting are understandably wary of the institution and may "test" the willingness and sincerity of those from whom they need to seek help before deciding to disclose more. A complaint may only hint at problems which the complainant may reveal in more detail if the complainant decides the investigator can be trusted and that it is safe to proceed.

An unsigned complaint may name an alleged harasser without providing details, such as the name of a victim, the specific subject and class period in which the harassment took place, or a specific work setting and circumstances of the harassment that would assist in identifying witnesses. Intense debate is generated by such a situation among the administrators who receive such complaints. Some administrators report that, when the accused is told of the accusation, even when it is made clear that no punitive action could be or will be taken, the desire to shoot (or at least discredit) the messenger is very strong and creates lasting suspicion and unpleasantness. Why bother to engender such animosity when no disciplinary action can result because of the insufficiency of the complaint? (In some institutions, if the investigation of an anonymous complaint yields enough information to sustain a formal complaint, the institution may initiate its own complaint against the alleged harasser.)

The argument in favor of sharing the complaint is threefold. First, all protestations aside, such notice has frequently been sufficient to stop conduct that constitutes harassment. Some individuals do not require much warning to decide that this "complaint" about them was too close for comfort and that they do not want a repeat. They know that the next time a complaint is filed about them, it may come from someone who is not afraid to provide specifics and who wants the institution to investigate and to take action. Second, even in circumstances in which sharing the anonymous complaint may not produce a needed change in behavior, it will help protect the institution and its administrators against charges of failing to act or failing to provide notice to employees of unacceptable behavior. Third, institution employees named in the complaint need to know when false complaints are being made. The false sexual harassment complaint, though rare, indicates that there is a student or fellow employee with some type of problem who has focused attention, albeit inappropriate, on an innocent individual. Knowledge of this fact, alone, may alert the person who has been falsely accused to exercise an increased level of caution about his or her interactions in the institution setting.

An effective way to share the complaint would be to offer it as information the employee needs to be aware of for his or her own protection. It cannot be cause for discipline, and it cannot be placed in an employment record. The administrator might suggest that the employee review the sexual harassment complaint procedure for his or her protection. The administrator should also keep a record of the steps taken to alert the employee to the complaint.

Be aware of the possibility that cumulative information will constitute notice sufficient to warrant an investigation. The victim and alleged harasser may be unidentified in a complaint, but the manner or pattern of harassment may have a unique character. A subsequent complaint by an individual who is willing to sign a complaint or is willing to name the alleged harasser, and describes the same or similar distinctive pattern of conduct, may reactivate an earlier complaint originally assessed as one that could not be investigated. A college affirmative action officer who was willing to promise anonymity to a series of complainants realized, too late, that the pattern of conduct alleged indicated that all were complaining about the same faculty member. By then, the institution was on notice of a widespread pattern of harassment but had already promised anonymity to all complainants.

A complaint does not need to name names to constitute notice of possible harassment and trigger an investigation. A signed complaint about the "department chair in my major" provides sufficient identification of the alleged harasser. Of course, the other "facts" of the complaint must still be assessed for specificity before a full investigation is instituted. Any complaint, however vague or confusing, that is signed or gives sufficient identification of the complainant should be investigated, at a minimum, by interviewing the complainant. If there is still an insufficient basis for investigating or the complainant will not cooperate sufficiently, treat this situation as a completed investigation that should be written up with findings (see Concluding the Investigation).

Delayed Reporting

Complaints may describe an incident that is obviously outside the time period in which a complaint is considered timely. *Do not assume* that the complaint does not require investigation. Interview the complainant and inquire about the reason for the delay. Promptly consult legal counsel and seek advice on whether to proceed with an investigation. There is increasing awareness on the part of legislators and courts that a victim's delay in reporting may be related to the alleged harassment. If certain elements of proof are satisfied, action may be possible on complaints that are outside the generally prescribed time frame. The key event for evaluating the timeliness of an investigation and determining whether action may be taken is the date the educational institution received notice of the complaint. Do not try to second guess state laws with respect to this issue; consult with counsel.

Save All Complaints in a Central File

Complaints should not be discarded because they are anonymous or insufficient on their face to warrant investigation. All complaints, whether or not they can be investigated, should be retained. They should be dated on receipt and retained for whichever of the following is the longest: (1) the time allowed by the Equal Employment Opportunity Commission (EEOC) and the Office of Civil Rights for delayed reporting, (2) the time allowed for delayed reporting by any state entity empowered with investigating sexual harassment complaints, or (3) the period of time required under any state public records act that may be applicable.

All sexual harassment complaints should be forwarded to an individual or office of the institution designated to assume responsibility for the physical retention of the complaints. Some institutions have an anonymous complaint form, knowing that many victims will never do more than make an anonymous report. Why should a institution encourage a report that cannot be investigated? The extent to which an institution demonstrates a positive commitment to eliminate harassment will be taken into consideration by state and federal agencies that may be asked to investigate a specific complaint against the institution. An institution administration that encourages the reporting of harassment indicates that it wants to fully address its obligation to eliminate harassment. Even anonymous complaints are useful to an institution that wants to seriously evaluate whether it is providing a climate that is free from the problems of sexual harassment. All complaints, even anonymous ones, should be accounted for in the collection and analysis of aggregate statistics by the institution. Such statistics—indicating the number and type of complaints filed; the number investigated and acted on, the general types of action taken; the nature of the complaints by characteristics of the complainant, the accused, and the conduct alleged—serve several purposes. The retained complaints provide a basis for determining the educational climate within the institution and a yardstick for measuring the effectiveness of the institution's efforts to educate about and eliminate sexual harassment. It is important to remember that educational institutions have an obligation under federal law to eliminate sexual harassment. This obligation is in addition to and independent of the institution's obligation to investigate specific complaints.

Create a Separate Investigation File

When it is determined that an investigation of a specific complaint will be conducted, a separate investigation file should be created. This file should not be part of an individual student's record or an employee's or faculty person's personnel file. An allegation of inappropriate conduct, absent a determination by authorized institution personnel that misconduct did occur, is not cause for discipline. Only when a fair investigation substantiates that misconduct has taken place can disciplinary action be taken. The mere inclusion of an allegation or of a report of an investigation in which the allegations were not substantiated in a permanent student record or personnel file could constitute discipline without just cause or due process and trigger complaints, grievances, or litigation. At the conclusion of an investigation in which allegations were substantiated, a document listing findings and related disciplinary action can be created specifically for inclusion in a student's record or someone's personnel file. A record should be kept of all complaints, by complainant name and by the name of the alleged harasser.

An investigation file of a specific complaint should include copies of all relevant institution policies and procedures. Specifically, policies that govern student, employee, vendor, or faculty conduct at the time the harassment allegedly occurred should be preserved. Policies that govern investigations, the retention of records, and the imposition of discipline and are in effect at the time the investigation is conducted, records or reports are created, or discipline is imposed should also be retained. If there has been a significant delay in reporting incidents of harassment that are investigated and substantiated, there may be an issue of which policies are applicable. If there has been a change in policies, both the old and new policies describing imposition of discipline should be reviewed. Do not overlook handbooks for faculty or students that may also contain guidelines or standards applicable to the investigation of sexual harassment. This compilation of materials is very important. When matters are litigated, several years may elapse before a trial takes place. Locating the applicable version of a policy or handbook which has been out of use for several years may be time-consuming and difficult.

Even though the investigation file is not part of an official student record or employee personnel file, access to the file should be restricted and carefully monitored. A listing by title or position of those who have a "need to know" and who may have access to such files should be delineated in a written policy. Further, when an investigation team is assigned to evaluate a specific complaint, a memo should specify by name and title those individuals who will have access to that particular file. It is also important to limit staff and clerical help to the smallest number necessary. Having staff and clerical help specifically assigned to assist in the investigation is preferable to letting the typing pool or general photocopying crew work with highly sensitive, confidential documents.

Investigation files may be discoverable as evidence if the matter is litigated. Settlements of sexual harassment complaints by the University of California at Los Angeles (UCLA) were recently the subject of litigation initiated by the *Daily Bruin*, the UCLA student newspaper. In addition to ordering that copies of settlement agreements between UCLA and plaintiffs be released as public records, the court ordered the release of witness interviews and other investigative notes and materials redacted to eliminate names. The court found that, because a public entity was a party to the settlements, release was necessary regardless of whether the plaintiffs wanted the settlements to be made public.

More litigation designed to force disclosure can be expected. Keep unnecessary personal comments out of the notes or investigative reports. Keep notes about questions for legal counsel separate from the main investigative material. Be aware, however, that reactions to witness credibility and observations of witness behavior are legitimate subjects for comment and should be included in investigative notes because they may form the basis for some of the investigation findings and conclusions (see section on Weighing Evidence).

Investigation Timeline

The best way to ensure that a complaint will be dealt with in a timely manner is to create a tentative timeline before initiating the investigation and to update it on a weekly basis. It is doubtful that any initial timeline can be an accurate estimate of the sequence of the investigation and time required, but the timeline will increase the likelihood that the investigation will progress without undue delay. When a revision is necessary, note the reason for the revision. A delay or a variance from the initial sequence or timeline does not produce a flawed investigation if there is a reasonable basis for the change. It may be necessary to consult legal counsel before proceeding to the next phase of investigation; a key witness may become unavailable; a law enforcement agency may become involved and ask that the institution investigation be delayed in furtherance of a criminal investigation; more witnesses may be identified than were originally projected; the pattern of misconduct may be more complex than was originally indicated.

Not all causes for delay will be considered reasonable. The illness of an investigator or other pressing administrative responsibilities of the investigator may require that another investigator take over. Availability of one witness does not always preclude another from being interviewed. Some reasons for delay, such as a refusal on the part of the complainant or accused to cooperate, may have significance for the findings of the investigation.

If, in the course of investigating a complaint, other complainants come forward or other alleged harassers are named, separate investigation files, identified by complainant and harasser, should be kept. These separate complaints will have different dates of filing or notice to the institution and should not be confused. Separate interviews do not necessarily have to be conducted, but, if interview notes from one investigation are placed in a file of another investigation, they should be carefully read and edited so that only information relevant to a given complaint is included in that file. If a separate complaint is revealed in the course of investigating one complaint, even when it is feasible and efficient for the same investigation team to conduct the second investigation, a formal decision for them to do so should be made. The new complaint should be treated in the same way that any complaint would be handled until the decision about the assignment of an investigation team is made.

Consult with Legal Counsel

Have a clear understanding before beginning the investigation of who may authorize communication with legal counsel and under what circumstances such communication may take place. All such communication should be put in writing. Communication to and from counsel should be kept in a segregated part of the investigation file. In general, these communications will be protected from disclosure in subsequent litigation provided they have not been disseminated beyond the circle of those who are authorized to act on behalf of the institution. Sending copies of otherwise discoverable information to legal counsel will not protect those documents, however. Not all matters on which legal counsel should be consulted can be anticipated at the outset of an investigation, but counsel should be notified that a specific investigation has been initiated. Counsel should be consulted about any procedural problems that arise, about any seeming conflict between laws or policies applicable to the investigation, before any documents are finalized for witness signature, before any "compromise" solutions are agreed to, and before any documents or specific information obtained from the investigation are released to individuals other than those authorized to act for the institution.

How to balance the First Amendment rights of free speech and symbolic expression of faculty and students against other institutional needs and concerns is a rapidly evolving area of law. The law does not prohibit all regulation of speech and speech-related activities within the academic setting, but legal counsel should definitely be consulted in any investigation where the behavior complained of includes complaints about academic as opposed to private speech. Provide counsel with weekly summaries of the investigation.

Inclusion of Advocates in the Investigation Process

A victim of sexual harassment has good reason to be angry and distrustful: distrustful of the institution; distrustful of any representative of the institution, including those assigned to investigate the complaint; ambivalent about coming forward and creating shock waves that may only serve to further disrupt the academic or work environment of the victim. Additionally, many victims are naive about the legal standards for conducting an investigation. These victims, especially if they are students, believe that, once they have complained and revealed the details they consider to be relevant, the matter can be quickly resolved with little or no additional participation on their part. A typical complaint to an investigator is, "I've already given this information to my dorm supervisor (committee chair/immediate supervisor/peer advocate, etc.). Why do I have to go through this all again and tell you too?"

Victims of harassment may feel they have become victims twice—first by the conduct of the harasser, and second by the investigation process. The presence of a support person or victim advocate can be of significant benefit to a victim, adding moral support and assurance that the victim is not alone in dealing with the process and securing his or her legal rights. The institution benefits because the likelihood of cooperation with the investigation process by the victim may increase.

When an institution trains, sponsors, or arranges advocates, however, it may be unintentionally incurring liability for the actions or failure to act, of those advocates. To the extent that advocates are associated with the institution, their neutrality or perceived ability to provide victim support is diminished. It is better that student groups, employee groups, or broad-based community groups train and provide advocates.

Even when advocates are not associated with the institution, investigators must distinguish those situations where an advocate's presence is permissible from those where an advocate's presence may compromise confidentiality. There is no problem having the advocate present in interviews in which information is sought from the victim or accused or at meetings when the complaint process or general investigation procedures are explained to the victim or accused.

There is a problem, however, when advocates receive information that should be confidential. The problem of unauthorized release of privileged information is most likely to arise in states where laws require release to the victim of information about specific disciplinary measures imposed on the harasser. These statutes generally authorize this release to the victim but are silent as to advocates for the victim. An exception would be the situation in which the results to be reported indicate that evidence of harassment has not been found. In this instance, an advocate's presence will be important, and the general information to be shared will not compromise confidentiality.

Structuring and Conducting the Investigation

At a minimum, an identified complainant should be interviewed in an investigation. A named harasser should also be contacted, but, remember that when the complaint or charges against an individual are anonymous, the institution administrator cannot impose discipline and should talk to the accused in the general terms detailed earlier. Some investigations will involve no more than an interview of the complainant and the accused. No witnesses will be offered by either side and findings must be drawn solely from the interview results.

When scheduling interviews, advise the complainant and accused that a support person may be present. The institution should clarify whether an attorney can be present and what role the attorney would play during the interviews. Most institutions that allow an attorney do not allow the attorney to participate, ask questions, or comment, but they may confer with and advise their client at any time. Physically arrange the interview setting so that the advocate can be seated near the complainant or accused but is slightly behind them; both should be facing the interviewer. With this arrangement, the interviewee will be less likely to take visual cues from the advocate and to frame responses based on advocate approval or disapproval. (See also cautions noted in the next section and under separate heading.)

Interview of Complainant

The investigator should have a prepared statement, which is drafted by the investigation team, for complainant and follows this general format:

> The purpose of this investigation is to follow-up on your complaint. We need to determine the details of what has happened. It is this institution's obligation to take allegations of sexual harassment seriously, to investigate promptly, and, where the facts indicate, to take action reasonably likely to end the harassment.
>
> For a complete investigation to be conducted and for action to be taken, if appropriate, your name must be given to_____ (the accused). It is not necessary for our investigation that you meet or confront _____ (the accused) in a face-to-face situation.
>
> You may have a support person present during any and all of our information-gathering interviews. If disciplinary action is to be taken, I can and will advise you of that action to the extent that the law permits, but I will caution you that such information should not be disseminated. At such a time, I would want to speak to you without any third person being present.
>
> It is against the law for anyone associated with this institution or with the accused to retaliate against you for your good-faith filing of a complaint of sexual harassment or for your good-faith participation in this investigation. Retaliation may be in the form of words or actions and would subject you to inappropriate conduct or tend to deprive you of a comfortable work environment or of the benefits of an education in some way as a consequence of filing or assisting in the investigation of this complaint. My caution to you about retaliation is a general one. I am not implying that I believe it will happen in this particular situation. If you believe you are being subjected to retaliation, you should immediately notify _____
> _____.
>
> I encourage you to limit conversation and speculation about this process with others. Rumors serve no one well. It is this institution's responsibility to investigate thoroughly before deciding whether action should be taken. You would want that same benefit extended to you if accusations were made about your conduct.
>
> I will maintain confidentiality about this matter to the extent permitted by law. I cannot guarantee complete confidentiality, however.

While an investigation in ongoing, it is best to ask the complainant to report retaliation to the head investigator. At the conclusion of the investigation, it is important to remind the complainant again about the need to report any retaliation that may occur after the investigation. Retaliation can occur whether or not a finding of misconduct has been made and whether or not disciplinary action has been taken. Allegations of retaliation require additional investigation and may result in findings that would require discipline, whether or not harassment was found to have taken place. The issue of confidentiality poses several problems. Unlike some anonymous complaints, which are too vague to put an institution on notice of a situation that can be investigated, information that is given in confidence may be specific enough to alert the institution to the presence of unacceptable and unlawful conduct. There is no clear rule about whether the position held or degree of authority exercised by the institution employee who receives the information determines whether the institution is on notice. The Office for Civil Rights appears to take the broad position that knowledge by any employee or agent puts the institution on notice. The institution itself can avoid problems by requiring that any employee who receives information about a possible incident of sexual harassment report this information in writing to the Title IX officer or individual designated to receive complaints of sexual harassment.

The institution should discourage any employee who may receive information about alleged harassment from making any promises of confidentiality. Further, the institution should avoid making promises to accept conditions that a complainant attempts to impose on information the complainant wants to provide. It is fairly common for a complainant to offer the names of a witness but to request that the witness not be told who provided his or her name. This situation requires considerable judgment. There is nothing wrong with asking a potential witness to participate in an interview without giving the name of the individual who provided the witness's name to investigators, but many potentially significant witnesses balk at disclosing any information if they are not told why they have been selected for an interview. As frustrating as it may be to pass up potentially useful information, the institution's investigator should tell the unwilling witness or unwilling complainant that the investigator will note that the witness or complainant had information to offer but would not provide it. Once this is expressed to witnesses, most will cooperate. This approach is a safer one for the institution than committing to promises that add uncertainty and inconsistency to investigation procedures and will complicate rather than assist with the resolution of the complaint. This dilemma underscores the need for sensitive, skillful, empathic investigators and interviewers. It also requires that the institution recognize that the interview process cannot be unnecessarily hurried. A victim will "size up" the investigator, and victim cooperation will be enhanced by the victim's perception that the investigator is effective and trustworthy.

Continuing the Interview

- Ask the complainant about the behavior that prompted him or her to file a complaint.
- Ask the complainant to describe anything he or she has done to deal with the offensive conduct before or since filing the complaint.
- Ask the complainant how he or she would like to see this matter resolved, but do not promise specific results.

Interview of Accused

When the accused is contacted to schedule an interview, inform him or her that a complaint alleging sexual harassment has been filed. Explain that you will discuss the complaint and investigation process with the accused. Advise him or her that the accused may want to have a support person or union representative present. The legal standard in National Labor Relations Board cases establishes the right of an employee to have a union representative present at any meeting which may reasonably lead to disciplinary action.

Assure the accused that he or she will have a right to respond to the accusations but do not go into any more detail before the face-to-face interview. Be prepared to schedule the interview within a day of the call. Allegations of any form of wrongdoing can provoke intense anxiety unrelated to whether the wrongdoing has actually taken place. A more cooperative, less adversarial atmosphere can be maintained if the investigator remains attuned to the accused's fears and anxieties as well as to the fears and anxieties of the complainant. The investigator can maintain better control of the investigation in a face-to-face situation which he or she has structured.

The investigator should have a prepared statement for the accused that follows this general format:

> A complaint has been filed that alleges you have sexually harassed _____ _____ (give the name of the complainant). This institution has the obligation to investigate this complaint and make a determination about whether the allegations are true. I will share the details of the complaint with you and give you the opportunity to offer any information in the form of statements, relevant records, or names of individuals who may have witnessed the incidents alleged in the complaint. You will be able to comment on any findings or recommended action before the findings are finalized and before any recommendations are made.
>
> You may have a support person present during any of our meetings.
>
> It is against the law for you to retaliate against_____ or any witnesses to this matter. Retaliation may encompass comments or actions initiated by you. Further, your friends may be found to have retaliated if they, through words or actions, subject _____ (the complainant) or any witnesses to inappropriate conduct which interferes with a comfortable work environment or the benefits of an education because of filing or assisting in the investigation of this complaint.
>
> I encourage you to limit conversation and speculation about this process with others. Rumors serve no one well. It is this institution's responsibility to investigate thoroughly before deciding whether action should be taken.
>
> I will maintain confidentiality about this matter to the extent permitted by law. I cannot guarantee complete confidentiality, however.

Review the complaint with the accused. Tell the accused the names of the complainant or complainants but only give the accused a copy of the complaint after any personal identifying information has been blackened out. The accused has a right to know who has made an accusation and what has been alleged, but the institution should not provide the accused with a copy of the complaint or any document which, if disseminated, would have the names of others involved. The complaint may include comments or statements that could be defamatory to the accused or others, and, if the accused choses to distribute this document, such distribution could create liability for the institution for republication of the defamation.

Before disciplinary action is determined to be appropriate, limit the written materials shared with the accused to a copy of the written complaint. Review witness statements in sufficient detail to allow the accused to respond, but do not supply written copies unless state law so requires. Even if there is no defamatory information in the complaint, dissemination of witness statements (including statements of the complainant) will have a chilling effect on witness participation. If disciplinary action is recommended for any permanent employee, that employee will be entitled to notice of the proposed action, all written documents not otherwise privileged that support the action, and an opportunity to respond. A permanent employee has an expectation of employment and therefore has a property interest in his or her position. Both federal and state laws support the provisions of notice and an opportunity to respond prior to loss of pay as elements of due process. Because allegations of sexual harassment are likely to affect the ability of the accused to find other employment, the same rights—notice of the complaint (including copies of all written documents, not otherwise privileged, that constitute evidence relating to the complaint) and an opportunity to be heard—may apply to a probationary employee. Although probationary employees do not have a property interest in their employment, state laws may recognize that they have a *liberty interest* (the ability to seek employment without unresolved questions of their good character), which would be impaired by allegations of sexual harassment, that had not been fairly addressed.

The only situation where a support person for the accused should be excluded would be a situation in which the complainants concerns were found to have been falsely filed intentionally. If disciplinary action against the complainant is to be taken as a result and reported to the accused, caution should be used in what is said to the accused if a third-party support person is present.

Continuing the Interview

- Give the accused the opportunity to comment. Do not limit the right to comment or provide information in his or her defense in the initial interview.
- Give the accused an estimate of how long the investigation will take. Explain that, as the investigation progresses, new information will be shared with the accused.
- If the accused denies the allegations, ask for whatever explanation or theory he or she has about why the complaint may have been filed.

Interview of Witnesses

Both the complainant and the accused may offer the names of witnesses who should be interviewed. It is possible that witnesses may come forward spontaneously or that several individuals, independent of each other, will complain about the same incident or incidents.

Additionally, all witnesses should be asked if they know of anyone else who may be a witness to the events or incidents in question.

Whenever the name of a witness is offered, ask the individual who has provided the witness's name if he or she is aware of any problems concerning the availability of that witness. A witness who is going on sabbatical and will soon be out of the country, is about to graduate, or is leaving to take another job should be interviewed as soon as possible. The interviewer is sometimes at a disadvantage in these interviews because the evidence could be developed more fully and logically if witnesses were taken in a different order. It is critical, however, to make contact immediately, and to obtain whatever information can be gathered. Explain that a follow-up interview may be necessary and that it may need to be conducted in writing or by phone. Having at least one opportunity to observe the witness face-to-face is important because it will provide some of the detail and nonverbal data that can be inferred from the totality of behavior rather than from mere words. Having a face to go with a name makes it easier to keep track of multiple witnesses. The face-to-face meeting will also allow the witness to feel more trusting about the investigator and will increase the likelihood that the witness will continue to be cooperative even at long distance.

In general, the next witnesses to be interviewed are the main witnesses of the complainant and then of the accused. Judgment about the order of witnesses is required here, depending on the facts offered by the two sides. Ask yourself, based on the particular facts, if there is any order of witnesses that would seem to facilitate understanding the facts more than some other order of witnesses. You will also need to decide, as facts are divulged, whether to check out new details with the complainant or accused or both first, or whether to interview marginal or "possible" witnesses first. The investigator should have prepared a statement for any witnesses that follows this general format:

> We are investigating a complaint about alleged misconduct on campus. Your name was given to us as someone who may have some information that would be helpful to the investigation. This institution takes complaints seriously and has an obligation to try to determine the facts of the situation and to recommend appropriate action. Please understand that no one has suggested that you did anything inappropriate.
>
> I encourage you to limit conversation and speculation about this process with others. Rumors serve no one well. It is this institution's responsibility to investigate thoroughly before deciding whether action should be taken. You would want that same benefit extended to you if accusations were made about your conduct.
>
> I will maintain confidentiality about this matter to the extent permitted by law. I cannot guarantee complete confidentiality, however.
>
> It is against the law for anyone to retaliate against you for your participation in this investigation. Retaliation may be in the form of words or actions and would subject you to inappropriate conduct or tend to deprive you of a comfortable work environment or of the benefits of an education in some way as a consequence of filing or assisting in the investigation of this complaint. If you believe you are being subjected to retaliation because you have participated in this investigation, you should immediately notify _____.

When listing potential witnesses, note who referred the witnesses and the incident or incidents they are believed to have seen. In many ways, the interviews of potential witnesses pose the greatest difficulty. Questions should not suggest testimony, yet some focus has to be given to the interview. Questioning of witnesses should proceed from general questions to more specific questions and will vary with the facts alleged in the complaint. An initial question could be, "Is there any conduct you have witnessed here that you believe may constitute sexual harassment of or discrimination against a student/employee/faculty member?" Depending on the response, it may be necessary to ask a more specific question such as, "Have you observed any conduct in your English 101 class from Professor Watson that you believe may constitute sexual harassment or discrimination?" If the witness feels that such conduct has been observed, ask for details. If the witness still answers in the negative, ask more specific questions based on the alleged facts such as, "This semester, have you ever observed the office manager in the accounting department touching other employees in a way that seems inappropriate?"

Another factor, which adds to the difficulty of interviewing witnesses, is the need for confidentiality. The complainant and accused, though for different reasons, will have knowledge of the extent of the complaint and a general sense of who the potential witnesses will be and why. An individual witness, however, will not necessarily be aware of the full circumstances that have led to his or her interview. Although the witness will be curious and want to know, there is little justification or need for the witness to know. Sharing unproven allegations with a witness to satisfy curiosity may lead to liability for defamation or feed rumors that flourish in such situations. Witnesses who want to give information only if all their questions about the investigation are answered pose a problem. Although some effort has to be made to maintain witnesses' good will, it is best to ask them to put themselves in the situation of the accused or the victim and recognize how important cooperation with investigators would be to them in such a situation. If you can still not ensure their cooperation, tell them you will note that their participation has been requested and you will note that they have refused to cooperate. Most of them will reconsider. Witnesses also must be cautioned that great care must be exercised in attempting to make inferences about the complaint or drawing conclusions from the questions asked.

Additional Procedures for All Interviews

Information for Follow-Up
Ask for the names, addresses, and phone numbers of any witnesses to the incident. Note which incident or incidents a particular witness may have observed. Tell each interviewee that it may be necessary to speak with them again. Ask about the best way to get in touch with them and assure them that no details will be offered to third parties you may need to go through to reach them. Ask them to contact you if they change their address or phone number.

Ask if they anticipate leaving the area or being unavailable for any extended period of time. If it appears that a witness will be unavailable, you should consult with counsel immediately about whether it is advisable to prepare a statement for the witness to sign under oath. If legal counsel feels this should be done, she or he can assist with the statement and formalities. Having counsel assist so that the interview statements of the witness become a signed statement under oath will be more likely to preserve the interview contents as evidence if the witness cannot be found at a later date because the rules for affidavits of declarations under oath vary from state to state.

Many interviewers have notes typed within a day or so of the interview and ask the party who gave the interview to review the notes and sign them. This approach may ensure greater accuracy in the notes but is not as legally useful as a signed statement under oath, should the witness be unavailable later. The signed statement may assist in focusing the witnesses testimony. Signed statements, whether or not under oath, will be discoverable if the matter is litigated.

Even complainants have been known to stop cooperating after investigations have begun. They will still maintain that harassment occurred but if they become disillusioned about the investigation process or the emotional cost to them, they cease to participate. The institution is still obligated to determine whether it can take action based on the information it has received even though the complaining witness will no longer cooperate. The statement signed under oath may protect the institution if action is taken on a complaint but the complainant ceases to cooperate.

There are disadvantages, however, to obtaining such statements. The statement can be used to discredit the witnesses' ability to recall or to be truthful by an opposing party in any subsequent legal action if the witness later wants to change or modify his or her testimony. Make this decision on the advice of legal counsel.

Opportunity for Questions
Give all parties interviewed an opportunity to ask questions. Introduce this opportunity with a statement such as the following:

> Because of the need to respect confidentiality and the rights of the parties involved, I may not be able to respond to all the questions you might have, but I would like to know whether you have any questions?

Record all questions asked and the responses given. Try to respond in general terms that reinforce the fact that the institution takes complaints seriously and reviews the general procedures for dealing with complaints. For all witnesses, note questions asked and answers given.

Standardized Interviews
A general list of questions can be prepared ahead of time. Many questions, or at least specific sequences of questions, will be repeated for other witnesses. Preparing a question sheet with room for recording the response will ensure thoroughness and uniformity of interviews and facilitate the organization of the interview results. Interviews can be tape recorded with the permission of the interviewee. If interviews are recorded, they should be transcribed within a few days and then destroyed. If retained, they will be discoverable in any subsequent legal action and will permit the trier of fact to second-guess the interviewer's conclusions from the conduct and demeanor of the witnesses and the content of the interviews. They should be viewed as a tool for facilitating the retention of interview details and not as a tool for delaying the preparation of official interview investigation notes.

Recording Impressions of Witnesses
At the conclusion of each interview make written notes about impressions of the witness and any other nonverbal events that were part of the interview that are relevant and need to be preserved. Include any observations about the credibility of the witness, the nervousness or ease with which the witness handled the interview, any observations about the conduct of support persons or the interaction of the witness and the support person. As interviewer, you may need to comment on such observations during the interview as a way of obtaining further information or clarification of responses. For example, a support person who has been expres-

sive in showing approval or disapproval of the complainant's responses should be questioned about the meaning of such conduct.

It is important to separate the valid, personal observations of the interviewer from the interviewer's personal judgment. Avoid any judgmental statements of personal values to witnesses (i.e., "Boys will be boys," "Professor Smith's career could be ruined," or "Mrs. Jones has been through a lot lately, and I'm sure she didn't mean any harm").

Sexual Conduct of the Victim

Many states have statutes that limit questioning about an alleged victim's past and present sexual conduct. The rules vary by the nature of the legal proceeding and the type of inquiry that is proscribed. It is best to request a written legal opinion from counsel before initiating the investigation or for the institution to have a standing request for information that can be made available to an investigation team. In contrast to inquiries about sexual conduct, the U.S. Supreme Court has said that dress of the alleged victim is relevant to the issue of "unwelcome" conduct. It is acceptable to note the appearance and attire of alleged victims and other witnesses who indicate that conduct was unwelcome. General attire and attire during complainant incidents whether it is self-reported or described by other witnesses or the alleged harasser, may be relevant. Interviewers may note interview attire as also having some relevance to the issue of "unwelcome conduct."

Weighing Evidence

The most common misconception held by those charged with investigating is the belief that no conclusions can be drawn from a situation or investigation in which the only evidence is the word of the complainant against the accused. A variation on this misconception is that the word of one in a position of authority, such as a teacher, supervisor, or administrator, will have more weight than the word of a student or lower-level employee.

The investigator should consider all available evidence, including factual information offered by witnesses, the investigator's observations of the witnesses conduct, and circumstantial information that supports or negates a witness's statements or has a bearing on the truthfulness of the witness.

If the investigation team concludes that some evidence is to be given more weight than other evidence or that nonverbal behavior should be weighed, there must be documentation to support these conclusions. Instead of discounting "gut reactions" or investigator "instincts," the investigator should ask, "Why do I have this sense?" Frequently the investigator will discover that observable events support those reactions and instincts.

Record nonverbal behavior, such as inappropriate laughing or gestures, that contradict the spoken word. Record general conduct observed at the interview such as asides to advocates, pressure or inappropriate prompting from advocates, threats made, attire of interviewees, physical observations that suggest the interviewee is under the influence of substances that may impair recall and judgment, and general observations about recall ability or ability to comprehend the process.

Record facts gleaned from records and other data that support the investigation team's conclusions. Relate the documentation to the conclusions supported by the documentation.

Concluding the Investigation

The full team of investigators should review all interview notes and list any information that needs clarification. Review lists of potential witnesses to determine that all have been interviewed. Make a list of facts relevant to the complaint that must be true for sexual harassment to have occurred. For each fact, list all the supporting data that has been obtained by the reporting witness or witnesses.

Suppose a female student has alleged that a male instructor lowered her final grade in World History because she did not submit to his sexual advances. Factual elements necessary to support a conclusion that sexual harassment did take place would include basic issues such as her enrollment in and attendance in that class during the time in question, his assignment to the class or lecture section in which she was enrolled, and information about her grades that would show that the final grade was lowered because of some event over which he had control. A check of institution records could verify her enrollment and attendance and his teaching assignment. Again, institution records would permit a comparison of midterm grades to the final grade and indicate whether an independent reading of her final paper or her final exam should be undertaken to further substantiate whether her final grade was lower than would be expected. Institution records could also substantiate her withdrawal from the class or verify that a petition for reevaluation of her grade was filed. Any such circumstantial evidence could tend to show that her final grade was less than she deserved. Other evidence which would substantiate her report could be statements of those who saw him show unusual attention to her, statements of those who heard him press her for sexual favors, or statements of a friend in whom she confided prior to filing the complaint. In addition, the investigator's evaluation of her credibility could also support these facts.

On the other hand, institution records may dispute some of these facts. Witness statements may indicate that she had been dating him and took the class expecting an easy grade or that she became upset over a breakup of the relationship because he began dating another student. Institution records may reveal a consistent pattern of dropping some classes each quarter or routinely petitioning for grade reconsideration. She may not seem as credible to investigators in her support of the claim as he is in his denial. Investigators may find that she changed details from one interview to the next in a manner that was not explained by nervousness or fearfulness. Witnesses may offer statements tending to show that she vowed to get even with him over some incident unrelated to sexual harassment.

Evaluate each fact separately to determine if it has been proven. The standard of proof, if the matter were to be litigated, would vary in exact wording from state to state but would be the standard of proof for civil litigation. This standard has been described as proof that something is "more likely than not" to have occurred. Another way of characterizing this standard is to imagine scales in which the balance is slightly tipped to one side.

A list should be made of verifiable facts that have a tendency, because they are direct evidence or circumstantial evidence, to substantiate that harassment took place. If there is disagreement among members of the investigation team, explore the basis for the differing opinions. Note any areas of disagreement and determine whether additional reasonable investigation could be pursued that would eliminate the disagreement. Obtain legal advice about any questions of law that must be answered to ascertain the facts.

Institutions vary as to whether the investigation team concludes its work at this point by turning written findings over to a decision maker. There are advantages to having a multilevel investigation process. The decision-maker acts as an overseer of the investigation. There is an opportunity for the decision maker to ask for additional investigation. The team should issue a written report recapping the complaint, the investigation timeline, the investigation steps, the facts that were determined to be true, and the facts that were determined not to be true. This report may or may not include a conclusion as to whether harassment took place. If not, the report will be forwarded to the decision maker who will have the responsibility for drawing conclusions and determining discipline and remedial measures, reporting recommended action to the complainant and accused, advising of appeal rights, and preparing any written disciplinary materials for student or employee files.

Evaluation of Evidence

When all information that is reasonably obtainable has been acquired, review the final list of facts. Next, evaluate these facts against the essential components of sexual harassment. Each of these components must be found to exist before a finding of sexual harassment can be made. The facts proven may vary from what has been alleged and still support a finding that harassment has occurred. For example, the evidence may not clearly support a finding of *quid pro quo* harassment but may support a finding of hostile environment harassment.

First, conduct of a sexual nature must have occurred. "Sexual" does not mean "erotic" but rather it means "sex based." A female instructor may believe that all males are intellectually inferior and incapable of earning an A in her class. This belief does not produce behavior based on sexual attraction or erotic behavior, but it does qualify as sex-based behavior.

Second, the conduct must have been "unwelcome." The issue of whether the conduct was unwelcome to the victim is generally a subjective standard. Unwelcome conduct is proven by the victim's statements and by conduct of the victim that would tend to support or deny that behavior directed toward the victim was unwelcome.

Third, if the sex-based conduct was determined to have occurred and to have been unwelcome, a determination must then be made as to whether the conduct would constitute harassment in the eyes of a reasonable person of the same gender as the victim. This standard is an objective one with a reference to a larger societal view than just the personal experiences of the victim.

Last, the harassment must act to deny the victim an educational or work benefit. This benefit may be as basic as the opportunity to work or learn in an environment free from discrimination.

If a conclusion is reached that harassment has taken place, then a final report must include facts that support this conclusion. If the facts support a conclusion that harassment has not taken place or there is insufficient evidence to conclude that harassment has occurred, a conclusion must be reached that harassment has not taken place. It is at this point in an investigation, when harassment has not been proven, that there is a tendency to let the matter drop without closure. Many institutions have been criticized by subsequent investigations by the Office for Civil Rights for failure to make findings of fact and failure to reach conclusions. As difficult as it may be, a final decision must be reached and communicated. A decision that sexual harassment has occurred should not be forced, but failure to make findings of fact is treated as failure to complete an investigation in a timely manner.

Communicating the Investigation Results

Whether the investigation team, an intermediate administrator, or the Title IX coordinator makes the determination of whether or not sexual harassment has occurred, the conclusions of the investigation should be shared with the complainant and the accused. The accused, who will have had an opportunity at various stages in the investigation to be apprised of evidence against him or her, may have a more detailed knowledge of the course of the investigation than the complainant up to this point. Once the investigation is concluded, however, meet separately with each to provide closure and to review the conclusions that will form the basis of action to be taken. Review the general steps taken in the investigation, the facts revealed by the investigation, and the conclusions drawn.

If harassment has been found to have occurred, meet first with the accused. This meeting gives the accused one last opportunity to comment on the investigation. The administrator who meets with the accused should be prepared to discuss proposed disciplinary consequences. A draft of the disciplinary document that will be placed in the student, employee, or faculty record should be prepared and shared with the accused. This document should not provide each and every detail of the investigation; include only that information that provides the basis or foundation for the discipline imposed. Do not include information about unsubstantiated allegations. As discussed earlier, keep a separate investigation file.

Note that many universities must, at this point, under general agreements with faculty, refer the imposition of discipline to a faculty or faculty/administration committee. The meeting with the complainant can include a general discussion of investigation results and of disciplinary consequences, or disciplinary procedures to be instituted. Consult state law before sharing disciplinary information about the accused with the complainant. It is important that institutions tell the complainant that action was taken and give him or her at least a general sense of what that action was. The information provided should be sufficient to allow them to protect themselves from retaliation or harm if the facts of the situation suggest that this will be necessary. Some states have statutes requiring that discipline of students for certain violent sex crimes be specifically shared with the victim.

Such statutes create an exception to the general presumptions of privacy regarding student records. It is critical that administrators share only information that is specifically authorized under these statutes. Dissemination of additional privileged information may result in an action for defamation if the statements are found to be untrue. Remind the complainant again to report retaliation even if there was a finding of no harassment.

The member of the investigation team or administrator responsible for follow-up should calendar a reminder to follow up with the complainant to determine whether the action taken stopped the harassment, or whether additional action may need to be taken. Consider and immediately act on any reports by the complainant that discipline has not been effective.

If the investigators conclude that harassment did not take place or that there is insufficient evidence to conclude that harassment occurred, discuss these conclusions with the complainant first. Especially in the situation in which the complainant has been a reluctant participant, the complainant may evaluate this as the last chance to cooperate more fully. If additional material that should be pursued is offered, extend the investigation. If not, meet with the accused and review the results.

When it is found that harassment has not occurred or that there is not sufficient evidence to prove that harassment has occurred, nothing should be placed in the personnel file of the accused. There should be no mention of the complaint, investigation, or results. Further, it is unlawful to discriminate against an individual simply because a complaint has been filed against him or her. Notify both complainant and the accused of any appeal rights they have within the investigation and discipline process.

Consistency of Disciplinary Action

Although it is important to note what discipline the complainant believes would be appropriate when a formal complaint has been filed, the measure of any discipline must include other considerations.

The disciplinary measures taken should be reasonably calculated to end the harassment. Any discipline should be appropriate for the offense and send a message that harassment will be disciplined in more that a token manner. Discipline should be consistent with discipline for other equally severe misconduct and similar to discipline for similar situations of harassment. Later offenses by the same individual should be disciplined with more stringent measures than a first offense.

When the accused learns that the findings will include a determination that harassment has occurred, the accused may want to negotiate the consequences or disciplinary action to be proposed. Exercise extreme caution about negotiating disciplinary consequences. When the institution permits the accused to withdraw or resign or negotiates some other compromise with the accused that requires the institution to stop the investigation before a conclusion is reached or before discipline is imposed, the institution puts itself in a precarious position. The institution cannot use an incomplete investigation to demonstrate that reasonable action has been taken to end harassment. It may be liable to subsequent institutions or subsequent employers for failure to warn others about the conduct of students or employees. At a minimum, a letter should be placed in the accused's file stating that he or she resigned while an allegation of sexual harassment was pending.

Records of Complaint Handling

The institution should maintain records of how sexual harassment complaints were handled. As a general rule institution administrators should follow up with a complainant at least once after an investigation is concluded. Administrators need to know whether initial disciplinary action was effective and stopped the harassment. If a complainant reports that the harassment has stopped, add this information to the investigation file. If a complainant reports continuing harassment, take additional action and, again, follow up with the complainant. The time between imposition of discipline and follow up varies from case to case.

Conclusion

The procedures described in this chapter are offered to help administrators who have responsibility for investigating complaints of sexual harassment get started on a task that may seem overwhelming as it is contemplated in the abstract. The information offered is a distillation of the experiences of many institution administrators and lawyers who have conducted sexual harassment investigations for academic institutions. In addition, some elements of these procedures have been crafted by the courts.

The first generation of individuals within employment and academic settings who understood that sexual harassment compromised employment and educational opportunities struggled to have sexual harassment recognized as a form of discrimination which government should maintain a commitment to eliminate. The second generation must now refine the methods and tools we use to educate about the problems of harassment and to deal with those who persist in acting in ways that interfere with the rights of others in the workplace and in academic settings.

The investigation procedures offered here contain many choice points for administrators. The history and experience of any given institution should be considered as these procedures are adapted so that each institution has a customized tool for investigating complaints. As with policies prohibiting harassment, institutions should disseminate investigation procedures. The opportunity for comment and feedback from students, staff, and faculty will increase the "buy in" of all concerned to the elimination of harassment, will add to the level of understanding of harassment, and will demonstrate the institution's commitment to dealing promptly and effectively with this serious problem.

11

MEDIATING SEXUAL HARASSMENT

HOWARD GADLIN

Introduction

Few topics divide those who are concerned about sexual harassment as much as mediation. Even those who work directly with people who have been harassed cannot agree on whether mediation is an appropriate approach for resolving sexual harassment complaints.

Although I have long been an advocate of the judicious use of mediation as a way of resolving some sexual harassment complaints, and I have used a mediation-inspired approach myself in more than 200 cases; my experience has deepened my own ambivalence about mediation even while it has strengthened my advocacy. In this chapter I draw on both my ambivalence and my advocacy in an attempt to define the possible uses of mediation as an approach to sexual harassment.

Critics see mediation as allowing institutions to cover up harassment and fear that it perpetuates the power imbalances that are central to the dynamics of harassment in the first place. "How can a mediated agreement between the harasser and the harassed possibly be fair?" they ask. When they think of mediation, they think of a less powerful, compliant, and/or intimidated woman being manipulated into accepting a secret agreement that lets off the hook a more powerful, hard-bargaining man who not only avoids formal punishment, but is also free to resume his predatory activities.[1] Not only does he escape sanctions, but administrators learn nothing about the harasser's activities and remain unaware of the institution's potential liability. Also, there is concern that confidential mediated agreements keep other current and potential victims of the harasser from learning about his actions.

Defenders of mediation believe that, when included along with other informal and formal means of pursuing complaints, it greatly increases the likelihood that women who have been harassed will come forward with complaints. They ask, "What good is a strong set of formal procedures if almost no one will use them?" Mediation, they claim, comes closer to meeting the interests of most harassment victims than formal adjudication or investigation. No procedure can be effective if it does not encourage victims to come forward, and they will not come forward if it does not meet their needs. When its defenders think of mediation, they think of a woman in control of her own complaint; empowered to confront a previously intimidating, more powerful man; and able to tell him exactly what was harassing about his actions or speech and precisely what the impact on her was. And, they imagine a mediator who is alert to power imbalances and sensitive to intimidation tactics and is in charge of the direction of a mediation session so that it does not become an extension of the original harassment experience.

Indeed, the defenders of mediation often point to its preferability by comparison with investigatory or adjudicatory processes which in many institutions are more abusive of the complainant than any informal process. By informal procedures I am referring to a wide range of approaches someone might take to stop sexual harassment short of filing a formal complaint in accordance with the organization's sexual harassment policy. Included here is speaking to or writing a letter to the harasser, speaking to one's supervisor, use of a third-party intermediary as a shuttle diplomat, and mediation. Most individuals who have first-hand knowledge of the formal procedures associated with sexual harassment policies acknowledge how horrendous an experience it is for the person attempting to pursue a sexual harassment charge. The power imbalances that exist between the harassed and the harasser are at least as strong in formal procedures as they are in mediation. Indeed, given the adversarial structure of formal procedures, there is every reason for the person accused of harassment to exploit his superior power to the greatest extent possible.

It should be noted, however, that most people accused of harassment also report strong dissatisfaction with their institution's formal procedures. The formal procedures for adjudicating or investigating harassment are often conducted by employees whose job responsibilities include protecting the institution and limiting its liability. Ironically, these investigator responsibilities often lead both accused and accusers to distrust the formal procedures. In some institutions harassment complaints are handled by a committee composed of the harasser's peers—for example, a committee of the academic senate charged with investigating complaints against faculty. In such circumstances, it is no surprise that students or staff might be reluctant to come forward with sexual harassment complaints. In general, one reason many women are reluctant to come forward resides in their distrust of the formal procedures as they are implemented within institutions, and the fear they will be slow, ugly, and biased.

By comparison mediation provides an opportunity for those targeted by harassers to come forward in confidence, to achieve a relatively speedy resolution of their grievance, and to come as close as is possible to returning to life as it was before harassment. The mediators, while also employed by the institution, are typically designated neutrals, less beholden to organizational priorities. Although it is rarely acknowledged in comparisons of mediation and formal procedures (hearings or investigations), the preferences of the partisans of either approach often are driven by their beliefs about which creates a better opportunity for fair and just treatment of the person who has been harassed. They often disagree as well about what constitutes a just settlement. Mediators tend to emphasize disputant satisfaction with the process and perceived fairness of the agreement. Opponents of mediation look for effective sanctions and some sort of public identification of the harasser.

To some extent the disagreements about the appropriateness of mediation as a way of resolving sexual harassment complaints replicate a more general debate about alternative dispute resolution (ADR). This debate features a wide range of theoretical, ideological, and practical differences regarding the relationship between various means of resolving disputes and the attainment of social justice, and is not likely to be resolved within our lifetime. In the meantime, most sexual harassment policies include some provisions for the informal resolution of sexual harassment complaints, and mediation is usually among the informal procedures offered to complainants. It is important to consider, then, the ways in which mediation ought to be structured to maximize its effectiveness and fairness. For example, there is general agreement among mediators that it is most effective when it is voluntary. A sexual harassment procedure requiring mediation would clearly be objectionable. But making mediation voluntary is no guarantee that it is appropriate. In addition, I believe there are ways in which the standard mediation format can be modified so that it is both responsive to the needs of those who use it and compatible with institutional goals and interests. Before examining those modifications, we must review some of the complexities of sexual harassment situations.

The Complexities of Sexual Harassment

It is not always easy to answer the question "What would be the best way for the institution to respond to this case?" Sometimes the more one knows about a particular situation, the more difficult it is to answer the question. In many sexual harassment situations, there is often sufficient ambiguity about the alleged harassment and/or considerable ambivalence on the part of the person harassed that formal investigations or hearings would be unsatisfactory from the perspective of the accused, the accuser, and the institution. Mediation is, I believe, especially suited for responding to the large proportion of harassment allegations where, given the rules of evidence that govern formal investigations or hearings, it is unlikely that the harassment charge would be upheld. Mediation can allow a person's complaint to be heard, understood, and responded to even when she might not win her case. It is acknowledged by almost everyone these days how much men and women differ in their understanding of what constitutes sexual harassment and their perceptions of what is going on when men and women interact. Speaking about those differences in a recent interview about mediation and sexual harassment, Albie Davis, Director of Mediation for the District Court of Massachusetts, and a skeptic regarding the use of mediation for sexual harassment, makes the following observation (see Sontag, 1994)[2]:

> Given that tremendous difference you can see how relationships, even those where people started out liking and caring about each other, end up turning sour. Small misunderstandings grow; maybe one person became obsessed and the other tried to pull away. Something that started out as friendship, or maybe even as a little *sub rosa* attraction, suddenly gets really loaded. I have seen situations where it would have been useful to air all of those dynamics and to try to get some kind of a fresh start.

Here she highlights perfectly the way differences between men and women contribute to an initially consensual relationship flipping over into sexual harassment. By highlighting the differences between men's and women's perceptions, I do not mean to imply that harassment is merely a matter of differences in perception and communication. There are many harassers who are masters at manipulating the ambiguities in social interaction, harassing their targets without leaving a trail of evidence clear enough to convict them.

Often it is the disparity in power between the two people involved that keeps the less powerful from raising the issue with the more powerful. How many junior faculty, or graduate students, or secretaries can safely and comfortably raise such issues with their senior colleagues, graduate advisor, or boss? Properly done, mediation can create a safe and supportive setting for raising these issues, and it can encourage the participants to view a situation from the perspective of the other.

In addition to ambiguity of circumstances, another problem for any system of handling sexual harassment complaints is the divergent interests of those who feel harassed, those accused of harassment, and the institution. Typically, people who have been harassed want (1) their story to be believed; (2) the harassment to end; (3) their privacy and reputation protected; (4) a speedy resolution of the matter; (5) reassurances that the harassment will not recur; (6) reassurances that others will not be harassed; and (7) their life to return to the way it had been before the harassment, and usually, as little contact as possible with the harasser. In addition, they generally do not want to be responsible for any disciplinary action against the harasser.

Most often people who have been accused of harassment want to know exactly what they are accused of, a chance to present their version of the story and to be given some credibility, a speedy resolution of the matter, their privacy and reputation protected, their career uninterrupted, as little contact as possible with the person accusing them of harassment, fair treatment (not to be assumed guilty merely because they have been accused), and a chance to get back to their life as it was before the charges. Institutions usually want to protect their reputations, to prevent negative publicity, to achieve inexpensive and speedy settlement of grievances, high employee morale and trust in the institution, and a means of preventing recurrence of sexual harassment.

When we consider as well that the intervention that might best meet the needs of the person harassed is not necessarily the intervention that will best meet the needs of the institution, the situation becomes stickier still. The victim's needs for prompt and confidential action and unqualified support often stand in opposition to the institution's obligation to respect equally the needs and rights of both the harasser and the harassed, as well as its responsibilities to create an organizational atmosphere in which harassment is unacceptable. The institution's ability to act appropriately is often complicated by the fact that many women who have been harassed express reluctance to get the person who harassed them in trouble. If someone who has been harassed is unwilling to voice her complaint without reassurances of confidentiality and nonpunitive intervention (if any), the institution is seriously constrained.

Complicating matters further is the threat of big money lawsuits. While acknowledging the possible advantages of a sexual harassment procedure that gives women the option of pursuing a complaint in confidence in a nondisciplinary way, there is tremendous fear that if the grievant is unsatisfied with the outcome, or has a change of heart with respect to a confidential, mediated resolution of a complaint, the institution's liability will be enormous. Indeed, after years of discussion about sexual harassment with upper management at many institutions, I am convinced that fear of liability is the overriding factor that shapes most institutions' policies and procedures regarding sexual harassment. That is why almost all policies focus on identifying, pathologizing, and punishing harassers rather than attempting to alter the organizational cultures and hierarchies of power, privilege, and pampering that sustain harassment. To be sure, most enlightened institutions will conduct some sort of "prevent sexual harassment" training workshops—occasionally quite extensive and sometimes very thoughtfully put together. They are, however, typically quite cursory in their treatment of the subject and so burdened by their obligatory status that the workshops quickly take on the quality of a ritual designed more to appease the gods who control lawsuits than affect the realities of interaction within those institutions.

Regardless of what influences any organization's approach, I would argue that prevention is the only satisfactory way of addressing harassment. A climate should be created to stop it before it starts, because once someone has been harassed any response to it is to some degree problematic. In part, this is because efforts to ameliorate the effect of harassment entail a painful reliving of the original experience, and at least a partial recreation of the power dynamics of the sexual harassment incident. In the long run, only improved management and workplace and educational environments that promote respectful interaction within organizations will eliminate harassment as a significant problem. One of the reasons I can support mediation as an appropriate approach to harassment is that mediation is structured to promote respectful interaction as a means of resolving differences. It is an example of the sort of interaction that must predominate if harassment is to be stopped. Indeed, when appropriately modified to take into account the dynamics of sexual harassment, mediation can be the antithesis of harassment.

Those who are wary of mediation assert that sexual harassment is just one manifestation of gender inequality. Until we address that inequality, harassment will continue. They fear that by turning harassment cases over to mediation attention and energy will be deflected from the issues of equality, and that we must choose between responding to individual situations or addressing structural factors. But, as Mary Rowe's recent writing[3] demonstrates, we need to take a systems approach to sexual harassment, simultaneously responding to individual grievances and addressing the structural inequalities that sustain harassment. Often critics imply that the availability of mediation dilutes the prospects for structural change by draining the energies that would otherwise go into protest and activism. I find it hard to imagine that the woman who is contemplating changing her major or dropping out of school because of harassment is less likely to become an activist if her complaint is mediated than if it is not. Certainly those of us who respond to individual complaints must address structural issues as well, but that does not imply that we would solve the structural problems better or more rapidly if we no longer worked with individual cases.

The Major Mediation Adaptations

There are four major adaptations of mediation that I consider essential in instances of harassment: (1) the availability of male–female comediation teams, (2) extensive use of premediation meetings and negotiations with each party, (3) active encouragement of the use of advisors by both parties, and (4) the availability of shuttle diplomacy as an alternative to face-to-face meetings.

Female–Male Comediation Teams

For the most part people involved in sexual harassment complaints are likely to feel more at ease and able to speak honestly with someone they assume can understand their perspective. Especially in harassment cases, people often test the waters before revealing all the details of their story and all aspects of what they are hoping for in the way of resolution. Also, male and female mediators sometimes differ in their sensitivity to nuances in communication from men and women, and even if they do not, people stressed by so charged an issue as harassment will often assume those differences. However, although it is important to offer male-female mediation teams, and even to encourage disputants to use them, I believe the choice of mediators should be governed by the disputants' needs. Often, concerns about privacy and confidentiality are so strong that both parties want as few people as possible to know about their situation. And, of course, much depends on institutional reputations. In many organizations there are individuals with reputations as effective and fair mediators and they are sought out by the disputants. Because one of the goals of mediation is the reempowerment of a person who has been disempowered by harassment, such preferences should be honored. Of course, there is a chance that the disputants might differ about the desirability of having two mediators, but in my experience once the parties have expressed a willingness to mediate, they have always been open to accommodating each other's needs regarding the choice of mediators.

Premediation Negotiations

The most important alteration of the traditional mediation format is the extensive use of premediation sessions. In most mediations, especially those that follow the norms of community mediation programs, the disputants are both present when they first tell their stories to the mediators. In a harassment case, since the story told by the person who feels harassed is also an accusation— "He harassed me when he..."—the person accused is almost always inclined to respond with a denial or a countercharge—"I didn't do that" or "She led me on." But beginning with point–counterpoint replicates exactly what occurs in the filing of a formal charge and initiating a hearing or investigation. The whole point of mediation is to transcend the limitations of that dynamic, especially when it favors the more powerful party in the dispute. The focus of mediation is on resolution, not fact-finding. To prevent the mediation from becoming merely an informal version of a hearing or investigation, and one in which there are fewer procedural safeguards at that, it is important to create a setting in which winning the argument is not the intent of the communication between the parties.

Recall that the person who turns to mediation as a way of resolving a sexual harassment complaint is typically seeking an acknowledgment of the impact of the harassment; an acceptance by the harasser of responsibility for exploiting power or violating trust; as well as a resolution that is prompt, private, protective of her position and reputation; a process with as little stress as is possible; and a restoration of her self-confidence. Ironically, a harasser is more likely to acknowledge the impact of his actions when he does not have to admit guilt in a formal sense; and he is more likely to take responsibility for his actions when addressing the person he harassed than he is when confronting a hearing panel or an investigator. In ambiguous cases, the harasser might leave mediation still believing he did not violate the policy yet recognizing that the other person was made uncomfortable and that his actions were inappropriate, offensive, or insensitive.

There are other reasons to meet privately with each party before bringing them together. A part of one's natural defensiveness, which is evoked when faced with an accusation, is anger directed at the accuser. Especially when the person accused is more powerful and of higher status than the accuser, he is likely to make threats and to attack the accuser. Although there is no reason to expose a person who has summoned the courage to raise a harassment concern to the vitriol of the person she is attempting to confront, there is good reason to want those feelings to be expressed. If they are not, the atmosphere for respectful communication cannot be established and there can be no negotiation. A considerable amount of the emotional managing of the dispute can occur in private sessions, allowing the mediators to bring the parties together at a time when they are reasonably confident that the actual mediation session will not be a psychological replication of the events that led to the harassment charge to begin with.

Similarly, the person who felt harassed may need to do considerable work in private to reach the point where she is ready for a face-to-face meeting with the person she feels harassed her. In a private session she can become comfortable stating her account of what happened and explaining the impact of the harassment. She can also clarify her goals for the mediation and set priorities among the interests she hopes to satisfy in the negotiation. In some cases, she may need to express a degree of hurt that she might not want to reveal to the alleged harasser or a degree of rage that might be counterproductive to achieving her goals in the negotiation. For example, I have worked with many women who spoke privately about past experiences with abuse that they wanted me to know about so I could better understand the impact of the harassment on them, even though they did not want the harasser to know about their history.

Finally, premediation sessions can allow for a degree of self-reflection and reality testing that might not be possible in the presence of the other party. Both parties can also use these sessions to raise issues and concerns they do not want the other party to be aware of.

In addition, it should be noted that premediation sessions afford mediators more latitude in their interaction with the parties than do joint mediation sessions. Especially in sexual harassment situations, disputants are on the alert for signs of mediator partiality. In private sessions mediators can raise difficult questions, explore hypothetical possibilities, and respond empathically to each party's personal predicament without undermining the perception of mediator fairness or neutrality.

The Use of Advisors

It is important to encourage both parties to seek the support and counsel of people who can serve as advocates for their interests. Although it may be a more humane encounter than a hearing or an investigation, a mediation session is also more directly personal and, therefore, often more immediately emotional. Both parties can benefit from more support than can be provided by the mediators who are obviously constrained by their roles. I always suggest that each person identify someone who can serve as a advocate and urge them to include that person in all the sessions associated with the mediation. Never have I had anyone question my explanation of why I could not play that role and even those who do not follow the suggestion are grateful for the offer because it acknowledges the strains associated with being a party to a sexual harassment complaint.

From the mediator's point of view, the advisors can help accomplish several of the goals of mediation. First, their presence invariably helps modify the power imbalance. Most often the victim who feels intimidated by the greater power of her harasser draws strength from her support person, both because that person is looking out for her interests and because she accepts her perspective on the situation without question. In my experience, the person accused of harassment is less likely to attempt to throw his weight around when his isolation is diluted by the presence of someone who is on his side, both because that person is looking out for his interests and because that person is unquestionably an ally. Both parties seem to turn to their support people for help in assessing what does and doesn't make sense from their point of view in relation to the negotiation. Of course, the support people too have to be educated about the process of mediation and its goals, but almost always I have found them to be more of an asset than a liability in terms of moving the disputants along toward a fair settlement while also helping them handle the emotional aspects of the mediation.

Shuttle Diplomacy

Although mediation usually means bringing people together face to face, that need not be the case. Many people express horror at the idea of having a woman who has been harassed meet face to face with her harasser. Indeed, there are women who make it very clear that under no circumstances would they consent to sit down at a table with their harasser. Such requests must be honored. In addition, there are some among those accused of harassment who are also reluctant to meet with their accuser. However, just because people are unable to meet face to face does not mean they cannot mediate their differences. There are two possibilities here, which for convenience sake I refer to as shuttle diplomacy. In both of them the mediator carries communications, proposals, and agreements back and forth between the disputants without there ever being direct communication between them. In the first variation of shuttle diplomacy, the mediation is structured like most mediations with both parties present at the same time but located in different rooms. The mediator goes back and forth from one party to the other until the session is over or an agreement or impasse is reached. In such mediations, it is especially important for each party to have a support person, if only to fill in the time when the mediator is working with the other party. In the second variation, closer to what we usually mean by shuttle diplomacy, the parties do not meet at the same time; rather, the mediator meets separately with each party until agreement or impasse is reached.

Although a mediator will always use shuttle diplomacy if either party prefers it, shuttle diplomacy is also an important alternative if the mediators, after working with each party in the premediation sessions, conclude that bringing the parties together would not be productive. Most important here are indicators that the person bringing the charge could not negotiate adequately on her behalf or that the person charged is not able to negotiate without resorting to intimidation, threats, or blatant exploitation of a power imbalance. The key is to avoid an abusive negotiation.

A word about reluctance to meet with one's harasser: Although it is crucial that we respect a woman's desire not to meet face to face with her harasser, I have found it important to inquire, when such a preference is first stated, as to the reasons for the reluctance. Oftentimes, the reluctance is tied to a specific set of concerns which, if they were met, would change the woman's feelings about a face-to-face meeting. For example, on learning they could be accompanied by a support person, many women are quite willing, sometimes even desirous of the opportunity, to "tell him to his face." Often, it is only the assurance that there will be certain ground rules and some protection against intimidation that is necessary for direct mediation to feel like a possibility. Ideally, a woman should be accompanied by her support person when the mediators explore her reluctance to meet the harasser face to face to be sure that she is not yielding to unconscious pressures from the mediators or even to her own tendencies to be cooperative.

Although an altered mediation process may not meet all the concerns and objections of those who in principle oppose its use with sexual harassment, it does allow the advocates of mediation to acknowledge the legitimacy of those concerns and to modify their process accordingly. These modifications are illustrated in the following annotated story of a recent sexual harassment grievance that I consider a successful resolution through mediation. It illustrates many of the complexities found in a majority of sexual harassment situations and it raises all of the concerns voiced by the antimediation camp—power imbalances, covering up the problem, recidivism, and limited sanctions for offenders.

A Case Study

When Joanna first called the office, she only wanted the answers to a few questions about the university's sexual harassment policy. "What does one do if she has a sexual harassment complaint about a teacher?" At that point it wasn't clear if she was calling for a friend or for herself. After a brief explanation from the secretary "she" became "I." "Where do I go? Who do I talk to? What happens to me? How much time would it take?" You could almost feel her poised to hang up the phone if the conversation went the wrong way, but you couldn't tell immediately which way was the wrong way.

We knew only that she didn't want to bring a charge; she didn't want to get him in trouble. She preferred not to give her name and, no, she didn't want to talk with one of the ombudspersons. The secretary reminded her that the Ombuds Office keeps these matters confidential and pointed out that it is often helpful to someone who has been harassed to at least come in and talk with us about the situation—there is no obligation to pursue a charge, no one would take her complaint away from her and act on it without her knowledge and permission.

The secretary also acknowledged that it must be a difficult experience to cope with on one's own. She finally said, "Well, maybe I should come in." "Why don't we set up an appointment, and if you don't come in, that's no problem?" Tentatively, Joanna agreed to come in the next day and she was even willing to leave her name. At this point, we knew only that her complaint had to do with a teacher.

When Joanna arrived, although somewhat tentative about being in the office, she relaxed as I repeated our pledge of confidentiality and our reassurance that we would not act without her knowledge and permission.[4] I asked if she would be more comfortable if another woman were present or even if she would prefer meeting alone with the associate ombudsperson, a woman. Without hesitation she assured me that wasn't necessary. She was very bright, quite relaxed with herself, and her friendliness was apparent even when she was being cautious. Joanna's story was pretty straightforward:

> After receiving notification of her admission to several graduate schools (she was accepted everywhere she applied, all of them excellent schools), she had gone to the office of one of her professors to let him know of her success and to thank him for his letters of recommendation. She had taken two courses with Professor Toma and done very well. The professor had supported her interest in graduate school and there had never been any indication that he had any interest in her except as a student. After talking about her acceptance letters and graduate school choices, he suddenly shifted the focus of their conversation and began talking about how he was attracted to her and suggested that they find some way to get together off campus. There was no physical contact and he was polite, even charming, but she was totally taken off guard, and repulsed. [If faculty knew how many students find their advances either humorous or repulsive, there would be much less sexual harassment.] Joanna had managed to extricate herself from the situation without giving any indication of how upset she was. The only person she told about the incident was her boyfriend, and if it had not been for his insistence, she probably would not have pursued the matter.

Once we began talking her anger and disappointment came quickly to the surface. We reviewed the full range of formal and informal options available to her; she dismissed everything that would involve formal charges or investigations. As we talked, Joanna returned over and over again to two main concerns: She wanted Professor Toma to understand how inappropriate his advance had been and how upsetting it was for her; and she wanted to know that he would learn enough from this that he wouldn't do the same to another student in the future. Of all the options, mediation seemed most appealing because it would allow her to speak for herself, but at the same time, mediation was daunting because she would have to meet with him face to face.

We talked about the concerns she had for a meeting—the ways in which he might be intimidating, his facility with language, the fact that he was the professor and she the student, and her uncertainty that she would be able to say the same things to his face that she was telling to me. I asked her to think about the kinds of things that could be done before and during the mediation to address these concerns so that it would not be a continuation of the harassment. From her perspective, she wanted a safe setting in which to confront him, one in which he could not intimidate her, throw around his status and power, or overwhelm her with smooth talk. Yet she felt very strongly that she wanted to be the person to confront him—shuttle diplomacy would not give her what she wanted from the process.

At that point we agreed that I would speak with him about her desire to address the incident in a nonadversarial manner, explain the process of mediation, and arrange for the three of us to meet. I urged her to approach the Woman's Resource Center for support and advocacy, explaining again that, as ombudsperson and mediator, I could not serve as her advocate. I encouraged her to bring someone who could serve as a support person with her to the mediation. Although appreciative of my suggestions, she decided to forego having an advocate. She did, however, decide to meet with someone from the Woman's Resource Center. Without using her name, I made those arrangements so that she only had to mention that I had referred her.

The next step was to contact Professor Toma. When I identified myself on the phone, he seemed curious that I was calling him; but as soon as I mentioned that a student had come to see me, he said, "Oh, you must be calling about...." We met within an hour of my call. At our initial meeting, after I explained the role of my office and the nature of mediation, he gave me an account of the events that differed very little from the one given by the student. Professor Toma was both remorseful and defensive—acknowledging that he had acted foolishly and reassuring me that, as a matter of principle, he did not get involved with undergraduates. (This was said in such a way as to imply, or at least so I inferred, that graduate students were another matter.) I reviewed with him the various options for handling sexual harassment complaints against faculty, reminded him again of the student's preference to resolve this without filing a formal charge, and asked him to take some time to think about how he wanted to respond before we went ahead with arrangements for mediation. We agreed to talk again before proceeding.

Over the years I have learned to be suspicious when someone accused of wrongdoing does not react with some self-righteous anger. This is especially so for people with status and power in an institution, and I knew he needed time to react to the accusation before I would risk letting the student be in the same room with him. It is important to note that this reaction has nothing to do with disputing the accuracy of the story told by the accuser. Sure enough, when he called back two days later, he was angry and much less apologetic than he had been in our first meeting. At that point I knew there was a chance that mediation, when we got to it, could be successful; without engaging his self-justification, there would be no hope of meaningful interaction between them at the mediation. Of course, the first step was to work through this stage with him, in private. To bring them together at this point would only mean subjecting her to his self-righteousness and intimidation.

We met for an hour and a half. Toma alternated between expressing rage about her making so much of so little and asserting that he had not violated the sexual harassment policy: It was a single occurrence, she was no longer his student, there had been no physical contact, and so on. I was pretty certain he had spoken with a lawyer. Given that he was a tenured faculty member, it is most likely he was right—Toma would probably be cleared if there were a formal grievance and investigation. Much of the meaning of what had transpired between him and the student was implicit. His inclination was to take a legalistic stance and deny that what he had done was sexual harassment. Although not quite saying it, he implied he was being victimized here.

My role, beyond the usual active-listening restatements of feelings and positions, was to help him develop a framework for comparing the relative merits of sticking to this legalistic approach versus opening himself up to a more genuine engagement with the student in mediation. Several factors brought him around to mediation. First was the fact that he was preparing a formal defense against a charge that was not being posed in a formal way. The student, in asking for mediation, was asking for interaction rather than investigation. He was someone who took his role as a teacher seriously, and I believe it was difficult for him actually to be as adversarial as he was saying he was. Mediation could allow him to interact as a committed faculty member who had, tempted by the student's attractiveness and deluded by his own misreading of her gratitude, made a serious mistake and abused the power of his position. To defend his innocence in a formal investigation he would have to play a very different role—that of the misunderstood professor. And, most likely he would have had to lie. Second was his concern to not have the matter become public. I think he was especially concerned about his wife, but he was also aware that despite promises of confidentiality, formal charges usually become known. Certainly it would be difficult to keep his wife from learning he was under formal investigation for a charge of sexual harassment. Although he could probably be cleared in any formal proceeding, it was his reluctance to be involved in a formal proceeding that provided incentive for him to enter the mediation.

Those who would prefer that all sexual harassment cases be referred to a formal process must keep in mind how significant a factor formal proceedings are in mediation. It looms as an option for the victim, thereby influencing the decisions harassers make about being cooperative with mediation, and it lurks in the mediation sessions: Most of the time the person accused of harassment has no idea about the willingness or unwillingness of the person harassed to pursue a formal charge should the outcome of mediation be unsatisfactory. The existence of the possibility of a formal charge influences the person harassed as well, in part by reminding her of a potential source of leverage should the harasser be unresponsive to her concerns in the mediation. Although she may not want to go the formal route, that option is always available, and an especially recalcitrant harasser might well push the person he harassed over the edge into a decision to pursue a formal charge after all.

Of course we must be alert to the analogous risks to the person bringing the complaint as well. No doubt the harasser, especially when he is a person of some influence within the institution and in his field, is in a position to do irreparable harm to the reputation and career of the person he harassed. Should she not be responsive to his concerns during the course of mediation, or should she be too vociferous in the pursuit of her goals, he could easily create considerable difficulty for her.

In any event, by the time we had explored all the options available to him and the implications of pursuing each one, Professor Toma committed himself to the mediation although he remained convinced that he would be exonerated if a formal charge were to be brought against him. This was a wonderful illustration of the way formal and informal avenues of complaint work together. Without a formal mechanism, there would have been no leverage to move him toward mediation. Without an informal mechanism, either the student would not have come forward or he would have prevailed.

We scheduled the mediation session. However, before bringing them together, I met again with Joanna to report to her about the outcome of my session with the faculty member, to explore further her concerns now that she had met with a support person, and to prepare for the mediation itself. Despite my urging but not surprisingly, her preference was still to meet with me without the support person present and to attend the mediation session on her own as well. Acting autonomously was very important to her, and she felt it was important to confront him by herself, with only the mediator present. This is not to say that the support person was unhelpful or unimportant: She had helped her prioritize her goals and had given her an additional perspective from which to understand sexual harassment and its impact on those who are harassed. In my meeting with Joanna, we identified the conditions she felt would facilitate her ability to speak for herself, anticipated things he might say or do to throw her off, and clarified what she was hoping for as an outcome of the mediation. She was both apprehensive and eager for it to be over. We arranged to meet at the mediation session the next day.

The mediation itself was somewhat anticlimactic. Joanna spoke first and quite eloquently described her disappointment in the way he had misinterpreted her gratitude for his support. She pointed out that Professor Toma was older than her father and made it clear how his actions had dissolved her respect for him. She spoke about how her sense of academic accomplishment and achievement had been undermined by his actions, introducing an element of uncertainty in her response to other professors. She reviewed her actions to help him see what her friendliness meant, perhaps, from my point of view, with a bit too much implicit apology for what he might have imagined as her role in all this. Finally, Joanna expressed her concerns about future students and how he might approach them. While she reiterated her desire to not get him in trouble, she was unsure about what he could do to reassure her that he would not repeat his behavior with someone else.

I had been expecting Toma to put up some sort of defense, most likely in the form of the sort of explanation that recontextualized the whole event and gave it a different spin, making each statement and action more innocent than they probably were. I have heard such alternate accounts more times than I care to mention, often having to swallow my skepticism and remind myself about the importance of face-saving and the dynamics of embarrassment. But, he surprised me by beginning with an apology that was built around an acknowledgment of what he had done. He took full responsibility for any misinterpretations of her friendliness and it made clear that she had never given him reason to believe she was interested in him. It was, he owned up, a construction grounded in his own desire. He was defensive only when he tried to convince her that his support for her as a student had been based on his respect for her academic ability and achievement and not a strategy to flatter her. He insisted that until she returned to thank him, he had never paid attention to her attractiveness and although she probably didn't believe him completely he was specific enough in his praise of her work that she knew at least he remembered more about her than her appearance.

It was more complicated when it came to her concerns about the safety of other students. Although Toma attempted to assure her that he had never acted this way with undergraduates, she remained, quite reasonably, skeptical. Still, Joanna did not want to go to the department chair, or as some who have been harassed do, ask for a sealed letter to be placed in his file, to be opened only should a subsequent harassment charge be raised. It was almost as if she was asking him to give her a reason to believe him, but his harassment of her had made it unlikely that he could offer her adequate reassurance that it would not be happen again.

In the end she was left with his promises. Throughout the process she had been unwilling to have anyone else learn about the harassment incident. Because his account of why he had come on to her hadn't really made sense to her, his explanation about why he could be trusted not to repeat his actions was equally implausible. But he had understood her enough, she felt, to bring the matter to a close. Although I am often quite skeptical of agreements that address the possibility of recidivism only with promises of clean living, both my private sessions with the faculty member and his conduct during the mediation gave me reasons to trust his word here. This trust was borne out several months later when he called asking for some additional readings on sexual harassment to distribute among members of a newly formed committee whose function it would be to address sexual harassment in the department.

Nonetheless, the resolution of this case does point to one of the dilemmas facing mediators of sexual harassment cases—how to ensure that the harasser does not use the confidentiality of a mediated agreement as a cover for continuing his harassment. Although it is true that most people who have been harassed mention a concern about other possible victims among the reasons they chose to come forward, addressing that concern while preserving confidentiality is a complicated matter. To be sure, an agreement can include a clause about the possibility of future harassment, but in most cases we need more than promises. Some agreements specify that the grievant would come forward to present a formal complaint should there be a later charge of harassment against the same person. Others involve depositing a sealed statement in a confidential file to be opened only should there be another harassment charge. Some policies protect the confidentiality of mediated agreements but allow the appropriate administrators to inquire of the ombudsperson about previous informally settled charges in the event of a later formal charge.

Although each of these options requires complex administrative manipulations, they can add teeth to clauses in agreements intended to protect others. My own preference is to conclude mediations with written agreements—they leave less room for differential recall about what exactly it was the parties agreed to. However, as is often the case with mediation, I am committed to tailoring the pro-

cess to the needs and interests of the disputants. In circumstances where both parties prefer not to have a written agreement, I feel impelled, after exploring with
them the implications of not having a written agreement, to honor their preferences. Of course, should they disagree about the form for expressing their agreement, then that too becomes an issue to be addressed in the mediation.

One of the ongoing debates among mediators is about whether and how to
incorporate the interests of unrepresented parties in mediation. In the field of environmental and public policy mediation, concerns have been raised that agreements can have significant and long-term affects on large numbers of people who
are not parties to the formal dispute. Some mediators advocate a very active role
for the mediator to ensure that larger public interests are considered and argued
for during the negotiations. At the very least, we should pose an analogous set of
questions to those who mediate sexual harassment cases. It is not enough to reassure oneself that both parties agreed to the process, attended "voluntarily," and
achieved a resolution that met both of their needs. As an ombudsperson, I have a
certain latitude for raising concerns about institutional and individual interests
that must be addressed in an agreement. Clearly this is one area that challenges the
advocates of mediation.

No doubt those who are opposed, in principle, to the use of mediation for set-
tling sexual harassment charges will not be satisfied by the arguments presented
and the proposed modifications of the mediation method. But even if they cannot
be persuaded, the objections raised point in the direction mediators must go to
ensure that their method does not serve purposes that are the opposite of those
that made mediation attractive to begin with—a prompt, confidential, creative,
effective, humane, educational, and empowering alternative to formal processes
for those who cannot or will not use them.

Having worked with literally hundreds of sexual harassment allegations, I am
convinced that framing mediation and formal procedures as antithetical to one
another undercuts efforts to address the problem effectively. In a well-designed
system the availability of each approach strengthens the effectiveness of the other.
I would never argue for a system that required mediation for sexual harassment,
nor for one that permitted no options other than mediation. At the same time, I
would be equally wary of a system that did not allow for the informal settlement
of harassment charges, and mediation is one of the most effective means to informal settlement.

Formal justice systems can offer only punishment, retribution, and stigmatiza-
tion of the offender. Although there are circumstances in which these are appropriate responses to harassment, formal procedures also take a tremendous toll on
those who have been harassed and the organizations in which harassment occurs.
Even though we have all assumed that punishment can reduce the frequency of
sexual harassment, there is no reason to believe there is a connection between punishment and the need for healing required by either the person harassed or the
organization. Anyone who has worked, taught, or studied in a department that has
endured a formal sexual harassment case can testify to the fact that many more
people than the two protagonists are affected by such cases. Relationships are
strained, allegiances are polarized, and trust is diminished. Formal procedures

cannot address these dynamics. Mediation **can**, both for the protagonists and for all those who care about the climates in their institutions. Mediation allows differences to be addressed without waging war. The potential effectiveness of mediation resides in the respect it affords both parties, the control it gives them over the resolution of their dispute, and its ability to construct a nonadversarial space in which "a remedial imagination," as my colleague, Carrie Menkel-Meadow calls it, can flourish.

Endnotes

1. Because some 85 to 90 percent of sexual harassment cases that come to me involve allegations by women of harassment by men, I will refer to the harasser as "he" and the harassed as "she." Of course, it is important to acknowledge that men are sometimes harassed by women and to note that there is also same-sex harassment. But to consistently use "he or she" in reference to both the harasser and the harassed distorts both the proportions and the dynamics of harassment in the real world.

2. Sontag, Karen, Sexual harassment and mediation: Is there a fit?—An interview with Albie Davis. *SPIDR New England News* II(3), Fall 1994.

3. Rowe, Mary P., People who feel harassed need a complaint system with both formal and informal options. *Negotiation Journal* 6 April 1990; and The Post-Tailhook Navy designs an integrated dispute resolution system. *Negotiation Journal* 207–213, 9 July 1993.

4. Most ombudspeople believe that there is, or ought to be, complete confidentiality with respect to communications between visitors to the office and the ombudsperson, and that this privilege belongs to the office not to the visitor. Some ombudspeople have agreements with their employers specifying that the organization will not call the ombudsperson in its own defense. These organizations recognize that the ombudsperson is not among those agents of the institution who are obligated to report or act on complaints of sexual harassment in the same way as others—managers, supervisors, and executives. This stance is supported by the belief that there is the need for at least one agency within an organization to which people can come without fear of having their story reported to others. Of course, like other professionals who claim a confidentiality privilege, ombuds people recognize a duty to warn when they learn of possible physical dangers. As of this writing, it has not been clearly established whether ombudspeople can successfully quash subpoenas.

12

AN EFFECTIVE, INTEGRATED COMPLAINT RESOLUTION SYSTEM

MARY P. ROWE

Probably everyone who is concerned with harassment complaints begins by looking for an "ideal" way to deal with harassment and discrimination. I believe, however, that there is no one best way. Each possible procedure for dealing with harassment has important disadvantages as well as important advantages. I believe this fact requires an institution to take a systems approach, one which looks at the organization as a whole, taking into consideration the interrelationships among its parts, rather than relying on just a single way to deal with harassment.

There are a number of reasons why there is no one perfect procedure. Different institutions have different missions. They exist within different and constantly changing legal systems, cultures, histories, and value systems. Different people have widely different views on what is moral and effective, especially with respect to the extent to which complainants should be allowed options for dealing with an offense. In a conservative, relatively homogenous school, senior administrators may believe, as a matter of principle, that all sexualized conduct must be reported. They may require mandatory reporting from every supervisor, and formal investigation of all rumors, concerns, and complaints. Some administrators believe all sexualized behavior should be outlawed—if necessary by expulsion of those involved in any kind of sexualized conduct. In a large, diverse university, administrators may believe in an educational approach, rather than punishment, at least for noncriminal offenses. They may encourage people who are offended—and bystanders—to consider speaking up in a civil and effective fashion, to deal directly with offensive behavior on the spot, at least for noncriminal offenses.

Probably the most important reason why there can be no one perfect procedure is that people who feel harassed are very different one from another. In particular, people who have been harassed typically have strong feelings about what they think should happen as a result of offensive behavior—and these strong feelings vary from person to person. For example, there is a small but significant minority of offended people who will only be satisfied with formal processes oriented toward punishing offenders. This group of people may not understand or want, and will usually distrust any attempt at reconciliation or "alternative" dispute resolution. They may ask for "one simple, clear process with clear, mandatory sanctions." On the other hand, a large majority of offended people will not choose and cannot be persuaded to try formal grievance procedures, and they will not enter into a process they think will disrupt their relationships at work or in school. In particular, they may refuse to use a process where they think "someone might get into trouble," and may quit or suffer in silence rather than use a process oriented toward sanctions.

In addition, because harassment, discrimination, and workplace mistreatment are so disruptive and damaging, it may be difficult to find positive solutions once harassment has occurred. Finally, because the evidence of offense is often minimal, it may be difficult to prove an offense occurred. Thus, many complainants find harassment procedures—perhaps especially formal procedures—unsatisfactory. The alleged harassers also typically feel great dismay. Bystanders often do not know all or even most of the facts about an alleged act of harassment and its aftermath; they also have strong but varied feelings about what is or is not a desirable complaint procedure, and they may be unhappy with whatever procedures they encounter.

In short, where there is only one procedure, even it is followed in a completely faithful and competent fashion, many people touched by harassment may emerge dismayed. On the other hand, sometimes good or very good resolutions can be found. I believe a systems approach is most likely to permit and foster good solutions. This chapter presents some ideas about an effective, integrated systems approach.

The Process of Design or Review of Harassment Policy and Procedures

All effective designs begin with the needs and interests of those who will use a given procedure or policy, a point constantly emphasized by quality management experts. In the case of a complaint system, design must begin with the first group whose interests are at stake—the complainants. Other groups also matter and must be considered, especially respondents, bystanders, and supervisors. But the first group of "customers" are those who feel offended. What do we know to be the interests of complainants? Common concerns and characteristics of complainants have been widely studied and are relatively well known. People who feel harassed and mistreated typically fear loss of privacy and dignity in the eyes of family, relatives, coworkers, or fellow students. They fear reprisal or other bad consequences for bringing a complaint. They hate the idea of risking their reputations at school and at work for the sake of a "single issue." For these reasons they may hate the idea of doing anything that will lead to an institutional record with their name in it.

Many are afraid they have insufficient evidence to be believed and that formal complaints will therefore be indeterminate and pointless. Many people who feel harassed say they "just wish to have the harassment stop, they do not want to rock the boat." Many say they fear they will be thought disloyal to the work unit or living group—that they will be found lacking in humor or be considered a poor sport. A number of people who feel harassed by words or expressions are very sensitive to the concepts of free speech and academic freedom and, therefore, do not wish to bring a complaint—or believe there is nothing they can do—where the offense is "only" a matter of expression.

Many people dislike going to a third party and many have strong feelings about which people they are or are not willing to trust with a concern or grievance. For example, they may be willing to talk about the problem only with a person of a particular race, ethnic group, gender, or background. They may feel better if they can be accompanied, for example, by a peer, although some will not want anyone to know they have had a problem. They often fear they lack the skills to deal with an offensive situation effectively, and many feel they are "losing concentration and are afraid their work is deteriorating." Perhaps most important of all, many people who feel harassed see their situation to be complicated, and, in particular, they may have a concern for maintaining a good relationship with the harasser, and with other colleagues, which they think will be damaged if there is an investigation.

There also are complainants with less common characteristics. Some of these speak about total distrust of the employer, the line of supervision, and staff offices. Some completely reject the notion of due process for the alleged offender and some just want revenge. Some appear to enjoy the dispute, or say they hate the dispute, but resist ever letting it go. Some are unwilling to take any action but believe the employer should "just handle the whole thing." Some feel so strongly about having an adversarial option that they ask for a formal advocate even for informal "problem, resolution."

Overall, I estimate that 75 to 95 percent of all men and women in a given institution or workplace will not willingly choose, or even cooperate with, a formal polarized grievance process when they feel harassed. These proportions vary greatly for reasons of cultural values, the context of an offense, the type of complaint, and so on. They simply do not see such procedures to be in their overall interest, even if they feel quite dismayed or angry about the harassment. On the other hand, probably 5 to 25 percent of men and women will ultimately only be satisfied by having a win–lose option oriented toward their rights—toward investigation and justice.

In short, offended people differ greatly from each other; however, many people who feel harassed share two characteristics—they fear loss of control over what will happen and most people strongly desire a choice of options. It is for these and the other reasons cited before that I suggest consideration of an integrated, systems approach in order to provide alternatives for dealing with harassment. In the following sections, I discuss providing options (and in most cases a choice of options), the review process itself, the coverage of an effective system, some characteristics of a fair process, and issues of accountability and support.

Provide Options and Choices

Although institutional systems will differ, an integrated dispute-resolution system might reasonably include five major sets of dispute resolution options, as well as other characteristics described in the sections on coverage of an effective system and on accountability and support. I present here a simplified version of a system that might well be presented somewhat differently in different organizations. Providing options for complainants can encourage effective, direct, personal action when appropriate, both to stop harassment and to prevent reprisal. Providing options will also provide alternatives that do not infringe on free speech; which may provide a greater possibility of protecting the privacy and other rights of complainants and respondents; which may foster personal responsibility on the part of supervisors, complainants, respondents and bystanders; and which help to emphasize education and prevention. Each of the following options is actually a set of possible actions, which might differ from place to place, or be configured in various ways. Each set of options has advantages and also disadvantages (see Chapters 8, 9, and 11).

The Direct Approach

In this informal choice, person-to-person negotiations are permitted and encouraged on a purely voluntary basis for most offenses that are not too serious in nature. This option can only work well where mandatory reporting and investigation of all rumors, concerns, and complaints is not required. The direct approach may be from complainant to respondent or from bystander to respondent, in person, or by letter, alone or with a colleague. The direct approach is only appropriate where the complainant or bystander prefers this option.

This option is especially appropriate for issues of offensive speech and expression. Using the direct approach is not an infringement on free speech because an offended person has the same right to protest that the original offender had to speak in the first place. The direct approach usually keeps more control in the hands of the offended person, usually provides more privacy, and often helps affirm the offended person's sense of efficacy. This option does not result in punishment, but rather responds directly to the commonly expressed wish that "all I want is for the harassment to stop." The direct approach will not result in an institutional record being made, which will seem like a disadvantage to those in the community who want the institution to keep a record of every act of harassment. On the other hand, the lack of recordkeeping will seem like an advantage to those complainants who do not wish the institution to have a record with their name.

The direct approach is an option that requires no investigation or evidence beyond the complainant's own word, because the disputing parties already know "what happened"—there is therefore no problem of needing further evidence. This fact may be especially important if the complainant believes it would not be possible to discover evidence other than his or her own word and is therefore worried about letting any third party know of the offense, lest they fail to believe the story. Moreover, a direct approach on paper may actually help to provide extra evidence if needed. If the offended person writes a note or letter and keeps a copy, the copy of the note or letter delivered to the offending person may later be used as evidence if the harassment does not stop. This possibility may also help where there is a real or perceived power imbalance, because the offended person will be in a stronger position after writing a letter—both in having more evidence and in having proof that he or she found the described behavior unwelcome. For a discussion on how a letter may be used to stop harrassment see Chapter 3.

Informal Third-Party Resolution

In this choice there is informal intervention or shuttle diplomacy by a third party who could be a supervisor, dean, bystander, ombudsperson, or other appropriate person. This option can only work well where mandatory reporting and an investigation of all rumors, concerns, and complaints is not required. However, the institution should make clear to the whole community that what happens after the use of this option may depend on the complainant's choice of who handles the complaint.

If the complainant asks a supervisor or another staff person to intervene informally, supervisors and most staff people must retain the ultimate right to decide in appropriate cases that there will be a formal investigation even if the complainant does not wish it. Cases of this sort might include allegations regarding known repeat offenses, egregious offenses, and concerns about reprisal. As the following further notes, I also believe the institution should provide a few people—religious counselors, ombudspeople, counseling deans, and health care practitioners—who are not required to act without permission, unless a life is at stake or there is a specific professional requirement to do so. This is because a great many people will not seek any third-party help at all unless they can be assured of privacy under all conditions except those of imminent serious harm. Informal resolution and shuttle diplomacy could include action by a supervisor, which falls within the ordinary scope of management responsibilities, such as reassignment of the duties of the offender, or counseling an offender, but does not include formal disciplinary action. Informal resolution also could include reassignment of the complainant, if the complainant requests such action.

For reasons of fairness, informal resolution should not result in formal disciplinary action against an offender. At many institutions, this also means that informal resolution will not result in an institutional record, which may be considered an advantage or disadvantage by the complainant, and is a factor that the complainant should think about in choosing an option. Informal resolution may, however, be appropriate when the complainant "only wants the harassment to stop." When the third party is an agent of the institution (e.g., not a bystander), he or she may be required or encouraged to write what happened for a confidential file; the name of the complainant would be omitted.

Many complainants prefer the informal third-party approach to either a direct approach, or a formal grievance procedure, both of which may be seen by them as too confrontational. If a supervisor is involved, this option permits the institution to take responsibility for getting the harassment to stop, for the institution to help prevent reprisal, and for the institution to help rearrange work responsibilities or other duties in such a way as to help the complainant get back to normal. It may be a good option when the offended person does not feel able to take action on his or her own. If a supervisor or other staff person intervenes informally to settle a concern about harassment, that person should also follow-up to see if the harassment has stopped or if another option will also be needed.

Classic Formal Mediation

This option is provided by a trained, neutral person who helps the parties in a relatively formal process—off the record—to come to their own settlement. This option too can only work well where mandatory reporting and investigation of all rumors, concerns, and complaints is not required. Classic mediation is only appropriate where both the complainant and respondent prefer this option—it should be purely voluntary for all parties who may opt out of the process at any point. Settlements, if any, may be on or off the record at the choice of the parties, but they usually are off the record. Settlements typically are not kept or monitored by the institution.

Classic mediation does not result in formal punishment of the offender. It does, however, provide a chance for the complainant to express his or her feelings and to ask for specific, custom-designed remedies. It gives the offended person a chance to try to explain the nature of the offense and its effects. Mediation is an option that will work even with "he said/she said" evidence because the disputing parties already know "what happened" and there is therefore no problem of needing further evidence. It provides an advantage for the complainant who wants to maintain control over a complaint, as well as maintain privacy. It may be a good option for complainants who think the offender needs a chance to take responsibility for changing his or her behavior. Mediation usually will not provide a chance for the institution to help unless the offender is a supervisor who is in a position to change work conditions as a condition of the settlement, and it will not result in an institutional record unless it is put on the record as a condition of settlement (see Chapter 11).

Generic Approaches and Systems Interventions

This informal choice provides generic responses for individual complaints. Again, this option can only work well where mandatory reporting and investigation of all rumors, concerns, and complaints is not required. In a generic approach, a quietly alerted department head might: introduce a video training program, disseminate striking harassment posters to local bulletin boards, conduct a "routine" departmental staff discussion about harassment, and/or send a policy letter to each member of a department without mentioning or addressing any individual but including common examples of behavior that is unacceptable. Generic approaches are usually appropriate if the complainant prefers this option or when a supervisor hears fragments of rumor and wishes to take action without investigating individual behavior.

In addition to providing the chance for generic approaches, an institution can pursue wider systems change to prevent harassment problems. For example, many institutions are now training all supervisors about how to deal with harassment they may observe and how to deal with complaints. Such training should require that all supervisors who observe or hear of harassment are responsible to see that some appropriate person—the complainant or supervisor or other person—stops the harassment, takes reasonable steps to prevent reprisal for complaints raised in good faith, and helps the offended person get back to normal.

Stopping harassment by means of a generic approach does not result in formal punishment of the offender. Generic approaches, however, can be used in a fashion that will protect the privacy of the complainant (and the respondent); for example, if the complainant alerts an ombudsperson who alerts the department head without using names. This approach is also appropriate if the complainant is especially concerned about having insufficient evidence of the offense or if the complainant is especially concerned about reprisal. In my experience, generic approaches work well to stop an (alleged) individual offense more than half the time at very little cost to anyone; and this option rarely results in reports of reprisal. However, anyone who knows of the original complaint should follow-up to see if the alleged harassment has, in fact, stopped and to see if other options are appropriate. Although records may be kept, a generic approach will not result in an institutional record of a specific alleged offender, and usually it does not provide a chance for an institution to help the specific complainant unless she or he was the one who raised the issue.

Formal Grievance Channels

This option includes formal investigation, adjudication, and appeal mechanisms, which should be provided by reasonably impartial persons within specified time frames and with appropriate opportunities for each side to be heard and to respond to the other side. This kind of formal process may be offered by disciplinary committees and hearing officers and also by campus police. Formal disciplinary action should require fair, prompt, and thorough investigation; impartial adjudication; and an opportunity for appeal. Formal grievance procedures are appropriate for situations where a supervisor knows of previous complaints against the same person, especially if the alleged offender has been previously warned, where the alleged offense is especially serious, where there is evidence or serious concern about reprisal, and in all appropriate cases where the complainant or respondent chooses this option.

The formal grievance process has these disadvantages: the institution cannot completely protect the privacy of all concerned, the complainant must give up control over how the complaint will be handled, and it may be difficult for the institution to find enough evidence to take the action it would like to take. In addition, many people think that formal disciplinary procedures are not appropriate with respect to matters of free speech and academic freedom. Finally, many people simply dislike all formal disciplinary procedures on principle, or for reasons of ethnic custom, and will try very hard not to use them.

There are, however, important advantages. Many people will trust a complaint system more if there is known to be a fair formal process as the "skeleton" holding up the system. This is especially true for the small but significant proportion of the population who believe formal grievance processes are the only appropriate way to deal with harassment, and for the small group of complainants who want revenge, but it is also true for many people who would never use a formal process themselves. Most people believe that formal disciplinary processes for serious offenses should exist. Formal procedures may be the only way to protect people who are unfairly accused, and the only way to end a complaint where the complainant finds it impossible to "let go." A formal disciplinary process may be the only way to provide an option for people who have been harassed and are unable or unwilling to act. A disciplinary process provides an option for an institution to track repeat offenders—a consideration that should be taken seriously by any complainant who is choosing an option and believes the offender may have offended others before.

An effective system provides for the possibility in suitable cases for "loops forward or loops back"—that is, from less formal to more formal options, or from more formal to less formal options. For example, a person, who has tried to deal directly with an offense in person or in mediation, might decide that a formal grievance would make better sense if earlier attempts at resolution were not satisfactory. Conversely, a person who brought a formal complaint through a grievance procedure might learn of other facts in the case and prefer thereafter to settle—in person, with the help of an informal third party, or in classic mediation—in cases where the institution finds this option appropriate. In some situations, the loops-forward or loops-back approach requires the approval of the institution or of all parties.

The Design and Review Process

The systems I have observed that appear to work most effectively are explicitly grounded in the core values of the institution. They typically were developed with widespread input from the relevant community, and they are periodically reviewed with input from the community. It may be, in fact, that processes of widespread discussion and review are the most effective harassment prevention mechanisms. Effective systems are designed and reviewed with an orientation toward prevention of unprofessional interpersonal behavior—ideally, with as much emphasis and resource allocation on prevention as on dealing with complaints. Given the apparently high correlation of alcohol abuse with harassment and other unacceptable behavior, it is not surprising that several effective complaint systems explicitly coordinate with programs on preventing abuse of alcohol. In addition, many effective systems are positively oriented toward building a climate of respect, as well as "negatively" oriented against harassment and discrimination.

Coverage of an Effective System

The United States—and all nations—are experiencing increasing diversity of values and opinions in the workforce and in academe. All groups, including white males, are seeking support in dealing with unacceptable unprofessional behavior. Looking forward to the twenty-first century, I believe that the most effective and efficient systems will be those that deal with a wide spectrum of concerns—from inquiry through serious offenses—and with all forms of unacceptable interpersonal behavior, including harassment on the basis of race, gender, religion, nationality, color, sexual orientation, disability, and age; and harassment that is simply plain human meanness and workplace or interpersonal mistreatment. Treating all forms of harassment as unacceptable may help reduce backlash from one group or another and may help an institution build a climate of respect. It may also permit complainants to define their concerns in a variety of reasonable ways. For example, a woman of color, complaining of sexual insult, might reasonably complain based on a matter of race, of gender or of "unacceptable unprofessional behavior."

An effective system should deal with all categories of personnel, including managers, as complainants and respondents, and that it must be able to handle groups as complainants or respondents. In addition, because many complaints about harassment are linked to other kinds of concerns and grievances, such as defamation, conflict of interest, nepotism, favoritism, incompetent supervision, academic dishonesty, and misconduct, and so on, an effective system must be integrated appropriately with all other dispute-resolution procedures at the given institution. I believe that many institutions will move toward adopting single integrated systems that can and will deal with any kind of dispute or complaint, while continuing to explicitly define certain forms of proscribed behavior like harassment.

Elements of Fair Process

There is much discussion among those who design internal complaint systems about the necessary elements of fair process. I believe that a fair process provides reasonable notice to all relevant persons of the kinds of concerns which will be handled, and how they are defined. There must be a clear policy about what is harassment and what is not. Policy should include many examples of unacceptable behavior. There should also be clear specification of management responsibilities such as work assignment or negative performance evaluation, which in and of themselves are not harassment. Malicious claims of harassment should be specified as serious offenses.

A fair system should treat reprisal for raising a concern in good faith at least as seriously as harassment. Policy should proscribe reprisal against any disputant and against witnesses for either side. Supervisors and specialized staff who handle formal complaints should be required to plan and take reasonable action to prevent reprisal and then follow-up with the complainant after the complaint is apparently settled to see if all is reasonably in order and that there is no known reprisal. The basic tasks for these complaint handlers should be seen to have several parts—to stop harassment, to prevent reprisal for complaints that are raised in good faith, and to put things back to normal for the complainant as well as is reasonably possible.

A fair system should provide for reasonable protection of the rights of both sides in formal grievance procedures. It should, where possible, include appropriate protection for privacy of complainants, respondents, and witnesses. It should encourage prompt complaints and prompt and thorough complaint handling. There should be an expectation that a respondent will have a chance to know the major elements of the charges against him or her, be given a fair chance to respond to the evidence and witnesses presented by others, and to present his or her own evidence and witnesses. The standard of proof and an expectation of thoroughness should be explicit for formal investigations. There should be no formal disciplinary action taken against a respondent without a fair and thorough investigation. If a fair investigation shows that harassment caused damage, the institution should take reasonable steps to put things back to normal for the complainant.

Accountability and Support

An effective system should be designed and oriented toward at least four separate roles: the complainant, the respondent, the bystander, the supervisor. The complaint system and the topics that will be covered by the system should be presented in common terms to each member of the relevant community or workforce so that each party—the complainant, the respondent, the bystander, the supervisor—knows his or her options and responsibilities and those of others, and that they have access to the same information about the system that is being given to other parties. An effective system has explicit special expectations about leadership in harassment prevention by senior administrators. In addition, having said that all four roles should be addressed, I believe the responsibilities of senior administrators and supervisors are, in many ways, the most important. With respect to harassment and illegal discrimination, everyone in the line of supervision should be held individually accountable to take reasonable action to prevent such behavior; to see that any such behavior that is observed or reported is brought to a stop by an appropriate person, including possibly the complainant or the supervisor; and to plan and take reasonable steps to prevent reprisal and bring things back to normal.

Because of the strong feelings of the majority of complainants that they wish to have options about how harassment is handled, because most offended people will not come forward in a system with mandatory investigation, and because mandatory investigations may unfairly damage some complainants and some respondents, I do not believe in mandatory reporting and investigation of all harassment complaints. To some extent, I differentiate this idea from the important responsibility of supervisors to see that harassment stops and to take reasonable steps to prevent reprisal. As said before, supervisory responsibility may, in fact, require thorough investigation if the alleged behavior is quite serious—for example, if the supervisor knows there have been other complaints of the same kind against the same person, especially if there has been a warning; if the complaint is about serious criminal behavior; or if the complainant alleges reprisal. But, in appropriate cases, a supervisor or staff manager should be permitted to support a complainant who chooses to deal with the matter directly. A supervisor should also be able, if asked, to deal with a matter informally as a third party, to recommend the option of classic mediation, or to take a generic approach when appropriate. In actual fact, options of this sort usually do stop harassment—at lower cost to the complainant and respondent.

The system should provide a variety of helping resources to each of the four parties or roles. Some resource persons should be available for support off the record. In my opinion, off-the-record resources should be expected not to act without permission unless there appears to be imminent risk of serious harm and no other option appears appropriate. These resources might include hot lines for people who wish to call anonymously, religious counselors, counseling deans, employee assistance, other health care practitioners, and internal ombudsmen. Calling such an office off the record should be announced in public brochures and statements as an action that does not "put an employer on notice." The system should also specify the resources—supervisors and appropriate staff offices—who will act if notified so that a problem will not fall in a crack once it has been reported. The system should clearly specify those who may be contacted off the record and those, by contrast, who are permitted and required to take action to see that harassment is stopped and that there is no reprisal. Differentiating roles in this way may permit offended people to make an informed choice about how and whether they may keep control over their concerns.

A system should provide a choice of complaint handlers (e.g., people of color, whites, both men and women) and a choice of people who especially understand issues of race and culture, gender, sexual orientation, disability, age, and religion, as sources of information and support. This is so a person seeking help may, if desired, find someone similar to himself or herself, and reasonably knowledgeable, as a helping resource. The system should also allow for information and support to a complainant or respondent in preparing or responding to a formal complaint, and accompaniment while making or responding to a formal complaint.

One of the most difficult questions in complaint system design concerns the amount of information that a complainant will be given after the institution looks into a complaint. The question is a difficult one because most institutions do not give out information about what happens in personnel actions or in dealing with complaints against students. An argument can be made that offended people are more likely to come forward if they know that prompt and fair action is taken against offenders. An opposite argument also is made that giving out information violates fair concepts of privacy, may violate certain laws, and also will discourage offended people from coming forward because other people may come to know of their complaint. In my experience both arguments are correct, albeit for different people.

On balance I usually suggest errors of omission—saying less rather than more. In general, complainants should be told the findings in the case and whether disciplinary action was taken. It is also helpful for institutions to present overall (identity-free) statistics that will help a community understand that the system is accountable. The system, thus, should provide for data collection and evaluation of the system, with summary information published in a manner that appropriately protects the privacy of individuals.

I also believe that a complaint system should be overseen by a specialized group—including, for example, appropriate persons from senior line management, personnel, security, student affairs, the medical department, employee assistance, equal opportunity officer, religious counselors, ombudspersons, legal counselors, and those responsible for housing—that meets regularly. This group should be available to talk about difficult and dangerous cases (e.g., people who stalk, who "won't let go," or who want revenge in an unreasonable way). As appropriate, this group can link the harassment complaint system to other systems inside and outside the institution and oversee, report on, and work to improve the system on a continuous basis.

Conclusion

In conclusion, I believe in an integrated systems approach for dealing with harassment within institutions. My reasons are both philosophical and pragmatic. On the philosophic side, it is ethically important to give most complainants at least some options and some choices about those with whom they will talk—and what will happen—if they feel harassed. As a matter of pragmatism, an institution must provide options, and in most cases a choice of options, if the system is to work. In my experience, because the majority of the population will reject any one single option that can be provided, an institution must provide more than one option if the majority of those harassed are to be able to take or seek effective action.

13

CROSS-CULTURAL
ISSUES AND INFLUENCES

ROBIN OAKS   *JOYCELYN LANDRUM-BROWN*

Introduction

Someone might well ask, "What possible relevance do cultural factors have to an academic institution's legal responsibilities for resolving sexual harassment complaints?" The question is a valid one and there is an equally relevant and compelling answer. Cross-cultural factors influence how people experience and react to offensive behavior, whether and in what manner sexual harassment is reported, how adequately complaint investigations are conducted, and how effectively complaints are resolved. Understanding how cross-cultural factors impact sexual harassment and complaint resolution will not only help administrators create working and learning environments based on respect, but also limit individual and institutional liability.

Anyone who actually handles sexual harassment complaints in the academic setting already knows that the simplistic legal definitions for sexual harassment inadequately address the complex social and cross-cultural factors affecting this discriminatory conduct. Although *sexual harassment* is a legal term, derived from a body of state and federal antidiscrimination laws, it manifests as a cultural phenomenon; characterized as behavior based on power, coercion, and oppression, its effects are far-ranging. The laws mandate that academic institutions must educate the academic community about sexual harassment, investigate complaints, and take the necessary action to ensure that this form of discriminatory conduct is eliminated. This chapter explores the impact of cross-cultural factors on sexual harassment and an academic institution's legal responsibilities.

Note: Many of the examples cited in this chapter refer to experiences of Robin Oaks as legal counsel advising and representing academic institutions in personnel matters and sexual harassment complaint resolution. Where reference is made to experiences "we" had, it is referring solely to legal work provided to academic institutions by Oaks and her legal associates. Although Joycelyn Landrum-Brown contributed information for specific portions of this chapter, she is not affiliated with the legal practice of Robin Oaks.

Unquestionably, academic communities reflect a myriad of cultures and sub-cultures, incorporating a multifaceted framework through which actions are filtered and checked as individuals interact in their environment. Culture affects how we function within an environment, act within role expectations, communicate, gather and process information, and make assumptions about the world in which we live. The problem with any discussion about cross-cultural issues, however, is that it may inappropriately foster stereotypic thinking or be dogmatically applied as a simple answer to address complex problems. In fact, a quintessential understanding of how cultural factors may influence sexual harassment recognizes that any cultural categorizing can never accurately reflect the reality of any given individual situation. Consequently, this discussion on cultural factors is presented with the awareness that it is inchoate; the intent is to foster dialogue and create a nascent framework that will provide a point of reference on which to build understanding about sexual harassment and encourage responsible action in academic communities.

Preventing Sexual Harassment

Although the high dollar judgments in sexual harassment cases usually are the result of an academic institution's failure to respond appropriately or at all to a complaint, under federal laws, such as Title IX[1] and Title VII[2], and virtually every state discrimination law, academic institutions must also take the necessary steps for prevention. For example, in California, the Education Code and the state employment discrimination laws set forth specific rules for disseminating information about sexual harassment to employees and students.

The Equal Employment Opportunity Commission (EEOC), which enforces Title VII, suggests that prevention measures should include affirmatively raising the subject of harassment, expressing strong disapproval, developing appropriate sanctions, informing employees of their rights, and developing methods to sensitize all concerned. Additionally, effective training of employees, students, faculty, and supervisors about sexual harassment is crucial to raising certain defenses that may insulate an institution from liability in a lawsuit.

It is obvious from the variations in legal opinions and court decisions on this subject that no definition exists that will accurately predict unlawful conduct in all cases. If each unique fact situation is considered on a case-by-case basis, how can people be educated to know what conduct is prohibited? Further confusion arises because the type of conduct that is being recognized by society and under sexual harassment law as discriminatory is rapidly evolving and changing. The problem is compounded by the fact that the law applies both an objective and a subjective standard to an analysis of whether a certain conduct constitutes sexual harassment.

The complainant's subjective or individual perspective is considered by focusing on the impact of the conduct, whether the complainant experienced the conduct as "offensive, intimidating or hostile" and whether it was "unwelcome." The *objective* standard applied under the law considers whether the conduct would be perceived as hostile, intimidating, or offensive from the perspective of an imaginary "reasonable" person in the same position as the complainant. The "reasonableness" standard assumes, however, that there is one cultural view that should or does predominate; in reality, people function within a spectrum of perspectives and cultural viewpoints. Although later in this chapter we will outline where the law does or does not recognize cultural factors in a legal analysis, people will better understand the true nature of sexual harassment if they are educated about what cultural factors affect our experiences.

When we teach people about sexual harassment, many react with frustration, even anger, when they learn that the law focuses on the impact of the conduct from the victim's subjective perspective, and discounts the intent of the person accused. The conundrum arises because discrimination laws attempt to protect two conflicting interests. One interest involves protecting individuality and recognizing differences. The other interest concerns a collective society's interest in identifying group interests and rights and preserving these interests based on such common characteristics as race, religion, or gender. A so-called standard of objective reasonableness applied by a judge or jury is somehow expected to provide a nexus between these interests. Unfortunately, by emphasizing an "either-or" approach in the court, which results in someone winning and someone losing, and by applying a dominant cultural standard, which is the interpretation of the judge or jury as to what is reasonable, cultural perspectives that are not identified by the dominant cultural norm are generally obscured.

It is clear that taking no preventive action or instituting superficial prevention training is neither prudent nor responsible. So what can be done to institute prevention measures to sensitize people realistically about sexual harassment? What can be done to increase understanding so that conduct can be modified before a hostile environment is created? At the very least, prevention measures should raise awareness that sexual harassment is not only about the law, but is also about cultural influences and power dynamics. When administrators, employees, students, and faculty are educated about the cultural influences affecting how we perceive and react to the world, an academic institution will both fulfill its legal responsibilities to send a message that sexual harassment is prohibited; and at the same time, it will increase the likelihood that complaints will be more fairly assessed, investigated, and resolved. Like a good insurance policy, prevention measures that comprehensively and honestly communicate the complexities about sexual harassment help to decrease the chances of improper conduct from occurring, ensure that effective action will be taken when problems arise, and strengthen the legal defenses to liability that can be asserted if litigation ensues.

At a minimum, the following four cultural concepts can be discussed in prevention training programs that target either the staff and student population generally or seek to specifically train investigators, administrators, and complaint officers:

1. Identity development
2. Modes of interaction with the world
3. Philosophical and cognitive processes
4. Psychological orientation

A brief summary of each concept with examples of how they relate to sexual harassment and the legal mandates for resolving sexual harassment complaints is provided in the following sections. Before discussing these cultural factors, however, it is important to understand exactly what is meant by the term *culture.*

Definition of Culture

Many scholars from different disciplines have attempted to define the notion of culture. Culture typically involves values, norms, beliefs, attitudes, folkways, behavior styles, and traditions. In general, culture can be described as a point of reference from which we construct our understanding of reality.

The definition of culture has evolved over time. At one point the focus was primarily on observable aspects such as dress, music, food, and folkways. In the United States during the 1960s, the focus on culture moved toward ethnographic variables including nationality, ethnicity, and racial classification. As a result of this shift, the definition of culture came to be associated primarily with racial/ethnic minorities. These trends have resulted in the unrealistic impression expressed by many members of the dominant culture who do not see themselves as having a "culture." This is particularly true of those individuals who chose or were forced to become "American" by abandoning their ethnic heritage and assimilating into the "melting pot." Therefore, those who have been influenced by or reflect the dominant cultural view may not readily recognize that their actions are culturally influenced. In reality, everyone is influenced by a myriad of cultural factors, evolving from individual family influences and the dominant societal culture as a whole. The framework of cultural factors create who we are and how we interpret and experience the world.

Another problem contributing to the lack of understanding regarding the influence of culture relates to how it manifests. Researchers have made distinctions between surface and deep-structure manifestations of culture. Typically, when cultural influences are considered, the emphasis is on surface elements such as dress, communication style, and customs. Little attention is directed to the deep-structural frameworks that include the values, assumptions, and philosophical views, that influence day-to-day interactions. It is the deep-structure cultural manifestations that have the most direct influence on sexual harassment. These elements are most clearly presented in the concept of worldview. *Worldview* involves the cognitive framework by which we create our understanding of our life experiences. The following are examples of deep-structure cultural concepts that are relevant to understanding sexual harassment and the controlling laws.

Identity Development

Identity development and gender role socialization patterns influence how people view themselves and others. *Role* is defined as a cluster of socially or culturally defined expectations that individuals in a given situation are expected to fulfill.

Anita Hill, speaking at the University of California at Santa Barbara, referred to the socialized patterns of identity development when she described sexual harassment as the manifestation of a culture of oppression; it is a learned behavior and as such can be unlearned.[3] It is important to recognize that laws reflect what a society or culture values and what behaviors it seeks to discourage through either criminal or civil sanctions. The scope of behaviors constituting sexual harassment and legal remedies have evolved rapidly as societal awareness has increased. Consequently, just as Anita Hill's testimony during the Clarence Thomas hearings heightened awareness of sexual harassment, as the dominant cultural view and the manifestations of power and gender dynamics shift, so changes the law.

Obviously, how men and women, boys and girls are expected to behave impacts all stages of sexual harassment complaint resolution. In our experience investigating, training, and advising academic institutions about sexual harassment complaints, it is not uncommon to hear comments reflecting gender role expectation such as "boys will be boys" or "she's just too sensitive, she can't take a joke."

Role identification issues may arise when credibility is assessed during investigations of sexual harassment complaints. Similar to the "rape myths" that prejudice the way jurors and the public perceive testimony in a rape trial, culturally derived assumptions also influence assessment of evidence in sexual harassment matters. Examples of culturally influenced myths that affect how people interpret behavior include the following: "women mean 'yes' even when they say 'no,'" "women bring false claims of sexual harassment to get even with a man who has spurned her," "the majority of women who are sexually harassed have bad reputations," and "if she really didn't want to have sex with her boss she would have just said no."[4]

Around the world cultures vary in how men and women are expected to behave in society. When referring to any racial or ethnic classification, it must be understood that each category covers a wide range of possible variations. For instance, the Asian cultural group involves many diverse ethnic populations, religions, and geographic territories, covering such areas as Korea, Japan, China, Southeast Asia, India and South Asia, Micronesia, Melanesia, Polynesia, and Hawaii. As a result, the descriptive term "Asian" is not very specific and is clearly an over generalization. With this caveat, researchers have noted that certain Asian religious traditions teach women to be subservient not only to their husbands but to all males.[5] One Vietnamese woman stated that she was taught to obey men and defer to their judgment unquestionably. In her culture, the teacher is more important than a parent. As highly honored members of the community, teachers recieve great respect. She stated that it is highly offensive and inappropriate to discuss sexual matters in public. When she arrived in the United States she was constantly embarrassed by the sexual content of conversations, television shows, and advertising. With such cultural views, it is easy to understand the difficulties that might exist for this woman if she were subjected to sexual innuendoes or overtures by a professor in the academic setting.

Additionally, "Asian" American women may be subject to gender stereotyping that characterizes them as exotic, submissive, demure, erotic, and manipulative.[6] For example, a white male professor from the mainland, teaching in Hawaii, had interpreted the traditional ethnic dress of a particular female professor as exotic. Based on his cultural expectations, he acted as though the woman's choice to dress in this manner was a sexual invitation to him individually, and he repeatedly made sexual advances to the woman despite her attempts to avoid him.

Another example of identity development involves machismo in the Latino culture. Although earlier research on traditional Latino culture focused on the rigidity of gender roles, more recently the research has suggested that gender roles within Latino families are much more diverse and dynamic.[7] The essence of machismo is a system of behavioral traits characterized by extreme "manliness" that avoids all roles or activities associated with women.[8] For women, *hembrismo* or marianismo is exemplified by extreme femininity and passivity. *Marianismo*, at its roots, is based on the Roman Catholic worship of Mother Mary, who is a virgin and the Madonna; the underlying concept is that women are spirituality superior to men and therefore capable of enduring all suffering inflicted by men.[9] This concept is exemplified in the expectation that a woman's role is to accept her husband's macho behavior and sacrifice herself on behalf of her family.

One affirmative action officer with years of experience in a government setting observed that many Latinos in the working environment are far more tolerant of interactive behavior engaged in by males from Mexican backgrounds than are those females who are influenced by the dominant culture. This officer, and many who function in similar positions, share the view that such different cultural perspectives and experiences create problems and real challenges for people who are mandated to respond effectively to discrimination complaints in culturally diverse work environments.

Whether conduct is tolerated, however uncomfortable, may depend on what is considered normal behavior or what role expectations exist. Where women are socialized into gender roles that reinforce submission and deference to males, they may accept intimidating conduct as part of the status quo and believe it must be endured.

In one situation at the university level, a male professor's conduct of dating, having sex with, and favoring his female students was condoned by the administration, despite protests, because it was considered normal behavior for an "attractive bachelor." Significantly, the administration's position was also likely influenced by the fact that the professor was nationally recognized in his academic field and the school had a higher investment in protecting the high-profile professor than in recognizing the impact of his behavior on a few students. Whether conduct is considered acceptable, normal, or offensive is directly related to cultural influences and values.

An interesting study conducted by Melissa Monson at the University of Nevada, which examined harassing conduct directed at video store rental clerks, reported that many of the female employees did not define offensive behavior as sexual harassment specifically because it was the norm and common.[10] That the conduct was "predictable" male behavior was interpreted as something that women had to tolerate. How men and women are culturally conditioned to believe they should behave is an integral factor in understanding the dynamics of sexual harassment and its relationship with gender role expectation and power in our society. All of these cultural influences have implications for understanding how people determine whether conduct is offensive and how response patterns to such conduct may vary.

When teaching people about these influences, it is important to emphasize that the intent is not to sanction discriminatory conduct simply because there is a culturally based influence or because it has been tolerated in the past. The case law clearly shows a trend away from accepting offensive conduct as reasonable simply because it historically was part of the traditional work environment, which may have been male dominated. Instead, raising awareness is intended to build a sense of respect for others and to encourage responsibility to act in a manner that fosters working and learning environments free of intimidation and oppression.

Modes of Interaction with the World

Modes of interaction with the world involve one's action orientation, relationships with others, and communication styles.[11] At its core, sexual harassment involves modes of interactions that reflect how people treat each other, how power is exercised, and how people function within a dominant cultural hierarchical framework. Many studies report that men and women communicate, interpret body language, and perceive the world through different cultural filters.

Deborah Tannen, author of *You Just Don't Understand,* concludes that men and women speak different gender dialects—women speak and hear a language of connection and intimacy, while men speak and hear a language of status and independence.[12] Communication between men and women may be like cross-cultural conversations. For instance, men typically interpret a woman's smiling as evidence of interest and a sign of sexual openness, whereas women usually intend a smile as a sign of politeness and friendly behavior.

As another example, in African American traditional culture, originally *rapping* referred only to romantic communications from a man to a woman intended as a means to win her affection and sexual favors.[13] Rapping styles and phrases as forms of social interaction may be interpreted as offensive or not, depending on a person's experience within a certain cultural context and what underlying message they believe the behavior is intended to send.

In traditional Native American cultures, elders, experts, and those with spiritual powers are highly valued. Ridicule and criticism of others should be avoided and harmony with nature is emphasized. In this culture, nonconfrontational communication styles are valued. Neither males nor females may directly communicate their negative reaction of offensive conduct; a "no" is not expressed overtly. Obviously, if a people not familiar with this culture act as though conduct were welcome unless they received a clear message otherwise, serious miscommunication problems could arise. Raising awareness of these differences in reaction styles is important not only for prevention training but also for those who must investigate, respond to, and resolve sexual harassment complaints.

Philosophical and Cognitive Frameworks

Philosophical and cognitive frameworks involve the information filters that affect each person's sense of reality. Philosophical factors include values such as individualism versus collectivism, and spiritual versus material beliefs. Cognitive frameworks involve problem solving, conflict resolution styles, and information-processing styles. For example, researchers have referred to traditional "Asian" worldview perspectives that emphasize varying degrees of maintaining tradition, reverence for education and family, fatalism, self-sacrifice, nonconfrontational styles, and behavior that prioritizes saving face and preserving honor.[14]

Many sexual harassment complaint officers have stated that when the complainant is influenced by an Asian culture, they have observed very strong family pressures not to report the harassing behavior, especially if a teacher is involved. Understanding these realities can help schools provide appropriate support for complainants and ensure that evidence is fairly and accurately gathered during investigations. Later in this chapter, we outline how hidden cultural influences may inappropriately influence how credibility is assessed and how investigations are conducted.

Psychological Orientation

Psychological orientation influences how a person relates to the world. It includes concepts of time, self, and others. For instance, if an individual's cultural view is from an "extended self," he or she may feel that taking formal action against harassment, particularly if the harasser is from the same cultural or racial group, will be harmful to the collective group. This perspective is reflected in the quote, "I am because we are, we are because I am."[15]

One situation at a university campus in California created much debate within the African American community. An African American male student was accused of sexual harassment and the African American female students were divided as to how much publicity they believed should be encouraged. Some felt the need to speak out against sexual harassment as a form of oppression and violence against women. Others feared that raising public awareness would foster the stereotypic views held by those in the white academic community against African American males. This incident is also illustrative of how people of color may experience oppression from more than one perspective and how these factors raise complex issues for sexual harassment complaint resolution.

Academic institutions can institute state-of-the-art policies and create procedures for complaints, but if there is no evidence of institutional responsibility, harassment will continue. Current statistics on discrimination lawsuits against schools confirm that people are frustrated with lack of institutional response; the problems will not go away unless they are attacked at the root. Instituting comprehensive prevention measures that include awareness of cultural dynamics will help build a predictable framework for appropriate conduct and foster environments based on respect. As the saying goes, an ounce of prevention is worth a pound of cure. Where the cost of defending lawsuits can be substantial and judgments often are thousands of dollars, effective prevention measures are worth the effort.

Reporting Sexual Harassment

The law requires that complaint procedures must "encourage complainants to come forward." Effective and prompt responsive action is required when the school knew or should have known about the misconduct. When supervisors/managers engage in discriminatory conduct, the institution is held strictly liable in most cases. Consequently, an academic institution is not insulated from liability simply because there was no "formal" reporting. Therefore, administrators should understand what dynamics influence whether someone will or will not report sexual harassment and what the warning signs are that a problem exists.

When the Office for Civil Rights of the U.S. Department of Education (OCR) investigates complaints filed against schools under Title IX, many of the cited inadequacies involve either a failure to advise students about available remedies or a failure to institute "prompt and equitable" complaint procedures. If administrators and those responsible for working with personnel and students are aware of how cultural factors influence timely reporting, they may be able to encourage reporting and early intervention before problems become lawsuits.

As the previous examples of cultural influences suggest, people differ in confrontational styles and responses to conflict situations. A person's beliefs about the justice system and procedures for redress are influenced by past personal and cultural experiences. Certain studies suggest that distrust of the justice system influences women of color to be less likely to report incidents of rape than white women.[16] Other studies report that African American women are less likely to bring sexual harassment complaints. Of those who did report, it was African American women who were more likely to report *quid pro quo* sexual harassment.[17]

Additionally, whether harassing conduct is reported may depend on whether the accused is from the same cultural background as the complainant. This may be related to a sense of loyalty to the racial or ethnic roots common to both, or may be influenced by whether the conduct is perceived as less offensive or familiar, and less intimidating. One female affirmative action officer, who was African American, stated that if a white male made sexual advances to her she would be far more suspicious than if an African American male approached her. Obviously, historical race and gender relations in this country, where slavery existed and women were considered property, play an integral part in influencing how offensive behavior may be perceived.

In another case involving an African American male professor who was making sexual advances to an African American female student, the student refused to file a formal complaint because she feared negative racial stereotyping against the African American community. Her individual problem relating to sex discrimination was weighed against her sensitivity to her African American roots and the racist stereotypes about African American males that she feared would be inappropriately highlighted by her individual complaint.

Kristin Bumiller, in *The Civil Rights Society*, writes about discrimination law systems.[18] She states that it is difficult to openly express protest or to label the conduct harassing because the very act of complaining forces a person to be identified as a "victim." Victims may be reluctant to come forward based on their word alone because they fear they will not be believed or taken seriously. If their societal experience includes being treated as "invisible" or "second-class," they conclude the system will not give great weight to their word alone without concrete evidence to support their testimony.

For women and men who do not represent the dominant culture or who have fewer perceived privileges, reporting discriminatory conduct requires that they trust a system that has historically treated them unfairly, as invisible entities, subject to stereotypic actions. As difficult as it is for any victim to take on the system and to be in the spotlight, it is far harder for those who are not from the dominate culture to do so.

Although studies show that both women and men believe that sexual harassment should be reported, when they are actually the recipient of the behavior, very different attitudes prevail. Women are typically socialized to avoid public attention and direct confrontation. Instead, they are encouraged to utilize avoidance techniques to resolve a conflict. Men may believe that they should resolve conflicts on their own, without outside assistance. Even stopping and asking a stranger for directions when driving is seen as an admission of "weakness" for many men. Further, in studies where male and female characteristics are listed, of the items associated with maleness, none was directly or indirectly related to sexuality, whereas femaleness is associated with sexuality in many ways. These stereotypes reinforce the view of men as organizational beings and women as sexual beings in the workplace. In a recent Ninth Circuit case, *Fuller v. City of Oakland*, the court recognized differences in male and female perceptions of intimidation and offensiveness. Interestingly, the court applied yet another variation on the reasonable person standard and concluded that whether the workplace is objectively hostile must be determined from the perspective of "a resonable person with the same fundamental characteristics."[19]

Such culturally conditioned expected behaviors, including gender role issues about sexuality and power, make reporting very difficult for men who are subjected to sexual harassment. In a study conducted by Beth Quinn at the University of California at Irvine, she reports that one male, who had been sexually harassed by his female supervisor, continually modified his story.[20] Initially, he stated that he felt very upset by his female supervisor's conduct. As the interview progressed and he verbalized more, he began changing his story to reflect a more generalized male role view, not his own perspective. He began adding qualifications such as, "But if I found her more attractive I might not have been so upset." As more cases surface involving male complainants harassed by either males or females in academic environments, more will be understood about how men experience and respond to sexual harassment. In many ways, the cultural factors relating to men as victims of sexual harassment involve unique factors. So, too, the cultural factors relating to harassment and discrimination on the basis of sexual orientation are only recently being understood, and victims of such harassment are finally being afforded legal protection and recourse in some instances.

Some recent studies by James Gruber suggest that efforts to encourage reporting may not be as complicated as one might suppose.[21] Gruber's work concludes that where policies and complaint procedures are strongly enforced by the administration and where the administration creates an environment that emphasizes the primacy of professional role obligations over ascribed gender roles, women are more likely to report and seek remedies for violations of discriminatory conduct. The implication of these studies is obvious: where the administration encourages professional respect and acts in a manner that confirms an intolerance for discriminatory behavior, people will report problems and resolve problems within the system, not seek redress in the courts. Only by knowing how cross-cultural influences may affect reporting can professionals responsible for preventing sexual harassment effectively fulfill their responsibility to truly encourage complainants to come forward.

Responding to Complaints

In addition to instituting preventive measures and "prompt and equitable" complaint procedures, an academic institution must respond appropriately to sexual harassment complaints by conducting fair investigations of the evidence. Further, particularly in public institutions, constitutional due process protections require a fair and unbiased evaluation of facts. Regardless of whether formal or informal options are pursued, once the administration knows or should have known of conduct constituting sexual harassment, it is responsible for taking the necessary action to end discriminatory conduct; this implies not only a thorough investigation to gather the relevant evidence but also an understanding of how evidence is evaluated to determine if the conduct constitutes unlawful discrimination.

Before exploring how cultural factors affect evaluating evidence in investigations, it is important to discuss how cultural factors influence whether the alleged conduct is first characterized as a sexual harassment complaint. Although the complainant may not label the conduct sexual harassment, it is the administrator's duty to recognize sexually harassing conduct and direct the complainant to the proper complaint officer. Often well-meaning administrators, either unaware of legal developments or blind to their own cultural biases, may not appropriately respond at this important phase.

In two recent Title IX cases filed in California federal courts, *Patricia H. v. Berkeley Unified School District*,[22] which settled for a substantial sum, and *Jane Doe v. Petaluma City School District*,[23] the plaintiffs asserted that the schools failed at the outset to recognize the alleged misconduct as sexual harassment. In the *Petaluma* case, the student told her counselor she was repeatedly being called names that had sexual overtones and yet he failed to apprise her of the sexual harassment complaint procedure or direct her to the Title IX officer. Although the harassing conduct of a sexual nature continued, at one point the counselor stated to the student's parents that "boys will be boys," words it is imagined, he may now regret having said. Almost two years later, after continual complaints to the counselor, the Title IX coordinator finally became aware of the pattern of harassment.

The legal definitions and varying common "working definitions" for sexual harassment are explored in other chapters in this book. What is important to emphasize in this chapter related to cultural influences is how the dominant cultural view influences how the legal definitions are interpreted. Whether conduct constitutes sexual harassment is determined by looking at the totality of the circumstances and the context in which the alleged incidents occurred. Whose cultural perspective determines what is relevant?

A *hostile environment* exists where the acts of a sexual nature are sufficiently severe or pervasive to impair the educational or employment conditions as determined from the viewpoint of a reasonable person in the victim's situation. Under Title IX, OCR considers the age of the victim, the frequency, location, severity, scope of acts, nature, and context of the incidents, and whether the conduct was verbal or physical. What culturally influenced factors determine the "reasonable person's" perspective?

In a significant California case, *Dept. of Fair Employment & Housing v. Univ. of California, Berkely, Amy Forga*,[24] involving a sexual harassment complaint by a female graduate student against a university professor and the University of California, Commissioner Phyllis Cheng's dissent evidences how people differ as to what is reasonable. She concluded, unlike the majority of the Fair Employment and Housing Commissioners, that "Given both the inherent nature of the teacher–student relationship and the particular circumstances of this case, then, I believe that complainant's perception of [*the accused professor's*] approaches was well within the parameters of a reasonable female graduate student." The university student was subjected to comments and conduct by the professor that had obvious sexual innuendos, and one incident of touching. The majority applied the so-called objective standard of a *reasonable female graduate student* and concluded that although her emotional well-being and ability to perform her studies were negativily impacted, given the nature of the complained-of conduct, they believed the extent of her reaction was extreme. The fact that there were divergent opinions as to what a reasonable female graduate student would conclude illustrates how reasonable minds differ. Commissioner Cheng asked, "How much more severe does unwelcome sexual conduct need to get before the commission would recongnize the existance of a hostile education environment?" Our legal system, by applying a dualistic process of guilt or innocence, may bring closure to a dispute but the result is far from precise, predictable, and perhaps even just.

Although, the United States Supreme Court, in *Harris v. Forklift*,[25] reconfirmed the applicable standard for sexual harassment under Title VII, the Court did not directly address the question of how anyone determines the kind of conduct that a reasonable person would consider sufficiently severe or pervasive to alter the conditions of employment and create an abusive environment. We all want to think that we are reasonable people; however, are we in reality applying our own individual standard of reasonableness that may ignore other equally reasonable perspectives?

Until this issue is decided by the Supreme Court, the circuits will differ as to what cultural factors determine whose perspective should be applied. Cultural differences based on gender were specifically addressed in a Ninth Circuit decision that has since been followed by some courts and governmental agencies. In *Ellison v. Brady*,[26] the court concluded that the applicable standard for a female complainant is whether a *reasonable woman* would consider the conduct sufficiently severe or pervasive to alter the conditions of employment and create an abusive working environment. If the victim is male, the standard is from the *reasonable man*'s perspective. The court reasoned:

> We adopt the perspective of a reasonable woman primarily because we believe that a sex-blind reasonable person standard tends to be male-biased and tends to systematically [*sic*] ignore the experiences of women. The reasonable woman standard does not establish a higher level of protection for women than men [*citations omitted*]. Instead, a gender conscious examination of sexual harassment enables women to participate in the workplace on an equal footing with men. By acknowledging and

not trivializing the effects of sexual harassment on reasonable women, courts can work towards ensuring that neither men nor women will have to "run a gauntlet of sexual abuse in return for the privilege of being allowed to work and make a living."

The court cited the cultural influences affecting its decision:

> American women have been raised in a society where rape and sex-related violence have reached unprecedented levels, and a vast pornography industry creates continuous images of sexual coercion, objectification and violence. Finally, women as a group tend to hold more restrictive views of both the situation and type of relationship in which sexual conduct is appropriate. Because of the inequality and coercion with which it is so frequently associated in the minds of women, the appearance of sexuality in an unexpected context or a setting of ostensible equality can be an anguishing experience.

This decision clearly reflects the view that culturally based gender differences must be considered when assessing whether conduct may constitute sexual harassment. As the Ninth Circuit acknowledges, there is a broad range of viewpoints even among women. The problem is there are many levels of cultural differences affecting women as a group that make it difficult to know whose perspective to apply.

Kimberle Crenshaw has written extensively about the problem of "invisibility" under discrimination laws for women of color.[27] Common legal categories, such as women and minorities, assume the whiteness of women and make invisible the woman who is also a member of a minority. Bell hooks [sic], a leading commentator on the situation of women in America, warns against the fallacy of sameness hidden in assertions like "all women are oppressed." She states,

> This assertion implies that women share a common lot, that factors like class, race, religion, sexual preference, etc., do not create a diversity of experience that determines the extent to which sexism will be an oppressive force within the lives of individual women. Sexism as a system of domination is institutionalized but it has never determined in an absolute way the fate of all women in this society.[28]

Susan Hippensteele and colleagues emphasize that, particularly in campus populations with diverse backgrounds, the understanding of sex discrimination must be expanded to include a working definition of ethnoviolence.[29] In studies of the University of Hawaii campus, which reflects perhaps the most ethnically diverse academic community nationwide, she concluded that racism has many faces—for women it manifests as sexual harassment, while for men it is exhibited in the form of physical intimidation. Her studies reveal that women of color experience intimidating and hostile conduct as a combination of racist and sexist conduct. Hippensteele also reports that how the intake officer or counselor weighs the importance of one form of discriminatory conduct over another influences how seriously the complainant's allegation is taken and how it may be resolved.

Examples of how cultural factors affect how people both characterize and experience conduct are included in a study conducted by Phoebe Stambaugh of the University of Arizona. Stambaugh's research studies women's reactions to sexual harassment and institutional complaint procedures.[30] She concludes that those who are subject to sexual harassment commonly share the feeling of being an "outsider." In particular being a racial or ethnic outsider amplifies the discomfort about working, especially, in environments dominated by white men. One woman with a Hispanic background stated that her white male supervisor exploited *both* her "femininity" and her Hispanic ethnicity. In the presence of her Anglo-European male and female coworkers, her boss often made fun of her animated personality, and joked about her "hot-blooded nature." Complainants noted three ways their complaints were rejected: (1) having their problems redefined, (2) having them referred out, or (3) having them disqualified from the complaint-handling process. In one example where the male complaint in-take officer downgraded the seriousness of the situation, the complainant reported that he said, "Tina, I think maybe he's just attracted to your accent. That's all. You know some men find women from your country irresistible. It's the accent, the look, the way you dress. He's just fascinated because, you know, you're kind of exotic."

In another situation reflecting experiences of women of color, one woman described the difficulty she had distinguishing where racism ended and sexism began.

> Looking back on things, I can see two different scenarios going on at once. With (the manager), it was sexual harassment and with (the administrator) it was race discrimination. It was very clear to me that my manager related to me in a sexual way. He only hired me for my looks. He just wanted a cutesy around. He liked looking at my butt and stuff. I can handle him. But the (administrator), to me, that was different. He liked to intimidate people and push them around. I felt like he treated me like dirt because I was a woman and Hispanic.

In the demand letter her attorney sent to the employer, because the attorney concluded that sexual harassment was a more tenable claim, race discrimination was never alleged. These are prime examples of how the intake person's analysis of the complaint and the complainant's subjective experience influence how the complaint may be characterized.

More court cases are directly incorporating cultural factors in determining whether conduct constitutes sexual harassment. As the understanding of sexual harassment grows and those in the legal field attempt to educate the judges, cases will reflect cultural factors that should be recognized.

An example of a court decision where the experiences of women of color were recognized is *Hicks v. Gates Rubber Co.*[31] In this case an African American female brought sexual harassment and race discrimination claims against her supervisor and employer. The plaintiff complained about harassing conduct that included racist comments, sexual overtures, and actual physical force. The court held that the harassing conduct should be considered in the totality. The proper assessment was to aggregate the evidence of racial hostility with the evidence of gender-based hostility. The proper question was whether the racist and sexist conduct considered as a whole created a hostile environment under Title VII.

Another important case that recognized how cultural factors may be considered in a sex discrimination claim is the recent Ninth Circuit decision in *Lam v. University of Hawaii.*[32] A woman of Vietnamese descent brought an action under Title VII against the University of Hawaii's Richardson School of Law, claiming that she was discriminated against on the basis of her race, sex, and national origin when she applied for a position at the school. The Ninth Circuit held that the lower court had incorrectly viewed racism and sexism as separate and distinct elements "amenable to almost mathematical treatment." Accordingly, the court decided that when a plaintiff is claiming race and sex bias, it is necessary to determine whether the employer discriminated on the basis of that particular combination of factors, not just whether there is evidence of discrimination against people of the same race, or, in the alternative, of the same sex.

The court reasoned that

> The attempt to bisect a person's identity at the intersection of race and gender often distorts or ignores the particular nature of their experience [*citations omitted*]. Like the subclasses under Title VII, Asian women are subject to a set of stereotypes and assumptions shared neither by Asian men nor by white women. In consequence, they may be targeted for discrimination in the absence of discrimination against [Asian] men or white women.

Although this case was not a hostile environment sexual harassment claim, it has important implications for how a particular cultural perspective might be evaluated under the reasonable person standard. Certainly, more awareness of the difficulties and realities that exist for certain complainants will expand the legal protections to those who may not represent the dominant cultural norm.

Fair and Equitable Investigations

A significant but often overlooked area where cultural factors are implicated involves how evidence is evaluated once a formal complaint is filed and an investigation is conducted. A fair and equitable investigation should be commenced to gather and assess the relevant evidence. Those responsible for the response and investigation stage of action should be trained to recognize their own cultural beliefs and values so that they respond in a neutral fashion and without hidden biases. Many well-intentioned administrators may not appreciate how certain ethnic minorities experience the world through the "dominant" culture. They may unwittingly apply their own culturally influenced cognitive frameworks, communication styles, and information-processing systems to arrive at conclusions that may ignore the reality of others. For example, an investigator influenced by his or her own cultural framework may conduct interviews in a formalized, direct questioning manner. Although on the surface this may appear appropriate, if the complainant has been taught to act in a nonconfrontational manner, as is emphasized in Native American or certain Asian cultures, the facts may never be fully revealed. If saving face is an important aspect of one's cultural conditioning, then there will be reluctance to talk openly about personal or intimate incidents or to admit conduct that may subject the person to ridicule or criticism.

Further, if an investigator is unaware of his or her own cultural influences, he or she may evaluate whether someone is telling the truth based solely on how the interviewee's account harmonizes with how the investigator might act. In a sexual harassment case we were asked to handle for a school district after the investigation had been conducted, we learned that the male and female investigators both had strong personal beliefs that a woman should confront the accused, not only in a timely fashion but assertively as well. Instead of asking questions in a open-ended manner, the complainant was grilled by the investigators with questions such as, "Why didn't you say something to the accused?" and "Is that all you did to stop the harassment?"

On many occasions individuals have shared with us their belief that Anita Hill must have been lying about the alleged conduct by Clarence Thomas, because "If it really happened, why didn't she come forward when it happened instead of waiting for so many years?" This is an example of a deeply rooted cultural myth that assumes if a woman does not make a prompt complaint then nothing happened. This myth has been applied historically to situations where women's testimony is involved, such as rape cases, yet the research shows that victim's rarely report sexual misconduct or crimes promptly.

Other studies of jurors' reasoning patterns in rape cases cite numerous stereotypic assumptions that lead to conclusions that are false. For instance, in one study a defendant was less likely to be found guilty if the victim had engaged in sex outside marriage, drank, used drugs, or had known the defendant. These studies confirm that culturally held assumptions may improperly influence factfinders.[33] Such hidden biases must be discovered and exposed or fair investigations will be compromised.

Understanding what the law considers relevant or not is important to conducting investigations that may later be scrutinized in court. For example, the California Fair Employment and Housing Commission considered a case[34] in which the cultural background of the witness was recognized in determining a credibility issue. In this sexual harassment case involving a Japanese American female, the defendant urged the Commission not to believe the testimony by the complainant's mother, in which she stated she had counseled her daughter to stay in the abusive working environment because she believed her daughter could not be employed elsewhere. The defendant contended that the mother and daughter had fabricated the allegation because no mother would counsel her daughter to endure the harassment. The Commission nevertheless concluded that the mother's testimony was credible because the cultural background of the family could logically support the mother's counsel to the daughter to tolerate the harrasment. Such overt recognition that cultural factors influence differing views are rare, however, in agency or court decisions.

Another strong culturally influenced aspect of sexual harassment complaints involves what evidence is relevant to determine whether the conduct was unwelcome by the complainant. Although in most situations the complainant will testify that the harassing conduct was unwelcome, the law evaluates whether the *behavior* of the complainant in fact proves she or he did not welcome the conduct.

In the landmark case, *Meritor Savings Bank v. Vinson*,[35] which recognized an action for hostile environment under Title VII, the Supreme Court also addressed certain evidence issues related to the element of "unwelcomeness" in a sexual harassment case. The Court concluded, contrary to the appellate court's holding, that the plaintiff's clothing and her disclosure of sexual fantasies were relevant evidence of whether the conduct was unwelcome. This aspect of the Supreme Court decision has led to a variety of interpretations by lower courts. Some courts have overemphasized the importance of how the complainant dressed in assessing credibility, perhaps reflecting deeply held culturally based myths. Additionally, because of the recognition that a complainant's sexual history may be unfairly prejudicial, especially based on the dominant cultural view of women and sexuality, most states severely limit or prohibit discovery of a plaintiff's prior sexual conduct with others. There is no question, however, that issues about clothing, women, and sexuality are interconnected and clearly influence whether a person is believed.

Determining what evidence is relevant often requires a legal evaluation of the totality of the circumstances. Although legal advice may be necessary at times, we have found it useful to assist investigators through focused training that introduces them to the complexities of evaluating credibility and exploring their individual cultural perspectives, and perhaps blind spots. Preventive efforts taken to train investigators properly beforehand will not only create strong defenses to liability but provide trust in the institutional complaint process.

Sometimes investigators fail to consider the underlying cultural dynamics and consequently fail to ask the important questions that might reveal a problem. As an example of how an academic institution may not have been sanctioned but nevertheless may have failed at their responsibilities, consider the following matter that was investigated by OCR. An African American female student was disciplined when she assaulted a white male student. The female contended that she hit the male student because he had been sexually harassing her. The male was not disciplined. The OCR held that the investigation was fair even though there was evidence that the female student had complained many times to her teachers before the assault and told them that the male student was "bothering her." The teachers said the female student never mentioned sexual conduct and, therefore, OCR concluded there was no evidence to support her contention of sexual harassment. What is interesting about this case is how the student's credibility was assessed. It would be logical to ask why the student wasn't questioned further when she reported she was being bothered. What cultural factors might have blinded the teachers to this obvious question or contributed to why they did not seek to prevent a problem from escalating?

Additionally, how information is gathered is very culturally influenced. Cultures differ in the amount of information that is explicitly transmitted through words versus the amount of information that is transmitted through the context of the situation, the relationship, and physical cues. "High-context" cultures, such as Native American, Arab, Latino, African American, and Asian, rely less on verbal communication than on understanding through shared experience, history and implicit messages.[36] Individuals from low-context cultures, such as Anglo-European, Swiss, German, and Scandinavian, typically focus on precise, direct, logical, verbal communication and are often impatient with communicators who do not get to the point quickly. Because of these different modes of processing and interpreting verbal or environmental cues, communication between high- and low-context cultures may lead to misunderstanding and difficulties. If those charged with gathering and evaluating evidence are aware of these differences, interviewing techniques can be appropriately modified to ensure optimum fact-finding.

Resolving Complaints and Imposing Discipline

After the evidence is evaluated and if a decision is made that sexual harassment has occurred, the law requires that the institution must take action reasonably calculated to end the harassment. The law requires the remedy to address the specific harassing behavior and also to consider what message the discipline gives to others about prohibiting sexual harassment.

Sometimes the accused will raise countercharges of discrimination such as racism or "reverse discrimination." For instance in the Clarence Thomas hearings, Thomas raised the countercharge of racism when he called the investigation "a high-tech lynching." It is very important that administrators not be confused by vigorously asserted countercharges. Particularly in the university setting, countercharges by the accused, such as academic freedom of faculty, disabilities, racism, violation of due process, and defamation, can lead to highly publicized and volatile situations in the context of a sexual harassment complaint resolution. Legal guidance can be helpful in weeding through the complexities; however, cultural factors are certainly implicated in how such complex situations are handled and assessed. It is interesting to consider that the ongoing legal battle pitting academic freedom rights against sexual harassment protections stems from the importance of the dominant cultural value in this country to protect First Amendment freedoms, at the same time recognizing the invidious harm of discrimination.

Remember, however, that simply because someone did not intend the conduct to be harmful, or that there was a cultural misunderstanding, will not operate as a defense to liability. In the well-known Eden Prairie case involving sexual harassment of young female students by young male students on a school bus, OCR stated that "disability cannot be a defense" to actions that have the impact of creating a hostile environment for others. Nevertheless, with the caution that students with special needs may implicate other legal concerns, OCR has stated that the factors a school can consider in student sexual harassment cases when "deciding the type of discipline to be imposed" include the following: the severity of the offense, the number of individuals involved, the age of the students, past disciplinary history, the special education needs of the individual, disability factors, and family situation.[37]

There are no easy answers for how to handle these situations. The law requires that the action taken was "reasonably calculated to end the harassment." Each matter should be considered on a case-by-case basis. In all cases, it is prudent to include follow-up monitoring after any form of discipline is instituted to ensure that the conduct has indeed stopped.

One other cultural consideration at the resolution stage involves the use of such alternative dispute-resolution processes such as mediation. Because the goal of mediation is not to place blame, but rather to find a solution to the dispute that addresses the needs or interests of both parties, communication factors are crucial to an effective resolution. We have found comediating sexual harassment disputes, where one mediator is a male and the other a female, is effective in building trust and rapport.

Mediators must be aware of the cultural influences that affect nonverbal communication, body language, power dynamics, confrontational styles, cognitive processing, and perceptions. If the parties have strong face-saving concerns, more effective resolution may occur with separate caucusing rather than face-to-face confrontation during mediation. Additionally, other factors, such as methods of questioning and information processing, may impact whether resolution through mediation is useful or effective. Such forms of resolution must be skillfully administrated and may be better suited for situations where power dynamics are not entrenched (see Chapter 11). In our experience, mediation techniques properly administrated may be a useful method for resolving problems before they intensify.

The law will evaluate whether the "discipline" instituted was reasonably calculated to end sexual harassment; however, when courts evaluate this question it is in hindsight. The bottom line is how effective the action was in actually stopping the discriminatory conduct. If considering cultural influences assists in a determination of what form of discipline will most effectively reach this goal then both the letter and the spirit of the law will be well served.

Conclusion

Voltaire once wrote in the *Philosophical Dictionary* (1764), "Let all the laws be clear, uniform and precise; to interpret laws is almost always to corrupt them." It is in the interpretation, application, and enforcement of sexual harassment laws that the challenge lies. Only by realistically addressing the underlying multicultural factors that influence sexual harassment complaint resolution can administrators identify and eradicate the abuses of power and inequities that exist. Through increased understanding of cultural influences, adminitrators will more effectivly fullfill their legal duties, institutional liability will be minimized, and working and learning environments free of discrimination will be created for *all* people in our cuturally rich academic communities.

Endnotes

1. 20 U.S.C. section 168.
2. 42 U.S.C. section 2000e.
3. Hill, Anita. Race and Gender Issues in the 90's, Speech on April 11, 1995 at the University of California at Santa Barbara
4. Torrey, M. When will we be believed? Rape myths and the idea of a fair trial in rape prosecutions, *U.C. Davis Law Review*, 24, 1013, Summer 1991.
5. Chow, E. N. The feminist movement: Where are all the Asian American women? In Asian Women United of California (eds.), *Making waves: An anthology of writings by and about Asian American women* (pp. 362–376). Boston: Beacon Press, 1989.
6. Bradshaw, C. K. Asian and Asian American women: Historical and political considerations in psychotherapy. In L. Comas-Diaz and B. Greene, *Women of color.* New York: Guilford Press, 1994.
7. Comas-Diaz, L. Culturally relevant issues and treatment implications for Hispanics. In D. R. Koslow and E. P. Salett (eds.), *Crossing cultures in mental health* (pp. 31–48). Washington, DC: SIETAR International, 1989.
8. Gonzalez, A. The sex roles of the traditional Mexican family: A comparison of Chicano and Anglo students attitudes. *Journal of Cross-Cultural Psychology* 13, 330–339, 1982.
9. Stevens, E. Machismo and marianismo. *Transaction-Society* 10(6), 57–63, 1973.
10. Monson, M. Defining the situation: Sexual harassment or everyday rudeness? Presented at Conference by Sociologists Against Sexual Harassment, August 1994.
11. Kluckhohn, F. R., & Strodtbeck, F. L. *Varia-*

tions in value orientations. Evanston, IL: Row & Peterson, 1961.

12. Tannen, D. *You just don't understand, women and men in conversations.* New York: Ballatine Books, 1990.

13. Smitherman, G. *Black talk: Words and phrases from the hood to the Amen corner.* New York: Houghton Mifflin, 1994.

14. Lynch, E. W., & Hanson, M. J. *Developing cross-cultural competence: A guide for working with young children and their families.* Baltimore: Paul H. Brookes, 1992.

15. Nobles, W. W. Extended self: Rethinking the so-called Negro self-concept. In R. Jones (ed.), *Black psychology,* 3rd ed. Berkeley: Cobb & Henry Publishers, 1992.

16. *See,* for example, Felsman-Summers, S. & Ashworth, C. D. Factors related to intentions to report rape. *Journal of Social Issues,* 4, 53–70, 1981.

17. Gruber, J. & Smith, M. An exploration of sexual harassment experiences and severity: Results from North America and Europe. Forthcoming in *Women and Work,* 5, 1996.

18. Bumiller, K. *The civil rights society.* Baltimore: Johns Hopkins University Press, 1992.

19. 47 F.3d 1522 (9th cir. 1995)

20. Quinn, B. The power of sex: An exploration of individual resistance of accommodation to sexual harassment law. Presented at the August. 1994 Conference for Sociologists Against Sexual Harassment.

21. Gruber, J. & Smith, M. Women's responses to sexual harassment: A multivariante analysis.

22. 830 F. Supp 1288 (N. D. Cal. 1993).

23. 830 F. Supp 1560 (N.D. Cal. 1993).

24. Case No. FCR 90-91 A8-0004S, N-39653, 93-08.

25. 114 S.Ct. 367 (1993).

26. 924 F.2d. 872 (9th Cir. 1991).

27. Crenshaw, K., *Feminist legal theory: Readings in law and gender,* Chapter 4. Boulder: Westview Press, 1991.

28. hooks, b. *Feminist theory: From margin to center,* Chapter 5. Boston: Southeast Press, 1984.

29. Hippensteele, S., Chesney-Lind, M., & Veniegas, R. On the basis of...The changing face of harassment and discrimination in the academy. In review to be published in *Women and Criminal Justice 18*(1), 1996.

30. Telephone conversation with Phoebe Morgan Stambaugh, Justice Studies, Arizona State University, Tempe, December 1994.

31. 928 F.2d. 966 (10th Cir. 1991).

32. 94 Daily Journal D.A.R. 16376 (9th Cir. 1994).

33. Torrey, at 1040-1041.

34. Case No. FEP 86-87, B4-0558se, L-41401, 91-16.

35. 477 U.S. 57 (1986).

36. Hall, E. T. *Beyond culture.* New York: Doubleday, 1976.

37. Telephone conversation with Edwards J. Sarzynski, Esq., Hogan & Sarzynski, Binghamton, New York, Jan. 1995.

14

A "CONSENSUAL" RELATIONSHIP

LESLIE IRVINE

Sexual harassment takes many different forms. Some are easier to recognize than others. This chapter provides a case study, a cautionary tale, even, of a more nebulous type of sexual harassment than is discussed in the rest of this book. Most readers would probably see the exchange of grades for sex, for example, as sexual harassment in its *quid pro quo* form. In all likelihood, most would also understand how a steady stream of sexually oriented jokes, remarks, and comments could create a "hostile environment"—another form of sexual harassment. There is considerable agreement about situations such as these. But sexual harassers do not always use such direct and obvious tactics.

Sexual harassment involves a wide range of often subtle behaviors, and there is less agreement about whether and in what sense some of these actually constitute harassment. Can an intimate relationship that appears consensual, for example, be considered harassment? What happens when the terms and currency of exchange become less tangible than trading sex for grades? What do we call it when the bargain involves not grades, but attention? What do we call it when seduction disguises the coercion? This chapter provides an argument in favor of a broad definition of sexual harassment, as I tell of my own experience in an ostensibly consensual intimate relationship and my attempts to make university administrators aware of the harm it caused me. I hope that my account will serve three purposes. First, I want to convince professors that consensual relationships with their students are wrong. Second, I want to persuade students that they, too, can be coerced into exploitive consensual relationships. And, third, I hope that administrators will realize their responsibility to make the university an environment in which learning can take place free of exploitation and coercion.

I understand sexual harassment as an abuse of power. Sexual harassers, as Dziech and Weiner (1984) tell us, "misuse the power of their positions to abuse members of the opposite [or same] sex." My definition of *power* comes from Max Weber: it is that opportunity existing within a social relationship that enables one to carry out one's own will even against resistance. Understanding consensual relationships as abuses of power requires a certain perspective on the notion of "resistance." People in authority have power by virtue of their position as gate-keepers for others. They control the distribution of resources, such as money, grades, status, or access, to important social networks. They seldom need to force or coerce compliance with the terms of distribution, for compliance comes through the social relationship. Subordinates understand—typically without being told—that they should please, if not obey, those in authority; *this* is power. Its subtle but coercive presence raises the question of whether those in subordinate positions can ever freely refuse a request from a person with authority over them. When the desire to please—or avoid displeasing—a person in power obscures one's ability to say no, "consent" becomes a meaningless term. In this formulation, an ostensibly "consensual" relationship in which one person has authority over another can qualify as harassment. A person in power can selectively distribute enough rewards to obtain consent. Attention, favors, status, and prestige may provide more acceptable routes to seduction than does force, but acceptability does not negate the coercion implicit in the trade.

I did not always understand the world in these terms. I seldom thought about power, least of all in my intimate relationships. But now, I live by this rule: Do not have sex with anyone you sometimes have to call Mister, Doctor, or Professor. I discovered that people who have honorifics before their names have more power than those who do not, which means they have greater access to resources that enable them to get you to see things their way. They can make you want to appeal to their expectations. They can get you to do things you would not have consented to with someone of lesser status. They can make you want to please them. They can do it so smoothly and gently that the word "manipulation" never crosses your mind. They can make it feel flattering. They can even make it feel like love. And, if you don't like the way it feels, they can make you think there is something wrong with you. They can also make others think there is something wrong with you, which makes it unlikely that anyone will believe your version of the story. People in power tend to see things in similar ways; after all, the system is organized to their benefit. Those with little power typically lack the resources to convince them otherwise. When the contest pits an individual against an institution, the institution has far more resources to make certain its definition of reality is taken as truth. The individual seldom stands a chance.

I learned all this the hard way. I had an affair with a professor that lasted two and a half years. An account of it follows, and I think most readers will find it an appalling example of exploitation. A person with power took advantage of my vulnerability, and the experience injured me in some fundamental ways. Years later, I still feel anger, shame, resentment, and humiliation. I have a reputation for being guarded and unmanipulable; however, I acquired my thick skin as a consequence of considerable self-doubt. When the relationship ended, I found it difficult to trust anyone—or myself—for some time. The experience made me wary of interacting with male professors. My circumspection has had its costs, but I so desperately want to avoid putting myself at risk that I see no other option.

I elaborate on much of this in what follows, but the account of the affair serves only as a subtext for another story. The *real* story I want to tell has to do with what happens when an institution has no policy regarding student–faculty relationships, and no procedure for reporting them. I was sexually exploited by a person who controlled my grades, my income, and my access to professional opportunities. When I gathered the courage to relive the shame and humiliation and disclose the relationship, I hoped that my disclosure would be taken seriously. I hoped that university administrators would understand the subtle discrimination implicit in sexualizing the classroom. But, in the absence of a policy that would lend credence to my version of the story, university administrators, including the affirmative action officer, could choose to wink at my exploiter and pretend the problem did not exist. Here is what took place.

In 1988, I was an advanced undergraduate student working on a degree in art history. I had returned to school after a long absence. I would turn thirty in November, and my six-year marriage was at the beginning of its end. I was struggling financially. A scholarship covered my tuition, but I had a hard time making ends meet. I had all the characteristic insecurities of returning female undergraduates. I had been well socialized to think of my professors as intellectually omnipotent. I wanted desperately to believe that I was smart—my ten-year hiatus from college had left me with serious doubts about my intellectual abilities—and I clung to my professors' evaluations as indicators of whether I had the right stuff. However, my intellectual aspirations did not relieve me of the need to know that men found me attractive. This combination of needs and desires left me extremely vulnerable to the attention I received from the man who controlled my grades, my income, and my professional future.

He was a thirty-nine-year old tenured professor of art history. He had a committed relationship with a female faculty member although he deceived me about the nature of this and numerous other entanglements he had during our relationship. Students considered his classes challenging and controversial. No one had an indifferent response to his classroom style; they either liked him or knew enough to stay away. He demanded a considerable amount of writing and critical thinking—a real contrast to the slide-memorization techniques of most art history classes. He packed his lectures full of references to sociology, philosophy, music, film, and the history of ideas. He learned each student's name within the first week of classes. He gave lively and engaging lectures. He moved around the classroom as he spoke and he covered the chalkboards with information. Students who took his courses seriously had richer intellectual lives as a result.

I was especially intrigued by his frequent references to sex and the emotions. Sex was a Rosetta Stone for him. Aesthetic experience, he said, was very similar to the experience of sexual intimacy. In his formulation, aesthetic experience involved something he called "annihilation of the ego," which he defined as the experience of escaping from the self. He said that art was made so that people could feel the emotions in powerful ways, and sex was the closest thing to aesthetic experience that most people had experienced. Understanding great works of art gave people the ability to overcome self-awareness and escape from reality in ways comparable to sexual fulfillment. It was fantastic and thrilling to be able to understand a work of art so that the experience felt like sex, he said. He seemed capable of feeling so much. I thought these were the most sophisticated ideas I had ever heard, and I was fascinated. The time between classes could not pass quickly enough for me.

He was very skilled at making it all feel so personal. It was like listening to a convincing sermon by an effective preacher. It was as if he knew my thoughts and desires. He used lots of eye contact, and, through it, he began to zero in on me in the classroom. He would often use students' clothing to illustrate principles of art such as color, shape, or line. He once called a female classmate in a tight skirt to the front of the room to illustrate the way the eye follows a curve. When he began to use *me* as an example, I felt simultaneously flattered and intimidated. His requests made me uncomfortable, yet, at the same time, I could not refuse because I wanted him to think well of me. I felt defenseless when he called the classes' attention to my short hair to make a point about gender-specific standards for attractiveness. I could not resist his request to show how the small tattoo near my right ankle drew attention down the leg. I was spellbound.

Sometimes students objected to some of the topics he chose to use. In his reply, he would always wrap himself in the flag of academic freedom. He would say that his tenure protected him from retribution against anything he might say in the classroom. He told us he had the right to talk about any ideas, no matter how controversial or seemingly unrelated to the course topic, and could use virtually any means to illustrate them.

I took four courses from him. During the second of those four semesters, I made an appointment to see him during his office hours. I wanted to tell him how much I was enjoying his course and learning from him. I knew that a lot of students found him threatening, so I wanted him to know he was getting through to some of us. Looking back, I understand how vulnerable I was to his attention. I remember wanting to impress him, yet I also remember feeling desperately ill-equipped to do so. Although I had earned an A in the first course I took, I felt certain he would remember only the inaccurate or shallow things I had written, or that he would recall only the times when I had failed to make an important point. I was even afraid I would make some dreadful grammatical mistake and expose my incompetence.

He recognized my vulnerability immediately, and he knew what to do about it. He closed his office door and asked his secretary to hold his calls. He made me feel important. He moved the conversation away from the class to more personal topics. He asked about my background. ("If you can just get people to talk about themselves," he would later tell me, "they're like putty in your hand.") He asked about my goals and interests in art history; curatorial work in a museum or gallery, I said. He offered me a highly coveted job as his research assistant in the university art gallery. It was a rare opportunity to earn some money at a job that would not detract from my studies. I would gain experience curating exhibitions and cataloging collections, working among people with similar interests. I knew he would think me foolish if I did not take the job. I could not refuse his offer, and I began to rely on him for my income as well as for grades.

Soon after I started to work for him, we met for racquetball on a Saturday. I should probably note that we played two games and he won both times. We talked for a while afterward, and, once again, he moved the conversation to personal topics: my marriage, my concerns, my experiences. I say "he" moved the conversation because he had control, and I understood that. He's smarter, I thought, he knows what to say. In those days, I doubted my ability to raise a topic worthy of discussion, especially in the company of someone better educated than I. I felt unable to make intriguing connections or recall significant names. I worried that I had not read the "important" books. His interest flattered me; he made me feel smart. He laughed at my jokes. He put his hand on mine. He touched my hair and commented on the bit of grey in it. It had been some time since a man had given me such undivided attention, and it felt good. He said he was glad that I was nearly thirty because it meant that I had enough experience to make up my own mind about things. He also made a point of saying that I had already earned an A from him; purportedly, I didn't need to impress him for a grade, so my interest in him was somehow "genuine." He convinced me that we were on equal footing in most ways; yes, he was a tenured professor, but what I lacked in status I made up for in experience, he said. I realize now that he was trying to convince me—and himself—that I had the ability to say "no" to him. In truth, I so wanted him to think well of me that I would have agreed to almost anything.

On Monday, he invited me to dinner and a movie. I could not refuse his offer of a luxury that I could seldom afford for myself. He offered me a momentary escape from the austere reality of my student life. I enjoyed the extravagant treatment, and I was flattered that he wanted to spend the evening with me. I asked him about his relationship with the woman on the faculty. I had heard from some students that they were married. Was this true? He told me they had a deep friendship and similar intellectual interests, but that he had no sexual interest in her. He said they were not married, although he admitted to having told *some* people they were, when it was convenient to have the legitimacy that people grant to a marriage. I found this intriguing and sophisticated and just what I would expect from such a person. I considered it yet another bit of mystery, and it excited me to even know about it. It should have alarmed me. I would later learn that this woman had another image of their relationship; in it, they were a monogamous, committed couple, building a life and a home together.

After the movie, we went to his office and had sex for the first time. We then began to steal opportunities for sex a few times a week, and our clandestine intimacy took place in whatever time and space he could arrange. I say "*he* could arrange" because, once again, he controlled the situation. He set the time; after all, he was the one who had to keep to a schedule. In my mind, his time *seemed* more important because it was filled with things like meetings with the president of the university or lectures at museums. He would fit me in between appointments or on a free evening. He would tell me how much he appreciated my ability to understand his scheduling difficulties and be spontaneous. I was happy to do it for him. I would take any time I could get with him.

At first we only met during the evening, then he began to suggest a morning here, or an afternoon there. Within a short time, I was "on call" for him for most of the day. He used my job illegally, as a way to make our time together legitimate. Because I worked for him, and, because he did most of his work at home, he could ask me to work there as well. Looking back, I see how he always had me arrive just as his partner was leaving for her office. She could see that I had been there—he protected himself from the accusation of having snuck someone in by appearing to have nothing to hide. And, she genuinely believed I had come to the house to work. In truth, we spent most of the time in bed. I filled out my time card as if I had spent the hours at work. The university, in effect, paid me to have sex with him.

When we couldn't meet at his house, he always seemed to know exactly where to find privacy. He attributed this to his eagerness to be with me, claiming that he sought places out just so we could be together. I would later learn that he had built up a long list of private places through experience with past and present lovers.

After about a month together, he invited me to go away with him. We would drive separately to a city about an hour away, have dinner, and spend the evening in a hotel. He had to give a talk early the next morning and had reserved the room so that he could be close. I would not have to pay a cent. Did I want to join him? I loved the city. I could pick the restaurant. This was another luxury I could not refuse; I could not have managed it for myself in those days. At dinner that night, he told me he loved me. I told him I loved him too. I would later realize that he had even set the terms of our love by defining the word for me. He insisted on unconditional love—love that endured no matter what—and he had a detailed argument to support his preference. He also insisted on monogamy, saying it was the surest way to guarantee intimacy. He referred back to the "annihilation of the ego" notion he had used in class and talked about the "moral high ground." I lacked the skills and the courage to provide a counterargument, so I agreed to his terms. I told myself he had already thought this through and he knew best. I had never known a man who seemed to have such easy access to his feelings, and it enthralled me. He called me his soul mate and said he had no interest in any other lovers.

Over the next two and a half years, I had other opportunities to travel with him. All of them involved abuses of his authority over me and illegal uses of university money. He contrived the arrangements to reduce the risk of our being seen together. After all, neither his partner nor my husband could find out, and we had to take care that no one from the university community saw us together— although, he said that, as my boss, he could ask me to drive him to the airport. So what if I dropped him off and got on a plane myself? Although I paid part of my airfare, everything else was covered by his research money. He would swoop me up, mid-semester, and take me away, saying he needed a "research assistant." In my experience, the relationship between these trips and academic research was very small. Apart from visiting art museums and having one or two brief meetings with gallery owners, very little actual research ever took place.

These trips took their toll on me as a student and as an employee. We would spend four or five days together, then return to our "normal" lives as if nothing had changed. But, from my perspective, something *had* changed. On one hand, having his undivided attention gave me several advantages over other students; our experiences and conversations gave me insights that I could not have gained in the classroom. My skills at oral argument grew sharper purely through practice with him. He also provided me with the opportunity to see original works of art, while most other students had to suffice with reproductions in books. On the other hand, our time together made the transition back to student life extremely difficult, and often quite sobering. He treated me differently than he treated other students by calling on me to the exclusion of others or by asking me to give lengthy analyses that other students saw as favoritism. He favored me unpredictably, however, and sometimes, without warning, he would treat me like just another student. Once, for example, I had to take an exam from him the day after we returned from five particularly passionate days together, days I had *not* spent studying.

I found it particularly troublesome that I couldn't mention the trips to other students for fear of arousing suspicion. The most exciting part of my life was also my most carefully guarded secret. I found this combination profoundly difficult to manage, and my strategy for doing so meant limiting my contact with other students. Most of them interpreted my caution as condescension. I had worked hard to make a comfortable place for myself in student life—no easy feat as a returning student—but the relationship slowly destroyed that comfort. It created an awkwardness between the other students and me, and, before long, I felt at ease only in the company of my lover.

The relationship destroyed the boundaries that I used to make sense of my life. I no longer "fit" as a student. Because my work usually involved having sex with my boss, I lost all sense of what it meant to be an employee. And, because I had to hide the fact that we were lovers, I didn't feel certain of that part of my identity either. I lost all ability to disentangle my feelings from my responsibilities as a student and employee. I felt disoriented in every role. I wanted him to continue loving me, and it obstructed my ability to say no to whatever he asked me to do. He exploited my confusion by asking me to do personal errands far beyond the scope of my job description or my student status. He asked me to do things that had nothing whatsoever to do with his courses or his research. I wanted to please him, so I complied with equanimity. He had me take his car in when the stereo needed repair and his shoes in to be resoled. He convinced me to indulge his taste for pornography by allowing him to have it sent under a pseudonym to my address. He would often call me at home late in the evening or on weekends with some urgent research that required me to change my personal plans and go to the library immediately. He used our relationship as a way to make exceptions in his treatment of me. He put off grading my essays; because he had so many others to grade, I would understand if he didn't get to mine immediately. (I never got some of them back.) Eventually, he told me that, because it was likely that I had done well anyway, I could count on getting As. Then, he even stopped calling on me in class; he said that, because we spent so much time together, I had purportedly become so much more advanced than the other students that I had "moved beyond" the classroom dialogue. I would only intimidate the other students, he said; we can talk later, in private, when the conversation can go faster.

One of the most appalling things he asked of me was to oversee his course evaluations and falsify any negative reports, and I performed this illegal task for several semesters. Many of his students used the evaluations as an opportunity to say he talked too much about sex and other topics unrelated to the course, and that he favored certain students—typically women. I photocopied blank evaluation forms, removed those with negative comments, and forged more positive handwritten responses to replace those I had taken out. Other women had done it for him before me—he admitted that much—and, I assume others have taken up the task after me.

Toward what would be the end of our two-and-a-half-year relationship, things began to change for me. I got divorced. If any parts of my marriage could have been redeemed, they were overwhelmed by the fact that my working-class husband stood little chance of competing with a tenured academic who could buy me dinner and take me on trips. I would not say that the affair caused the divorce, but it certainly made it easier for me to go through with it. My life changed in other ways too. I got my Bachelor's degree and, with that, stopped taking courses from my lover. I changed disciplines and entered a graduate program in sociology—though I remained at the same university. Through sociology, I began to learn about gender inequality and the dynamics of power. I came to realize that the balance of power between student and professor is tilted in such a way that a student can never really give informed consent to a sexual relationship with a professor. I began to see that consensual relationships outside the classroom are extensions of what happens inside the classroom. There the professor is always in control of the situation, always the expert, and always determines what will be taken as correct. And, I understood that inequality between men and women exacerbates that difference in power.

Around the same time, I began to notice the many other female students who flocked around him and did similarly odd errands for him at similarly odd hours. I had an awakening of sorts. I had paid little attention to them before, but suddenly, I began to wonder what we were all up to. I questioned him about these other students and the power he seemed to have over all of us. He denied any sexual involvement with the others and claimed that he only wanted to foster their intellectual growth. He assured me that I was "special." Then, I learned firsthand that he had ongoing sexual relationships with as many as eight of these students. When I confronted him with this bit of information, he again denied it. He told me that this one only needed career guidance, another one had a daughter who wanted to be an art historian, yet another happened to have an extra ticket for a concert, and so on. He convinced me that his involvements were innocent, and I believed him because I wanted to trust him. He was so adept at getting me to see things his way that, when I once asked him about a bruise he had that looked suspiciously like teeth marks, he succeeded in convincing me that he had been hit by a tennis ball. He could always get me to believe that the woman he had seen on a particular night had sought him out for academic advice, and that they had only had their conversation in a restaurant because he was hungry.

Finally, I had *incontrovertible* evidence he was sexually involved with another student, and I again confronted him. I asked him if we could meet at a specific time and at a certain restaurant. This request caught him off guard because, until then, he had always set the terms of our time together. When I arrived at the restaurant, he complemented me on my appearance. I told him I felt quite good too. He said he was waiting for the other shoe to drop. I gathered my courage. "You have set the terms of this relationship," I said, "and convinced me that you were also following the same rules. In truth, you have been violating the rules behind my back and, in doing so, have not allowed me to have all the information I need to truly give informed consent." My voice started to rise and I saw anxiety on his face because, for the first time in our relationship, he did not control the situation. He accused me of turning against him, even after all he had done for me. He said I had taken advantage of him, used him as a resource, and then moved on. He said that feminism had "ruined" me, making it impossible for me to have fun. I ended the relationship that day.

The feelings I had after that entailed far more than those that typically accompany a breakup. After all, he had used his power over me to get me to do things that were illegal and to treat me differently than he treated other students. For a long time, I went around feeling naive, humiliated, and ashamed. Many of his colleagues knew the extent of the errands I ran for him. I have since learned that he confided to them that I would do things like take his shoes in for repair because I was so thankful for everything he had done for me, or because I had a hopeless crush on him. He would laugh about this poor lovesick student behind my back. Many of his colleagues were also my professors, and the humiliation I felt in their presence was great. I was ridiculed by students who were aware of what was going on. My emotional attachment to him earned me the title "Professor X's pitbull," as though I could not think for myself, only defend my master on command.

I also felt tremendous anger and betrayal. I felt betrayed because he denied me—his student—a fair opportunity to learn by having my ideas critiqued in an unprejudiced manner. I was angry that he denied me—his employee—the right to say "No, I'm sorry. I can't go to the library for you tonight." I felt angry because I was denied the opportunity to have the professor who knew my work better than anyone else recommend me for graduate school and academic honors.

It took me about a year to recover from all this. During that time, I began to understand the extent of the manipulation I had experienced. I had once believed that the classroom was a place where I would have an equal opportunity to learn. I now knew that some students have an advantage on the basis of sexual attractiveness. I had once believed that the currency of exchange in the classroom was grades, and I thought that I would receive mine on the basis of intellectual merit. I now knew that some grades bore little relationship to what happened in the classroom. I had also believed that professors structured lectures and course topics to elucidate a subject. I now understood that some professors tailor their lectures to appeal to potential sexual partners. My disillusionment was profound.

I stopped feeling foolish and started realizing I had simply been vulnerable, and someone had failed to respect that vulnerability and had instead used his power to exploit it. I began to understand why most women are silent about sexual exploitation and why most feel they will risk too much by speaking out. They are afraid of being embarrassed, afraid of being hurt. Because of their silence, it is easier for other women to be exploited in the future. Each one believes that she is alone in her feelings of anger, betrayal, and shame. I became willing to relive those feelings so that other women would not be exploited in the future. I was about to leave the area to start a Ph.D. program at another university in another state. I had little to risk by going public. I was ready to make sure that the university knew how he abused his power by sexualizing the classroom. I wanted the administration to know he had abused his role as professor, advisor, and employer. More than wanting them to *know*, I wanted them to *do* something to protect others from similar experiences.

My first step was to look in the university catalog for some statement of policy about student–faculty involvements so that I would know how to go about reporting one. I could not find anything of the sort, not to mention any procedure for reporting. I didn't know where to begin. I started asking vague questions of trusted faculty members; although most of them considered relationships with students a bad idea, they knew there was no policy against them. What should I do if I wanted to report one? To whom should I speak? The answers ranged from the president to the director of women's studies.

I decided to write a letter to his dean, with copies sent to his chair, the provost, and the president. I wanted them to know he was using the classroom for seduction. In the time I was involved with him, I knew or knew of *eight* other students who were ensnared through the same technique. I saw it as an ongoing pattern of exploitation in which he used the classroom as a supply center for intimate relationships. I wanted his employers to know that he *continually* abused his professional privilege by engaging in sexual relationships with his students.

I wrote a lengthy letter, and followed it with a second one revealing details I left out of the first. I explained how the intellectual seduction had begun in the classroom, how it had become personal during the meeting in his office, and how it became a *fait accompli* when he traded on his ability to give me a rare job opportunity. I wrote about how he had convinced me that I was a consenting adult, able to rationally choose or refuse his attentions. I told them about his ability to provide dinners, movies, and trips to someone who could barely make ends meet. I told them about the errands he had me run under the cover of my job. I told them about the other students who had also been involved with him, in the hope that they would see that he was enacting a pattern of exploiting his students sexually. I asked that my identity be kept confidential, and that they inform me of what they were going to do with this information. I waited. What happened over the course of the next fourteen months is a model of institutional incompetence and bureaucratic bungling.

Only two of the four administrators even responded to my letters. This alone astonished me and should have prepared me for the tactless treatment to come. When I took business courses in high school, I learned that one should *always* acknowledge a letter, even if only to pass the buck. Evidently, only the chair and the provost had learned this bit of bureaucratic etiquette. They thanked me for the information and said that, if they needed to know more, they would contact me. I did not hear from them again. The dean and the president did not respond. I did not know how to interpret their silence. Records would later show that the university counsel wrote me, although I did not receive that letter for more than a year.

Four months passed, and I received the first indication that any action had been taken on the issue. It took the form of a letter from the professor's attorney—an alarming item to find in one's mailbox under any circumstances. The attorney threatened to charge me with libel and said that I could be required to compensate this professor for damages. She also said that my request for responses to my letters constituted intentional interference with his contract with the university. She admonished me to refrain from any further actions. So much for confidentiality and being kept informed.

Two more months passed without communication. I wrote to the president asking for information. Six weeks later, I received a letter from him, in which he wrote the following:

...You expected more response than the University was able to provide. In matters such as those you raised, our response is limited by prohibitions imposed by the law. For instance, under [state's] open record law, there is no provision to keep your letters confidential. Under [state] law, there are very few matters deemed confidential. Moreover, under well-established principles of due process, it is a basic tenet that those accused of wrongdoing have the right to confront the accusations. Therefore, it was impossible to keep your correspondence confidential...results of investigations concerning charges of sexual misconduct against an employee of the University fall under one of the few areas covered by the confidentiality provisions of [state] law. Therefore, we cannot provide you with information concerning the results of our investigation. We can, nevertheless, inform you that the matter was referred to our University Affirmative Action Officer and appropriate action has been taken.

Essentially, he gave me the university's policy on student–faculty relationships: anyone filing a complaint against a faculty member must tell all, but will be told nothing. The complainant's personal history will be photocopied, passed around in committees, read aloud at meetings, and handed off to attorneys. Having endured this, she has no right to know what purpose her actions served; the law protects the faculty member and the university. The complainant should just trust that the affirmative action officer will take appropriate action.

I was outraged. If they could not provide any information about the results of the investigation, they were accountable to no one and their "investigation" was a sham. I felt doubly humiliated, first by a professor who exploited me, and then by administrators who failed to take that exploitation seriously.

The president had mentioned a letter from the university counsel, which I had not received. I wanted a copy, but had no grounds for thinking that a letter to her would get me anywhere. I decided a registered letter might increase the likelihood of a response. I sent one, and it was eventually returned to me unclaimed. Two months passed, and I wrote her again, also sending it by registered mail. Still, I got no response.

Then, that summer—a year after my first letter—interest in student–faculty involvements was renewed following the University of Virginia's new policy concerning consensual relations and the pace of other universities considering such policies increased. A friend sent me a copy of a newspaper article in which the university president and provost were quoted as saying that student-faculty relationships were just not a problem at their university. They had not heard of any faculty members dating students. Nor, they said, had any student complained of sexual harassment by an instructor in at least the past several years. Once again, I was outraged. I called the reporter who wrote the article and told him that the president and the provost had lied. I told him my story, and he took quite an interest in it. I sent him copies of my correspondence. I provided the names of a few women students I thought I could trust to corroborate my story by telling him they had also had affairs with this professor; however, the only one who would speak to him told him that I was crazy.

Within days, an article appeared in a local paper. In it, the administrators admitted that, yes, they *had a few* complaints, but because my relationship had been "consensual," they felt there was nothing they could do about it. The affirmative action officer was quoted as saying that he did not think my claim that the classroom was being used for seduction warranted investigation because it had not been a hostile environment. He also thought that sex with students was just one of the perks of the job; he said my story was evidence that the classroom was "a great hunting ground" for professors who wanted sexual relationships. Evidently, he saw no correlation between "hunting" and "hostility." I was at a loss to figure out where consent fit in.

The day after the article appeared, I received a phone call and a letter from the university counsel. She asked for more information; more accurately, she *pleaded* for it, emphasizing the seriousness of the situation. She said she wanted "specific answers to specific questions." She urged me to call her office collect. I did so, and my call was not accepted. I wrote to her, explaining that I would cooperate in any way I could. I never heard from her again. I never learned what "specific questions" she had. A reporter from another newspaper contacted me to do a more in-depth article. She interviewed me over the telephone and, once again, I provided copies of my correspondence. The article never appeared. Officially, that is the end of the story.

Unofficially, of course, the tale continues. I still face consequences of the experience. I have difficulty trusting myself to choose appropriate partners. I distrust male professors and am wary of meeting them in their offices. Before accepting a research assistantship with another professor at another university, I questioned other women about that professor's character, arousing their suspicions about me. My wariness is so intense that, on being appointed a teaching assistant, I immediately checked the departmental manual for any guidelines for student–faculty relationships. I was relieved to see that the department had a clearly delineated list of duties students are prohibited from performing for faculty, such as personal errands and any chores not directly related to the specific course in which they assist.

The experience has made me suspicious of administrators. I am skeptical of the efficacy of any policy on student–faculty relationships, given the imbalance of power and the vulnerability of women students. And, perhaps the most frustrating consequence of all, is that I live with the knowledge that no policy yet exists to protect women at that institution. I was just a moment of trouble, an inconvenient item on the administration's agenda. The problem still has no name.

I realize that everyone reading this knows exceptions to the rule: Every department has its tale of the faculty member who married a student and lived happily ever after. Sometimes, things do work out. But, far more often, the less powerful person loses, and usually, that person is a woman. Consensual relationships between students and faculty members are demonstrably discriminatory in their impact. Pretending that they are not a problem denies all women equal access to education. How many women feel comfortable in a classroom in which the professor is evaluating his women students' bodies? How fair is a professor's grading when he is seeking a sexual relationship with one or more of his students? What is the impact on a student's self-confidence on discovering that a professor's praise for her work has been motivated by his hidden agenda of sexual exploitation? What are the consequences for the women who reject the professor's advances? How does he treat women he does not find attractive? How many women drop his classes because they don't know how to fend off advances without jeopardizing their grades? How many women withdraw from classroom interaction (and jeopardize their grades) because they are uncomfortable with the kind of attention paid to them by the "hunter" at the front of the room? How many women learn to mistrust male professors as a consequence of being "hunted" in a classroom or a faculty office? And how does that mistrust hamper their pursuit of advanced degrees?

Consensual relationships between students and faculty constitute one of the more "slippery" areas in the debate about sexual harassment. One could argue that adults should have the freedom to become intimate with whomever they choose. When the issue is framed as one of choice and consent, it could be argued that the university has no business interfering in consensual relationships between two adults. I argue, however, that, because students have relatively little power in the university setting, their ability to truly choose and give consent is questionable. One's ability to give consent depends largely on one's ability to say "no." Within the framework of a relationship where one partner has control over another's grades, earnings, or access to professional opportunities, the less powerful partner has little ability to say "no," and consent becomes irrelevant. When one partner cannot withhold consent from another, the relationship becomes potentially coercive and disruptive, and it moves into the realm of harassment.

I began this essay with a rule—don't become intimate with people who have significantly greater social power than you—and I end it with a plea. The rule is intended for those on the margins of power. It serves as a warning to look critically at social arrangements and to try to understand their politics. In the classroom setting, we students must understand that professors have considerable power over our lives. They have the power to make us want to please them, and my rule places a limit on the kind of pleasure we can provide. But the bulk of the burden for preventing sexual harassment and its attendant discrimination should not rest on the shoulders of those who are typically its victims. Those who are close to the centers of power must also do their part. It is a privilege to command the deference of others, and the legitimacy of those positions of privilege depends largely on the actions of those who occupy them.

This is where the plea comes in: I urge students, faculty, and administrators to consider both the impact that consensual relationships have on students and the ethical implications such relationships have for the profession. Although many believe that educational programs are enhanced by the existence of policies concerning consensual relationships, I believe that banning consensual relationships altogether is an ineffective and laughable strategy. A more effective approach would involve creating educational programs that inform students and faculty about the potential exploitation and harm that arises from the power differential in consensual relationships. Opening up this discussion would create an environment in which consensual relationships could be reported. This would, in turn, require procedures through which faculty members could remove themselves from positions of power over students before pursuing intimacy with them.

Administrators must abandon their benign perspective and recognize that they have an ethical responsibility to educate students and faculty about these critical issues. Universities need innovative policies on consensual relationships in order to protect students and preserve the integrity of the profession. Carefully crafted policies, consistently applied, can prevent other students from experiencing what I endured. In the absence of such a policy, people in power made a fool of me. A set of rules could save others from the same fate.

Reference

Dziech, Billie Wright, & Linda Weiner. 1984. *The lecherous professor*. Boston: Beacon Press.

15

ANATOMY OF A LAWSUIT
JEAN JEW v. UNIVERSITY OF IOWA

MARTHA CHAMALLAS

As a law professor who specializes in antidiscrimination law, I am often asked why so few women who claim they have been sexually harassed ever report the harassment, file a formal complaint, or sue. In response, I often mention what has been called the *second injury*, the injury sexual harassment victims experience when they bring their claims to court. The harsh treatment of Anita Hill as a complaining witness before the U.S. Senate Judiciary Committee was but one dramatic example of the cruelty of sexual harassment disputes. The strategy of discrediting the plaintiff is unfortunately a staple in sexual harassment litigation. Despite attempts to focus the legal inquiry on the actions of the defendant, rather than on the behavior of the plaintiff, lawyers know they must warn prospective sexual harassment plaintiffs that they too will be put on trial. Even successful plaintiffs may question whether the costs of victory are too high.

The case that has been the most influential, in my experience, is the lawsuit Professor Jean Jew brought against the University of Iowa. Sometimes I consider Jew's case to be a complete victory; she won in the courts, she changed public opinion in our community, all the while insisting that she should not be forced to find a new job in a more hospitable environment.

Sometimes, however, I regard Jew's case as a warning that legal claims of sexual harassment offer only limited prospects for social transformation. Jew's victory was exacted at an extremely high cost. Jew fought the University for more than a decade and was treated cruelly by an institution which, during the lengthy ordeal, professed a commitment to sexual and racial equality. As Jew acknowledged, her public stance was made possible only because she was relatively privileged in terms of education, economic and social position and had no partner or child who might also suffer from the stress and ostracism that accompanies such a lawsuit. I also regard Jew's case as special, in the sense that certain unusual factors, including grassroots organization and extensive press coverage, combined to overcome formidable institutional resistance to her claims.

Note: An earlier version of this chapter was first published in *The Yale Journal of Law and Feminism*, 6, No. (1). Reprinted by permission of The Yale Lournal of Law and Feminism, Inc.

As a matter of law, Jew's case is significant because it is one of only a few cases in which a faculty member has successfully argued that her academic department constituted a hostile working environment.[1] It is significant as a case study of gender hostility in a predominantly male working group of elite professionals in which the harassment was every bit as virulent as that which occurs in factories and at construction sites. It is significant as a painful yet powerful demonstration of how race and sex discrimination intersect to create distinctive burdens for women of color. Finally, the case is significant for what it reveals about the interplay between law, litigation, and grassroots activism.

Harassment and Discrimination

Jean Jew is a research scientist. She grew up in Mississippi and went to undergraduate and medical school at Tulane University. She is first-generation Chinese American. Those who know Jew often describe her as serious, hard working, and very devoted to her career. In 1973, shortly after receiving her M.D., she came to the University of Iowa as a post-graduate associate in the Department of Anatomy. She was twenty-four-years old. A year later she was placed on the tenure track. At that time she was the only woman in a faculty position in a basic science department in the College of Medicine.

Jew came to Iowa as part of a research team from Tulane. Her mentor was Terence Williams who had been recruited to head Iowa's department of anatomy. At Tulane, Jew had already worked extensively with Williams in the field of the nervous system and electromicroscopy. Before the Tulane group ever arrived, the anatomy department at Iowa was fractionalized and morale was poor.[2] The tension grew after Williams became department head. Some of the older faculty members, in particular, did not like Williams or the way he ran the department. Faculty members complained that he would not tolerate disagreement with his views, and many feared Williams would try to get rid of people who were not on his side.

Jew suffered from her association with Williams. Beginning the first year and lasting thirteen years thereafter, Jew was the subject of rumors that she and Williams were having a sexual relationship and that Jew was given preferential treatment in the department because of the relationship. The slander campaign was extensive, reaching students throughout the College, as well as staff and faculty in other parts of the University. There was even gossip about the alleged relationship at national and international meetings of anatomists and neuroscientists. Throughout these years, Jew insisted that her relationship with Williams was professional and friendly only. Despite the persistence of the rumors, Jew did not distance herself from Williams; she continued to socialize with him and his wife and they collaborated on a number of research projects.

At times, the comments about Jew turned vicious. One startling aspect of her case was the crude treatment of Jew by some of the male faculty in her department. She was called a "stupid slut," a "dumb bitch," a "whore," and a "chink"—sometimes even to her face. She was the subject of sexually denigrating graffiti and cartoons, which appeared intermittently in the men's room and on a bulletin board outside the office of a faculty member. She was also defamed in an anonymous letter sent to a male colleague describing Jew in racist, lewd terms such as "Chinese pussy."

The situation reached a critical point when Jew became eligible for promotion to full professorship. By the time the faculty met to vote on Jew's promotion, Williams had been pressured to resign as head of the department, and his supporters were now in the minority among senior faculty. The committee voted five to three against Jew's promotion. Two of those voting against Jew's promotion were the same faculty members who previously made sexual slurs about her. One of these men repeated his slur to another full professor on the very day of the vote, referring to Jew as a "whore." One of the others voting against Jew complained that she had received professional advantages denied to him, and a fourth person in the majority remarked during the discussion about Jew that "women and blacks have it made." The stated reason for the denial of promotion was that Jew had not established independence in her research, implying that her long-standing collaboration with Williams had been costly to her career.

Administrative Inaction

Even before the denial of the promotion, Jew took her complaints to administrators in the College of Medicine and to the central administration of the University. When Jew approached the vice president of Academic Affairs, she told Jew that nothing could be done and that Jew would only make things worse for herself by pursuing a complaint. The Dean of the College of Medicine told Jew that a single woman in a small town such as Iowa City had to realize that she lived in a "goldfish bowl environment."

After she was denied promotion, Jew hired Carolyn Chalmers as her lawyer and filed a formal complaint. Chalmers, then a partner in a small public-interest law firm in Minneapolis, had gained a reputation as a successful feminist litigator by winning a suit on behalf of women faculty against the University of Minnesota.[3]

To avoid litigation, the sides agreed to convene a panel of three faculty members to investigate Jew's sexual harassment complaint. The panel was chaired by a lawyer on the faculty of the College of Business who had been active in several women's organizations on campus and had been called on frequently to serve as a representative of women's interests on committees at the University. The other two panel members were male faculty members from the College of Medicine. Both parties approved each of the panel members. The hearings conducted by the panel were quite formal—the testimony of witnesses was sworn and transcribed. The panel's report concluded that Jew had been defamed and harassed because of her sex and recommended that immediate administrative action be taken on her behalf.

At this point, the University intensified its resistance to Jew's claims. It never implemented the panel report, nor did it take steps to repair Jew's reputation. It allowed the case slowly to proceed to trial—a process that took six years. During those six years, Jew became active in groups concerned with women's issues on campus. She worked with a diverse group of faculty and staff studying affirmative action in other colleges within the University and was elected chair of the Council on the Status of Women. Through such work, a group of women, including myself, came to respect Jew and to believe her account. When the cases proceeded to trial, we were prepared to watch them closely.

The Trials

The federal trial lasted twelve days, with Judge Harold Vietor presiding as the trial court, without a jury. The University was officially represented by two lawyers from the Office of the Attorney General. Because the trial was in Des Moines, a hundred miles from campus, few people from the University attended. The newspaper coverage was not extensive. The *Des Moines Register* carried a few stories, but the local paper never assigned a reporter to cover the trial.

The University's litigation strategy was to discredit Jew by trying to show she had indeed been sleeping with Williams and that the rumors had a basis in fact. The theory of defendant's case was that Jew had incited or provoked the harassment and that the response to Jew did not constitute a sexually hostile environment. The litigators demonstrated little concern for how their trial strategies might undermine the University's stated position of promoting the advancement of women and condemning racist behavior on campus. The effect was very intimidating to observers, like myself, who followed the legal developments.

In a variety of ways, those defending the University alerted faculty and staff that the only institutionally loyal course of action was to side against Jew in the litigation. In a memorandum, a lawyer from the central administration instructed the medical faculty not to speak with anyone about the case. Persons who appeared on the plaintiff's potential witness list were called by counsel from the Attorney General's office and asked sharp questions about the substance of their testimony.

In addition to denying that particular harassing incidents had ever occurred, the University tried to prove that Jew was in some way responsible for the sexual slurs made by her colleagues. At trial Jew was asked whether she had ever had a sexual relationship with Williams. When she responded negatively, the University tried to impeach her testimony by introducing medical records from her gynecologist showing that Jew had been using birth control pills during the period in question. Over the plaintiff's objection, the judge allowed University counsel to ask Jew if she had a prescription for birth control pills from 1973 to 1978. Presumably to cast aspersions on Jew's character, in a written brief to the court, the University stated that Jew's sister, who was also employed by the Department of Anatomy, had once been a Playboy bunny and referred to Jew as a claimant "without a conscience."

Before the opinion was handed down in the federal case, Jew's state defamation claim against Professor Robert Tomanek was tried before a jury in Iowa City. Although the University was not a defendant in this action, the state paid the legal fees and ultimately the entire damage award for Tomanek. Like the defense in federal court, the strategy in state court evidenced no regard for what an all-out battle against Jew might mean for other women at the University or for the reputation of the University. For example, the defendant challenged a prospective juror for cause simply because she had taken a women's studies course. The defendant disputed the testimony of a woman, a former associate dean for the College of Liberal Arts, who stated that the personal vilification of Jew violated several University policies. Through the testimony of the former vice president for Academic Affairs and a University lawyer, the defendant took the position that even sexual and racial slurs fell within the bounds of academic freedom because they were made in the context of an intradepartmental dispute.

In the federal harassment case, the truth of the allegations about any sexual relationship between Jew and Williams was arguably only indirectly relevant as evidence that Jew's conduct somehow provoked or incited the harassment. In the state defamation case, however, truth was clearly a defense and the defense again set out to show that the rumors were true. The defense produced a witness who claimed she saw Williams having sex with a woman in the Department of Anatomy library. She assumed the woman was Jew because, she stated, the woman had "yellow legs." To show that the witness's testimony was distorted by racial stereotypes, Jew's attorney conducted an experiment for the jury. She asked them to compare her bare "white" legs to those of her client's.

The defense strategy in the state trial drew on the sexual stereotype that all close interactions between men and women must have a sexual dimension. At one point, Tomanek's counsel asked a witness whether she knew of any other male/female research team in the department besides Jew and Williams. The witness could think of only one other team, which happened to be a husband and wife team. The insinuation carried an ominous message for junior women faculty trying to establish a record of research, especially because there were no other women in Jew's specialty with whom she could have collaborated.

Legal Victories

Jew's first major victory came from a state jury, which held Tomanek liable and awarded Jew $5,000 in actual damages and $30,000 in punitive damages. In contrast to the federal trial, the state trial and the verdicts were covered extensively by the local and campus newspapers. Each day a contingent of faculty and staff supporting Jew attended the trial, became familiar with the incidents, and discussed the implications of the defense strategy for our professional lives at the University.

Shortly after the start of the fall semester in 1990, Judge Vietor issued his opinion in the federal case. The twenty-page ruling was decidedly favorable to Jew: Vietor found that Jew had been subjected to sexual harassment, that the harassment was serious, and that the University had failed in its duty to take prompt remedial action. These findings entitled Jew to affirmative relief from the sexually hostile environment, including the distribution of the court's opinion and the earlier faculty panel's report to top University officials, all College of Medicine department heads, and all faculty and staff in the department of anatomy. Vietor also determined that the harassment of Jew had tainted the decision to deny her promotion and took the relatively unusual step of ordering her retroactive promotion to full professor, along with lost back pay. The issue of attorney's fees was reserved for a subsequent hearing in which the court would determine the amount Chalmers was entitled to recover for her representation of the prevailing party in a Title VII suit.

After all the years of speculation and rumors, Vietor issued the simple finding that "[t]here had never been a romantic or sexual relationship between Dr. Jew and Dr. Williams."[4] He also dispatched the University's provocation defense by finding that "Dr. Jew did not, by word or deed, invite the type of comments made about her and Dr. Williams.... Indeed Dr. Jew has conducted herself throughout her employment at the University as a serious and committed teacher, scholar and member of the academic community."[5]

In addition to clearing Jew's name, Vietor's opinion contained a thorough and detailed account of the incidents that formed the basis of Jew's claim of a hostile work environment. In clear, dispassionate prose, Vietor's narrative painted a vivid picture of the cruel and unprofessional way some of Jew's colleagues treated her, a picture that shocked many who thought that doctors and professors did not act this way. He also had little positive to say about the University's handling of Jew's complaint; his understated comment that the University's response was "ambivalent at best"[6] would later be quoted repeatedly and would serve to pressure the University to change its course of action.

Perhaps the most important aspect of Vietor's opinion was his analysis of the sex-based nature of the hostility directed at Jew. The University had taken the position that Jew's harassment was not really sexual in nature. According to the University, the central problem was the animosity toward Williams. The University claimed that Jew suffered not because she was a woman but because of her political alignment with the detested department head. Vietor rejected this argument, reasoning that among the faculty who supported Williams, only Jew was accused of using sex to further her career. The men on the "wrong side" in the department, those who aligned themselves with Williams, did not have their achievements so diminished. Vietor also stated that the rumors about Williams and Jew did not have the same affect for each. The slanderous statements portrayed Jew as trying to use sex, rather than merit, to advance. Although the rumors charged Williams with being unethical, no one questioned his competency as a researcher. No one asserted that it was Jew's talent that made their joint projects successful. Vietor's complicated and nuanced assessment of the effect of the rumors and harassing statements negated the University's argument that life in the Department of Anatomy was equally bad for men and women. His assessment also saved a classic case of sexual slander from being classified as having no connection to sexual harassment.

The Jean Jew Justice Committee

Initially there was only moderate publicity on the ruling. Various newspapers in the state carried stories announcing and describing the judgment, but there were no editorials or in-depth coverage. Privately, individuals and groups of faculty and staff urged University administrators to put an end to the matter and not to pursue an appeal. The two top administrators, who were relatively new on the job, professed an inability to stop the ongoing litigation.

The University's decision to appeal the case to the Eighth Circuit Court of Appeals provided the impetus for political mobilization on behalf of Jew. In an official statement by the Board of Regents, the University claimed that Vietor's order violated the free speech rights of faculty members and placed it in the position of "policing the statements and behavior of faculty members in ways that appear inconsistent with academic life and constitutional protections." Immediately after the public announcement of the appeal, the Jean Jew Justice Committee was formed. The core group included leaders in feminist circles, as well as men and women who either knew Jew personally or had followed the case. By word of mouth, the group grew into a diverse coalition of people intent on forcing the University to drop the appeal. It took as its primary mission the job of informing the University community and the state about the facts of the case. The group quickly conducted a fund-raising effort that generated more than enough money to pay for mailing and advertising costs. In retrospect, the most important action taken by the Justice Committee was the distribution of a copy of Judge Vietor's opinion to every faculty member at the University.

The impact of the mailing was profound; in response, over 200 people signed a full-page ad in the campus newspaper urging people to judge the facts for themselves by reading Vietor's opinion. Many of those signing the ad had never before been associated with feminist causes; it was becoming clear that outrage over the University's response had reached beyond the political left.

Over the next several weeks, the newspapers in the state finally began to comment on the case. All the editorials were critical of the University; many expressed scorn and disbelief at its refusal to end the suit. One columnist, who styles himself "the old reporter," had particularly harsh words for the University; he referred to the behavior of the administrators as "sickening" and "disgusting" and suggested that the press had been reluctant to cover the story because it was too "raw" to report in "family newspaper[s]."[7]

With increased print media coverage, the sentiment within the University began to shift radically and the view that it was on the wrong side gained widespread support. Individual departments and the Faculty Council passed resolutions condemning the appeal; eighteen members of the math department wrote a letter to the campus newspaper calling for the University to drop the appeal and issue an apology.

The Settlement

Only hours before a public forum scheduled by the Jean Jew Justice Committee to mark one month since the filing of the appeal, the parties settled the case. The lawyers from the Attorney General's office were supplanted in the last round of negotiations by private counsel representing the president of the board of regents. The final agreement gave Jew everything she had won in the district court and more: Jew was retroactively promoted to full professor, given back pay, and compensated for her state defamation judgment and pending state civil rights claim. Of great importance to a financially strapped university and state government, under the terms of the settlement, Chalmers was paid $895,000 in attorney's fees. The terms of the settlement were made public, in contrast to many discrimination settlements in which the plaintiff gives up the right to disclose the content of the parties' agreement. It was clear that Jew had won; the settlement did not require her to compromise on any of her initial demands.

Beyond the specific litigation demands, however, it was considerably less clear what Jew had won from the University. The president of the University issued a formal statement: "Dr. Jew deserves our apologies and our respect for her stand." He did not, however, embrace her publicly in any other way and delegated to others the responsibility of implementing that part of the court order requiring the University to create an environment free of sexual hostility. Most significantly, the University instituted no disciplinary action against Tomanek and refused Jew's request to transfer his tenure line outside the Department of Anatomy. Like most institutions worried about their public image, the University of Iowa was not inclined to reflect publicly on what had happened and simply wanted to put the case behind it. The public statements of University officials spoke of healing rather than assessing.

Explaining the University's Resistance

A case as painful, prolonged, and politically significant as Jew's deserves to be examined closely for what it reveals about the conditions under which such events can occur and the importance of law and litigation to social change. Now that several years have passed since Jew's victories in court and the University's capitulation, I find myself constructing a guardedly optimistic appraisal of the case. In retrospect, I think that the University's resistance to Jew's claim—and perhaps the callousness of its defense—was predictable given the dominant attitudes and structural conditions at the College of Medicine and in the larger University community.

Why did the University oppose Jew's complaint of sex discrimination? As simple as it sounds, I believe that several of the key people at the University who opposed Jew's claim—men and women—did so because they believed Jew was dishonest, unscrupulous, and undeserving of support from the University. They believed the rumors about the sexual relationship and were even willing to come to the aid of crude professors like Tomanek, simply to show that the University would not give in to "bad" women. The deeper question is why these administrators and others would believe rumors that failed to persuade the faculty panel members, the jury, or the federal judge.

Sexual and Racial Stereotypes

The rumor campaign against Jew was as successful and as persistent as it was because it drew on deep-seated and harmful stereotypes about professional women and about Asian academics at U.S. universities. In contrast to the official fact-finders who were constrained to base their judgment solely on the evidence presented, many within the University community making less considered judgments were apt to be influenced by stereotypes.

The false narrative constructed about Jew was believable in part because of its familiarity. Jew was portrayed as a cold, conniving woman whose success was due to her sexual relationship with a man in power rather than her achievements as a teacher and researcher. The narrative drew on both sexual and racial stereotypes. It supported the stereotype that women sleep their way to the top; that women are not really good at science and if they achieve in that area, it must be because of the talents of men; that women of color are promiscuous; and that Asians over achieve in their jobs, but are not truly talented or creative. As Vietor's opinion recognized, it was no fortuity that the vilification of Jean Jew took a sexualized form. Vietor pointed out how attacks on Jew were cast in sexual terms, while criticism of Williams, as department head, were regarded as political or professional. This aspect of the litigation demonstrates how sexual harassment can reduce women to sexual objects, diverting attention from women in their roles as professionals.

To the community beyond the College of Medicine, the racial dimensions of Jew's harassment were not as prominent as the sexual component. Only after Vietor's opinion was disseminated, for example, did many people learn for the first time that Jew is Chinese and that her ethnicity was also the subject of her opponents' ridicule and abuse. It is telling, however, that the sexual attacks on Jew were often racial in nature (e.g., "Chinese pussy"). Jew's harassment took on a specific sexualized and racialized form because she is a Chinese woman. It is impossible to understand the nature of her sexual harassment apart from her position as a racial minority in a predominantly white department. Her case exemplifies what scholars have described as the "dual vulnerability" of women of color.[8] For Jew, the dynamics of racism and sexism in her department intersected to produce a distinctive type of harassment that cannot simply be labeled either sexual or racial.

The University's litigation strategy traded on these racial and sexual stereotypes by depicting Jew as an unworthy plaintiff, while at the same time attempting to discount the sexually and racially specific nature of the harassment. The defense proceeded on the assumption that the harassment of Jew would not be actionable if the rumors about the sexual relationship between Jew and Williams were true. Implicit in the defense theory was that Jew could have forfeited her right to work in a nonhostile environment because of her sexual conduct. The University's attempt to defeat her claim by proving that her conduct incited the harassment, however, lacked substantial legal support. Although Judge Vietor made the factual finding that there had been no sexual relationship, the finding was not essential to his legal conclusion that Jew had been sexually harassed. The law requires only that the discriminatory conduct be sufficiently severe or pervasive to create a hostile or abusive environment. The defense strategy of portraying Jew as a "bad girl," unworthy of legal protection, responded more to conventional notions of morality than to legal requirements.

Tokenism

It was also critically important to explaining the University's resistance that Jean Jew was a token woman in the College of Medicine. I use the term *token* here in the sense that social scientists who have examined structural barriers to equality use the term to mean a woman (or a member of a minority group) who is the only woman or one of only a few women at her level in an organization.[9] Stereotyping is more likely to occur when women are rare in an organization. In highly imbalanced settings like the College of Medicine, the numerical many dominate the few and are able to typecast women and reduce their chances for advancement. Jew was cast into the role trap of "seductress," a common fate for young, attractive token women. Token women are often taken under the wing of a powerful man in the group. This close alliance then becomes the subject of resentment by other men, and the token woman risks being treated as a "whore" and a sexual object simply because she is a rarity in the group.

The scarcity of women professors at the College of Medicine also meant that Jew's promotion would be judged entirely by a group of men. By pointing out this structural feature, I am not assuming that if any woman had voted on Jew's promotion, the result necessarily would have been different. Women in male-dominated environments often do not resist the status quo and certainly some women at the University of Iowa went along with and helped to construct the University's defense. However, the total absence of women in the decision-making process at the College of Medicine made it more likely that sexist stereotypes about Jew would play a role. I doubt whether many men in the department empathized with Jew, or feared that the kind of rumors that were going around about Jew might some day be directed at them and damage their careers. The role trap into which Jew was cast did not have a male counterpart.

Male Perspective

The third element that explains the University's resistance to Jean Jew's claims is the perspective embraced by its administrators. The administration approached the situation in the Department of Anatomy from a male-centered perspective, treating the problem from the beginning as managing competition among men—the men who supported Williams and the men who were against Williams. In this narrative, Jean Jew was invisible, or at best a minor player. The administration responded to Jew's complaint of denial of promotion and sexual harassment as if it were a sideshow, one more manifestation of the personnel problems surrounding Williams in his department.

The University lawyers argued that this case had nothing to do with sex, despite the repeated sexual slurs and the mistreatment of the sole woman professor. The tragedy of the case is that the University never seemed to care much about losing the talents of Jean Jew, despite her promising early career and despite the University's stated commitment to affirmative action. By taking Williams as its central focus, the University failed to understand the environment of the Department of Anatomy from Jew's perspective—from a woman's perspective. Even at the last stages of the case when the Board of Regents announced it grounds for appeal, it expressed concern only for the free-speech rights of the male faculty members who had abused Jew. This academic-freedom argument turned the victimizers into the victims and was the product of a partial male-centered viewpoint. The erasure of Jew as the real party in interest, coupled with the denial that this case was really about sex discrimination and sexual harassment, made it easier for the University to play hardball and to deploy offensive stereotypes that it would not have used in everyday discourse.

Understanding the Victory: Lessons from One Case

I doubt that Jew changed many minds at the College of Medicine, the central administration of the University, or the Attorney General's office. However, Jew was victorious; she forced the University to settle on her terms. Although she would likely have prevailed on appeal, Jew's victory was greater because she compelled the University to recognize her injury and her power, rather than simply abide by the terms of a court order. In this one case, a complicated set of factors combined to overcome the University's resistance.

Feminist Legal Doctrine

Jean Jew's case is remarkable for what it reveals about the importance of incursions of feminism into the law in the last two decades. The cause of action for sexual harassment—particularly the recognition of a sexually hostile environment—had been created in the late 1970s by feminist activists and scholars.[10] Although men can be sexually harassed, the meaning of harassment is largely shaped by women's claims and the chances of being harassed are much greater for women. When Jew came to Iowa in 1973 and first suffered harm from her colleagues, no court had granted recovery to a sexual harassment victim. When Jew first complained to the central administration at the University of Iowa in 1979, there were no federal guidelines defining harassment and no national policy condemning the practice. When Jew first filed suit in 1985, there was no Supreme Court opinion recognizing hostile environment claims. Only the cumulative efforts of many plaintiffs like Jew made it possible for Jew to articulate her harm as a legal injury and to secure a legal judgment. The irony of Jew's long ordeal is that it took almost that long for the law to catch up with injury.

Feminist Lawyering

Jew was fortunate to have had the benefit of a talented feminist lawyer who displayed extraordinary dedication to her case. Even though Chalmers and her firm were ultimately compensated for the years of litigation, few lawyers would take such risky cases, because only the winning party recovers attorney's fees.[11] The relationship that developed between Jew and Chalmers was a rare one and exceeded the normal professional connection: Chalmers maintained close contact with Jew for the entire period in which she represented her, even when little was happening in the case. Jew was also an unusual client: She developed a sophisticated knowledge of the law and learned a great deal about the workings of the University bureaucracy through her work on the Council on the Status of Women. Most important, she built a network of support through her efforts on behalf of other women.

An Authoritative Narrative

The University was unable to defend its position in the face of the authoritative narrative written by Judge Vietor. The opinion gave a compelling account of what happened in a manner detailed enough and clear enough to give readers a feel for the situation as he perceived it. It was a well-written narrative as well as a judicial opinion. As a white male federal judge who was not labeled as a liberal, Vietor's opinion was particularly credible. Jew was also fortunate in that she did not have to confront a series of news stories or other publicity contesting Vietor's narrative. One article in the campus newspaper written while the appeal was pending focused on Williams' bad history as a department head and restated the rumors of sexual favoritism, with no mention of Vietor's factual finding that there had never been a sexual relationship. This story, however, was not taken up by the other papers which generally stuck to Vietor's account. A campaign of counterpublicity for the University's position never materialized.

Political Mobilization

The most important element in Jew's ultimate victory was the political pressure exerted by the Jean Jew Justice Committee. The mere issuance of Vietor's opinion did not have an immediate impact. For over two months, there was no public outcry and little media interest. Instead, it was the publicity campaign of the Jean Jew Justice Committee that activated the opinion and gave political momentum to the case. Vietor's words spoke for themselves only after the wider public actually read portions of the opinion and the case became the topic of sustained media attention. Both the authoritative narrative and the political mobilization were essential ingredients in getting the University to change its course. For Jew and for many others on campus, it was an exhausting—even if ultimately triumphant—effort.

Postscript

Jean Jew's case had a radicalizing and dispiriting affect on me. I still find it hard to believe that the University contested Jew's claim that she was unfairly denied a promotion, while conceding that some of the men sitting in judgment had called her sexually derogatory names. Whatever else the case might come to mean, the fierceness with which the University defended its position is a graphic reminder that sexual harassment victims have much to lose by simply invoking the legal process. The privileges of education, rank, or social position did not protect Jew from a scripted defense that called her character into question and invaded her privacy. The lesson that stays with me is that it takes both legal action and direct political agitation to sustain even limited victories in this highly contested area of women's rights to dignity and economic parity.

Endnotes

1. *See*, e.g., *King v. Board of Regents of the Univ. of Wis. Sys.*, 898 F.2d 533, 538 (7th Cir. 1990).
2. Much of the account of Jew's treatment is taken from the case report. *See Jew v. University of Iowa*, 749 F.Supp. 946 (S.D. Iowa 1990).
3. *Rajender v. University of Minnesota*, 546 F. Supp. 158 (D. Minn. 1982).
4. 749 F. Supp. at 948–49.
5. Ibid. at 951.
6. Ibid. at 959.
7. James Flansburg, Being ashamed of the U of I. *Des Moines Reg.*, Nov. 3, 1990 at 7A.
8. *See* Kimberle Crenshaw, *Race, gender, and sexual harassment*, 65 So. Cal. L. Rev. 1467 (1992).
9. *See* Rosabeth Moss Kanter, *Men and women of the corporation*, 208–10 (1977).
10. ~ Martha Chamallas, *Writing about sexual harassment: A guide to the literature*, 4 UCLA Women's L.J. 37 (1994).
11. At the time of the litigation, plaintiffs alleging sex discrimination could not recover either compensatory or punitive damages under Title VII. Jew's prospects for monetary gain were small because her claim for back pay was not very large. The Civil Rights Act of 1991 now allows sex discrimination plaintiffs to recover damages up to a maximum of between $50,000 and $300,000, depending on the size of the employer. 42 U.S.C. 1981a (b)(3)(Supp. III 1992).

16

UNTYING THE GORDIAN KNOT OF ACADEMIC SEXUAL HARASSMENT

SUSAN J. SCOLLAY   *CAROLYN S. BRATT*

Near the conclusion of a sexual harassment workshop we were conducting for a university's orientation and training program for new graduate teaching assistant (TAs), one of the male teaching assistants in the audience emphatically declared that allegations of sexual harassment have become the "whiplash injury of the 1990s." He went on to assert that the university's responsibilities were to defend him from unfounded charges of sexual harassment in order to protect the academy from the dangers of "political correctness." His remark provoked angry responses from female TAs and elicited nods of agreement from a number of other male TAs in the room.

Despite its brevity, this vignette captures many of the major thematic threads that are intertwined in the issue of academic sexual harassment. For example, one of the threads is the complex constellation of legal responsibilities and ethical duties that flow from the dual nature of the academy as both an educational institution and employer. The potential of conflict between and among long-standing academic values (e.g., academic freedom, instructor autonomy, individual needs, organizational interests, and legally protected privacy and free speech rights) is another thread that may be more aptly described as a rope given the intricate interaction of these values. Issues of organizational culture, the (but sometimes not so) silent male norm, the systemic sexism of the academy, and the challenges of working within traditional organizational structures while attempting to implement the broad-based institutional changes necessary to eradicate sexual harassment in academic settings are other tangled strands of the problem. These threads are so inextricably interwoven that those who attempt to address sexual harassment in the academy often feel as if they are trying to untie the mythical Gordian knot.

If college and university decision makers are going to be successful in fashioning policies for their campuses that untie the knot of sexual harassment, the conflicts that need to be addressed and resolved in their remediation efforts must be clearly identified. That task is daunting enough. False conflicts—issues interjected into the sexual harassment debate that serve as either intentional or unintentional distracters from the real problem—must be recognized and avoided. In this chapter, the major threads in the sexual harassment knot are examined in some detail. False conflicts are untangled from the knot of sexual harassment, and the true dilemmas and substantive challenges inherent in dealing effectively with the multifaceted problem of sexual harassment on campus are discussed.

The Duality of the Academy

The dual nature of the academy is close to the very core of the sexual harassment "knot." Similar to the TAs in the workshop who were by definition both teachers and students, colleges and universities are simultaneously employers and educational institutions. Like other employers, the academy must comply with the dictates of state and federal laws prohibiting sexual harassment of employees, but as educational institutions they have additional legal responsibilities and clear ethical duties. For example, in addition to being responsible for sexual harassment of their employees by supervisors and co-workers, colleges and universities bear responsibility for sexual harassment of students by either institutional employees or other students. The typical nonacademic employer has no legal responsibility for the harassment of its customers by other customers. In addition, certain ethical duties vis-à-vis the students flow from the essential nature of colleges and universities as institutions of higher learning. At its most basic and fundamental level, an institution of higher education stands in a fiduciary relationship with its students such that it is ethically bound to ensure that learning, not sex, is the essence of faculty–student interactions and that the student's personhood is, at all times, respected. In pursuit of the fulfillment of these responsibilities, colleges and universities must sort through the potentially conflicting demands of various rights, interests, and values.

Conflicting Rights, Interests, and Values

The statements made by the male TA in the introductory vignette highlight some of the conflicting rights, interests, and values inherent in dealing effectively with sexual harassment on campus. First, the TA's characterization of the problem and the institution's responsibilities demonstrates that the individual interests of the various parties to a sexual harassment dispute and the responsibilities and duties of the institution are not likely to be coterminous. Universities and colleges face the challenge of structuring institutional procedures for handling complaints of sexual harassment that are at once responsive to the complainant's needs, protective of the accused's rights, and in harmony with both the institution's legal obligations and its heightened ethical duties. That task can be particularly problematic when the complainant "needs" confidentiality and the alleged harasser has the "right" to know the charges that have been made. A similar lack of symmetry can exist between the "needs" and "rights" of the individual parties and the "duties" imposed by law on the university or college. For example, if the complainant is satisfied with simply talking with someone in authority about the alleged incident and does not want the institution to take further action, the college or university may nonetheless have the legal responsibility to investigate; to stop the harassment; and, if necessary, take appropriate action against the alleged harasser. At the same time, an educational institution may feel constrained to respect the privacy rights of its adult employees and students to form intimate relationships of their own choosing with each other, yet worry about the ethical implications of such faculty–student relationships. Should an amorous faculty–student relationship go awry and allegations of sexual harassment follow, the academic institution is responsible for sorting out and determining if the power imbalance inherent in faculty–student interactions was an inappropriate influence in the "choosing."

Despite his sloganeering, the TA's comments also raise the issue of "academic freedom"—another essential variable in the equation of academic sexual harassment. As an institutionally venerated value, "academic freedom" stands at the heart of the academic enterprise. Traditionally, it is a value of which colleges and universities, as well as the courts, have been extremely protective. Yet, at some point, the individual's right to academic freedom may impinge on the right of students to an educational experience free from sex discrimination. If so, the institution's ethical duty to ensure that its students receive a substantively—as well as a formally—equal education may justify inroads into the individual's right to academic freedom. These are just two of the myriad of conflicting values and duties colleges and universities must address in their efforts to develop and implement effective policies concerning sexual harassment on campus. All such conflicts must be resolved within the prevailing culture of the academy which itself contains formidable challenges and constraints on the development and implementation of policies that successfully address academic sexual harassment.

Institutional Culture and Systemic Sexism

As an accurate microcosm of the larger academic community, the audience response to the male TA's statements is as instructive as the statements themselves. Those who publicly objected to his remarks were all females, and those who exhibited support for the speaker and his opinions were all males. The correlation between gender and individual audience member's responses illuminates more than just the unmistakable reality of a chasm between female and male students' attitudes about the existence, frequency, severity, and importance of academic sexual harassment. It also illustrates basic differences in the perceptions of those who are most likely to experience academic sexual harassment and the perspectives of those who are most likely to be in a position to do something constructive about sexual harassment. No studies have shown that incidents of false allegations of sexual harassment are more likely to be made than false allegations of other forms of sex discrimination. Yet, if those in positions to do something about academic sexual harassment (administrators, professors, TAs) perceive of themselves only as potentially unjustly accused perpetrators, and not see either themselves or others as possible victims of sexual harassment, institutional attention and scarce organizational resources and energies may well be invested in efforts to uncover and prevent false allegations rather than in much more needed initiatives to prevent and punish sexual harassment.

The opening vignette is also illustrative of the almost intractable nature of resistance on campus to attempts to address and remedy the problem of sexual harassment. The training program had the imprimatur of the university, and our presentation was replete with empirical evidence documenting the depth and breadth of the sexual harassment problem on campus. Nonetheless, the speaker rejected the very "fact" of the existence of sexual harassment in the academy. In expressing his disagreement in the fashion he did, the TA also cast aside the rational, data-based discourse traditionally revered by the academic community in favor of derisive sound bites that trivialized the issue and left no room for reasoned discussion and dialogue.

The existence of academic sexual harassment is really a symptom or manifestation of an institutional culture and organizational climate on campuses across the United States that can be most accurately described as "systemically sexist." Not only are the administrative and instructional staffs of most colleges and universities male dominated, but the academic culture in most institutions of higher education is both male-defined and male-normed. Only when this fundamental reality is recognized, acknowledged, and changed can campus resistance and other, more systemic impediments to the elimination of sexual harassment be addressed and eradicated. However, such self-reflection and change are exceedingly difficult to bring about when institutional leadership is comprised primarily of individuals who because of their gender (male), race (white), and sexual orientation (heterosexual) are immune from any "felt" experience with the fundamentally sexist nature of the academy.

Organizational Structure and Change Efforts

The limited nature and effectiveness of institutional efforts to address sexual harassment in academia are also apparent in the opening episode of this chapter. Despite the pervasiveness of the problem and the complexities of fashioning effective solutions, our one-hour session constituted the totality of the information and training that new teaching assistants at the university received on sexual harassment. As is true at an overwhelming number of institutions, once these new TAs entered their respective classrooms and closed the doors, there would be little, if any, ongoing supervision of their behavior and interactions with students. Even if one could reasonably assume that all the TAs in that audience heard, and, in good faith, intended to heed, the message to refrain from engaging in sexually harassing conduct, that is, no guarantee such conduct will not occur. After all, TAs are likely to model their behavior as instructors on the classroom conduct of their own teachers. It is unfortunately true, however, that those role models often created highly sexualized classroom climates and engaged in sexually harassing behavior toward students. In the absence of meaningful supervision and ongoing training, TAs may unintentionally engage in sexual harassment as they intentionally replicate the behavior of their role models.

The problem of sexual harassment in the academy will not be solved by simply instituting longer and more intensive orientation sessions or by monitoring the classroom behavior of instructors. Much more extensive efforts must to be undertaken (see the following). The reality is, however, that any meaningful organizational change is extremely difficult to achieve within the traditionally atomistic and diffuse authority structure of the academic community of scholars. Legalistic and highly directive initiatives that may succeed in stemming sexual harassment in nonacademic work settings are fundamentally at odds with the decentralized and nonhierarchical structure of the academic community; the high value that community places on individual freedom and instructor autonomy; and the long-standing, laissez-faire tradition in that community of tolerance for idiosyncratic behaviors.

Finally, while many of the thematic threads that make the knot of academic sexual harassment so difficult to untie successfully can be teased out of the vignette introducing this chapter, the episode does not illustrate directly other, existing structural barriers to remedying sexual harassment in a university or college setting. The duties and responsibilities of an institution's affirmative action (AA) office provide one example of these other structural barriers. Most academic institutions assign the AA office two different, and at times bipolar, roles—institutional protector and institutional enforcer. In the former role, the AA office attempts to protect the educational institution from the consequences of noncompliance with laws prohibiting sexual harassment by educating staff and students as well as by monitoring and reporting on institutional behavior. In its role as enforcer, however, the AA office is also charged with ferreting out and punishing violations of those same legal prohibitions against sexual harassment. Given the severe time and resource constraints faced by campus AA offices, one or the other of these roles must dominate, and in many institutions the one that wins out is the role of protecting the institution from the consequences of its own noncompliance.

When woven together into the knot of sexual harassment, these thematic threads create a variety of false conflicts and true dilemmas for college and university decision makers. Institutional policies and practices that are effective in defining, documenting, punishing, preventing, and eventually eliminating academic sexual harassment can only be developed if the false conflicts are recognized and the true dilemmas are resolved. An analysis of some of the most troublesome conflicts and dilemmas appears in the following sections, with suggestions for addressing them.

Academic Freedom, Free Speech, and Equal Educational Opportunity Without Regard to Sex

Academic freedom and First Amendment free speech issues invariably arise during discussions about how to eliminate sexual harassment from universities and colleges. That's not surprising. Although academic freedom is not an explicitly identified constitutional right, it has long been viewed by the U.S. Supreme Court as a special concern of the First Amendment. The academician's freedom to speculate, experiment, and create depends on the robust and wide-open exchange of ideas and information that is at the core of the First Amendment's protections against government-sponsored abridgments of free speech. What is surprising, however, is that too often when "academic freedom" is invoked or "free speech" is interjected, the discussion of sexual harassment ends. Often, the academy simply accedes to the bald assertion that if enacted and applied, a sexual harassment policy addressing speech would violate the academic freedom or the other free speech rights of an alleged harasser.

It is true that the U.S. Constitution offers significant protection of free speech, and its higher education counterpart, academic freedom. A debate concerning the type of sexual harassment policy an institution should adopt need not be stifled, nor should enforcement of a sexual harassment policy against an alleged violator be called off merely because "free speech" or "academic freedom" is invoked. The First Amendment's free speech guarantees are not absolute, and academic freedom does not erect an impenetrable shield that places all faculty conduct beyond the pale of scrutiny. A thorough and sensitive analysis of the particular free speech or academic freedom claim may reveal a false conflict instead of a true dilemma. That is, the enforcement of the institution's sexual harassment policy addressing speech against a particular person may not be incompatible with the rights granted by the First Amendment or the protections afforded by academic freedom. (For additional discussion of the legal issues surrounding academic freedom see Chapter 2.)

For example, the claimant may not be within the class of people entitled to assert the right of academic freedom or the institution against which the right of free speech is raised may not be bound by the commands of the First Amendment. Typically, academic freedom inures only to the benefit of faculty members, not other institutional employees or students. The free speech protections of the First Amendment are available to faculty, other institutional employees, and students, but only if the institution is a public university or college. (At the state level, the California legislature has granted First Amendment rights to private colleges.)

Even when a claim of academic freedom is raised by a faculty member, it still must be closely scrutinized before the institution accepts it as either an obstacle to enactment or a bar to enforcement of a policy prohibiting sexual harassment. Faculty members can only legitimately claim the protections afforded by the notion of academic freedom when they are functioning in their roles as educators and scholars. For example, if a faculty member engages in sexual harassment of a secretary, federal and state statutes requiring nondiscrimination in employment because of sex have primacy. In such a situation, there is no conflict to resolve because the value at the core of academic freedom (the protection of ideas and information as a step toward truth) is not even implicated.

Neither should a careful analysis of a claim of academic freedom be dispensed with merely because the faculty member's conduct involves a student rather than an employee. The first step in the analysis is to determine whether the alleged academic sexual harassment is of the *quid pro quo* or hostile environment variety. Federal discrimination law prohibits *academic quid pro quo* sexual harassment defined as unwelcome sexual advances, requests for sexual favors, and other verbal or physical conduct by a faculty member (or administrator) when submission to such conduct is made either explicitly or implicitly a term or condition of the student's academic advancement or submission to or rejection of such conduct by the student is used by the faculty member as the basis for an academic decision (e.g., grades) affecting the student. When such conduct occurs, academic freedom is not compromised by punishing the sexual bribery and sexual coercion of a student by a faculty member. Indeed, the very integrity of the teaching and learning process academic freedom is intended to protect would be severely eroded if such conduct could be shielded from censure by the invocation of the doctrine of academic freedom.

A student allegation that a faculty member is guilty of environmental sexual harassment (i.e., hostile environment), however, can present a true dilemma to the institution. By definition, academic environmental harassment occurs when a faculty member engages in unwanted sexual behavior that has the purpose or effect of unreasonably interfering with the student's academic performance or creates an intimidating, hostile, or offensive academic environment for the student. Unfortunately, because the definition lacks the particularity and clarity of the definition of quid pro quo harassment, it allows considerable latitude for interpretation, which in turn causes confusion and ambiguity regarding the exact parameters of the prohibited conduct. The lack of precision in the definition becomes particularly problematic for a college or university when it is alleged that prohibiting environment sexual harassment may impede the robust exchange of ideas embraced by the concept of academic freedom.

The claim of academic freedom is at its strongest when invoked to protect the legitimate academic judgments of a faculty member. These are judgments made in furtherance of the institution's educational mission, and the invocation of academic freedom serves to preclude second-guessing by institutional authorities or the courts. If the educational process is to be effective, faculty members must be free to challenge the student's, and society's, most cherished and fundamental beliefs and ideas by employing in their classrooms whatever teaching–learning strategies and methodologies they, in their professional judgment, deem most advisable. Recognizing the paramount importance of academic freedom in the classroom, however, does not permit the institution to abdicate all responsibility for enforcement of the law's prohibitions against environmental harassment. It is consistent with one of the central reasons for the concept of academic freedom, education of students, to judge faculty members' conduct vis-à-vis their students by a higher standard than that of the ordinary person in the street. Because they are the intellectual guides and counselors for their students, faculty members cannot be permitted to use their position and influence to exploit students for private advantage; to pursue a private sexual agenda unrelated to any legitimate educational objective; or to create, or permit, a classroom environment so charged with sexual hostility or intimidation that the individual student's ability to learn is seriously jeopardized.

Balancing these competing interests is delicate, but not impossible. For example, a faculty member who singles out particular students in any instructional setting as targets for sexual comments cannot lay claim to immunity from the institution's sexual harassment policy by invoking academic freedom. No legitimate educational objective is at issue. In contrast, a faculty member who raises, with a legitimate educational purpose, controversial, and even unproved, theories concerning the relationship between sex and intelligence in a psychology class cannot be censured under the school's policy prohibiting environmental sexual harassment no matter how offensive some of the students might find it. Academic freedom protects wrongheaded theories as well as those which are currently accepted as true. The limit here, of course, is to the discussion of such theories. Were an instructor to use a theory of sex-based differential intellectual capacities in the classroom to the detriment of either female or male students, academic freedom protections would not apply. Similarly, institutional policies prohibiting environmental harassment do not prevent the art historian from showing relevant slides of art that involve nudity or explicit sexual acts regardless of the offense they might cause to student sensibilities unless the slides have no educational purpose or effect and the context becomes one of denigrating women rather than educational.

In balancing faculty claims of academic freedom against student claims of environmental harassment, the touchstone must be education. A reasonable nexus must exist between the conduct the faculty member seeks to protect by invoking the shield of academic freedom and the accomplishment of a legitimate educational objective. If such an analytical paradigm is used, genuine academic decisions intended to facilitate the teaching–learning process will be protected. However, faculty conduct in the classroom that focuses attention on sexual characteristics or sexual behavior in a context in which sex would otherwise be irrelevant would violate the student's right to be free from sexual harassment in the classroom. Identifying impermissible environmental harassment by reference to the nexus, if any, between the conduct at issue and the furtherance of a legitimate educational goal is a cogent approach to resolving this particular dilemma. It strikes a fair balance between protecting faculty conduct that contributes to the education of students and faculty conduct that has no educational value and pollutes the students' learning environment.

Some institutional policies that might seem to be effective methods for eradicating sexual harassment on campus can create real dilemmas because of the free-speech rights guaranteed by the First Amendment. For example, if a public university or college attempts to regulate peer harassment by adopting so-called "speech codes" for its students, the First Amendment's general prohibitions against government-sponsored restrictions on speech are implicated. Moreover, free speech claims can be raised by faculty members or other institutional personnel charged with violating a school's policy against environmental harassment because of hostile and harassing speech or conduct.

As in the situation involving the competing claims of academic freedom and nondiscrimination in education because of sex, the seeming conflict between regulating peer sexual harassment through the use of restrictions on speech and the First Amendment's prohibitions against such restrictions may be more apparent than real in many situations. Although it is without question that freedom of speech protects many forms of speech and conduct that constitute expressive speech, it is equally true that the First Amendment does not protect all speech all of the time from all governmental regulation. The task for the academy is to distinguish between sanctionable speech and protected speech and then adopt rules that are narrowly drawn to regulate only that speech it has the constitutional right to regulate. If a university fails to engage in this type of precise line drawing, its regulation is likely to be invalidated by the courts. A public university or college may not attempt to prohibit broad classes of speech, some of which may be legitimately regulated, if in so doing a substantial amount of constitutionally protected speech is also prohibited.

The starting point for such an institutional undertaking is the distinction in First Amendment jurisprudence between content-neutral and content-based restrictions on speech. A *content-neutral* restriction is one that limits speech without regard to the message being conveyed. *Content-based* restrictions, on the other hand, limit speech because of the message conveyed. The former type of restraint on speech is more likely to be found constitutionally permissible than the latter form of restriction.

The permissibility of a university speech regulation that falls into the content-neutral category is determined by balancing the First Amendment's commitment to the principle that debate on public issues should be uninhibited, robust, and wide-open against the competing institutional concern that led to the enactment of the regulation. A series of Supreme Court cases clearly permits schools to adopt time, place, and manner restrictions on speech and conduct that interferes with the opportunity of other students to obtain an education. A speech restriction of this type could, permissibly, take the form of a general prohibition against classroom conduct including, but not limited to, the use of sexual epithets and other derogatory references to sex by students that materially disrupts class work, involves substantial disorder, or the invasion of the rights of others. In the classroom setting, such speech has only minimum value in terms of the historical, philosophical, and political purposes of the First Amendment; whereas, the institution's interest in preventing interruptions and disruptions of educational activities is substantial.

Under current constitutional law, a public university or college can only adopt content-based restrictions on speech if the limitations fall within one of several well-defined and narrow classes of unprotected speech identified by U.S. Supreme Court decisions—fighting words, obscenity, libel, and commercial fraud. It is axiomatic that a regulation expressly prohibiting sexually harassing, intimidating, and demeaning speech in both classroom and nonclassroom situations is a content-based restriction on free speech. Typically, such restrictions do not survive constitutional challenge because they are not tailored precisely enough to meet the law's narrow definitions of fighting words, obscenity, or libel. Those that do survive constitutional scrutiny address only a very small part of the problem of peer sexual harassment because the restriction has to be so narrowly drawn. For example, *fighting words* are defined as words that constitute a direct assault on the person of the hearer of the type likely to provoke the average person to engage in a fist fight. The generalized advocacy of gender hatred would not fit within that definition although individualized taunting could depending on its severity. However, regardless of the limitations inherent in using one or all of the recognized exceptions to the free speech guarantees as a means of reaching to sexist speech on campus and in the classrooms, it is incumbent on the academy to use whatever avenues are constitutionally available to it to try to ensure equality of educational opportunities without regard to sex. Sexually harassing speech prevents some students from participating in the life of the university community and developing their intellect fully by undermining their dignity and stigmatizing them. If fighting words are all words that can be constitutionally regulated, then, at least that much should be done. It should be noted in this context, however, that the male norm inherent in the court's current definition of fighting words precludes legal prohibition of speech that many women would define as harassing. Given that the average woman is not likely to resort to a fist fight in response to objectionable speech, this class of permissibly regulated speech has limited value in efforts to prohibit much gender-based hate speech on campus.

In light of the very real limitations imposed on a public university's ability to remedy environmental sexual harassment by prohibiting sexist speech, alternative means must be developed to address the issue. At a minimum, colleges and universities should initiate civilized, nonpolarizing, continuing conversations within the academic community concerning how sexually harassing speech undermines the integrity of the academy as a place where knowledge is both transmitted and pursued. When words are used as weapons, when the form of the utterance cuts off all possibility of reply, what contribution has the speaker made to exposition of ideas?

Privacy, Power, and the Sexualization of the Teaching–Learning Process

Educational institutions confront a true conflict when they attempt to unravel the issue of the permissibility and regulation of amorous faculty–student relationships. There is an inherent asymmetry in faculty–student relationships caused by the differing status of the individual participants that militates against the idea that such relationships are formed consensually. Even if consensual, the sexualization of the student–teacher relationship fundamentally alters the nature of that relationship for the participants in ways that are inimical to the continuing role of the teacher as the student's intellectual guide and counselor. Such a role requires a type of "distance" or objectivity that is not possible, or for that matter, necessarily desirable, when two people are participants in an amorous relationship. The relationship also creates the appearance of potential favoritism and unfair advantage for the student who is involved romantically with a faculty member. Thus, an amorous relationship between a faculty member and student can adversely affect the teacher's relationship with other students and jeopardize those students' education. And, from just the perspective of university self-interest, such relationships have the ongoing potential for creating institutional liability for sexual harassment. If the relationship falls apart and the professor's advances become unwelcome, institutional liability for sexual harassment is possible. Consent, once withdrawn, is not a defense to subsequent unwelcome sexual conduct.

At the same time, however, the right of an adult to engage in intimate decision making is at the heart of the protections afforded by the notion of the right of privacy. Constitutional protection from government-sponsored interference with such decision making has been variously justified as serving such core values as "autonomy…over the intimacies of personal identity;" the "right to be self-determining;" respect for "individual dignity," "human dignity," or "individuality;"

and the "right of personhood." All of these values are in keeping with the purposes of educating students. An attempt to forbid adults from making a decision as highly personal as deciding when, where, and with whom to form an intimate relationship may transgress the very essence on what it means to be a human being. However, the right of privacy is not absolute. It does not protect against every kind of governmental intrusion into the individual's decision-making process. A substantial, important governmental interest can justify a narrowly tailored limitation on a person's right of privacy, including the person's right to choose a partner with whom to form an intimate relationship.

At one extreme of the debate are those who assert that there is no such thing as a truly consensual amorous relationship between a faculty member and a student. The proponents of this viewpoint argue that all such relationships must be prohibited because the faculty member has all the power and the student has nothing with which to bargain. At the other pole are those who deny the existence of any power differential at all. The adherents of this position believe that an institution of higher education need not intervene in an amorous relationship between a faculty member and a student because the very existence of the relationship is the proof that it is consensual. As in most polarized situations, the truth lies somewhere in between these extremes.

By virtue of their position, faculty members do have power over their students. In its most readily apparent form, that power includes such things as the giving of grades, the awarding of scholarships, and the approval of courses of study. Another less apparent, but in some ways farther reaching, manifestation of this positional power, is the faculty member's ability to directly and indirectly influence the student's future success. This is especially true in the case of graduate students who are heavily dependent on the goodwill and support of their major advisor in securing postgraduate employment and advancement within their chosen profession. The mystique associated with being a faculty member also subtly contributes to students' perception of the faculty member as powerful. In addition to the psychological power that faculty members have over students by virtue of their position, there is a type of economic power that a faculty member wields. It is the "economic" power that flows from the unequal distribution of information and knowledge that in academia is the "coin of the realm." Finally, the trust a student places in a faculty member who assumes the role of intellectual mentor further distorts the power dynamic of the faculty–student relationship in favor of the faculty member.

In the typical amorous relationship between the male faculty member and a female student, the issue of whether the student "consented" is complicated by more than just the power differential between the participants. In such a situation, consent may only be in the eye of the beholder. Studies show consistently that men and women perceive and experience sexual harassment very differently. Often, men do not label their behavior as sexual harassment despite the fact that the women who are the objects of the behavior report experiencing it in that way. Any attempt to assess the issue of consent must also take into account the reality that women's socialization and economic dependency may make them "submitting" rather than "consenting" adults.

Despite all of the real concerns about consent in amorous relationships between faculty and students, the absolutist position that denies every faculty the right to form an intimate relationship with any person who happens to be a student is problematic. In addition to raising potential violations of the student or faculty member's right of privacy, the argument rests on the essentialist error of false universalism because it attributes to all women the characteristics of some women. It is no doubt true that many female students who enter into amorous relationships with male professors do not do so totally of their own volition because the inherent power differential in student–faculty relationships and because their socialization as women overrides their absolute free choice. However, common sense tells us that there are factors that can mitigate the extent of the power differential; and there are women whose histories, personalities, and socialization experiences make the issue of consent less troublesome.

Certainly, the sheltered woman who enters college directly from high school may be particularly vulnerable to overreaching by an intimidating professor who coerces her assent to a sexual relationship by his formal authority and position. The savvy, returning female student who has a firm sense of self and self-worth, however, may not need or want the institution to assume that she cannot enter into a consensual relationship with a faculty member. A "one-size" institutional response to all amorous faculty–student relationships in the form of a blanket prohibition just does not fit all.

Colleges and universities must devise policies for dealing with amorous relationships between faculty and students that are as responsive and as narrowly tailored as possible to accommodate these competing concerns and the variety of possible factual permutations. The cornerstone of any such policy is the admonition from the highest level of authority that such relationships should be avoided. Department and college-based discussions of the ethical dilemmas these relationships create for faculty, the threat such relationships pose to the integrity of the educational process, and the problematic nature of truly informed consent could be used to buttress official condemnation.

The problems arising from faculty–student amorous relationships transcend the particular individuals involved. Such relationships can compromise the impartiality of the faculty member in teaching and evaluating other students as well. Even if the relationship does not result in preferential treatment and the giving of an unfair advantage to the student involved in the relationship over those who are not, the appearance of impropriety is often so strong as to taint the teaching–learning process. A college or university can address this problem by adopting a rule similar to its antinepotism policy. A faculty member involved in an amorous relationship with a student would be required to disclose the relationship and the identity of the student to the appropriate administrator. The institution would then implement an alternative, objective method of evaluating the student's performance. In some instances that would mean having another faculty member grade the student's work or even a faculty member from another institution. In those situations in which an alternative grader is not a viable alternative, the institution could insist that the professor employ some form of anonymous grading to protect the other students in the class from possible favoritism. Certainly, in situations in which the student can obtain the necessary coursework from other faculty members, the faculty member can be precluded from teaching future classes to a student with whom she or he has an amorous relationship.

A hard-and-fast rule either forbidding or permitting all faculty–student amorous relationships would, of course, be easier to administer than any of the suggestions here. However, the issues of privacy, power, and the integrity of the university as an educational institution are so inextricably interwoven into the problem of faculty–student amorous relationships that the potential conflicts are not amenable to a simple, single solution in many instances (see Chapter 2).

Institutional Change in a Systemically Sexist Culture

The analysis of the vignette introducing this chapter suggests that the Gordian knot of academic sexual harassment is composed of many threads. All of these threads contain potentially conflicting interests that must be addressed both when an institution is developing policy and procedures for academic sexual harassment and when it is applying its policy and procedures to an alleged incident on campus. It is important to recognize, however, that even if the contemporary academy could balance and resolve the multitude of competing and conflicting interests, rights, needs, and values at work, the resultant response to academic sexual harassment would be flawed at best.

A number of characteristics inherent in the academic culture come together to inhibit the eradication of campus sexual harassment and to preclude the implementation of effective responses to and remedies for this particular form of sex discrimination. One of these inhibiting characteristics is the academy's version of classism that separates the educational institution's community into at least three, clearly distinct, and differentially valued groups (faculty, students, and administrative/other staff). With differential value comes differential power and the license to use that power. As the discussion of faculty–student amorous relationships suggests, drawing clear lines between legitimate and inappropriate expressions of positional power and privilege can be problematic within the academy. Thus, by the very way it is structured, the scholars' class system creates a variety of opportunities that are ripe for sexual harassment. For example, the academic caste system defines the majority of institutional employees as something akin to "second-class" citizens who are in the service to the "upper-class" academic personnel. Most often, these class distinctions make it is institutionally acceptable for faculty, graduate assistants, students, and other academically related individuals to perceive and treat secretaries, lab technicians, and other nonacademic staff as the proletariat of the community.

The potential for success of even well-intentioned efforts to clarify and sort out legitimate from inappropriate expressions of class power and privilege is made more problematic by the separation of academic and administrative decision making and authority in the governance structure of the academy. The dual system that exists both reflects and reifies class divisions. It creates and maintains an artificially deep chasm between academic issues and administrative functions.

Administrative decision-making and authority structures tend to be formal, clearly defined, centralized, and vertical. Consequently, the process of administrative decision making and problem solving and the products of that process are often legalistic in content and bureaucratic in style. In contrast, academic decision making and problem solving tend to be ambiguous, informal, decentralized, and nonhierarchical. The results of that process are likely to be both minimalist in content and laissez-faire in approach.

Because the issue of campus sexual harassment has both academic and administrative elements, it can get caught in the "orchestrated anarchy" created by the dual-track institutional authority, decision-making, and governance structure. Administrators talk legal liability, regulations, and procedures relative to sexual harassment, and faculty debate issues of rights, freedoms, and privilege while pursuing a course of enlightened self-interest. Though influenced by faculty opinions and interests, official institutional policies and procedures are eventually crafted by administrators and revised by legal counsel who perceive their role as risk-managers, not as guardians of the integrity of the educational process. Minimalist policies expressed in legalistic, bureaucratic language that rarely attempt to do more than insulate the faculty and the institution from liability for academic sexual harassment are the most likely results of such a process.

Entrenched and institutionalized sexism is intertwined with the threads of academic classism and the bifurcated decision-making structure of the academy. Whether it is tactful to acknowledge or not, institutions of higher education are both a product and a reflection of the society which they serve and within which they function. As such, the academic culture of our colleges and universities exhibits, mirrors, recreates, and sustains the systemic sexism of contemporary society. Although academic classism and the dual nature of decision making in the academic culture constitute serious impediments to the eradication of sexual harassment on campus, systemic sexism is at once the most basic, the most influential, and the most resistant to change.

Sexism is the most fundamental impediment to eliminating academic sexual harassment because institutional equal opportunity and affirmative action rhetoric notwithstanding, the academy remains an essentially single sex institution. It is male-dominated, and that domination exerts itself in both numbers and power. In the vast majority of colleges and universities, virtually all top-level decision makers are men as are the majority of faculty, particularly the senior faculty. Women, though present in greater numbers since the advent of federal equal employment opportunity and affirmative action mandates, remain concentrated in the lower-status, lower-level, and lower-paid positions in the academic community. As a consequence, women's voices are often silent; their insights are ignored; and their values are absent from high-level decision-making positions, influential institutional committees, and other policy-setting bodies.

The sexism systemic in higher education is the most influential of the various culturally based impediments to the eradication of sexual harassment on campus because our academic institutions and culture are essentially male in nature. Clearly, colleges and universities continue to be male-dominated. More basically, however, their structure, policies, procedures, and values remain overwhelmingly reflective of the male experience. Thus, the male life pattern, male perspective, and male example are used automatically as the baseline and the determinative criterion for interpreting the campus world, defining institutional policies, and making administrative and academic decisions.

An analysis of some of the most common elements of institutional sexual harassment programs reveals some reasons for the limited success of institutional efforts to eradicate academic sexual harassment. Workshops, staff training, and professional development programs are the most common mechanisms colleges and universities use to raise the issue of campus sexual harassment with their employees. Less often, such programs are directed at students. The typical training–education session and program ranges from one to three hours in duration. Within such a limited time frame, not much more than rudimentary awareness-raising can be accomplished. Few institutions follow up these initial efforts with ongoing sessions over an extended period of time. Further, the target audiences for these sessions are not likely to include the most important or influential people on campus. As in the opening vignette, many institutions provide a quick introduction to academic sexual harassment for teaching assistants, faculty, and/or staff members. Far fewer provide systematic programs for current faculty, staff, administrators, or students. Fewer still mandate participation in such programs by anyone. The sessions usually concentrate on legal mandates and outline legally prohibited behavior. Many programs seem designed to frighten attendees into compliance by emphasizing potential institutional and legal sanctions for those found guilty of violating the law. Few institutions allocate the time and resources to these training sessions that are really necessary to delve into issues of culture, socialization, societal sexism, and the other complex and difficult issues that arise from academic sexual harassment. A wealth of research exists on continuing adult education and staff and professional development that documents the general ineffectiveness of such short-term and negative approaches.

Those institutions that do offer workshops or professional development sessions on sexual harassment for current employees often target potential attendees who are in the groups more likely to be victims rather than perpetrators. In essence, many institutional training efforts concerning the issue of sexual harassment on campus target teaching assistants, new faculty, support staff, and even mid-level supervisors are among the least powerful and influential within college or university community. Although it is important to train these people, they are not the ones who by their own behavior can encourage, foster, and stimulate far-reaching changes in the institutional climate. More training is needed for senior faculty members and people with institutional power in the university community.

Additionally, most on-campus educational programs on academic sexual harassment are conducted by women; efforts should be made to involve men in facilitating such workshops. This is NOT to say that women should not exercise a leadership role in institutional efforts to eradicate academic sexual harassment. The fact is noted to raise the question of who should be talking to whom about this issue. A plethora of research documents that, overwhelmingly, sexual harassment is not a phenomenon of women's behavior. Women know about it because they experience it, but typically sexual harassment is about men's behavior. As long as men accept, tolerate, or even simply ignore the sexually harassing behavior of other men on campus, institutional efforts to eliminate that behavior are bound to fail.

However, even the very best, one-shot, three-hour workshop targeted at the most powerful and influential members of the academic community and conducted by men for men would not by itself change the entrenched elements of academic sexism that often find expression in acts of sexual harassment on campus. Similarly, verbal or written public pronouncements concerning the inappropriateness and unacceptability of sexual harassment on campus and in the classroom from the highest administrative levels, although important, are not a panacea for eliminating the problem.

The preceding discussion is not intended to say that academic sexual harassment cannot be eradicated from college and university campuses. It certainly can be. To do so, however, will take a much more substantive, concerted, broadly based, well-funded, and long-term effort than most institutions have put forth to date. Colleges and universities must acknowledge and accept that academic sexual harassment is simply one form of systemic sexism and recognize that it cannot be addressed effectively in isolation from the context within which it occurs. The eradication of sexual harassment from college and university campuses requires fundamental changes in the prevailing sexist organizational culture and institutional climate.

The particulars of that effort to address systemic sexism and to change the culture and climate of the academy are implicit in the critique provided above. In essence, to change the inherently sexist nature of academic culture requires forceful and consistent, formal and informal leadership, involvement, and support at every level of the institution. Overtly sexist behavior can be eliminated IF the institutional leadership declares that such behavior is unequivocally unacceptable and implements an educational program. This declaration must be made in a variety of ways and in many different forums. It must be made within the context of substantive, long-term institutional change effort and as a companion to that effort. At a minimum, this change effort needs to include:

1. Ongoing education programs for all groups within the campus community (students at all levels and full- and part-time faculty, administrators, and staff)
2. Multi-session training for all supervisory personnel, including academic administrators
3. Men talking with men, both formally in educational programs and training sessions and informally in everyday interactions
4. An effective mechanism to handle complaints, including informal and formal procedures
5. Vigorous recruitment, hiring, and promotion of women until they are equitably represented at all levels and in all segments of the institutional community
6. Analysis, critique, and where needed, revision of all institutional publications to ensure they do not communicate, either blatantly or subtly, sexist messages and images
7. Incorporation of the issues of sexual harassment–sexist behavior and affirmative action–equal employment opportunity into all institutional assessment and evaluation mechanisms (teaching evaluations; faculty, staff, and administrator performance and merit reviews; and unit/departmental reviews) with clearly articulated, actively enforced, and generously supported systems of incentives, rewards and sanctions.

Conclusion

When all is said and done about the complex threads, competing responsibilities, and conflicting interests inherent in the issue of academic sexual harassment, the most responsible and effective way to address it may be in terms of the fundamental interest at stake in all the discussions, debates, and decision making. The *raison d'être* of the academy is, after all, the educational well-being of all students. The development and adoption of a professional code of ethics for the academy is one way to help focus attention on this overarching principle of equal educational opportunity for our students.

The effectiveness of any code of academic ethics depends on the willingness of current members of the academic profession, both faculty and administrators, to accept, agree to, abide by, and support the enforcement of the code's provisions. Would-be academicians need a stake in the code as well; and as graduate students, they should receive specialized educational experiences focusing on academic ethics. Such training should be similar to the specialized ethics education law students traditionally receive during law school and that medical students are given as a part of their professional education. Continuing education and training in academic ethics for academicians and administrators working in college and university settings is necessary to ensure the continued relevance and viability of such a code.

It is clear that if the academy does not take the self-monitoring responsibilities inherent in its traditional autonomy more seriously, the institution stands to lose both that autonomy and the privilege of self-regulation. But the justification for the development of an academician's code of professional ethics goes much deeper than the danger of a potential loss of autonomy and increased external regulation. The academy needs a vigorous and demanding formal codification of its ethical standards in order to protect the integrity of the teaching and learning process. The debates and discussions that would necessarily precede the development of such a code could be used to explore the issue of ensuring equal educational opportunities for students in a very different way than is currently used to determine particular institutional policies and regulations. Instead of identifying the minimum that the institution is legally required to do, we could define what we aspire to be as educators and scholars.

17

RECOGNIZING SEXUAL HARASSMENT

LINDA VADER GRATCH

An important achievement of the past fifteen years has been the public recognition of the reality of sexual harassment both in the workplace and in institutions of higher learning. Moreover, there is now sufficient consensus about the specifics of sexual harassment that guidelines can be provided in terms of clear behavioral examples (Shoop & Hayhow, 1994). Despite such progress in recognizing the reality of sexual harassment in public life, however, difficulties continue to exist. One problem that is often overlooked in dealing with sexual harassment in the university setting concerns the issue of "labeling." What accounts for the differences, for example, between someone's experiencing unpleasantness and labeling that unpleasantness "sexual harassment"? For that person, once an event carries a particular label—particularly one for which there are legal implications—a whole set of actions becomes necessary. The issue of labeling sexual harassment is the subject of this chapter, and it is a complex issue for many individuals in the university environment. On one hand, real progress has been made in terms of clarifying law and policy at universities regarding sexual harassment. For many reasons, however, making further progress regarding communicating that policy and eradicating the behaviors will require deeper understandings both of the functions and complexity of the university setting, and of how individuals build and utilize schematic thought mechanisms to process the sexually harassing situations they witness (Bargh, Raymond, Pryor, & Strack, 1995).

It is always surprising to find that people can be exposed to the same information about an event but generate quite different descriptive labels. An example from a recent study elucidates this point. I conducted a study in which undergraduates read seven scenario examples of university sexual harassment. Students were asked to decide whether they believed these were indeed representative of sexually harassing situations, and *why* (Gratch, Murff, & Ferguson, 1995). The scenarios for the questionnaire were taken from the university's pamphlet on sexual harassment, and were considered by the university as representative of sexually harassing behaviors. One scenario reads: "An instructor used sex-stereotyped references and depictions in lectures and made jokes about sex. The better looking the woman was, he suggested, the more help she would get. He often commented on the clothes and figures of the women students."

This scenario is a clear example of what is called a "hostile learning environment." In this type of situation, students are unfairly and inappropriately exposed to a constant barrage of sexual innuendo in the classroom. When students' opinions were first measured in 1991, only 60% of the students thought this represented a sexually harassing situation; by 1994, almost 78% identified and labeled the scenario appropriately. When asked *why* they decided as they did, those who responded "yes, this is an example of sexual harassment" said things such as: "He did not have any respect toward his female students and some would be offended by his remarks." or "The instructor's comments were offensive and derogatory toward the women in his class, thus inhibiting their capacity for learning" or "No one paid their money to hear that type of talk in class; it is disrespectful to the women students because we just want to be treated as serious and normal human beings" or finally, "The professor may believe he is simply lightening the mood, when he is in fact embarrassing the women by showing sexual attention to them and creating a disturbance." To the students who labeled this scenario as representative of sexual harassment, this situation was clear, unwanted, and showed complete disrespect for the students in the class.

Almost 40% of the total student sample in 1991, however, did not label this scenario as an example of sexual harassment (this decreased to 22% by 1994). They explained their decisions *not* to label it as sexual harassment in the following ways: "He is not being serious" or "These were made in a passing way" or "He just used it in a lecture" or "He is probably just fascinated by all women" or finally, "He was just talking about how better looking women get better things." Clearly, these students excused the behavior or were unable to understand the seriousness presented by this hostile learning environment. Because of their inability both to recognize the negative aspects in the event and to the label the event appropriately, they would be disabled in a number of ways. First, they would be unable to report this type of behavior as sexually harassing were they to be recipients of such actions. Second, they are accepting of stereotypes about women. Third, they might be more likely to become perpetrators of sexual harassment themselves because of the fact that the logic underlying their decisions not to label this event sexual harassment suggests that "being fascinated by women" or "not being serious" constitutes reasonable thought.

A second type of sexual harassment found in the university setting is called *quid pro quo*, and is characterized as a "bargain" proposed either implicitly or explicitly by the harasser to the victim: if the victim will surrender her or his body in the way that is requested by the harasser, the victim can *have* something she or he wants (or might *lose* something she or he wants if noncompliant). One of the scenarios on the questionnaire that represents quid pro quo is: "A male student was uncomfortable about the way the male teaching assistant (TA) in his composition class touched him. When the student had to meet with the TA to discuss his work, the TA told him the only time he could meet was at his apartment in the evening." Again, the majority of students in this sample were able to label this event as representative of sexual harassment (83.20%), and this ability improved between 1991

(77.99%) and 1994 (87.14%). Those who did label it as an example of sexual harassment justified their decisions by saying things such as: "Absolutely no one has the right to touch anyone else if they don't like it" or "Teaching assistant work should be done in a school atmosphere…and any touching is wrong" or "It seems like a bribe to me" or finally, "It seems like the male teacher is trying to get close to him."

Those students who did not label this scenario as sexual harassment believed, on the other hand, that "It might be lust or being attracted to that certain person" or "Maybe the TA was telling the truth about his only available time to meet" or "It depends on how the TA touched the student…the student may have a slight case of homophobia" or finally, "The male student should have told the TA in what way he liked being touched." These kinds of comments reveal a very different response from those who clearly understand what sexual harassment represents. Some seemed to be captured by the nature of the touching (the idea that lust is OK, or that the TA just needs to offer the type of touching preferred by the student) rather than by the fact that touching between the TA and the student could constitute a clear case of sexual harassment. Others were thinking of the possibility that a meeting-time conflict might be a real problem, and chose not to keep the unwanted touching expressed in the scenario in mind. Finally, many of those who did identify the event as an example of sexual harassment may have done so primarily because it was male-on-male harassment. This is revealed by comments from male students: "No man will touch me!" or "I would beat him up if he tried to touch me!" In other words, it is unclear from their comments whether they understood the fact that it is the *touching* in power situations like this that constitutes sexual harassment—not the fact that the TA and student were both male.

Cases such as these two are not uncommon in the university workplace. Classes are sometimes taught in such a way that they present a hostile learning environment to students; and faculty, staff, and students can find themselves in working/learning situations in which they are confronted continuously with sexual innuendo and unwanted sexual touching. Serious difficulty can arise when individuals find themselves in situations like those described above, but are unable or perhaps unwilling to clearly recognize or label situations as sexually harassing. There are often high emotional and physical costs associated with dealing with the stress of sexual harassment on a daily basis; being unable to label the stressors appropriately prevents the individual from taking action and might lead to victims blaming themselves for the harassment.

In an ideal sense, universities should be model settings where education, productivity, merit, and equity are maximized for all involved—students, faculty, and administrators. Sexual harassment, however, exists as a constant threat to the realization of these ideals. Managing a problem like sexual harassment in the university setting is difficult because of (1) the potential for abuses in power, favoritism and exclusion; (2) the organizational environment and its status differentials among students, faculty, and administrators; (3) the varying levels of awareness and sensitivity of individuals within universities; and (4) men are attracted to each other (Merton, 1968).

This chapter addresses these issues with a particular focus on how the complex difficulties of labeling instances as sexual harassment challenge the system's efficacy. Research suggests students, in particular, often are unable to accurately label offensive behaviors as sexual harassment—even those situations that have been selected carefully by universities as model examples of sexual harassment. Other research indicates that this labeling difficulty is not restricted to students, but includes faculty and administrators as well. Considering these problems in labeling, how can we appraise and manage our problems with sexual harassment in the university? If students attend classes in hostile learning environments and they are uncomfortable but unaware that it is sexual harassment, it is difficult to assess the incidence of sexual harassment. Given that discovering a reduction in officially reported incidence rates is one of the ways we measure policy success in the university, labeling difficulty becomes a serious problem. Grievance hearings may be held without adequate understanding by all of the participants in the academic community at large if they cannot adequately recognize and label sexual harassment as such. Education programs and workshops may neglect the probability that attendees may have varying perceptions. Finally, policy may fail to take into account the difficulty of communicating its directives. Therefore, the principal goal of this chapter is to highlight how the complexity of the setting, coupled with the variety of awareness levels, makes managing the problem of sexual harassment at universities difficult.

The University as a Complex Setting

The university is a very complex setting, because of the varieties of individuals who participate in the setting, and also because their power and participation roles are quite different. Faculty come to the university to work, and students come to learn. This is the manifest function of the university—its primary intended function (Merton, 1968). Usually, working and learning are compatible and complementary activities. There are situations, however, in which the way someone *behaves* in her or his work interferes with the *learning* (or working) process of others. In other words, individuals may feel intimidated in the university setting, not invigorated. This is the sort of problem that is at issue regarding the type of sexual harassment called *hostile learning environment*. Students and faculty alike are protected by Title IX in that they have the right to learn and work in an environment that is free from sexual hostility, intimidation, and discrimination. Current research notes, however, that universities are not fulfilling this promise very well for many students. For example, Mazer and Percival (1989) surveyed students and found that 78% of female students and 72% of male students found hostile learning environments problematic at universities. Some faculty charged with this type of sexual harassment, however, have used academic freedom arguments to support their behaviors, saying that the sexual harassment speech codes unfairly restrict their teaching in the classroom.

For example, Graydon Snyder, a professor of the Chicago Theological Seminary, told a *Talmud* story in class in which a man falls off of a roof, lands on a woman, and "accidentally" has intercourse with her. Snyder described how the accidental nature of the act revealed the man's innocence and lack of intent to cause harm (Johnson, 1994). Students, feeling that the way he told and used the story of rape made learning in his class difficult and unpleasant, charged him with creating a hostile learning environment and violating the speech codes associated with sexual harassment. Objectively speaking, one can imagine how this story could have been used in a classroom situation without causing a hostile learning environment. For example, it could have been used to describe historical changes in the law or how female participation in the writing of the law has created progress and change. What seems to be at issue here is the *way* Professor Snyder delivered this story, and the resulting offensive and sexual hostility felt by the students he taught. At some point a case like this one may reach the Supreme Court.

Other unpublicized examples reveal differences in how faculty and students label what happens in the classroom. Again, at the heart of these tensions between faculty and students is that the student believes the style or theme is sexually hostile and disruptive; the professor believes her or his style of teaching or subject matter is acceptable. Most often, however, the cases are clear in their superfluous use of sexual innuendo. One such case occurred in a graduate education class in which the professor was discussing how important it was to use all one's resources to gain the attention of students in the classroom. The example he chose was how, if one were a large-breasted woman, she could garner full student attention by just raising her shirt (and he demonstrated) (Anonymous, personal communication, January 4, 1995). In a women's studies class, a male student was offended by the use of a book about child sexual abuse. He complained that the use of the book and the discussion of the perpetrator's actions constituted a hostile learning environment. Further, he suggested that the discussion unfairly targeted men and sexualized the classroom in such a way that he could not feel comfortable (Anonymous, personal communication, January 3, 1995).

These different kinds of cases highlight the tension that can arise out of not having a shared understanding of what constitutes a hostile learning environment. Certainly universities are places that value academic freedom and the First Amendment—without it, subjects like sexual harassment could not have been studied! However, not everything a professor would want to say in a classroom—or anything a university would want to display—would warrant First Amendment protection. There are many ways a faculty member might violate the rights of a student (or vice versa) by what she or he might say, and while there is controversy in the courts and among sexual harassment prevention experts regarding these issues, some scholars believe that sexual harassment speech codes are vital, and do offer necessary and significant protection, especially for those who have been disenfranchised and systematically excluded from the educational system. Lewis's view is that because they have been excluded from the system, they are less able to recognize abuse and less skillful in speaking up, and therefore need the force of law to protect them from sexual harassment (1994).

To conclude, the idea of *uncensored voice* is indeed essential to the process of discovery and teaching—it means that the professor and the student have the freedom to express their thoughts and beliefs. However, if through that free expression a whole class of people is intimidated and feels robbed of its opportunity to learn and participate in the educational system, the whole point of the activity of education is lost. Resolving dilemmas like this in the university is difficult. The tensions are real and there is sometimes valid support on both sides (e.g., certain subjects like sexual harassment do need to be discussed even though they may make individuals feel uncomfortable). What administrators need to remember is that the goal of the university is to promote learning and discovery. Those things that impede that goal need attention—if a professor is engaged in gratuitous sexual comments or behaviors in class, then swift action should be taken. For both the student and the professor, helping them distinguish between necessary comments (those constituting academic freedom) and those that create pain in others is important.

Mislabeling Sexual Harassment as Love-Seeking

A second aspect of the university setting that makes it complex with regard to sexual harassment and labeling issues is the fact that "universities often serve as a meeting ground for people seeking marital partners" (Schaefer & Lamm, 1995, p. 19). Sociologist Robert Merton (1968) would call this a *latent function* of the university. In other words, while the manifest function of the university is to offer an education to its students and a professional setting within which to work for its faculty, an unintended or latent function would be to meet appropriate and compatible romantic partners. Research on romance and the worksite has documented that over 70% of all male and female workers have either dated or married someone met at work (Petrocelli & Repa, 1992). Research suggests that proximity, shared values, stimulating surroundings, and a readiness to develop a relationship enhance the possibility that individuals will come to feel close to one another (Hatfield & Sprecher, 1986). Behavior that occurs mutually between two romantically involved individuals is not sexual harassment. However, the fact that so many individuals in the university setting may be seeking romantic relationships poses problems in the management of sexual harassment (Loftus, 1995). Some individuals are so geared toward thinking of love and partnering that, when they observe behaviors that might be construed as sexually harassing, they tend to normalize it, and perceive it as relationship-seeking behavior. Unfortunately, this framework does not distinguish between relationship-seeking and sexuality-seeking behavior. Women may be more likely to engage in the former, and men the latter. Research suggests that a history of romance between two people seems to legitimize in others' eyes social-sexual behaviors that otherwise could have been perceived as sexually harassing (Summers & Myklebust, 1992). In this case, some people see victims of sexual harassment as more complicit, and view perpetrators as less guilty where there is evidence of a prior romantic relationship. Other research exploring this interplay between relationships and sexual harassment in the university context supports this claim (Reilly et al., 1982; Weber-Burdin & Rossi, 1982)—that when a prior relationship existed between individuals engaged in a sexual harassment scenario, it was far less likely to be interpreted by experimental subjects as sexually harassing. In other words, the aversive behaviors in these scenarios were interpreted as arising from normal partnering issues and conflicts, not from the imposition of sexual power and status over others.

It is common behavior in a university setting for one student to ask another to come over after school. Additionally, if they are dating or flirting, they might touch or look at each other in sexual ways. The real key to interpreting these overtures, of course, is how *wanted* these behaviors are by the recipients. That is always the litmus test of all sexual harassment cases. This fact (relationship-seeking pervades the university context), though, suggests that individuals' judgments regarding potential sexual harassment scenarios—both when they are the participants and when they are observing the actions of others—are quite likely to be affected by the guidance offered by this relationship-seeking way of thinking.

Louise Fitzgerald and her colleagues at the University of Illinois (1988) have found individuals are quite likely to be utilizing a relationship-seeking framework to describe their sexual behaviors in the university. They surveyed male university faculty and found that 26% reported sexual involvement with their students; 11% had attempted to stroke, caress, or touch students. These are relatively high percentages of male faculty who admitted sexual involvement with students; however, only one man reported he had sexually harassed someone. So from these data, while it seems clear that the male faculty have indeed engaged in sexual behaviors that have a high likelihood of affecting their students' lives and educations, they have chosen to interpret these experiences as mutual, consensual relationships.

This interpretation of consensuality made by the male faculty members differs markedly from interpretations made by students in another study by female graduate students (Schneider, 1987). Indeed, some of them had dated male or female faculty (13%), but more than 60% had interpreted at least one incident during their graduate student careers as sexually harassing. This suggests that because the graduate students characterized the majority of incidents as sexually harassing, they were clearly *not* thinking in the mutually responsive relationship framework but rather were classifying them accurately as negative via a sexual harassment framework. In other words, they were able to recognize and label these events as sexually harassing and contributing to the *latent dysfunctions* of the university—something that, if left unchecked, would serve to harm the equilibrium of the system (Merton, 1968). When individuals are able to accurately interpret events and gestures as sexually harassing—in other words, form a knowledge framework that allows them to label the power, threat, abuse, and unwantedness that are inherent in sexually harassing incidents—they are less likely to be misled by relationship-seeking interpretations. So being aware that these conflicting knowledge frameworks exist—and that they may serve to impede the process of labeling—is important. Part of the education of the university community regarding sexual harassment is to build in its participants this willingness to process "unwantedness" through the sexual harassment framework such that improper and inappropriate behaviors can be more accurately identified and, in turn, managed.

Many changes have occurred in recent years with regard to perceiving sexual advances as unwanted—these can be seen most clearly in the culture at large in the discussions of date rape and marital rape. In the past, if it *appeared* to the male that there was compliance, interest, or seduction on the part of the woman, or if there was a sanctioned relationship (such as marriage or engagement) of any sort that included rights to the other's body—no wrongdoing was even possible in the eyes of either the law or the public. Now, however, the perception of sexual advances— even *parts* of advances—as unwanted is legitimate in *any* relationship, legally sanctioned or not, and the logic of holding absolute power over another's body is disappearing. Individuals now believe they can choose to participate or resist further participation at each moment in their sexual relationships. This is a major change in the culture's thinking and, of course, is not yet shared by all. However, there are several current university models where policy has been written to manage this issue (c.f., Antioch College). It is important to incorporate this newer way of thinking into how universities handle the education of its employees and students with regard to sexual harassment (Mazer & Percival, 1989). For example, it might be helpful in workshops and educational materials to suggest that individuals engaged in or pursuing romantic relationships keep current with what their partners want by clearly discussing their level of involvement. This might help reduce misinterpretations and possible litigious situations.

Variety and Status Differentials of People in the University Setting

The university setting is shared by many different types of people who markedly vary in their power and status. Given that sexual harassment involves formal or informal uses of power, it is important to review the ways in which labeling problems differ for people in the university. Students (both graduates and undergraduates), faculty (tenured and untenured), staff (clerical, technical, and professional), and administrators (elected and appointed) all experience sexual harassment. The likelihood of experiencing and accurately labeling a situation as sexual harassment among faculty women seems governed in part by the power individuals have in the system—but almost in a counterintuitive way.

In another study, faculty women also were found to experience sexual harassment at higher levels—and label it more accurately—than graduate students (Brooks & Perot, 1991). For example, faculty women were found to experience each level of sexual harassment—as identified by the Sexual Experiences Questionnaire (SEQ) (Fitzgerald et al., 1988)—to a greater degree than did graduate students. They also were more willing to label these experiences as examples of sexual harassment. Both groups, however, labeled at generally very low levels. In other words, they could identify these incidents as aversive, but did not label them as sexually harassing. Two categorical examples are as follows:

1. Of those women who recognized the fact that they had dealt with an unwanted attempt to touch or fondle, only 27% of the faculty women and 20% of the graduate students labeled it as sexual harassment.
2. With regard to forceful attempts to touch or fondle, only 42% of the faculty women as opposed to 0% of the graduate students labeled it as sexual harassment.

These data suggest that while university women could recall dealing with aversive sexual behaviors of others, they were unlikely to use the overt label of sexual harassment, even when the level of harassing behavior was quite serious.

It is possible that this seeming inability to label the unwanted situation as sexual harassment is in part a reluctance to label the event. Once an event is labeled as an illegal activity, it may suggest a greater "call to action" that cannot be as easily ignored. Also, once it is labeled, it places the labeler more clearly in the position of a victim, which is an uncomfortable self-characterization for many people. (See Gratch, 1995, for a discussion of the reluctance of labeling sexual harassment situations for female police officers.) Finally, labeling and reporting sexual harassment by female faculty involves a recognition that the academic situation is less than perfect—a difficult admission for individuals to make about their work settings.

This same tendency in the professional women with higher status to recognize and label more sexual harassment than the lower status female graduates students appears to be found also between female graduate students and female undergraduate students (Fitzgerald et al., 1988). Graduate students tend to have closer and more personal associations with faculty, and they tend to be older than undergraduates. These factors might be responsible for their greater relative problems with sexual harassment (Lott et al., 1982).

A final manifestation of this phenomenon can be seen among undergraduates. Third- and fourth-year students tend to experience more aversive sexually harassing situations than first- and second-year female students (Mazer & Percival, 1989). Because students, in general, are relatively powerless in the university system, they tend to deal with their harassment through silencing themselves (not reporting), by avoiding enrollment in or dropping problem courses (Bailey & Richards, 1985), or by changing their majors (Wilson & Krauss, 1983). For reasons such as these, the problems students have with sexual harassment often go unreported. Much of the data suggest that general experiences with sexual harassment increase with higher status in the university: first- and second-year female students experience and label the least, and higher-status faculty women experience and label the most. (The length of time one is in the university may account for higher-status persons, such as faculty, experiencing more sexual harassment than lower-status first- and second-year students. These people simply may have been there longer.)

Levels of sexual harassment for students might be higher than they appear, however. Students' strong tendency not to label the aversive behaviors as sexual harassment influences the documented incidence figures drawn from officially reported sexual harassment—and can make it appear to those who monitor system changes that legally defined sexual harassment is occurring at far lower levels than it is in reality. Although undergraduate women often acknowledge in survey data that they have experienced a variety of aversive behaviors, they tend not to label it as sexual harassment and would not, in turn, report it. (However, many students who do label sexually aversive experiences as sexual harassment also do not want to report them because of fear of retaliation, not wanting to engage in an adversarial process, fear of being blamed for the behavior, and so forth.)

There are other power relationships existing in the university that also reflect the power of being male in this culture rather than the formal power associated with professional status found in the university. For example, Elizabeth Grauerholz (1989) of Purdue University found that almost half of the 208 faculty women she surveyed had experienced some form of sexual harassment by male students: although the faculty women had more formal power than their male students, the students had more cultural power (called *contrapower harassment*). Informal power and prestige "overcome" the formal power of a female faculty member (Gutek & Morasch, 1982), and encourage one kind of sexual harassment that has more to do with being male in the culture than having formal power in the university.

Organizational Demographics as Affecting Labeling

One final factor relevant to the complexity of the university setting that affects sexual harassment labeling in the university is its organizational demographics, or the proportion of the minority group to the majority group (Kanter, 1977). In university settings, women most often represent the minority group, particularly at the higher professional levels. For example, virtually all faculties are predominately male rather than female, most graduate programs are somewhat more male than female, and most undergraduate programs are roughly equivalent. When women make up less than 15% of the total group, they tend to be regarded as *tokens* (Kanter, 1977). They are likely to suffer greater amounts of stress, experience strong negative stereotyping, and be excluded from informal networks. This tokenism also seems to affect the likelihood that events will be successfully labeled as situations of sexual harassment. In a study done by Sheffey and Tindale (1992), researchers asked undergraduates to judge the likelihood that "ambiguous" and "potentially threatening" sexual behaviors were indeed sexual harassment. Behaviors that took place in male-dominated (vs. female-dominated) workplaces were more likely to be judged as sexually harassing. Students tended to view these behaviors in token environments as threatening and sexually harassing. This may be because of the fact that in token settings, workplace negativity, hostility, stress, and stereotyping is highlighted.

What makes the impact of organizational demographics more compelling on sexual harassment labeling is that the incidence figures just discussed—the fact that more female faculty can label it sexual harassment than graduate students, and more graduate students can label it than undergraduate students—appear to reveal a consistent inverse relation to the female–male sex ratios in the university. The more token or male-dominated the group is, the more able the females are to label sexual harassment (faculty); the more even the group is relative to sex ratios, the less able the females are to label the events (undergraduate students). It may also be that because there is a higher incidence of sexual harassment when women are fewer in number, the women may recognize the behavior more clearly as sexual harassment.

A recent conflict that occurred at the Harvard Law School (59 tenured professors: 54 men and 5 women) reflects the greater awareness afforded by tokenism. When someone wrote a parody of a feminist legal scholar's work (who recently had been murdered), the females on the faculty were angry; the males called it *accidental* and *unintentionally* offensive. In describing what they believed to be the causal factors for this event (and the stark differences between the females' and males' opinions about it), the female faculty have suggested that it is the unequal numbers that have created an atmosphere that encourages derogatory treatment (Butterfield, 1992)—and they had no trouble recognizing that they had experienced it.

In summary, it appears that one factor that might affect an individual's ability to label sexual harassment is the organizational demographics of the setting—the more token the group is, the more harassment they sustain, and the more able they are to label the incident accurately. The important thought for university administrators to keep in mind regarding organizational demographics and sexual harassment is that a relationship exists. In other words, when uneven numbers occur at the token rate, harsh stereotyping and hostility tend to grow.

Factors Associated with Raised Awareness

A number of studies have focused on discovering which factors are associated with a raised awareness of sexual harassment. Several studies have found that students who have had firsthand experience as victims of sexual harassment are likely to perceive it as more common for other students (Mazer & Percival, 1989). They also are significantly more accurate in labeling sexual harassment scenarios (Gratch, Murff, & Ferguson, 1995).

A second factor that seems to be associated with raised awareness and sensitivity is the high profiling of sexual harassment cases in the media. For example, since the time of the Clarence Thomas/Anita Hill hearing, there has been a 112% increase in complaints to the EEOC (Noble, 1994). It has been suggested that the media—through its television coverage of the hearings—educated the public on the subject of sexual harassment. This media education served to increase awareness and sensitivity to the important issues relevant to sexual harassment labeling, and to alert individuals that they have the right to object.

Of all the factors likely to impact labeling accuracy, gender appears to be the most powerful. Females are more skilled at labeling sexual harassment, and they tend to notice subtlety and details that are vital to accurate judgment and reporting (Dietz & Murrell, 1992; Jensen & Gutek, 1982; Reilly, Lott, Caldwell, & DeLuca, 1992; Valentine-French & Radtke, 1989). An interesting study conducted by Cindy and David Struckman-Johnson (1993) at the University of South Dakota illustrates how college males and females reason differently about unwanted and coercive sexual situations. They constructed scenarios in which either a male or a female acquaintance came to study in a college dormitory and he or she touched—either gently or forcefully—the other's genital area. Both heterosexual and homosexual situations were included in the study. Results revealed that female students reacted more negatively in general to the scenarios than did male students, and they were able to distinguish between the two conditions of force. Those females who had very negative attitudes toward casual sex reacted most negatively to the scenarios. Male students, on the other hand, were much less negative about the scenarios in general, and in fact, tended to see the scenarios as sexually arousing. Also, the college males were unlikely to perceive the difference between forceful touching and gentle touching. Both male and female students tended to react negatively to the same-sex scenarios.

This study points to the possibility that males and females initiate the appraisal process of coercive sexuality differently. Females appeared to attend more to the details of the situation; for example, they made an effort to distinguish between the levels of force. Also, they processed the scenarios as unwanted, especially when they themselves viewed casual sexuality as not acceptable. Males clearly were thinking in terms of the relationship schema discussed earlier—they found the scenarios arousing, and perhaps as a result, failed to find it necessary to distinguish the levels of force. This study presents further evidence that the schemata males and females have developed around heterosexual encounters are different and serve to prime them to view the nature of events in markedly different ways. Both males and females in this study read the same scenarios, but what they saw and how they reacted was quite different.

The fact that this can happen—that two people, a male and a female, can be presented with the same information and yet see quite different things—is vital to dealing with sexual harassment issues. If this difference is compounded by other things, such as fears, motives, and feelings, then selectively perceiving information, filtering out details, and remembering others is highly likely. It would be important to keep this in mind when trying to understand individuals' differing memories for information and reactions to reported situations of harassment. A useful strategy to aid in controlling for individuals' differences in memory, perception, and memory degradation would be to create recordkeeping forms that could be widely distributed and easily obtained for recording the details of sexually harassing situations. Details recorded at the time of the event are more dependable than those recorded after a period of time has elapsed, primarily because they are less likely to have been degraded by schematic and script memory (Martin & Halverson, 1983), although for many reasons, those who are sexually harassed may often wait days, weeks, or months before reporting the harassment.

Factors Associated with Lower Awareness

Endorsing stereotypic sex roles appears to be a significant factor, then, in college students' abilities to take sexual harassment seriously (Dietz & Murrell, 1992). In particular the traditional college women with high self-esteem are more accepting of sexual harassment and are least aware of its potential harm (Malovich & Stake, 1990). Perhaps their seeming indifference toward recognizing the negative aspects of sexual harassment is because of the cultural support they get by identifying with traditional values or their self-esteem may act to make them less vulnerable to the effects of sexual harassment. Maybe they feel strong and confident in their current roles as traditional women, and are in the throes of feeling secure and proud at being traditional in a world that is constantly in turmoil regarding the shift away from traditionalism (Birnbaum, 1975). As already pointed out, undergraduates have experienced the lowest amounts of the more serious types of sexual harassment, and are least able to identify clear examples of sexual harassment (Jaschik & Fretz, 1991; Mazer & Percival, 1989), so factors like firsthand experience with sexual harassment (or life experience, in general) have not yet had an opportunity to have an appreciable impact on their abilities to label harassing situations (Bremer, Moore, & Bildersee, 1991). It is also a possibility that these traditional women are denying the existence of sexual harassment. They maintain a traditional view in which sexual harassment does not exist or occurs only when "women ask for it."

Another factor associated with lowered awareness in labeling involves the race of the complainant. Very little data are available regarding race and how it affects the labeling of sexual harassment events. However, the impact of race can be seen in how it affects EEOC judgments. Data suggest that the sexual harassment cases of many more African Americans (vs. Caucasians) are resolved as having "no reasonable cause" (Noble, 1994). Possibly, prejudice has "spilled over" into the EEOC, encouraging the agency to selectively interpret African American cases as less important or serious, or perhaps to view their cases with a relationship schema. It may be that the race of the victim, when African American, may make it difficult for others to label sexual harassment as such (see Chapter 13).

Conclusion

The issue of protecting the university environment from the unbalancing effects of sexual harassment and discrimination is important and complex. It is important because it threatens the university's manifest function, which is to provide a quality education to its students and a professionally stimulating environment for its faculty. It is complex because it necessitates a shared ability to recognize sexually aversive behaviors as illegal, and to label them as sexually harassing. Clear policies and laws serve to establish the initial ground rules for common understanding, yet they have not managed to eradicate the problem of sexual harassment in the university.

At the heart of those factors that militate against the elimination of sexual harassment in the university are labeling problems. People can have problems labeling aversive sexual behaviors as sexual harassment because of individual factors such as their gender, whether they have had firsthand experience as victims of sexual harassment, their self-esteem, their religiosity, their professional status level, their liberal versus traditional attitudes toward women, and their use of sex-role stereotypes. Their abilities to label sexual harassment can be affected also by properties of the setting such as the organizational demographics of the setting or subsetting, the impact of the media, and the status of gender in the culture.

Cognitive factors also affect the likelihood that one will or will not label aversive sexual behaviors as sexual harassment. As described here, individuals are primed to process sexual information using a relationship framework, particularly given that one of the latent functions of the university is to provide a meeting place for individuals to form relationships. This tendency can be an impediment to the accurate labeling of sexual harassment.

Finally, there are motivational factors that affect labeling—once an individual labels an event as sexually harassing, it creates a "call to action" for which the individual may or may not be emotionally, financially, or professionally prepared. Support needs to be available for the individual to cope with the negative consequences that sometimes accompany action. Faculty and staff who observe sexual harassment, and label it as such, have an obligation to do something, if only to pass the information on to someone else who will presumably stop the behavior.

A further complicating factor in the management of sexual harassment in the university, one that makes the university setting unique, relates to the tension in the classroom between freedom of speech and concerns for offering individuals protection from sexually harassing discrimination. It may be necessary for universities to develop specific policy in this area because a general sexual harassment policy may not address ways in which sexually harassing faculty behavior in the classroom subverts their educational mission.

Managing sexual harassment in the university setting requires far more than adopting policy. Educational efforts to help people understand what behaviors are labeled as sexual harassment are critical. The numerous complicating factors and functions associated with the act of accurately labeling an event as sexually harassing must be incorporated into training and educational materials. Further progress toward eliminating sexual harassment in the university setting will come in the form of this more elaborate approach.

References

Bailey, N. J., & Richards, M. M. (1985). Tarnishing the ivory tower: Sexual harassment in graduate training programs in psychology. Paper presented to the American Psychological Association, Los Angeles.

Bargh, J. A., Raymond, P., Pryor, J. P., & Strack, F. (1995). Attractiveness of the underling: An automatic power sex association and its consequences for sexual harassment and aggression. *Journal of Personality and Social Psychology* 68(5), 768–81.

Birnbaum, J. A. (1975). Life patterns and self-esteem in gifted family-oriented and career committed women. In M. Mednick, L. W. Hoffman, & S. Tangri (Eds.), *Women and achievement: Social and motivational analyses.* New York: Halsted Press.

Bremer, B. A., Moore, C. T., & Bildersee, E. F. (1991). Do you have to call it "sexual harassment" to feel harassed? *College Student Journal* 25(3), 258–68.

Brooks, L., & Perot, A. R. (1991). Reporting sexual harassment: Exploring a predictive model. *Psychology of Women Quarterly* 15, 31–47.

Butterfield, F. (1992, April 27). Parody puts Harvard Law faculty in sexism battle. *The New York Times*, p. A8.

Dietz, U., & Murrell, A. (1992). College students' perceptions of sexual harassment: Are gender differences decreasing? *Journal of College Student Development* 33(6), 540–46.

Fitzgerald, L., Weitzman, L., Gold, Y., & Ormerod, M. (1988). Academic harassment: Sex and denial in scholarly garb. *Psychology of Women Quarterly* 12, 329–40.

Gratch, L. (1995). Sexual harassment among police officers: Crisis and change in the normative structure. In A. V. Merlo & J. M. Pollock

(Eds.), *Women, law, and social control* (pp. 55–77). Boston: Allyn and Bacon.

Gratch, L., Murff, W., & Ferguson, D. (1995). Students' accuracy in labeling university examples of sexual harassment. Paper presented at the Annual Meeting of the American Psychological Society, New York.

Grauerholz, E. (1989). Sexual harassment of women professors by students: Exploring the dynamics of power, authority, and gender in a university setting. *Sex Roles* 21(11/121), 789–801.

Gutek, B. A., & Morasch, B. (1982). Sex-ratios, sex-role spillover, and sexual harassment of women at work *Journal of Social Issues* 38, 55–74.

Hatfield, E., & Sprecher, S. (1986). *Mirror, mirror…: The Importance of looks in everyday life.* Albany: State University of New York Press.

Jaschik, M. L., & Fretz, B. R. (1991). Women's perceptions and labeling of sexual harassment. *Sex Roles* 25(1/2), 19–23.

Jensen, T., & Gutek, B. A. (1982). Attributions and assignments of responsibility in sexual harassment. *Journal of Social Issues* 38, 121–36.

Johnson, D. (1994, May 11). A sexual harassment case to test academic freedom. *The New York Times*, p. D23.

Kanter, R. M. (1977). *Men and women of the corporation.* New York: Basic Books.

Lewis, A. (1994, March 13). The First Amendment, under fire from the left. *The New York Times*, Sec. 6, p. 42.

Loftus, M. (1995, March/April). Frisky business. *Psychology Today*, 34–41, 70–85.

Lott, B., Reilly, M. E., & Howard, D. R. (1982). Sexual assault and harassment: A campus community case study. *Signs* 8, 296–319.

Malovich, N. J., & Stake, J. E. (1990). Sexual harassment on campus: Individual differences in attitudes and beliefs. *Psychology of Women Quarterly* 14, 63–81.

Martin, C. L., & Halverson, C. F. (1983). The effects of sex–stereotyping schemas on young children's memory. *Child Development* 54, 563–74.

Mazer, D. B., & Percival, E. (1989). Students' experiences of sexual harassment at a small university. *Sex Roles* 20, 1–22.

Merton, R. K. (1968). *Social theory and social structure.* New York: Free Press.

Noble, B. P. (1994, May 22). At work: Unhealthy prospects for women. *The New York Times*, Sec. 3, p. 23.

Petrocelli, W., & Repa, B. K. (1992). *Sexual harassment on the job.* Berkeley: Nolo Press.

Reilly, M. E., Lott, B., Caldwell, D., & DeLuca, L. (1992). Tolerance for sexual harassment related to self-reported sexual victimization. *Gender and Society* 6(1), 122–138.

Reilly, T., Carpenter, S., Dull, V., & Bartlett, K. (1982). The factorial survey: An approach to defining sexual harassment on campus. *Journal of Social Issues* 38, 111–19.

Schaefer, R. T., & Lamm, R. P. (1995). *Sociology: A brief introduction* New York: McGraw-Hill.

Schneider, B. E. (1987). Graduate women, sexual harassment, and university policy. *Journal of Higher Education* 58, 46–65.

Sheffey, S., & Tindale, R. S. (1992). Perceptions of sexual harassment in the workplace. *Journal of Applied Social Psychology* 22, 1502–20.

Shoop, R. J., & Hayhow, J. W. (1994). *Sexual harassment in our schools: What parents and teachers need to know to spot it and stop it.* Boston: Allyn and Bacon.

Struckman-Johnson, C., & Struckman–Johnson, D. (1993). College men's and women's reactions to hypothetical sexual touch varied by initiator gender and coercion level. *Sex Roles* 29 (5/6), 371–85.

Summers, R. J., & Myklebust, K. (1992). The influence of a history of romance on judgments and responses to a complaint of sexual harassment. *Sex Roles* 27(7/8), 345–57.

Valentine-French, S., & Radtke, H. L. (1989). Attributions of responsibility for an incident of sexual harassment in a university setting. *Sex Roles* 21, 545–55.

Weber-Burdin, E., & Rossi, P. H. (1982). Defining sexual harassment on campus: A replication and extension. *Journal of Social Issues* 38, 111–20.

Wilson, K. R., & Krauss, L. A. (1983). Sexual harassment in the university. *Journal of College Student Personnel* 24, 219–27.

Bibliography

Anderson, M. (1991). *Impostors in the temple.* New York: Simon & Schuster.

Baker, D. D., Termstra, D. E., & Larntz, K. (1990). The influences of individual characteristics and severity of harassing behavior on reactions to sexual harassment. *Sex Roles*, 22 (5/6), 305–25.

Caplan, L. (1994, November 14). Who lied? *Newsweek*, pp. 52–54.

George, P. (1994, April 9). College study finds sexual harassment high among faculty. *The Houston Chronicle*, p. 18A.

Honan, W. (1994, September 17). Professor ousted for lecture gets job back. *The New York Times*, sect. 1, p. 9.

Margolin, L. (1990). Gender and the stolen kiss: The social support of male and female to violate a partner's sexual consent in a noncoer-cive situation. *Archives of Sexual Behavior* 19, 281–91.

Murray, K. (1994, September 18). At work: A backlash on harassment cases. *The New York Times*, Sec. 3, p. 23.

Slade, M. (1994, March 27). Sexual harassment: Stories from the field. *The New York Times*, Sec. 4, p. 1.

Struckman-Johnson, D., & Struckman-Johnson, C. (1991). Men and women's acceptance of coercive sexual strategies varied by initiator gender and couple intimacy. *Sex Roles* 25(11/12), 661–76.

Thomann, D. A., & Weiner, R. L. (1987). Physical and psychological causality as determinants of culpability in sexual harassment cases. *Sex Roles* 17, 573–91.

18

ADVOCACY AND STUDENT VICTIMS OF SEXUAL HARASSMENT

SUSAN K. HIPPENSTEELE

> *The experience of being sexually harassed wipes away all that we as students achieve—it negates the importance and value of that which is the essence of education—intellectual achievement—and reduces the learner role to one of irrelevancy. The most painful part of this experience for me was the realization that my intellectual abilities were not being questioned, they were being dismissed as unimportant.*[*]

Introduction

In 1990 the University of Hawai'i[1] at Manoa (UHM) appointed a Sexual Harassment Task Force of students, faculty, staff, and administrators to revise its 1983 sexual harassment policy and procedures. This action was part of a settlement with the U.S. Department of Education's Office for Civil Rights (OCR) in a controversial sexual harassment complaint brought against the institution that included charges that the institution's policy violated students' rights under Title IX. Sexual harassment of students had been the subject of heated debate as students, women faculty, the faculty union, and the university administration became increasingly polarized, and articles in two student papers and a local daily challenged the handling of student complaints. Some students, in particular, claimed that their allegations of sex discrimination and sexual harassment had been trivialized, and investigations of their sexual harassment charges against faculty were biased.

Of significant concern to students was a perceived lack of access to information about sexual harassment complaint filing and accessible complaint procedures for those who believed they had been sexually harassed. The Sexual Harassment Task Force responded by developing procedures which included a

*Excerpt from Sexual harassment: The personal is political, in *VOICES: The Hawai'i Women's Newsjournal*, Winter 1989–1990.

program of formal advocacy for student complainants. Although the Task Force initially recommended developing a student advocacy program independent from the administration, the position was ultimately created as a full-time, tenure track (union-excluded) faculty position within Student Affairs. The revised procedures were implemented during the summer of 1992 and I was hired as the first Student Advocate in Spring of 1993.

With only a brief job description and few models of student advocacy to choose from, the Student Advocate program at the University of Hawai'i evolved to (partially) fill a gap in student services that few realized was so immense. In the first three years, I assisted nearly 150 students in filing formal and informal complaints of sexual harassment and compiled statistics on over 100 additional complaints and inquiries brought by students who wished to remain anonymous. Discussions I have had with victims' advocates from institutions throughout the United States suggest that these data are not unusual—when information about sexual harassment is made available and adequate support systems and advocacy for victims are created, students become less reticent in voicing their complaints and objections to sexual harassment on campus.

Throughout this chapter I will use the term *victim advocate* to identify an individual who has a formal role and the authority to work on behalf of student victims of sexual harassment within their college or university. I refer to *victim supporters* as those who have no formal role within their institution's sexual harassment complaint procedures but voluntarily offer crucial emotional support and encouragement along with practical advice and assistance to students who have been sexually harassed.

Advocacy in Context

The term advocacy means different things to different people and there are many variations of it developing on college campuses across the country. Yet at most institutions, advocacy with any real structural integrity remains suspect to victims and the institution—and rightly so. Victims' advocates are, by their very nature whistle blowers, and large bureaucratic entities will generally serve to undermine the effectiveness of employees whose role or job duties bring them in conflict with the employer. But on campuses, such as the University of Hawai'i where victims of assault and discrimination demand action, accountability, and voice, the social context can evolve to allow alliances between sexual harassment victims and advocates that affirm and protect victims (Herman, 1992), and struggles by advocates to maintain clarity of purpose within the institution can be successfully realized.

I base my role as Student Advocate on a loosely defined counselor–advocate model created by the Task Force three years earlier and am also guided by my previous experience as a victim of sexual harassment. Several years ago as a student at the University of Hawai'i, I filed a formal sexual harassment complaint against my graduate advisor and am personally familiar with the difficulties inherent in pursuing internal and external grievance processes. I provide support counseling, therapist referral when warranted, information on internal university and external agency filing options, and representation throughout informal and/or formal complaint processes. I have found that most students who have been sexually harassed initially need a sounding board—someone who will listen supportively and provide them an opportunity to express conflicting feelings surrounding their experience and desire for resolution. With an opportunity to problem solve in a safe, confidential environment and ready access to administrative and civil rights and procedures, student victims can make informed, well-reasoned decisions regarding the options they wish to pursue. The counselor–advocate model provides important in-house continuity for victims, most of whom need to take positive steps to remedy the discrimination far more than they need to endlessly revisit the traumatic, harassing events themselves.

As the Student Advocate, I am usually the first or second point of institutional contact for a student alleging sexual harassment. About 75 percent of the students I work with self-identify as victims and call my office directly. The remainder are referred by faculty, staff, or their peers. Of the 250 student complaints I have documented during the past three years, roughly half involved peer harassment. The remainder consist of complaints against faculty, staff, and administrators.

Students frequently make contact individually to discuss their personal experiences with sexual harassment after attending a sexual harassment prevention seminar and about half of the students who come to see me about being sexually harassed "just want to talk." Many students already have ideas about how to handle the harassment on their own and are simply seeking confirmation that their ideas are sound, but when a student does decide to file an informal or formal complaint, I generally assist them in preparing their documentation of allegations; represent them throughout informal resolution proceedings; and/or represent them in investigation interviews, hearings, and other meetings related to internal or external formal complaint processing. I have found no significant correlation between perpetrator status (peer, faculty, staff, administrator) and the student's choice of resolution option, although contextual factors of the incidents (location, relationship between victim and perpetrator, reputation of the perpetrator within their academic unit, etc.) do appear to influence the likelihood of achieving a successful informal resolution to the complaint.

Taking Sides

A 20-year-old Asian American transfer student from a small community college on a neighboring island called me after reading a story about sexual harassment in the local paper. She told me she had read about my position in the paper and wished she had known about my office earlier. When she came to Honolulu her parents had told her to watch out for trouble in the dorms and downtown and insisted that she go to any one of her teachers at the first sign of trouble. Teachers, for this young woman, were analogous to parents and could be trusted unequivocally. When she did go to a teacher for help after an argument with her boyfriend, he told her she should not be dating such young men. This trusted professor in his mid-forties suggested that she would be better off dating "more mature men like [himself]." The shame and betrayal she experienced over this incident made school such an overwhelmingly threatening place that she left.

Most students expect their university to be a safe place to learn; professors to provide teaching, mentorship, and personal examples; and peers to offer opportunities for mutually satisfying social experiences and growth. Students sexually harassed in college confront many demons. It is not uncommon for a student, new to campus and confronting sexual harassment for the first time, to be devastated by the loss of idealized images of college as a haven from the grim realities of the rest of the world. In my experience, many identify the experience as a personal failure—a potent illustration of their inability to "make the grade." To successfully come to terms with the trauma of sexual harassment they must mourn the loss of their academic ideals and meet the challenge of revising their visions of the future. At the most basic level they must reconcile the harasser's betrayal with their own vulnerability to abuse. Beyond this, loss of trust, confusion over self-worth, fear of academic and/or administrative reprisal, concerns about the future, shame, guilt, isolation, and anger haunt those who remain to finish school—unfortunately, untold numbers of students who experience sexual harassment at school quit.

Sexual harassment is antithetical to society's expectations of higher education—our ideals about academia and academic relationships. It is morally impossible to remain neutral about sexual harassment on our campuses. Because the topic provokes such intense controversy, most of us have had ample opportunity to express strong feelings about the subject, one way or the other. It is likely that everyone reading this book has already "taken a side," so to speak. The side we choose reflects what we know about sexual harassment—personal experiences we have had as victims or witnesses, our familiarity with civil rights laws and Equal Employment/Affirmative Action (EEO/AA) guidelines, myths and stereotypes we hold about victims and perpetrators, our beliefs about sex and gender roles, rumors we have heard about false or frivolous complaints or witch hunts against male faculty that circulate on campuses, personal experiences as the accused in a sexual harassment case, and so on.

Overview

I have three primary objectives in writing this chapter. The first is to contribute to current discussions about ethnically identified student victims of sexual harassment. I will do this by offering anecdotal data that reflect the definitions, experiences, context, responses, shared feelings and expressed needs of students whose race, ethnic background, sexual orientation, citizenship, and socioeconomic status represent the diversity of students attending the University of Hawai'i. My second objective is to introduce ideas about student advocacy and expand the framework for discussing sexual harassment of college students to include a victim's advocate perspective. I will talk about the ways advocates can support student victims and effect the resolution of students' experiences of sexual harassment. My third objective is to stimulate interest in developing student advocacy programs on campuses that have not yet done so by outlining what a knowledgeable, caring, supportive advocate can do to help mitigate the impact of sexual harassment on a students' academic career and future.

This chapter is not a treatise on battling the system, although I acknowledge that those who choose to provide advocacy and support to victims of sexual harassment often have to do just that. Nor will I emphasize the importance of recognizing the procedural and ultimately legal implications of a competent and judicious sexual harassment complaint. Although an effective student advocate must be well versed in Title VI, Title VII, Title IX, and numerous state statutes related to civil, employment, and administrative law, these and other references to crucial procedural issues are addressed elsewhere in this book.

Framing Advocacy

The Context on Campus

Numerous "how-to" books and manuals have been written to guide institutions in their efforts to prevent sexual harassment and avoid legal liability. Yet educational efforts on college campuses are often inspired not by a deeply held conviction that students' rights to an educational environment free from sexual harassment should be ensured, but rather by the desire to avoid costly litigation and institutional embarrassment. Title IX requires that institutions provide accessible complaint procedures and a level of assistance that allows students to file complaints of sexual harassment. Title IX does not mandate that institutions provide students alleging sexual harassment with emotional support or in-house advocacy.

   Through discussions I have had with victims' advocates across the United States, I have come to believe that many faculty members and administrators on many campuses (including those with student advocacy programs in place) often feel that offering any sort of help to students who allege civil rights violations by a member of the institution is analogous to promoting anarchy. Yet encouraging such strategies and even adopting formal programs of advocacy for complainants is not only consistent with the *intent* of Title IX, it can ultimately help institutions meet important institutional and legal goals. I believe that providing serious and committed support to students who have been sexually harassed is the best way an institution can manage the conflict that inevitably occurs when a student's early efforts to resolve their complaints of sexual harassment are stymied. The question should not be whether it is in the best interest of the institution to actively support and encourage the effective resolution to a student's grievance, but rather how to inform all members of the campus community of the practical strategies for doing so.

Supporting Victims

There are numerous places victims of sexual harassment can go for support on most college campuses. Faculty and staff working in women's studies departments, university women's centers, and the dean of students offices are generally familiar with academic literature pertaining to sexual harassment in education and many individuals who hold positions in these departments and programs have acted as supporters to student victims of sexual harassment for years. Some campuses also have social science experts in the field available to counsel and advise student victims. On my campus an informal victims' support network of mostly women faculty and graduate students has existed as long as anyone I know can remember. Some of the strategies of resistance to sexual harassment they have employed over the years are legend in our campus community, serving as inspiration to young, less experienced, but equally enterprising victims and supporters. (My own inspiration came from talking to women faculty members who had spent months patrolling the halls in front of one notorious harasser's office during his office hours, catching his eye whenever they could to make their presence known, and standing guard with their arms crossed outside his closed door when he was alone with a female student.) It was this network that initially challenged the institution to formalize advocacy for student victims as its members began to recognize that the environment on campus was changing in ways that made these types of informal resistance essentially obsolete.

The milieu through which discrimination is justified depends on the relative status of the victim of the abuse. In the case of sexual harassment, its very pervasiveness continues to discourage many people from viewing it as discrimination at all (Stellings, 1993). Most victim supporters and sexual harassment experts have lived for a long time with accusations that we promote a political agenda, lack objectivity, or are trying to "work out our personal problems under the guise of scientific inquiry." As these challenges to professional and personal credibility and integrity take root, many supporters and advocates seek refuge in the legalistic aspects of discrimination that discourages personal narrative and emphasizes a more distant and objective relationship with victims. Many of the unique characteristics that identify a victim's experience of harm from sexual harassment are lost in this process. Sexual harassment remains a joke to many and the burden of consequences (along with the burden of proof) rests with victims of sexual harassment rather than with perpetrators.

One very important step for those who find themselves supporting a student who has been sexually harassed is to clarify their role within the system. Being mindful that an advocate is neither an investigator nor a decision maker will help tremendously. In training seminars I encourage employees to be supporters to student victims of sexual harassment and remind them that:

1. Students generally disclose experiences of sexual harassment only to faculty and staff they like and trust
2. Coming forward with an allegation of sexual harassment is a terrifying experience
3. Students often believe faculty and staff know everything there is to know about sexual harassment and the institution's procedures for dealing with it
4. Questions about specifics and requests for details can sound censuring to students under these circumstances
5. Institutions should have trained staff to determine the merits of individual cases
6. Federal law requires that institutions make every effort to investigate and resolve problems of sexual harassment

This last point means the institution may be subject to liability if employees hamper the Title VII, Title IX, and/or states' statutory enforcement process in any way.

When Support Is Not Enough

It is easy to underestimate how important the initial response of an advocate or supporter is to students who has shared their story of sexual harassment for the first time. Although the experience of being influenced by a confidante's response to our problems and concerns is common to most of us, the circumstances surrounding disclosure of an experience of sexual harassment are unique. Students who have been sexually harassed will use the reactions of the people they tell to interpret their own feelings and responses to the abuse. Often confronting their own beliefs about sexual harassment for the first time, students soon come to recognize that many of the people they talk to in their educational institution have already taken a side before they even hear the student's story. (Most students I work with have either "trusted their gut" about who to talk to or desperately experimented with different people in an attempt to get help.) They understand almost instinctively that their experience is life changing and that their decisions about what to do or what not to do about it will have a significant impact on their future.

Most of us normalize sexual harassment in our own lives to some degree. We apply rules and strategies for resolving personal disagreements to sexual harassment because we have learned to try to evade or ignore its systemic influence on our lives. Institutional strategies of conflict resolution and mediation, for example, generally presume a third party's ability to mediate through existing inequities in status and power. And although campus mediators and conflict resolution staff are increasingly used to resolve sexual harassment complaints, many are unfamiliar with the psychosocial and often material consequences of sexual harassment on victims.

In my experience, mediation conducted within an institution often does not effectively mitigate the power differential between a student and a professor. Although mediation may, theoretically, appear to be appropriate for resolving some types of grievances, I do not advocate its use in any form for sexual harassment complaints involving student complainants and faculty respondents. Many disagree. Those interested in a more detailed discussion of the potential advantages of shuttle-mediation for resolving sexual harassment complaints are referred to Chapter 11.

At my institution, students have historically had few opportunities to avoid individuals who are part of the grievance process and either ignorant or insensitive to the marginalization victims experience. Direct and even indirect contact with such people through well-intentioned but often controversial programs, such as mediation, is one of the ways students can feel revictimized by a resolution procedure. Supporters may not have the expertise or status within the institution to effectively influence a grievance or resolution process that is not appropriate to the circumstances or to the victim's needs. Further, students are frequently required to make a case against a harasser using terms and language that are unfamiliar and intimidating to them. Those students who file formal complaints are often expected to tell their story again and again, sometimes answering questions and recounting painful or humiliating experiences to groups of people they have never met before. Although having supporters buffers a student victim from some of the consequences of the complaint or resolution process by validating her or his experience, developing ways of balancing the emotional with the administrative consequences of articulating a grievance in a personally meaningful way remains a significant challenge for most student victims.

Victim Identity in Context

Sexual harassment of students on campus can only be understood by factoring race, ethnicity, sexual orientation, class, age, and other social characteristics that coalesce to provide a context for the victim's experience (Crenshaw, 1993). But sometimes encouraging victims to articulate these intersections places their opportunities to file a grievance and win within the institution at risk. Decision makers and even investigators may not clearly recognize or acknowledge the harm that occurred to the victim or appreciate the importance of examining the complex relationships between these different forms of discrimination.

For many students, standing up and publicly decrying one's own victimization by a powerful professor or even by a less powerful peer through a formal or informal complaint process is not even an option. Such a move feels antithetical to their position of lesser status within the academic hierarchy. Calling up the local women's center or campus counseling office can be a similarly unappealing strategy for many women. Many ethnically identified women perceive sexual harassment as a white women's issue and suspect the strategies employed to defend victims and their rights (Crenshaw, 1993). On most campuses, relatively few people are aware that many of the named plaintiffs in precedent-setting employment discrimination cases involving sexual harassment—Mechelle Vinson, Carmita Wood, Kerry Ellison, and others—have been African American. On many college campuses, women of color often view in-house, traditional caregivers and programs as untrustworthy (DeFour, 1990), and marginalizing (Crenshaw, 1993). Further, women who need time and space to sort out their feelings and think about options may find the confrontational stance against sex discrimination employed by many women's advocacy groups uncomfortable or even threatening; many choose less visible strategies for dealing with their experiences of sexual harassment on campus.

Lesbians frequently feel invisible as victims of sexual harassment, as well. Pervasive disapproval and hostility toward homosexuals contributes to a climate of secrecy, anxiety (Schneider, 1982), and invisibility for many lesbians on campus. The stigma of being "outed" increases *closeted* (unwilling to disclose their sexual orientation publicly) lesbians' vulnerability to sexual harassment and other forms of discrimination and many are frightened into subordinate, dependent behaviors (Pearlman, 1987). Although very few studies have examined the sexual harassment of lesbians, Schneider (1982) found that lesbians consistently reported more hostile environment experiences than heterosexual women (82% v. 69%), suggesting too that the increased likelihood of lesbians to be perceived as "single" also contributes to the probability that they will be harassed. Many of the lesbians I have assisted at the University of Hawai'i were concerned that in voicing their objection to the sexual harassment they experienced, people would recognize them as lesbians. Others have been incensed that the harasser presumed heterosexuality.

Less invested in male approval, affirmation, and economic support than heterosexual women, many lesbians are more comfortably critical of social practices such as sexual harassment that subordinate and oppress women (Pearlman, 1987). And, because lesbians' primary emotional and sexual attraction is to women, lesbians who are sexually harassed by men rarely experience the emotional or physical boundary confusion common to heterosexual victims of male perpetrators. Yet sexual harassment grounded in heterosexist assumptions reinforces a lesbian's position as an outsider at school, and confirms the difficulty many lesbians have in managing and controlling their sexual identity in a heterosexually defined environment (Schneider, 1982).

The Role of an Advocate on Campus

For racial and sexual minority women, sexual harassment is just one more component of an already marginalizing experience on campus (DeFour, 1990; Weiner, in Dzeich & Weiner, 1990)—further compounded by the general view that racism and sexism are mutually exclusive (Crenshaw, 1993). Most white, presumably straight, women supporters and advocates lack the experience to fully comprehend the complexity of sexual harassment commingled with race and/or sexual orientation oppression, thus few women of color or lesbians expect influential people within the institution to be sensitive or responsive to their sexual victimization. While it has been ten years since Linda Weiner suggested that people were becoming increasingly comfortable making sexist, racist, and ethnocentric slurs and that such expressions of hostility contribute to the difficulty racial and sexual minority students experience confronting sexual harassment, her words still ring true (Dzeich & Weiner, 1990). Strategies that deal with sexual harassment as a unidimensional phenomenon and deny the experiences of victims who are subject to multiple forms of oppression (Crenshaw, 1993) cannot be effective for those persons.

An advocate must challenge those responsible for the discrimination *and* those who have traditionally provided student victims with support and remedy. To be effective, advocates must champion students' rights to assert unique experiences and needs, rather than simply help them frame and argue an administrative case against a harasser. Helping students make clear distinctions between working through a complaint procedure and pursuing a resolution that will be personally satisfying to them is fundamental to the role of the advocate.

For those students who do pursue complaints, maintaining realistic expectations through the unpredictable and often discouraging developments of a grievance or resolution process requires constant vigilance. A student subjected to sexual harassment commingled with racism and/or homophobia needs that experience to be validated by a person within the university so that using the university antidiscrimination policies will not be so damaging.

A couple of years ago I worked with an openly bisexual Asian student who was sexually harassed and assaulted by a male professor who appeared to find her bisexuality titillating. Over the course of several research meetings with the professor this student, 21 years old at the time, became suspicious of the professor's intent. Because the professor's lesbian colleagues kept conveniently showing up during their meetings, the student confronted the professor and suggested that she was quite capable of managing her own social life and felt that his manipulation of their professional time together was disrespectful and insulting. A couple of days later, after a department social event, the student was raped by the professor, who told her during the assault that she had been "teasing" him with her bisexuality all along. The student initially wanted to talk to me primarily because I am a lesbian.

She had little faith that justice would be served through institutional remedies because she believed no one would understand the full import of what had happened to her, as a bisexual student.

Most students do not expect the vigorous denial or detailed countercharges that harassers frequently make. It is easy for a student to become embroiled in conflict over a harasser's accusations—some of which may not even be related to the initial allegations of discrimination. Helping a victim understand that this response is merely a continuation of the lack of personal and professional ethics that precipitated the incidents of discrimination in the first place is ultimately more useful for three reasons. First, it enables students to maintain and assert their own personal and professional ethics throughout the grievance process, limiting the revictimization that commonly occurs when victims of sexual harassment are forced into a defensive posture after filing a complaint. Second, this strategy encourages victims to distance themselves somewhat from the grievance process so they are less invested in winning. And third, recognizing dirty defense strategies for what they are allows students to feel good about their own participation in the process, whether they win their case or not.

The Changing Face of Sexual Harassment

The Need for Common Definitions

Paludi and Barickman (1991) correctly point out that common definitions of sexual harassment are important because they both educate members of the campus and help victims identify their experiences as sexual harassment. Like all of us, students rely on information from many sources to determine what sexual harassment is and what it is not. But the subordinate status of students in the classroom, specifically, and on campus, more generally, often has a profound impact on student's feelings and reactions to sexual harassment at school.

Fundamental intersections between sex, race, class, and sexual orientation have always characterized sexual harassment on college campuses. The strength of these relationships within the more readily recognized language of connections between sexuality, gender, and power (Stimpson, 1991) fuels the historical explanation regarding the perniciousness of sexual harassment in academia. The overlap between various forms of discrimination sometimes further confuses victims and their advocates or supporters who may rely on inaccurate assumptions about a victim's experience to gauge and validate the appropriate responses to a harassing experience. An advocate must be ready to recognize and accommodate the dynamic factors sex, race, class, and sexual orientation create for individual victims.

As women of all racial and ethnic backgrounds gain status within academia, and the sexual harassment of lesbians and gay men is acknowledged, common definitions of sexual harassment which accommodate a broader range of sexually harassing experiences will develop. For example, repetitive jokes, comments, questions, or slurs about a heterosexual person's sexual practices are accepted within the standard definition of hostile environment sexual harassment. Yet as I write this chapter, debates continue over whether similar expressions about a lesbian or gay man's sexual orientation violate sexual harassment policies and procedures or even are considered objectionable. To compound the difficulties for lesbians, bisexuals, and gay men, few states provide protection from discrimination on the basis of sexual orientation and many lesbians, bisexuals, and gay men are frequent targets of sexual harassment because of their sexual orientation.

The inevitable expansion of the common definition of sexual harassment should ultimately improve the effectiveness of the definitions as tools for intervention and prevention. But until they incorporate a broader range of victims' experiences of sexual harassment, effective advocates must recognize and teach others to recognize that common definitions are often based on false assumptions about the heterogeneity of victims and the stereotypes we hold regarding sexual harassers.

The Student Victim: Experiences and Response

Any student can be a victim of sexual harassment. One need only to look at the faces in a typical college classroom to see the face of the typical student victim of sexual harassment. Even with over 250 cases in my files, I cannot predict the nature, range, or impact of a harassing experience based on any recognizable characteristic of "a victim." Although most who file sexual harassment complaints are women, victims are also male, straight, gay, bisexual, married, dating, happily single, young, middle-aged, old, large, small, and from every racial and ethnic group represented on campus. Each student defines and talks about the experience of sexual harassment as an individual. Some articulate the racist dimension of their experience first, some believe they were victimized because of their age, others because of their sexual minority status. Many young adults who are sexually harassed grew up thinking that sexual harassment was a thing of the past. All experience a range of conflicting emotions: guilt, sadness, confusion, fear, shame, and anger. Stambaugh accurately characterizes this common period of personal upheaval as "emotional vertigo."[2]

Understanding the uniqueness of student's experiences of sexual harassment is crucial to helping them (Dzeich & Weiner, 1990). Harassers themselves defy stereotypes and are often infinitely creative in their strategies of harassment. There are innumerable ways of sexualizing the learning environment. As Dzeich and Weiner so lucidly discuss in their classic text, *The Lecherous Professor,* teachers sometimes use elaborate overtures masked as academic or professional interest in students' welfare to increase their vulnerability to sexual harassment. Some students understand the underlying intentions of the professor and choose to ignore or less frequently confront them. Many students, however, are unaware of the intent because it is so incongruous with their expectations of an academic relationship.

Graduate students are particularly vulnerable to strategies that isolate them from peers and other faculty and increase their dependency on the abusive professor because of their reliance on letters of support and their need to develop reputations for collegiality through their graduate training. One 23-year-old bisexual Caucasian, born and raised in the continental United States, was seeking admission to a graduate program at the University of Hawai'i. Just separated from enlisted military service, she began working with a faculty member she had been encouraged to meet because of the similarity of their research interests. This professor agreed to take her on as a student. He characterized her insight into their shared area of interest as brilliant and her feminist politics as a problem with other members of the department. Some weeks later the professor informed her (before official word went out) that she had been admitted, in spite of significant opposition from the entire department, because of his strong advocacy for her work. He cautioned her against raising personal concerns or interests with other members of the department. After months of praise, compliments, and professed disbelief at the lack of professional foresight on the part of his colleagues, the professor began inquiring about the student sex life. He told her his sexual fantasies and insisted that she tell him hers. When she refused, he indicated that she suffered from a sexual problem with men and suggested that, as her mentor, he was responsible for "helping her through it." He told her he could not concentrate on his work when she was around because she was so provocative and sexy. This student waited almost a year before pursuing a complaint, charging the professor sexual harassment and ongoing retaliation against the professor because she believed what he had told her about other faculty members' views regarding her work and "feminist" ideology.

Victim advocates and supporters must carefully analyze their personal biases and experiences with sexual harassment when (or ideally before being) confronted with the actual face of a victim and the identity of a harasser. It is important to balance respect for the student's perceptions of harm and desire for remedy with a recognition that the impact of the sexual harassment can go beyond the student targeted by the abuse. Sometimes the most difficult conflicts will stem from a student's desire to take no remedial action at all and the advocate's desire to improve the situation of all students.

I recently worked with a young local (born and raised in Hawai'i) woman of mixed Asian ancestry who was being harassed by a professor born and raised in Korea. Her complaint outlined the professor's racially derogatory comments about her intellectual abilities, repeated compliments about her appearance, attempts to fondle her in his office, and his allusions to her ethnic heritage and cultural practice as a means of maintaining her silence about the harassment. The student was unaffected by his presumptions of her "filial piety." In discussing complaint options, however, she was very clear about not wanting to pursue anything formal because "Korean men are just like that" and "he will never stop anyway—it's in their blood." She wanted her complaint on record just in case the professor tried to run her out of school. Although ethnic stereotypes may be more easily spoken in Hawai'i than in many parts of the United States, they serve to increase awareness of the complex influence ethnic (including gender, sexual minority status, etc.) assumptions and misconceptions have on our responses to sexual harassment, and provide fertile ground for their maintenance as a mode of defense.

Advocating through *Grievance Procedures*

One problem identified through research conducted at UH is that while victims of sexual harassment have ready procedures (and in some cases direct advocacy) for pursuing complaints, there is no similar procedure for those who are victims of racism (Hippensteele, Chesney-Lind, & Veniegas, 1996). Thus, decisions of complainants who have been subjected to multiple forms of discrimination must often be based not on the "worst" part of their experience, or even the most salient, but on factors such as the ease and clarity of various grievance procedural options available to them, accessibility of assistance in using them, and even the institution's relative familiarity with its own policies.

An international student recently came to see me because her supervisor first harassed and then retaliated against her after she confronted him about his behavior. For many months, she said, he had been trying to spend time with her outside of work. He had invited her out socially several times and consistently tried to persuade her to attend school-related functions with him by saying that "this is the American way to get along." He even used her lack of fluency in English to trick her into agreeing publicly to share a jacuzzi with him—she thought he had asked her to share a vegetable dish with him.

Because of the limitations of the grievance process on my campus, I was compelled to advise the student to pursue her institutional complaint as one of sexual harassment, even though she was clearly experiencing discrimination that was also, and perhaps more fundamentally, related to her national origin. This complaint was ultimately resolved to her satisfaction, in part because her experience of sexual harassment commingled with race and national origin discrimination was validated through our conversations.

Toward Resolving through Advocacy

A recent study of 926 students at the University of Hawai'i supports other research findings that a significant majority of students who experience sexual harassment seek nonconfrontative ways of dealing with the problem. The UH data suggest that many talk to friends, avoid contact with the person, and/or ignore the attention. The reasons for the silence vary: fear of retaliation at work or in class, fear the working climate will deteriorate; fear of unsatisfactory grades, recommendations, or evaluations were the ones most commonly cited (Hippensteele et al., 1996).

Some of the students in the UH study did seek direct paths to resolve their complaints. Eleven percent told a university official about their problem. Of that number though, over 80% reported that this action made no difference and nearly 5% said it made things worse. Only 13% felt that telling their story to someone within the institution had improved the situation. The results of this study are not atypical. My discussions with victims' advocates from around the country confirm that the most difficult problems victims' supporters confront involve challenging deeply ingrained institutional practices that effectively deny victims access to the very resources and information that would help them the most.

For instance, Title IX mandates institutional procedures that are "fair and equitable" and that allow students full access to complaint processes and rights to appeal. Yet my own reading of over 40 university sexual harassment policies from around the United States suggests that few make information about prior complaints against a harasser known to current victims, even though such disclosure is clearly justified through Title IX. Further, crucial information regarding remedies is often withheld from a complainant because of privacy concerns asserted by harassers. (The University of Hawai'i has struggled with this issue for several years now in what became a statewide debate, producing several legal challenges to state "sunshine laws" by public employee unions—including the two university unions representing faculty and staff—attempting to guard their members' "right" to privacy.) It is, of course, unlikely that a complainant will be able determine whether they are satisfied with the outcome of their grievance unless they know what corrective action was taken by the institution. When student victims of sexual harassment are given conflicting messages about the intentions of the institution in providing a remedy to the discrimination, achieving an effective resolution to their complaint is further complicated.

Unfortunately, few of the sexual harassment policies and complaint procedures I reviewed appeared to be designed with meaningful remedies to the discrimination in mind. Although most include important language regarding the need to eliminate sexual harassment from the campus community, institutional responsibility for providing corrective action is frequently addressed through a general laundry list of punishments a policy violator may have to face. Without exception, victims I have worked with initially wanted to recapture the valued academic relationship they lost when they were sexually harassed. When they first come forward with a complaint, their desire for corrective action usually begins and ends with an apology from the harasser and acknowledgment of the feelings the behavior elicited. Yet while most complaints are currently handled informally, I have only been able to learn of a handful of cases handled by EEO/AA offices, advocates, or supporters that were resolved so simply. It has become quite common for a student's allegations of sexual harassment, even in the absence of formal charges, to spark a volatile and angry episode and little chance of a nonadversarial resolution to the student's complaint.

At the University of Hawai'i, I am frequently confronted with student victims of sexual harassment who do not want to report their experience out of loyalty to the harasser because of his (or her, theoretically) race, ethnicity, or sexual orientation. For example, I recently met an 18-year-old white man struggling to end what he felt had been a consensual relationship with a faculty member in his department. He expressed confusion and remorse for having caused the professor (who was 19 years his senior) pain when he left, but felt that the professor's repeated attempts to contact him at the department laboratory were having a negative impact on his ability to work and on his relationships with other students in the department. Although neither the student nor the professor in this case were closeted, the student felt immense loyalty to the professor because he was gay. He was quite concerned that a formal complaint would subject the professor to unfair treatment by the institution because of his sexual orientation. The student recognized that the professor needed to be held accountable for his extremely unprofessional conduct, so we devised an informal resolution that incorporated several educational meetings between the professor and me, which eventually proved effective in ending the harassment. In this case, the professor was motivated by his desire to regain the student's respect.

The politics of university relations can be excruciatingly complex for victims of sexual harassment. They must negotiate conflicting territories of experiential and legal definitions while weighing the personal and professional impact of describing oneself as a victim. Understanding the context through which the sexual harassment of students can be ignored, or worse, condoned, is the first step toward correcting the numerous ways victims are harmed by these experiences.

What Advocates Can Do

At the time of my hiring, several articles appeared in the campus and local newspapers about the creation of my position as advocate for students. When I arrived for work the first day, two women were waiting in the hall outside my office. The first told me she had been in the country for one year and had to complete her degree as quickly as possible because her family did not have enough money to support her in the United States for more than two years. She tried but had difficulty controlling her emotions enough to tell me her story of sexual harassment without crying. She described how one of her professors had repeatedly propositioned her and after months of refusals had cornered her in the lab and grabbed her from behind, pinning her to the wall with his body. After her escape she notified a female instructor who immediately spoke to the harasser. He denied everything to the instructor who was his lover at the time. An "A" student, the young woman decided to try again with the department chair who, on hearing her complaint, suggested that she change her field of study.

The second student I met with that day was far less upset than the first. She was a nontraditional student returning to school after raising three children. A professor twenty years younger than her had begun the annoying habit of putting his hands down her shirt to look at her jewelry while the class was taking an exam. The student told me she had a feeling that his behavior was inappropriate but wanted to make sure before trying to figure out what to do.

In the case of the nontraditional student, she and I were able to devise a satisfactory strategy for resolving a complaint that involved a verbal intervention by the student during the next class exam within a couple of hours. Many complaints are satisfactorily resolved in similar ways. But a significant number of student's experiences are not so simple. Perhaps 10 percent of all the cases I handle involve complex circumstances requiring dozens of hours of counseling to prepare and present a formal complaint. The first story I heard that first day developed into one of the most difficult and frustrating cases I have ever handled. The student was unfamiliar with U.S. laws and found the option of filing a formal complaint against her professor completely outrageous. Good-faith efforts to resolve the situation on her own before coming to see me had resulted in severe retaliation that escalated rapidly. The student had earnestly explained to each person she met that she had no intention of filing a complaint and my subsequent attempts to informally resolve her grievance proved futile. She eventually transferred to a new program. The institution was unwilling to investigate her allegations without a signed statement of complaint against the professor, although legally they are bound to stop harassment, even if there is no written complaint. The best I was able to do was validate this woman's experience and help maintain her academic standing through her program transfer. My assurances to the administrator in charge that the institution's refusal to formally investigate was illegal had no impact—she was certain the student would not "make a fuss." Even without press coverage, I can receive as many as three new complaints in a day.

Obviously, the personal and professional demands of providing support and advocacy to victims of sexual harassment can be formidable. A crucial step in preparing to help a student deal with sexual harassment is to identify and acknowledge the depth of our own emotional reactions to them and to their experiences. The intensity of the initial response to a victim of sexual harassment catches most people off guard. Unwitting advocates may find themselves reacting with doubt, pity, anxiety, guilt, frustration, or even anger at the victim for getting them involved. Coming face to face with a student alleging sexual harassment by a colleague or even a friend can be both personally and professionally threatening. Many academics respond by denying the relevance of their feelings and depersonalizing the problem. But accepting strong reactions to sexual harassment as a legitimate part of the advocacy process dramatically improves the chance that an advocate will be able to help the victim, who needs earnest, genuine, caring support more than anything else.

Few students have access to information they need to make informed decisions about how to resolve an experience of sexual harassment. An advocate within the institution can help leverage students entering complaint/resolution processes in important ways. Because of their greater familiarity with institutional power dynamics and idiosyncrasies, an advocate will be able to provide answers to questions students may not know to ask. Students are certainly aware of the controversy around bringing charges of sexual harassment, but may not understand that their ability to effectively resolve a sexual harassment complaint can depend on the personal commitment of individuals with key positions within the procedure. Students are unlikely to even know who these people are, much less whether they can be trusted to make tough, courageous decisions. At this point in the evolution of sexual harassment complaint handling, on many campuses the most damaging part of a sexual harassment experience for a student can occur after she or he begins to look for remedies. Yet the powerlessness victims often experience through the complaint/resolution process can be mitigated by a sensitive advocate who acts on the old adage "information is power." To students who are trying to regain the trust and faith they have lost in an institution and the people who work at it, knowledge also leads to healing. I suggest that advocates provide students with answers to the following questions—whether they ask them or not:

- How did the sexual harassment grievance process develop at the institution?
- Have complainant's been satisfied by the outcome of their grievances in the past?
- What support services on and off campus exist for students who have been sexually harassed?
- What are the student's filing options?
- What external options for filing complaints exist?
- How are these procedures accessed?
- Who are the people responsible for implementing the policy and conducting the investigation (names, titles, locations of offices, etc.)?
- How long is an investigation supposed to take?

- Who represents the complainant through the process?
- What informal options are available, and how do they work?
  - Things the student can do
  - Things the institution can do

These questions are ordered in a way that will facilitate creating a narrative or history of sexual harassment at any institution. They reflect the main concerns students have raised with me as they make decisions about resolving their sexual harassment complaints. The first three questions essentially provide a context for what can otherwise feel like a barrage of disjointed facts about complaint options, time frames, complaint forms, and so on. Most of the students I have worked with since developing and using this narrative/historical strategy seem to experience less confusion about the complaint procedures and express more positive feelings, such as a sense of autonomy and personal control, as they move through the process.

When a Case Is Tried through the Press

Distortions of actual cases run rampant in the hypervigilant environment of a university campus. The drama surrounding allegations of sexual misconduct by a professor offers profound intrigue. Public fascination with the controversy often makes confidentiality for victims impossible to maintain. In my experience, the lack of control students have over their own story once it becomes grist for the rumor mill can cause enormous difficulties for complainants who find themselves unwittingly revisiting feelings of helplessness that are surprisingly similar to those they experienced when they were initially harassed. These feelings are compounded by concerns over gossip and factual misrepresentations, particularly when media get hold of a case. It is important for advocates to help victims acknowledge and then manage the fear and anxiety campus (or wider public) notoriety will likely produce.

Six months after closing a complicated case involving a graduate student who had charged a former professor with coercing her into a consensual relationship and retaliating after she ended it, a professor in another department began using this case in his classroom lectures as an example of how women regularly and "falsely accuse men of sexual harassment after being romantically involved with them in order to ruin their careers." The misrepresentation of the facts of this case (which the student had won) and other derogatory comments about victims of sexual assault, compelled students in the class to object—several of them knew the student involved and the facts of the case the professor had cited. The atmosphere created by the professor through this lecture had such a profound impact that several students in the class came forward to file a discrimination complaint against him for creating a hostile environment. One of the students also disclosed allegations of sexual coercion by the same professor whose lecture had so seriously misrepresented the earlier case. She believed his comments during that class had been designed to intimidate her into silence by denigrating victims.

Nearly two years later, this case remains unresolved for the students. Each is comforted by her conviction that fighting discrimination without compromising values or personal ethics is a worthy endeavor, but none feel they received a satisfactory outcome to their grievances by pursuing university complaint procedures. As their advocate, I was unable to effectively fight the collective resources of the faculty union and some administrators who insisted (publicly in some cases) that this case revolved around violations of the professor's rights to academic freedom. Eighteen months after bringing the original charge, the student alleging sexual coercion by the professor filed a lawsuit in federal court.

Whenever a specific case of sexual harassment becomes public, students are deeply affected by the controversy; some become more willing to come forward with their own story. More often, they move deeper underground, fearful that their situations will later become fodder for jokes, rumor, and nasty innuendoes. In 1989, after months of frustrating attempts to effectively resolve my own complaint of sexual harassment at the University of Hawai'i, I eventually went public with my charges of retaliation and procedural violations by the institution. Because I am now employed by this same institution I regularly meet women whose career paths have also kept them at UH after graduation. Many recount horrendous experiences of sexual harassment from their graduate student days and, in response to my query most tell me that they decided against filing a complaint because of "what the university did to you." These remarks are painful to hear. The decision to make my case public was difficult and the potential "chilling" affects on other students who were experiencing sexual harassment was a big concern. But, I believe the pressure exerted by campus and community groups as a result of the publicity was instrumental in encouraging the rapid changes the institution made to its policies and for the increased scrutiny of these procedures that persists today. Employee supporters and advocates for students who have been sexually harassed serve as important reminders to other members of the campus community who do not know or who choose to ignore their institution's history of sexual harassment.

Raging Debates or Debates About Rage

The number of women (and increasingly of men, as well) who have been sexually harassed at school suggests that it is more of a normative experience than a unique one. We have more than a decade of research about victims. Who, where, how, and by whom are questions that elicit relatively succinct responses these days. Even questions about the elusiveness of a reasonable definition of sexual harassment have become much more easily addressed with the steady accumulation of case law dealing with both quid pro quo and hostile environment harassment issues. Yet debate over whether sexual harassment is a serious problem for victims rages on.

Across the country a few students have spoken up, gone public, named a harasser publicly, or filed suit. These women symbolize enormous strength, conviction, and courage to other sexual harassment victims. Most came forward hoping for support, loyalty, and advocacy that they did not receive. They have earned our gratitude and deserve an honored place in history. However, they are not the norm; most victims suffer in silence. Further, because most of the women whose voices are heard on campus are presumed to be white and/or middle-class, this is the face we have come to recognize when we hear about sexual harassment on campuses.

Throughout academia, the cultural diversity versus academic freedom arguments tend to converge on the issue of individual rights. Many professors who enter into these debates do so expecting their participation to carry an authorizing function. Their role on campus as the ultimate arbiters of information and ethical standards has only recently met challenge and many yearn to revisit earlier times when social and professional boundaries within the academy were not so clear. Some hope to redefine their relations with students, paradoxically through the very authoritative traditions they claim to resent. Such expectations are not entirely illogical to those accustomed to a lengthy tradition of autonomy and self-regulation in the classroom (Dzeich & Weiner, 1990), but from the student's vantage point, the professor *role* and the professor *person* are generally indistinguishable. For those college students who are sexually harassed at school, debates over whether the problem of sexual harassment on campus is significant is insulting, to say the least.

Sociologist Carol Smart identifies the apex of these debates as that which enables us to articulate the nature and validity of knowledge when truth is no longer absolute (Smart, 1990). The difficulties inherent in challenging one group's truth with anothers' are profound. Formerly useful dichotomies—women and men, of color and white, gay and straight—no longer carry currency as we become more sophisticated in our understanding of multiculturalism. The need for a language and a politic accurately reflecting the multitude of experiences represented in academia has never been more compelling. Making a constructive debate even more difficult is the fact that few colleges and universities have a grasp of the relationship between racism, sexism, and homophobia on their own campus or the scope of their combined impact on students' experiences of sexual harassment.

Maivan Lam, a friend and colleague who teaches at City University of New York law school, has repeatedly described the current state of campus discrimination as "second generation" (i.e., those who seek to discriminate are aware of the landscape and how to "fit in" to avoid early detection as undesirable elements in our midst). The victims with whom I have discussed second generation sexual harassment often find the concept enormously useful as a way to make sense of the their feelings of confusion and powerlessness. Stanley Fish (1994) describes Lam's second-generation phenomenon as a "speaking in code," which allows bigotry and discriminatory practices in academia to be perpetuated by liberals and conservatives alike who cloak themselves in the language of tolerance and equality while perpetuating their own often discriminatory self-interest; merit, rigor, standards, and excellence are the current code words for the more refined sentiment against many whose voices and perspectives challenge the traditions of academia (Matsuda, Lawrence, Delgado, & Crenshaw, 1993).

The historic utopian values of the academy (freedom of thought, expression, and speech; model symbols of individual rights and respect for others; and so on), which protect rights that, in the main, reside with and protect white male faculty, are now in unavoidable collision with the need to address the rights of nonacademic majority members (Hippensteele, et al., 1996). To many, academic freedom is currently being used as a license to speak and behave irresponsibly. There are few, if any, professions that provide the opportunity to exert such extensive control over others as has been given to university professors. Unfortunately, such unparalleled professional power requires a level of self-regulation and a standard of professional ethics that is often sadly lacking on contemporary college campuses. Supporters and advocates must combine resources and strategies to meet the growing and increasingly complex needs of students who are sexually harassed on campus.

Campus policies and procedures that can accommodate the needs of ethnically identified victims of sexual harassment, such as those whose stories I have recounted above, require increased sophistication: most students do not complain formally about sexual harassment and many never tell anyone that they have been discriminated against at all. Some are intimidated by those who harassed them, some do not want to call attention to themselves, and some fear retaliation and feel nothing will be done to remedy their situation if they do come forward. Often, these fears are borne out. Until victims and perpetrators both become confident that acts of sexual harassment and retaliation will no longer be tolerated, efforts to prevent sexual harassment will be futile.

Weiner (1990) suggests that the depth of sexism on campuses today creates in victims' advocates, counselors, and supporters a second order of sexual harassment victims: those whose personal history of opposing institutionalized racism, sexism, and homophobia increase their vulnerability to retaliation and burnout when they support others' battles. Although it is certainly true that "backlash" politics contribute to the context in which students and their advocates and supporters experience and object to sexual harassment, those who object are, at the most basic level, activists; and activists generally find personal strength in eliciting and creating reactions from opponents. Campus activism remains an important means through which subordinate members of any organization press for institutional change and reform (McKee, 1994).

Most institutions struggle to maintain policies and procedures adequate to the task of providing victims of discrimination with avenues for redress without overburdening administrative systems. The result is rarely satisfactory to complainants or to the institutions. Campuses are finding themselves embroiled in crises that might have been avoided through policies that (1) validate the complexity of ethnically identified students experiences, (2) effectively communicate information about complaint processing that will help students make informed choices about their options, and (3) recognize and respond to students' needs for support and advocacy in resolving sexual harassment complaints. Assuming that sexual harassment is experienced as the same phenomenon by all victims masks the complexity of the problem especially for students who identify their experiences as commingled with racism, classism, and/or homophobia.

The experience of sexual harassment is alienating and frightening. A university is a formidable adversary. Students who pursue sexual harassment complaints should be commended for their courage. Most students who object are isolated and vilified. Providing in-house advocacy for student victims of sexual harassment dramatically enhances an institution's responsiveness to sexual harassment and its ability to mitigate the damage sexual harassment causes in students' lives. Effective advocacy improves student victims' ability to articulate their complaints within the system and enables them to balance efforts to win complaints with their efforts to remedy the discrimination. Advocacy may also decrease the chances that adversarial relationships between victims and the institution will develop as informal resolutions that meet victims' needs may be achieved more readily. Students are more likely to feel that their experience of sexual harassment has been validated when they have an advocate within the system who confirms their unique experience of the harm. There is much work ahead as we struggle to create an academy that permits all students to study, learn, and create in an environment free from sexual harassment.

Endnotes

1. The correct English spelling of Hawai'i includes the 'okina (or glottal stop). The state completed the transition to the use of okina and other pronunciation marks, revising all street and highway signs, state letterhead, etc., to reflect more accurately the pronunciation and inflection of the Hawaiian language.

2. The author would like to thank Phoebe Morgan Stambaugh, the School of Justice Studies, Arizona State University–Tempe for "emotional vertigo" and for her careful critique and insightful comments on earlier drafts of this chapter.

References

Crenshaw, K. W. (1993). Beyond racism and mysogyny: Black feminism and 2 Live Crew. In Matsuda, M. J., Lawrence, C. R., Delgado, R., & Crenshaw, K. W. (eds.), *Words that wound: Critical race theory, assaultive speech, and the First Amendment.* Boulder, Westview Press.

DeFour, D. C. (1990). The interface of racism and sexism on college campuses. In Paludi & Barickman (eds.), *Ivory power: Sexual harassment on campus.* New York: SUNY Press.

Dzeich, B. W., & Weiner, L. (1990). *The lecherous professor: Sexual harassment on campus.* Urbana, IL: University of Illinois Press.

Fish, S. (1994). *There's no such thing as free speech.* New York: Oxford University Press.

Herman, J. L. (1992). *Trauma and recovery.* New York: HarperCollins Publishers.

Hippensteele, S. K. (1991). Sexual harassment in academia: Scenario construction and gender differences in students' behavioral definitions and judgments. Published dissertation (Univ. Microforms, Int'l, Ann Arbor MI).

Hippensteele, S. K., Chesney-Lind, M., Veniegas, R. (1996). On the basis of the changing face of harassment and discrimination in the academy. *Women and Criminal Justice* 8(1), 1996.

McKee, S. (1994). Simulated histories. *New Perspectives: Critical Histories of Graphic Design* 28(4), 328–43.

Matsuda, M. J., Lawrence, C. R., Delgado, R., & Crenshaw, K. W. (eds.) (1993). *Words that wound: Critical race theory, assaultive speech, and the First Amendment.* Boulder, Westview Press.

Paludi, M. A., & Barickman, R. B. (1991). *Academic and workplace sexual harassment.* New York: State University of New York Press.

Pearlman, S. F. (1987). The saga of continuing clash in lesbian community, or will an army of ex-lovers fail? In Boston Lesbian Psychologies Collective (eds.), *Lesbian psychologies: Explorations and challenges.* Urbana, IL: University of Illinois Press.

Schneider, B. E. (1982). Consciousness about sexual harassment among heterosexual and lesbian women workers. *Journal of Social Issues* 38(4), 75–98.

Smart, C. (1990). *Feminism and the power of law.* London: Routledge

Stelling, B. (1993). The public harm of private violence: Rape, sex discrimination, and citizenship. *Harvard Civil Rights–Civil Liberties Law Review* 28, 183–216.

Stimpson, C. R. (1991). Overreaching: Sexual harassment and education. In Paludi and Barickman (eds.), *Academic and workplace sexual harassment.* New York: SUNY Press.

Weiner, L. (1990). Introduction. In *The lecherous professor: Sexual harassment on campus.* Urbana, IL: University of Illinois Press.

19

THE ROLE OF THE PRESIDENT IN SEXUAL HARASSMENT PREVENTION

ROBERT L. CAROTHERS　　　　　*JAYNE E. RICHMOND*

Among the most important responsibilities of a college president is the work that supports and builds the climate, the environment, the culture of the campus. If the campus community is to be efficient and effective in the learning process for which the university exists, that culture must balance freedom and responsibility, respect for the rights of the individual, and respect for the rights of the greater community.

A college or university president typically employs both power and influence to achieve the goals he or she has set for the institution served. The president makes decisions that set priorities, allocate resources, reward performance, and sanction inappropriate actions. The president adds assistantships in the psychology department, defers roof repairs for the athletic facility, promotes a brilliant young professor of mathematics ahead of the usual schedule, and awards an honorary degree to a controversial physician in the community.

But the president also makes important statements about values in more subtle ways as well. She or he attends a night of the film festival sponsored by the Gay and Lesbian Alliance, pins the bars on the shoulders of newly commissioned graduates of the ROTC program, agrees to speak at the local Rotary meeting, and arrives in time for lunch. The president meets with the athletic coaches at the beginning of the fall term and talks about sportsmanship and the kind of behavior expected of them on the sidelines. And, the president meets with the campus police and talks about their mission. People begin to know what the president is about.

When it all works, there is a harmony about the president's activities, those spoken and those unspoken. Themes emerge, values are established, and these have a way of working their way into the campus culture, even when opposed at various times by diverse elements of the community. Power reinforces influence, and influence makes the exercise of power possible.

Such a position makes the president uniquely able to confront the difficult and complex web of issues that exist around sexual harassment. Establishing the values which inform the university's handling of these issues also allows the president to protect the rights of all concerned without becoming the arbiter of particular cases. As in most things on campus, an investment of time and personal vigilance establishes the attitudes that make it possible to maintain a positive climate with a minimal use of coercive power, an exercise rarely altogether effective in a community in which individual freedom is so highly celebrated.

Creating a Quality Environment

Balancing these often competing rights around issues of gender, power, and exploitation—all containing great emotional content—begins with an open discussion of the problems that exist on campuses; the traditions which have given rise to them; and the philosophical, moral, legal, and political questions intertwined in resolving them.

New college presidents are always surprised—and often dismayed—to discover that their every word, whether pronouncement or casual comment, is widely quoted and carefully dissected. Moreover, what is not discussed will be noted as well. Thus, if a president is to help create a campus climate free from harassing behavior, the first step is simply to talk about it, to say that it is OK for administrators, faculty, staff and students to acknowledge that sexual harassment probably is occurring on the campus. After all, we know, that approximately 30 percent of all undergraduate women experience some form of sexual harassment by at least one professor or staff member during their college years. Acknowledging the problem exists is only a first step, however. Publicly proclaiming that we will not attempt to cover it up or deny it, to close our collective eyes to it, or to accept it, is the next step. Now the campus conversation is legitimate, is not disloyal, and can be carried on in a positive and constructive manner.

Having established that perspective on the subject, the president can build the process by which the campus community can define and learn about harassment. Because a campus is in some ways a mobile and transitory community, this process of building understanding about which behaviors are acceptable and which are unacceptable is never-ending. There is always a new class of students (first-year students and graduate students) and new staff, faculty, and administrators who must learn institutional policy and the realities that lie beyond the words. This process of orientation and acculturation can take many forms, but if we expect it to result in complete understanding and consequently more appropriate behavior, it must be clearly established and broadly communicated.

This is where the president's leadership in both word and deed is very important. The rise of sexual harassment as a controversial campus issue has been accompanied by a delicate shift in the legal, political, administrative, and personal foundations for many diverse decisions which the president is required to make. Indeed, the topic has influenced the role of the president in such a pronounced way that today he or she is likely to have a new consciousness that all decisions send messages and set the tone with regard to mutual respect between and among members of the community. Further, as the president becomes more and more involved in cases of a nature that was unknown in the past, a legal perspective alone, without the ability to understand the social and personal sides of the issue, will not be enough. Just how seriously the president regards issues of sexual harassment will be quickly gauged by nearly everyone in the community.

For example, one is not on campus very long before discovering that a clear test of what a university values is what it funds. The importance of a particular effort or initiative will be measured by whether the training program is done cavalierly by people with too much to do already, or whether it is well planned and well executed.

> Does the program announcement come accompanied by a letter of explanation and endorsement signed by the president?
> Does the president make at least several appearances at training sessions?
> Is training in sexual harassment prevention provided for the entire community, including the highest administration and all staff members?
> Is sexual harassment defined broadly enough to include student peer harassment, and are student leaders and the general student body included in these discussions?

For students, faculty, and staff, this sort of introduction to the issues should be a standard part of the campus orientation. It should be didactic and experiential, allowing for reflective observation and for role-play observation and practice. This way the information is made personally relevant and, as a result, more meaningful.

But, we will not be successful in creating a productive climate in the campus community by focusing only on those who are newcomers. Nor can this strategy have full impact if responsibility rests exclusively in one area, such as with the president. Although the president must be clear about what he or she will or will not stand for, one chief responsibility is to spread a sense of "mission" about sexual harassment prevention throughout the leadership of the university. This includes both the formal leadership (vice presidents, deans, department heads, and program directors) and the informal leadership (senior faculty, union stewards, student senators, athletes, and other students). The task of the president is to make sexual harassment prevention an important issue and to empower and inspire other leaders to carry a conversation to all corners of the campus.

There is a language necessary for this kind of conversation. We believe the most effective approach has a personal quality to it, an openness to talking about one's own learning about sexual harassment, and a willingness to acknowledge the complexity of this problem. The president who frankly acknowledges the difficulty of transforming a university climate will be better able to empower others who deal with sexual harassment, both directly and indirectly, ensuring that responsibility for this issue is widely shared. Certainly, eradicating sexual harassment from campuses requires everyone's effort.

The president can also contribute greater attention to harassment issues by pursing an aggressive hiring policy, placing more women in positions of influence and authority. Many of the things we say and do that have a "chilling effect" are part of a traditional culture often described as the "old boys club"—a set of assumptions which too often do not include women or their perspective. But the old boys' club functions best in a state of homogeneity; it has difficulty doing business around a table where women, minorities, and/or disabled people sit. Although it is clearly not the responsibility of women alone to end gender bias or sexual harassment, nonetheless, when a female dean sits with the Council of Deans, the conversation is different; when the second female dean joins the group, a different perspective is often articulated with new force and confidence. In such a council, not only is there likely to be less tolerance for harassment, there is also likely to be greater reinforcement for those who "do what's right," who become leaders in the campaign to create a nurturing and fair environment for both students and staff.

Although the president has the responsibility of protecting both the members of the community and the institution itself, someone should be able to give expert counsel and technical assistance to the president and to the campus community at large on matters of procedure and due process. Together they must ensure that there are policies and processes, both formal and informal, that are known to the community. These policies must include well-established procedure, due process, and protection of the rights of the victim and the accused. And, at the very least, there must be a monitoring process to evaluate the effectiveness of these policies.

Frequently, this person is identified as the campus affirmative action officer (AAO). If the president assigns responsibility for leadership with regard to sexual harassment issues to the officer, the president must be certain that there is a meeting of the minds between the two about the role each will play. There must be clarity about whether the AAO is responsible for developing and implementing policy as an extension of the president, whether the AAO is an activist functioning as an investigator of grievances and a prosecutor of offenders, or something else altogether. More important, that person needs to help all the rest of us to think intelligently about the complexity and the ambiguity often inherent in sexual harassment cases. The roles played at various times by such an officer can be confusing, and even contradictory. Without some clarity with regard to role, the AAO may become everyone's adversary, left without the credibility needed to solve these difficult problems, or indeed to be an advocate for those making a claim.

Because we recognize that there are at least two goals in dealing with and in ending sexual harassment—protecting the institution from liability and developing and maintaining a climate of positive respect in the workplace and in the classroom—we believe it is best to think of the AAO as an educator, responsible for helping the formal and informal leaders of the institution do their jobs more efficiently and effectively. For example, an effective sexual harassment policy must grapple with many hard questions of parameters such as the following:

> Where to draw the line between acceptable and unacceptable behavior in the complex arena of human relationships.
> When is a sexual relationship consensual?
> When does it stop being consensual?
> What constitutes saying no?
> In the areas of speech, what choices of language may create a sense of pain or of anger such that learning is impaired?
> Where does one person's right to express himself or herself freely end and another's right to work or study free of intimidation begin?

These questions are not simple and we cannot rely only on the legal system or guidelins proffered by the courts to set the direction for how we will move institutions toward greater tolerance and understanding. Rather, college and university representatives, including presidents and faculty, should articulate the parameters central to the issue, with clarity and vigilance, so that the lines of acceptable behavior are drawn.

For example, an enduring policy statement on freedom of expression made in the 1975 report of a Yale University committee and incorporated into the *Yale Undergraduate Regulations* says:

> Even when some members of the university community fail to meet their social and ethical responsibilities, the paramount obligation of the university is to protect their right to free expression. . . If the university's overriding commitment to free expression is to be sustained, secondary social and ethical responsibilities must be left to the informal process of persuasion, example, and argument.[1]

Stephen Sample, past president of the State University of New York made a powerful point as well in a call to the entire university community to speak out against all intolerance. President Sample said, "As long as we let those small moments pass without calling attention to the injustice they represent, the threat to justice everywhere will continue. Only by vigilance in our daily lives can we help make justice everywhere possible."[2]

If a sexual harassment policy is to accomplish the legitimate goal of protecting people from the harassing behavior of others while preserving the largest degree of personal freedom possible for all, then the community at large must believe that the policy is well considered, the result of reasonable people thinking together with full recognition of competing perspectives and competing interests.

Traditions and Challenges

Colleges and universities have unique traditions rooted in the nature of the work we do and our powerful commitment to academic freedom, the nearly unlimited right of faculty members to conduct their research and express their thoughts without prior censorship or fear of reprisal. At heart, academic freedom is the right to tell the truth, as the professor or the student sees it, limited only by the common law of libel and slander and the "clear and present danger" principle which Judge Holmes articulated nearly a century ago. Under the flag of academic freedom, we strive to protect each member of the community from charges of heresy of one sort or another and to keep the campus discourse free from political or religious interference which would intimidate or silence unpopular or expression.

On the other hand, there are also certain standards of civility which prevail in each culture, and on college campuses at least, these are normative in nature rather than absolute. For many women—and for some men as well—the traditional standards of verbal usage have included expressions which are often offensive or demeaning or intimidating, and which together can create the kind of "chilly" learning environment that subverts our teaching mission. One of the ways the president can lead in this difficult area is by openly discussing the process of balancing an equal commitment to academic freedom and sensitivity to language and practice that can be detrimental to the learning process.

Among the most important traditions in the academy is the centrality of the mentoring process, the often intimate relationship between faculty and students. Sometimes, as the old saying goes, all that is needed for learning is Mark Hopkins on one end of the log and his student on the other. Indeed, all of the more recent work on the learning process for undergraduates—the development of the "Wingspread Principles of Good Practice," for example—emphasize that the single most important variable to success is the amount of time students spend with faculty members in and out of class.[3] More and more, we understand that involving students with faculty as they practice their professions as scholars and researchers and as people providing service to the community is one of the most effective ways of connecting students to the academic enterprise and motivating them in professional growth and development.

But teaching and learning at their best are passionate processes. Faculty members who really care often develop an emotional investment in their students, an investment that is both professional and personal. Students who admire and appreciate their teachers often develop a similar regard for these mentors. Indeed, to the degree we are successful in increasing the amount of active and collaborative learning going on at colleges and universities—closing the traditional gap between those who "profess" and those who sit passively in lecture halls hoping to absorb the tide of words flowing over them—we can surely predict that there will be more such professional and personal involvement between faculty and students, most of it entirely appropriate and desirable. As a best result of such collaboration, mutual respect and appreciation between students and faculty should increase. Conversely, a closer and more intense interaction between students and faculty can also bring out conflicts of perspective and of values that one party or the other may take beyond the limits permitted. There remains the potential for sexual harassment to increase in these setting.

Just as harassment itself is an expression of power, an accusation of inappropriate sexual behavior has a significant power of its own. On campus today many men fear that power to accuse. There is uncertainty—sometimes real and sometimes feigned—about just what jokes or stories are allowed now, about language usage, about touching, and more. There is a growing fear on campus among some men that interaction with women is dangerous except on the most precise terms, a sense that men are now more exposed to false or unfair accusations of harassment. An unfortunate result is the increasing withdrawal of men from many of the mentoring roles so important to the professional and personal growth of women. If we are to preserve this very positive element of our tradition, we must not only have a sexual harassment complaint and resolution process in which men as well as women have confidence, but more important, educational programs so that men understand precisely what behavior is sexual harassment.

Finally, ours is a tradition where faculty members have had the ability to do their work with great autonomy, to rule nearly supreme within the confines of their classrooms and laboratories. Teaching, it is said, is the second most private thing we do. Faculty members are largely unsupervised, and they bring to their relationship with students the power of the grade and the ability to give or withhold recommendations for jobs or graduate school, as well as access to their professional networks. The consequence, then, is that between faculty members and students there is a huge imbalance of power and far too many illustrations of instances when faculty have used that power in an abusive way. Because we wish to sustain the important traditions of academic freedom, faculty autonomy, and mentoring, the president has an important responsibility to ensure that fear and sexual harassment do not undermine the viability of each.

Complaint and Resolution

From the president's perspective, the goal of a complaint process is to end a harassing situation with the utmost dispatch in the most confidential way possible. Perhaps the most fundamental duty of the president is to ensure that the learning climate on campus is positive and productive. The presence of sexual harassment can infect that climate very quickly, contaminating the basic elements of trust necessary for learning. At the same time, the president has a nearly equal duty to ensure that the process which resolves conflicts on the campus is both fair and perceived to be fair. It must meet the tests of due process which the campus community and ultimately the courts will expect, while shielding all parties from the damage that can easily flow from charges, true and false.

One area of increasing concern is in the relationships between and among students. These are sometimes the most difficult to manage or give guidance to. At least for students of traditional age, college is a time of social exploration and experimentation. Away from home for the first time, many students find themselves somewhat adrift from the moral standards enforced in their family. The rules of engagement are not always clear, and ambiguity can lead to sexual harassment and charges of sexual harassment.

The president must be concerned about how coverage of harassment charges will be handled by the media and about the reactions from various university stakeholders. She or he will want to balance a desire to maintain an openness to the discussion of harassment on campus with the demands of the media for specifics on cases, especially in this time of nearly rabid tabloid journalism. Well before such cases are reported on the six o'clock news, the president will want to have educated the trustees, government officials, alumni, and parents to the fact that while there are instances of harassment in all organizations, at the university, these are dealt with quickly and appropriately. When a specific story breaks, the president wants and needs their confidence that the desired learning and working environment will be quickly restored.

Another part of the discussion has to do with actual sexual relationships between staff, or staff and students and how appropriate guidelines are to be established. For the president, these are particularly muddy waters. There is an inherently exploitative situation any time there is a power differential, as when as senior professor is involved with a new assistant professor, an administrator with a staff or faculty member, or when a professor is dating a student. In such cases, the argument goes, the university should attempt to regulate sexual relationships where there is this imbalance of power between the partners, especially where there is a special relationship of trust involved.

A number of institutions—the University of Virginia has received the most notoriety for its efforts—have enacted policies which attempt to enforce such restraint. Other universities have put faculty and staff on notice that there is a presumption of exploitation on the part of the individual with more power whenever a complaint of harassment is filed by a person of lesser power or authority who was previously engaged in a consensual relationship. Establishing a presumption of exploitation accepts the realities of human relationships; acknowledges the constitutional protection of the right of free association; and, at the same time, provides institutional cautions about the possible consequences of such relationships. Establishing these criteria also has the advantage of notifying everyone in the university that exploitation will not be tolerated. This, then, may deter the development of some problematic relationships. As in each of these strategies, the best results come from the educational process that surrounds the development of these policies and the campus orientation to them.

Another difficult area for the president to deal with involves fund-raising and alumni affairs. Here particularly, where women have risen quickly in the field, there is considerable potential for harassment. The relationship between a development office and a donor can be a very personal one, and the process of cultivation can easily create both impressions and circumstances that make the development officer vulnerable to inappropriate advances. The behavior of an alumnus or a corporate executive with the capacity to make a substantial gift to the university may be difficult to control at times. The university should ensure that development officers and alumni staff have appropriate training in this area, so that they are prepared to manage these situations with personal dignity while completing their challenging assignments. The president, however, must sometimes take quick and clear personal action to protect staff members from inappropriate or exploitative behavior.

Conclusion

Today, there is a generally positive movement in achieving a climate where people are more willing to grapple with the issue of sexual harassment. Unquestionably, there is a new level of consciousness among students and employees with regard to unacceptable behavior and a greater willingness to take legal action to ensure protection from exploitation. Women, gay men and lesbians, people of color, and people with disabilities have led the way in being more assertive about their rights to study and work free from harassment. There is both better understanding of and support for those seeking redress of grievances. The public in general is more willing to discuss issues of harassment of all sorts, so painful experiences that once would simply have been endured are now being brought to the attention of university officials. Accusations of sexual harassment are much more common today, reflecting both this new consciousness and a new sense of the power of people to end inappropriate behavior directed toward them.

For all of these reasons, the existence of an effective informal conflict-resolution process is immensely important to the campus and to the president. Such a process can protect both the individuals and the university from public exposure that can be damaging.

We want a sexual harassment policy that is both settled and flexible, well understood in its purpose and confidential in its operation, seeking the resolution of problems and the restoration of a productive learning and work environment. Making this policy work effectively depends on an informed community that can recognize inappropriate behavior, articulate concerns, and then address the matter without fear of retribution. And, because sexual harassment most often occurs in situations where there is already an imbalance of power, we need a process that protects the rights of complainants, those who serve as advocates for the complainants, and those accused.

At the same time, we also need to make it clear, both on the campus and beyond, that the great majority of men and women at institutions do behave in ethical and sensitive ways. As we counsel students that they have the right and the obligation to identify harassment and speak out against it, we also need to celebrate the many faculty and staff who have taken roles that support the advancement of women and men through fair and sensitive means.

Much has been made in the past few years about "political correctness" (PC); that is, behavior, language, and even thoughts that conform to certain "liberal" ideological standards. The debate about "PC," joined at the national as well as local levels, has in it a certain "gotcha" mentality—people on one side of the debate identify and criticize sexist attitudes, language, and pedagogical styles, while those on the otherside point to the orthodoxy, the lack of humor, and the flirtation with censorship that characterizes those who are "correct." It is predictable that some members of the campus community have attacked any sexual harassment policy as a codification of "politically correct" thought, but in fact persons of all political persuasions have a stake in seeing that women and men are not exploited. Again, a broad and open public dialogue which seeks to define sexually harassing behavior—including behavior that is essentially speech—will be healthy for the community as a whole, ensuring a productive learning community, and avoiding infringements on academic freedom and freedom of speech.

In the end, however, all our best efforts are not likely to eliminate sexual harassment. The problem is rooted deeply in the interplay of power and sexual dynamics, among the most complex problems in the human experience. Thus, discussion of sexual harassment, attempts to raise consciousness regarding its negative effects on work and learning, and imposition of policy and procedure to deal with harassment when it occurs are necessarily continuing activities. In grappling with sexual harassment at universities, we must recognize the dangers to academic freedom inherent in our efforts and weigh these dangers carefully. Yet we are convinced that the best way to protect these freedoms is to keep the discussion open, because fear of facing this problem only keeps it festering in the dark, poisoning the academy itself, including its traditions of personal and professional freedom.

The conclusion we have reached is that another freedom—the freedom from sexual harassment—must be a value fully integrated into the institutional mission and culture. Efforts to do so must be purposeful, deriving from a specific plan of policy, procedure, training, enforcement, and evaluation. If we are successful in treating these matters openly, without rancor or intimidation, the entire campus environment can be improved and learning, the institution's purpose for being, significantly enhanced.

Endnotes

1. From the *1975 Report of the Committee on Freedom of Expression at Yale*, chaired by Professor C. Vann Woodward, pp. 10–12.

2. From Viewpoint of the president, *The Spectrum*, SUNY at Buffalo, 4 Dec. 1989, p. 11.

3. Chickering, Arthur W., & Gamson, Zelda F., Seven principles for good practice in undergraduate education, *The Wingspread Journal* 9(2), June 1987.